Gender and Public Relations

Although there is a small body of feminist scholarship that problematizes gender in public relations, gender is a relatively undefined area of thinking in the field and there have been few serious studies of the socially constructed roles defining women and men in public relations.

This book is positioned within the critical public relations stream. Through the prism of 'gender and public relations', it examines not only the manipulatory, but also the emancipatory, subversive and transformatory potential of public relations for the construction of meaning. Its focus is on the dynamic interrelationships arising from public relations activities in society and the gendered, lived experiences of people working in the occupation of public relations. There are many previously unexplored areas within and through public relations which the book examines. These include:

- the production of social meaning and power relations
- advocacy and activist campaigns for social and political change
- the negotiation of identity, diversity and cultural practice
- celebrity, bodies, fashion and harassment in the workplace
- notions of managing reputation and communicating policy.

In extending the field of inquiry, this edited collection highlights how gender is accomplished and transformed, and, thus how power is exercised and inequality (re)produced or challenged in public relations. The book will expand thinking about power relations and privilege for both women and men and how these are affected by the interplay of social, cultural and institutional practices.

Christine Daymon is Associate Professor of Communication Management at Murdoch University, Australia. She is co-author of the successful Routledge book *Qualitative Research Methods in Public Relations and Marketing Communications*, now in its second edition.

Kristin Demetrious is Associate Professor in Public Relations at Deakin University, Australia. Her first book is *Public Relations, Activism and Social Change: Speaking Up* (Routledge, 2013).

Routledge new directions in public relations and communication research
Edited by Kevin Moloney

Routledge New Directions in Public Relations and Communication Research is a new forum for the publication of books of original research in PR and related types of communication. Its remit is to publish critical and challenging responses to continuities and fractures in contemporary PR thinking and practice, and its essential yet contested role in market-orientated, capitalist, liberal democracies around the world. The series reflects the multiple and interdisciplinary forms PR takes in a post-Grunigian world; the expanding roles which it performs; and the increasing number of countries in which it is practised.

The series will examine current and explore new thinking on the key questions which impact upon PR and communications, including:

- Is the evolution of persuasive communications in Central and Eastern Europe, China, Latin America, Japan, the Middle East and South East Asia developing new forms or following Western models?
- What has been the impact of postmodern sociologies, cultural studies and methodologies which are often critical of the traditional, conservative role of PR in capitalist political economies, and in patriarchy, gender and ethnic roles?
- What is the impact of digital social media on politics, individual privacy and PR practice? Is new technology changing the nature of content communicated, or simply reaching bigger audiences faster? Is digital PR a cause or a consequence of political and cultural change?

Books in this series will be of interest to academics and researchers involved in these expanding fields of study, as well as students undertaking advanced studies in this area.

Public Relations and Nation Building
Influencing Israel
Margalit Toledano and David McKie

Gender and Public Relations
Critical perspectives on voice, image and identity
Edited by Christine Daymon and Kristin Demetrious

Gender and Public Relations
Critical perspectives on voice,
image and identity

**Edited by
Christine Daymon and
Kristin Demetrious**

LONDON AND NEW YORK

First published 2014
by Routledge
2 Park Square, Milton Park, Abingdon, Oxon OX14 4RN

Simultaneously published in the USA and Canada
by Routledge
711 Third Avenue, New York, NY 10017

Routledge is an imprint of the Taylor & Francis Group, an informa business

© 2014 Christine Daymon and Kristin Demetrious

The right of the editors to be identified as the authors of the editorial material, and of the contributors for their individual chapters, has been asserted in accordance with sections 77 and 78 of the Copyright, Designs and Patents Act 1988.

All rights reserved. No part of this book may be reprinted or reproduced or utilised in any form or by any electronic, mechanical, or other means, now known or hereafter invented, including photocopying and recording, or in any information storage or retrieval system, without permission in writing from the publishers.

Trademark notice: Product or corporate names may be trademarks or registered trademarks, and are used only for identification and explanation without intent to infringe.

British Library Cataloguing in Publication Data
A catalogue record for this book is available from the British Library

Library of Congress Cataloging in Publication Data
Gender and public relations : critical perspectives on voice, image, and identity /edited by Christine Daymon and Kristin Demetrious.
  pages cm. – (Routledge new directions in public relations and communication research)
Includes bibliographical references and index.
1. Public relations. 2. Sex role. I. Daymon, Christine editor of compilation.
II. Demetrious, Kristin, 1958- editor of compilation.
HM1221.G46 2013
659.2–dc23   2013002975

ISBN: 978-0-415-50555-0 (hbk)
ISBN: 978-0-203-43601-1 (ebk)

Typeset in Times New Roman
by Cenveo Publisher Services

Printed and bound by CPI Group (UK) Ltd, Croydon, CR0 4YY

Christine: For my god-daughter, Luisa Miller, whose radical creativity challenges and inspires me.

Kristin: For the students, and for the practitioners, trying to make sense of things.

Contents

Contributors ix
Foreword xiii
LANA F. RAKOW
Acknowledgements xvi

Introduction: Gender and public relations: making meaning, challenging assumptions 1
CHRISTINE DAYMON AND KRISTIN DEMETRIOUS

1 Surface effects: public relations and the politics of gender 20
KRISTIN DEMETRIOUS

2 Caring about public relations and the gendered cultural intermediary role 46
ANNE SURMA AND CHRISTINE DAYMON

3 Interrogating inequalities perpetuated in a feminized field: using Critical Race Theory and the intersectionality lens to render visible that which should not be disaggregated 67
DONNALYN POMPPER

4 Gendered performance and identity work in PR consulting relationships: a UK perspective 87
LIZ YEOMANS

5 Mothers, bodies, and breasts: organizing strategies and tactics in women's activism 108
C. KAY WEAVER

6 Celebrity, gender and reputation management at the BBC 132
JANE ARTHURS

7 Campaigning for 'women, peace and security': transnational advocacy networks at the United Nations Security Council 156
IAN SOMERVILLE AND SAHLA AROUSSI

8 Gender, culture and power: competing discourses on the Philippine Reproductive Health Bill 177
MARIANNE D. SISON

9 'I want to voice out my opinion': bringing migrant women into union work 198
MAREE KEATING

10 'Mammography at age 40 to 49 saves lives; just not enough of them': gendered political intersections in communicating breast cancer screening policy to publics 221
JENNIFER VARDEMAN-WINTER, HUA JIANG AND NATALIE TINDALL

11 Ex-journos and promo girls: feminization and professionalization in the Australian public relations industry 247
KATE FITCH AND AMANDA THIRD

Index 269

Contributors

Sahla Aroussi Ph.D. is a post-doctoral researcher and a member of the Law and Development research group in the Faculty of Law, University of Antwerp. Her work has appeared in the *International Journal of Feminist Politics* and the *International Journal of Human Rights*. Her doctoral research was on the implementation of UN Security Council Resolution 1325 in peace agreements. Her current research interests include women's rights, transitional justice, peace agreements and power sharing.

Jane Arthurs Ph.D. is Professor in Television at Middlesex University in the UK. She has published widely on women, sexuality and the media from feminist approaches. Her books include *Television and Sexuality: Regulation and the Politics of Taste* and *Women's Bodies: Discipline and Transgression*. Recently, she has focused her research attention on charitable campaigns about trafficked women, leading to publications in *The Handbook of Gender, Sex and Media* and the *International Journal of Media and Cultural Politics*.

Christine Daymon Ph.D. (Kent) is fascinated by the qualitative research process, especially the use of ethnographic and feminist approaches to study how public relations affects the lives of communication practitioners and the cultures of organizations. Co-author of the successful Routledge book *Qualitative Research Methods in Public Relations and Marketing Communications*, now in its second edition, she is based in Australia at Murdoch University, where she is an associate professor, leading an international project on cross-cultural learning and communication, and directing a collaborative China–Australia research centre investigating media and communication in Asia.

Kristin Demetrious Ph.D. is Deputy Head of School in the School of Communication and Creative Arts at Deakin University, Australia. Her research is concerned with social change, struggles for meaning making and its cultural intersections, particularly with media industries, communities and notions of citizenship. Her research in gender stems from her observations in the teaching of public relations, as well as a desire to achieve higher ethical standards in the field. With a background in community work and activism, Kristin is an experienced media and communication practitioner who has operated her own consultancy. Her first book is *Public Relations, Activism and Social Change* (Routledge, 2013).

Kate Fitch is a senior lecturer at Murdoch University, where she chairs the Public Relations programme. She received a national teaching award in 2011 for her development of the public relations curriculum and its focus on work-integrated learning. Prior to joining the university, Kate worked in public relations roles in the arts, government and community sectors. She has published extensively on public relations topics, including social media, social responsibility, culture, gender, pedagogy and education, and public relations in Singapore.

Hua Jiang Ph.D. (University of Maryland) is an assistant professor at S.I. Newhouse School of Public Communications, Syracuse University, NY, USA. She teaches public relations undergraduate and graduate courses, such as principles of PR, PR campaigns and PR theories. Her research areas include relationship management, work–life conflict, public relations leadership, social media, global public relations and public diplomacy.

Maree Keating Ph.D. is a lecturer in the College of the Arts at Victoria University, Melbourne, Australia. She co-ordinates the Communication and Public Relations programme, and lectures in organizational communication, public relations campaigns and gender, work and society. She has worked internationally as a country programme manager and gender policy adviser for Oxfam and in Australia as a trade union teacher, advocate and researcher. She currently researches narratives of change and resistance among low-paid women workers.

Donnalyn Pompper Ph.D., APR is an associate professor in the School of Media and Communication at Temple University, Philadelphia, PA, USA. She is an internationally recognized scholar of social identity intersectionalities of age, ethnicity/race, gender in organizations, and in mass media representations.

Lana F. Rakow Ph.D. founded and directs the Center for Community Engagement at the University of North Dakota, where she also holds the position of Professor of Communication. Prior to completing a Ph.D. at the University of Illinois, Urbana–Champaign, Lana practised public relations for a university, a trade association, and a corporation. Her research, which includes four books, has been focused on feminist theory, gender and technology, community, and higher education. In 2010 she was awarded the Teresa Awards for the Advancement of Feminist Scholarship by the Feminist Scholarship Division of the International Communication Association.

Marianne Sison Ph.D. is Deputy Dean (International) and a senior lecturer at the School of Media and Communication at RMIT University in Melbourne, Australia. Her research interests include international public relations, corporate social responsibility, organizational values and culture, and internal communication. She was educated at the University of the Philippines, the University of Florida, and RMIT University. Originally from the Philippines, Marianne moved to Melbourne in 1989 where she lives with her husband, Miguel, and two sons, Antonio and Francisco.

Ian Somerville Ph.D. is a senior lecturer in the School of Communication, University of Ulster. His work has appeared in *Public Relations Review*, *Public Relations Inquiry*, the *Journal of Communication Management* and *Corporate Communication: An International Journal*. His research interests include PR in post-conflict societies, activist PR, and sport and social exclusion. He is on the editorial board of *Public Relations Review* and *Public Relations Inquiry*, and is Vice-Chair of the Organizational and Strategic Communication Section of the European Communication Research and Education Association.

Anne Surma Ph.D. (Warwick) lectures in the English and Creative Arts programme at Murdoch University, Australia. She has also worked in private industry as an editor, writer, workshop facilitator and consultant, advising on communication strategy and practice. She is the author of two monographs: *Public and Professional Writing: Ethics, Imagination and Rhetoric* (Palgrave, 2005) and *Imagining the Cosmopolitan in Public and Professional Writing* (Palgrave, 2012).

Amanda Third Ph.D. is a senior lecturer at the University of Western Sydney, Australia, where she is a member of the Institute for Culture and Society. She has published in scholarly journals and edited collections on cultural studies and gender studies topics, including: the gendering of public relations; popular cultural representations of female terrorists; and young people's everyday use of technologies. Amanda leads a research programme in the Young and Well Cooperative Research Centre (youngandwellcrc.org.au), which has received Australian federal government funding for 2011–2015.

Natalie T.J. Tindall Ph.D., APR is an assistant professor in the Department of Communication at Georgia State University, USA, where she teaches strategic communication. Her research areas include diversity in public relations, gender and work–life balance/conflict, fundraising and organizational identity.

Jennifer Vardeman-Winter Ph.D. (University of Maryland) is an assistant professor in the Jack J. Valenti School of Communication and an affiliate faculty member in the Women's Studies programme at the University of

Houston, TX, USA. She teaches public relations theory and management, issues management, and critical and cultural public relations. Her research areas include risk and health campaigns, gender and identity in public relations, and cultural studies and research methods.

C. Kay Weaver Ph.D. is a professor in the Department of Management Communication and Pro Vice-Chancellor of Postgraduate Research at the University of Waikato, New Zealand. She has published many articles and chapters advocating critical approaches to the examination of public relations theory and practice, and is co-editor of *Public Relations in Global Contexts* (Routledge, 2011). Kay has taught across the fields of public relations, communication, media and film studies in the UK and New Zealand.

Liz Yeomans is the co-editor of the popular international book *Exploring Public Relations* (Financial Times/Prentice Hall, 2013 [2006]), which is now in its 3rd edition. A principal lecturer at Leeds Metropolitan University, UK, her doctoral work has involved developing perspectives in PR drawing on gender and emotional labour theories within the sociology of work. Liz is a member of EUPRERA's Women in PR project team. Previously she worked in communication management positions for British central and local government.

Foreword

Lana F. Rakow

What does gender mean to public relations, and what does public relations mean to gender? We have long needed the attention this volume brings to the question, and I am thankful that editors Christine Daymon and Kristin Demetrious have taken up the challenge. The answer, it turns out, is more interesting and important than most scholars of either gender or public relations have understood. The editors and contributors open up new insights into the taken-for-granted approaches to gender and public relations that have guided feminist scholars in the field of public relations and that have eluded the attention of other scholars for at least the last forty years. Indeed, even more recent interest in turning the gaze of critical theory to public relations has tended to slight the importance of the question when challenging traditional relationships of power through an understanding of the practice and consequences of public relations.

Written by feminist scholars (or those with sympathies to feminist scholarship) with organizational experiences inside and outside of public relations, this volume's significance to both feminist scholarship and critical public relations scholarship derives from its anti-essentialist approaches to both gender and organizations. First, the authors understand that the widespread existence and role of organizations should not be taken as a fact of contemporary life but rather as an issue to be recognized and challenged. Organizations, and more specifically large bureaucratic public and private institutions, generate the fundamental physical and cognitive structures that orchestrate and accomplish daily life, from the production and flow of human traffic to food and energy and consumer goods. These organizations are both the result of systems of meanings and the generators of meaning through routinized and legitimated practices involving deployment of human and environmental resources. In short, organizations are in the business of the organization of meaning. The definition Daymon and Demetrious use to define public relations sets the stage for this important shift in understanding organizations. They define public relations as 'a communicative activity used by organizations to intervene socially in and between competing discourses in order to facilitate a favourable position within a globalized context'. This non-essentialist approach to public relations and organizations is a first step in their project to understand and disrupt power relations in society, power relations in which gender is a critical linchpin. Contributions that call our attention to alternative organizational forms that challenge the social order, from women's activist groups to labour unions, reveal the shortcomings of the dominant approach to public relations (which assumes corporate public relations as the standard of practice), as well as highlight the difficulty of creating inclusive spaces for the participation of all groups, even where challenges to relations of power are at stake.

Second, the book leads to a greater understanding of how gender, too, is an organized system of meaning. As Christine Daymon and Kristin Demetrious make clear in their introductory chapter, gender is not a pre-given and binary characteristic of human biology and psychology, even if understood to be somehow inflected by race, class, and other contemporary categories of difference. They instead see it as a 'fluid and negotiated process performed through every social interaction'. Chapters that demonstrate how sexuality, race and ethnicity, and class are not additions to an understanding of how gender differences are constructed and carried out but integral to them should challenge our deepest assumptions about gender. Chapters that point to competing discourses about gender should remind us that gender is not only about the self but about a system of differentiation used to make sense of the worlds in which we live – from division of mental, physical, and emotional labour in the home, workplace, and civil society to assumptions about the function and capabilities of all that is living and inanimate.

With these challenges to notions of gender and organizations in mind, we are able to see how the focus of much prior feminist attention on the role of women in public relations has been limiting and inadequate to understanding the full range of associations between gender and public relations. As chapters in this volume point out, even where the role of women in public relations is considered, it is more complex than is often assumed. In addition to re-examining the role of women in the traditional arenas of public relations, we need to look at how women have used public relations, if defined as strategies of persuasion, through their own organizations and collective action. Finally, we need to look beyond women in public relations and women's use of public relations to see the importance of considering women as objects of public relations and gender as an outcome of organizational discourse.

Therefore, this volume rightly urges us to attend to public relations rather than either to embrace it as a lucrative career option or to dismiss it as a tool of oppression utilized by powerful institutions. The editors show us a third way. This volume might be seen, unexpectedly, as having a 'rescue mission': that is, the editors and contributors are not advocating for an abandonment or the overthrow of public relations practices, nor a reform from within that will make public relations a better career for women, but rather foresee the possibility of rescuing its practices so that they may be put at the service of more liberatory and socially transformative purposes. This is a tantalizing consideration. We should all be thankful that we now have this volume to start us on the path to that transformation.

Acknowledgements

The act of compiling a book, especially an edited book, is always done in concert with others. In this, we would like to thank our panel of insightful reviewers for their willingness and enthusiasm to read and comment on the many contributions (and various iterations) submitted for inclusion in this collection. Their input – especially that of Beth Pengelly – has been invaluable in shaping our own ideas and arguments, as well as those of our co-authors. We also thank Elizabeth Braithwaite for editorial support.

Our appreciation extends to the following reviewers: Beth Pengelly, Jane Arthurs, Estelle Barrett, Geoff Boucher, Peta Bowden, Rhonda Breit, Adam Brown, Jo Fawkes, Kevin Moloney, Judy Motion, Louise North, Jeannie Rae, Barry Richards, Richard Stanton, Anne Surma and Elspeth Tilley.

Thanks go to the Centre for Memory, Imagination and Innovation for providing useful funds in the book's production, and to the staff at the School of Communication and Creative Arts at Deakin University for their generosity and support.

Introduction: Gender and public relations
Making meaning, challenging assumptions

Christine Daymon and Kristin Demetrious

The idea of compiling an edited collection around gender and public relations was seeded at the 'Radical Public Relations: Alternative Visions and Future Directions' roundtable held at the University of Stirling in 2008. This meeting of international scholars had a shared purpose, paradigmatically, to challenge dominant positivist understandings of public relations and open new research agendas by paying attention to the social and political contexts in which public relations is situated. Thematically, the roundtable focused on the cultural effects and critical power relations in and between public relations and society. This book furthers these aims by exploring gender within and through public relations in order to generate new strands of knowledge that will challenge the status quo. As such, the intention is to open new avenues of research and new ways of thinking about public relations.

Over the last fifty years or so, gender research employing critical feminist approaches has theorized women's experiences and elevated the status of this knowledge to destabilize, and at times rupture, hegemonic beliefs that have invisibly systemized inequality and exploitation. With the social positioning of women (and other under-represented groups) as a core objective of feminist research, it has sought to question the sometimes dormant, underlying values and assumptions that have invisibly served to invest research. In rejecting narrow absolutism and reductionist science, and in seeking to be open to multiple, sometimes competing, approaches to understanding (Reinharz and Davidman 1992: 3–4), research inspired by feminism has contributed to the development of new knowledge and social practices, as well as the nourishment of ideals. In recent times, these have become embedded to a large extent in contemporary social life. Thus the impact of feminist activity, with its focus on gender, has been profound, but at times confronting, and subject to intense resistance and disapproval. For example, early criticism of feminism was based on arguments about the extent to which feminist actions helped or hindered women and whether or not they rotted the social fabric as a consequence. Later criticisms emerged from within the ranks of feminists themselves who objected to the way that only some women benefited from feminism-inspired social change: for example, the protection of women's sexual rights helped empower white, heterosexual women, but it didn't help sexual or racial minorities; also, improving access to work helped child-free or wealthy women, but not those with large families. At times, feminist activities were subject to considerable entrenched hegemonic resistance, such as in the early 1980s when there was a move in the USA to introduce an Equal Rights Amendment (ERA). Although the legislation was designed to elevate the legal status of women, it was women themselves who spearheaded a campaign to oppose the legislation. The success of the campaign driven by Phyllis Schlafly was described by the *New York Times* as a 'public relations coup' (Warner 2006):

> When it was approved by the House and Senate and sent to the states for ratification in March 1972, its success seemed assured. Thirty state legislatures ratified the amendment within a year. Presidents Nixon, Ford and Carter all lent their support. Yet in 1982 the ERA died, just a few states short of ratification. By then, it had become linked in the public mind with military conscription for 18-year-old girls, co-ed bathrooms and homosexual rights.
>
> (Warner 2006)

Opposition campaigners claimed that sexual 'equality' would lead to a blurring of the differences between the sexes and, among other things, remove women's right to stay at home, to be dependent and to devote themselves to raising a family. In contrast, feminists in support of the ERA (including the prominent legal activist Catharine A. MacKinnon) argued that, rather than eradicating gender differentiation in favour of gender sameness, for them equality meant eradicating gender *hierarchy*:

> We stand for an end to enforced subordination, limited options, and social powerlessness – on the basis of sex among other things ... Our issue is not the gender difference but *the difference gender makes*, the *social meaning* imposed upon our bodies – what it means to be a woman or a man is a social process and, as such, is subject to change. Feminists do not seek sameness with men. We more criticize what men have made of themselves and the world that we, too, inhabit. We do not seek dominance over men. To us it is a male notion that power means someone must dominate. We seek a transformation in the terms and conditions of power itself.
>
> (MacKinnon 1987: 22–23)

The ERA example is of interest because it reveals through the arguments and counter-arguments of the opposing and supporting groups (including their public relations activities) that the fundamental social rights of women have been hard fought, and the process of winning has required the careful unpicking of profoundly entwined discourses, laced, among other things, with differing notions of morality, femininity, race and class. This constructed a powerful hegemonic acceptance in North American society that rendered the social and personal wellbeing benefits of the feminist movement not only invisible but dangerous to and threatening of the social order. It also demonstrates that a deeper understanding of the communicative process around gender is central to the renegotiation of the social and strategic role of public relations – a central aim of this book.

Despite the setbacks, criticism of and resistance to the feminist movement over the years, there is no doubt that gendered power relations were disrupted by feminist activity, including gender research from a feminist lens, with real social consequences that impacted on how both women and men lived and worked. Yet social change that leads to reform is never a closed narrative, nor linear. Fluid and dynamic, it is interrelated to, and responds with, changing contexts, cultures and milieux through which new combinations of thought and action emerge, generating new dilemmas and new challenges. As such, reform is perpetually in motion and must be subject to revision, because at times, despite appearances, thought that was once subject to interrogation may merely return to much the same social space from whence it came. While public relations as an occupation in modernity has been socially and culturally situated alongside the broad thrust of the feminist movement (such as the second wave of feminism which saw women's status in areas like pay and conditions upgraded), nonetheless there remain many hidden hegemonic assumptions around gender in public relations which continue to be both unquestioned and unchallenged. In this introductory chapter, we identify some of these issues and questions, and note how they are addressed by the various authors in this book.

We define public relations as a communicative activity used by organizations to intervene socially in and between competing discourses in order to facilitate a favourable position within a globalized context. This definition highlights the political role of public relations in seeking to influence the meaning making process purposefully. As an occupational domain, the public relations industry exerts significant influence and power in society through the production of meaning, the commoditization of discourse and the creation of consent (Demetrious 2008; Weaver, Motion and Roper 2006). Primarily, it operates on behalf of corporate entities and governments, although it can also be employed by third-sector organizations, such as not-for-profits and ephemeral organizations and individuals.

However, its role and relationship to society is not one that is understood particularly well, either within its own ranks or externally (Demetrious 2013; Coombs and Holladay 2007). Designed to intervene in the decision making process, public relations is intrinsically political and sits uneasily with many of the central tenets of democratic society. Thus, when statements manufactured by public relations circulate invisibly through the public sphere, working through a growing repertoire of media, modes and texts, tensions are manifest. On the one hand, they are evident in the idea of an individual in modern society who has agency to deliberate and to contribute to public debate and decision making; and on the other, they are evident in the notion that public relations plays a role in directing thought, shaping meaning and developing social practice in ways that might compromise both agency and criticality.

Public relations as a field of academic inquiry has been tightly bound to the processes of production, the development of useful tools and apparatus, the planning and allocation of resources in putting together and distributing a text, be it a brochure, a media release or a tweet, and to theorizing counter-attack when it meets resistance. Other research fields centre on the consumption of the text, how the audience received it, and whether it worked. Public relations' focus tends to benefit large organizations like business and government and often articulates to the powerful professional associations which accredit its courses. As a result, academic inquiry in public relations has been accused of anti-intellectualism and of being overly concerned with vocational outcomes. In respect to the development of public relations education in Britain, Jacquie L'Etang has written:

> Education had the potential to increase respectability and status which practitioners desired and to provide theoretical knowledge to underpin a specific expertise … 'education' quickly became synonymous with training (processes, procedures, and routines) and practitioners; interest in education was purely instrumental.
> (L'Etang 1999: 283)

In failing to explain how public relations interrelates and works with the sociological and the cultural and the political, its conventional, positivist knowledge bases are wanting and limited. Internally, the mainstream lens in public relations is inadequate to excavate meaning that sheds light on its tensions within and between other cultural forms or to interrogate questions about how reform can be achieved to lessen public relations' emphasis on creating consent (often involving the suppression or silencing of certain voices and meanings). When gender issues have been acknowledged (which is rare), researchers have tended to concentrate on the 'feminization' of the occupation and gender inequalities in the workplace. While not dismissing these as unimportant, this narrow field of inquiry overlooks some of the powerful cultural forces and interrelationships that position men and women in relation to the occupation. In effect, conventional knowledge has been on an instrumental trajectory where it has paid little heed to the hidden workings of gender, presenting theories and data as if they were gender-neutral. Numerous books and articles about public relations have masked the ways that gender can and sometimes does shape the type of data that is collected and the empirically based theoretical conclusions that have been drawn.

The silent acceptance of gender 'neutrality' extends also to the lecture halls and curricula of public relations degree programmes. Much public relations education can be viewed as functionalist because it has a predisposition towards '*techne*' and the production of useful tools or artefacts to reach 'publics'. For example, public relations education at a university level places great store on students acquiring technical expertise, which is often validated through positivist quantitative methods (for example, programme planning and evaluation, as well as the production of tactical devices such as media releases) rather than a critical examination of their social and political impact and context or how these socially constructed 'objects' link to and limit epistemological possibility (Demetrious 2012; Daymon and Demetrious 2010). Examples are public relations management plans, communication audits, social media releases, newsletters and the like. The absence of reference to gender in teaching is not actually gender neutrality; instead it reifies an implicit male-biased perspective which is also evident in some other disciplines, as Marta Calás and Linda Smircich (1992) have shown. Just think, for example, how the use of supposedly gender-neutral language can hide or exclude the voices of those who do not fit the dominant and conventional disciplinary forms of thinking and practice. While there is a place for the instrumental, practical and vocational, when this is the sole focus of the curriculum, graduates are unprepared for the realities of the workplace and unequipped with the critical tools required to resist the gendered lines that may limit or demark their career choices. Greater attention to gender must be embedded into public relations teaching as it is impossible adequately to understand the social construction of public relations and therefore disrupt its associated hegemonic assumptions without closely examining its gendered nature. If graduates are to contribute as responsible, caring citizens of democratic societies, and also as critically aware public relations professionals, then it is incumbent on university teachers to develop their understanding of difference, care and equity, not least in relation to gender, in order to nurture the sensibilities of students with regard to the complexities of ethical public relations to society.

Although gender issues have been segregated from the central intellectual debates in the field of public relations, there is nonetheless a small corpus of published work which shows that gender inequalities do exist in supposedly gender-neutral communication practices, and that gender bias is evident in the assumptions of traditional public relations theorizing. Much of this work emanates from scholars and teachers in North America, including Linda Aldoory (2009, 2005; Aldoory and Toth 2002; Aldoory *et al.* 2008), Carolyn Cline (Toth and Cline 1991; Cline *et al.* 1986), Pamela Creedon (1991, 1993), Larissa Grunig (1988, 2006; Grunig *et al.* 2000, 2001), Linda Hon (1995; Hon *et al.* 1992; Choi and Hon 2002), Suzanne Horsley (2009), Julie O'Neil (2003, 2004), Donnalyn Pompper (2007, 2011, 2012), Elizabeth Toth (2001; Toth and Cline 2007; Toth and Grunig 1993), and Brenda Wrigley (2002, 2006). These researchers have focused their research on issues such as salary discrepancies, the under-representation of women in senior positions, and gender (and racial) stereotyping, mostly in relation to the workplace. Importantly, they have drawn our attention to relations of inclusion and exclusion which privilege some at the expense of others, such as men over women, and white women over women of ethnic backgrounds.

However, the significance of such work could be strengthened if in future researchers were to question the core concepts embedded in research, because this then would lead to the present social order being challenged and potentially destabilized, rather than tacitly accepted. Theresa Russell-Loretz (2008) argues that there is a certain disciplinary myopia in current public relations gender research which could be overcome if researchers were to turn towards other disciplines where feminist theories are well developed and thus able to yield greater heuristic value. The use of such theories and methodologies has the potential to assist public relations scholars both to challenge and to reimagine the notion of gender, and better contextualize the lives of those they explore, and thus raise important new questions and lines of inquiry. We and the contributing authors to this book have sought to undertake this type of feminist-inspired research.

In furthering Russell-Loretz's idea, Lana Rakow and Diana Nastasia (2009) wrote about the power of feminist sociological thinking to analyse public relations. They suggested that gender issues cannot be sufficiently addressed until scholars apply a *critical* feminist lens to their investigation. To do this, they argued that researchers need to uncover and reflect on the assumptions that undergird research, by problematizing concepts such as gender, power and injustice, and by focusing on the political consequences and effects of public relations. A handful of researchers writing from or about regions outside North America have made a start in this direction. We refer here to the work of Romy Fröhlich and Sonja Peters (2007) in Germany; Katharina Tsetsura (2011, 2012), a Russian based in the USA; Christine Daymon and Anne Surma (2012) in Australia; and the Australian, New Zealand and European authors (some of whom feature in this book) who published in the interdisciplinary special issue that we edited in 2010 on gender and public relations in the online journal *PRism*. While some of these scholars might not consider themselves 'critical feminist public relations' researchers, all would nevertheless claim the moniker of 'critical' scholar. Joanne Martin (2003) has helpfully articulated some of the differences and similarities between feminist and critical lenses, noting that both seek to reveal tacit and obvious gender inequalities, and to reduce or eradicate these. However, put simply, feminist scholars tend to place gender as the fulcrum of their analyses (with race, class and ethnicity as secondary emphases), whereas critical theorists often have class as the crux of their research, giving less emphasis to the others (Martin 2003: 66–67).

In our editorial for the special issue of *PRism* (Daymon and Demetrious 2010), we outlined a critical feminist lens for exploring the notion of gender which we described not as a universal, fixed and unchanging demographic status but rather as a fluid and negotiated process performed through every social interaction. Thinking about gender in this socially constructed way positioned us to take note of situated power relations, privilege and struggle, for and by women as well as men, and how these have been and continue to be affected by the interplay of social, cultural and institutional practices. These include public relations in its role of producing meanings, shaping identities and realities and orchestrating consent to domination, subjugation or liberation. As our thinking developed over the course of editing this book, we were compelled to pay more attention to the intermeshing of gender struggles with other hierarchies of power since these too are linked in the lives of individuals and communities who are subject to public relations. In this book, then, we see gender intersecting with and inseparable from race, nationality, ethnicity, class, sexuality, age, ableness and location. But we step back for a moment and explain how we reached this position and some of the work that influenced our thinking.

In 2009, the Australian philosophers Peta Bowden and Jane Mummery made the point that 'feminism has no proper boundaries: as an adaptive responsive movement it is still ongoing, still responding to new circumstances and problems' (Bowden and Mummery 2009: 8). Because of this they suggested that the feminist project may be better understood as consisting of 'multiple feminisms' (p. 8) which include not only major, historical, theoretical approaches – such as liberal, socialist, radical, anti-racist and postmodern, as we noted ourselves (Daymon and Demetrious 2010) – but also dynamic, multifaceted positions and strategies which are constantly evolving in order to counter the different problems faced by women (and other oppressed groups) in different contexts. This led us to ask the question: how best might we study this methodologically, and what might feminism tell us about public relations and its gendered context?

To respond to this question we began with the text by Lana Rakow and Diana Nastasia (2009), who had comprehensively outlined how the ideas of the feminist sociologist Dorothy Smith might be applied to an analysis of public relations, and the value of doing so. They argued that Smith's work is able to direct the gaze of public relations researchers to how our gendered world is accomplished and the potential role of public relations in that process. Smith's influential book *The Everyday World as Problematic. A Feminist Sociology* (1987) is a compilation of her thinking over many years. She writes of how she became frustrated through the 1970s and 1980s with the exclusion of women from the making of culture. This included their silencing in the intellectual realm of sociology, a discipline in which she was steeped. She asserted that historically in America women have been treated differently from men because of the dominance and authority of 'the male voice' (p. 29) which excludes women from the production of knowledge. Masculinized thinking, she claimed, is legitimized and buttressed by society's governing structures. Such pervasive power is a form of 'ruling' which regulates social relations because it shapes social discourse and meaning.

At this point, we can see that public relations, in its corporate guise, is an integral element in society's relations of ruling whereby it uses communication texts to perpetuate ideologies that Smith declares are implicitly gendered. A core problem for Smith is that this form of knowledge or consciousness represents life as neutral, impersonal and universal, and ignores the 'particularized ties of kinship, family, and household' as well as relationships that are anchored in specific locations (p. 3). Women have become used to seeing themselves according to this abstracted male-biased conceptual scheme, and thus their personal autonomy to realize their dreams and desires is limited. At the same time, they live with a different, contrasting knowledge which is grounded in their actual experiences outside the dominant social order. Smith stated that away from her teaching and writing about sociology, her own lived world was like 'coming down to earth' (p. 7). Here she was immersed in family relations, leisure relations, emotional ties, friendships and the personal goings-on of everyday living. Here meanings were grounded in experiences. All women, Smith claimed, live with a 'bifurcated consciousness' (p. 6), moving in their everyday lives between meaning shaped by the dominant relations of ruling, and meaning that is implicated in the local particularities of home and family. This notion is at the core of Smith's feminist methodology. She advocates doing research from the standpoint of individuals in order to analyse the social relations in which each person's world is embedded, including how these have produced contradictions in our ways of understanding ourselves and our realities. Knowledge gained from research of this nature is subversive because it is grounded in the standpoints and actual experiences of actual people and thus contrasts with knowledge which is vested in the relations of ruling.

The writing of North American philosopher Sandra Harding also had a significant role in shaping our thinking. A highly influential feminist scholar, she is credited with bringing feminist analyses of how meaning is constructed to centre stage in feminist theory (Bowden and Mummery 2009). Like Smith, she asserted that systems of knowledge which traditionally have been seen as universal are in fact biased towards men. For us, the power of her ideas lies with her methodology, which promotes the use of individuals' lives as grounds to criticize dominant knowledge claims and thus highlight gendered oppression as it intersects with race, class and cultures within dysfunctional social orders. Notably, she incorporated anti-racist and anti-imperialist analyses into her work (e.g. 1998, 2008) in order to conceptualize an inclusive, democratic understanding of knowledge making. Harding advocated grounding research investigations in the lived experiences of women because she considered that this would reveal a way of seeing reality that differed from the conventional. In this way, the 'partialities and distortions' (1991: 121) of dominant visions of social reality would be decreased. Doing research from a feminist position, she maintained,

> teaches women (and men) how to see the social order from the perspective of an outsider ... Feminism teaches women (and men) to see male supremacy and the dominant forms of gender expectations and social relations as the bizarre beliefs and practices of a social order that is 'other' to us. *It* is 'crazy': we are not.
> (Harding 1991: 125; italics in original)

In other words, as Bowden and Mummery have explained, 'the experience of the marginalized can give them an epistemic advantage because their lives spark lines of investigation that are invisible to those in the top strata' (2009: 30). Bowden and Mummery have reminded us that if we are successfully to unravel exclusion and disadvantage from a biased social order, then we need to pursue questions about 'who is marginalized, whose experience has been mistakenly interpreted, sidelined or left out of consideration, and whose has dominated and why' (p. 26). And, we would argue, we also need to ask: what is the role of public relations in promulgating exclusion or inclusion, and on behalf of whom and why?

By drawing on the work of these scholars, we have come to realize that the principles and methodologies of feminist thinking can apply to the study of any form of disadvantage, not only that of women, as Rakow and Nastasia have indicated:

> We can see the contours of a critical feminist public relations theory. It would be concerned with *public relations in the lives of women* rather than with *the lives of women in public relations*, and would be focused on the consequences of all institutional discourses, including public relations, on women and other outsiders, rather than on their proficiency using institutional discourses. It would see power not simply nor only in the relations between individual women and men within an organization, but in the structure of society in which powerful institutions produce and enforce meanings about the social order and the place of groups of people within it.
> (Rakow and Nastasia 2009: 272; italics in the original)

Our research and theorizing, then, must take account of the meanings and experiences of those affected by public relations in its real conditions of complex and gendered interrelationships. Research might start with the interconnection (and consequences) of public relations in and on women's lives, but then again it might use a feminist position to consider the public relations experiences of men who are not members of dominant groups, such as indigenous communities or those steeped in poverty. Further, public relations should be regarded as a discipline that cannot be 'created' in the abstract because its theorizing is not neutral.

Therefore, in selecting chapters for inclusion in this book, we chose authors who were keen to explore how public relations penetrates and organizes the experiences and meanings of individuals and groups, whether they are producers of public relations, publics or others affected in some way by public relations activities. The various chapters employ no single, monolithic perspective but instead draw on a wide range of interdisciplinary feminist positions to express their pluralistic, and sometimes conflicting, concerns, despite some similar intentions and inflections in their research. Some of the major feminist thinkers whose works inform the following chapters are Joan Acker, Judith Butler, Carol Gilligan and Arlie Hochschild, among others. Through the accounts presented by the contributing authors, we seek to offer in this collection a critique of public relations in its corporate guise, but also to show its emancipatory or subversive potential for meaning making. In this way, we want to raise awareness of the hegemonic power of society's ruling relations and its interrelationship with public relations, an occupation which exercises considerable social and political power and that influences meaning making through its media-related and economic status.

Social topographies of critical feminist public relations

Without seeking to reify critical feminist public relations as a single homogeneous approach or meta-theory, it is important in understanding gendered investments in public relations to outline some emerging contours and some key concepts. Outlining such an approach will also assist future researchers to understand public relations in a critical feminist light. Therefore, this section broadly sets out how research in the book has been situated, its socially transformative cultural effects and what these reveal in terms of the political and social investment in, and implications of, public relations.

Researching lived experiences

Critical feminist public relations research is both 'critical' (in terms of power relations) and 'political', by speaking about and to the lived experience rather than a theoretical ideal. As scholars working from this position, our role is to make visible and audible the personal and collective gendered meanings and experiences of those involved in and with public relations, and also the experiences of those who are affected by public relations, including those previously invisible or silenced, who are often women. And because it is important not to assume *a priori* ideas about women and men but instead to acknowledge the nuances, complexity and interrelationships of gender, we begin by problematizing the concept of gender instead of taking it for granted. For example, Lana Rakow and Diana Nastasia (2009) urge us to challenge the woman/man dichotomy which has been presupposed in previous research, when the status of women has been contrasted with that of men, and subsequent recommendations made for more equal opportunities for women. In contrast, they point out, 'there are women as well as men who willingly or unwillingly contribute to the reification of patriarchy, capitalism, Western racism, and colonialism, and there are women as well as men who do not support or accept these' (p. 267). Scholars then need to present a more critical awareness of gender, acknowledging that it is much more complex than a simple dichotomy, and that there are differences between and among women, as well as men.

This subtlety is illustrated by Kristin Demetrious (Chapter 1 of this book), who investigates how the sexual aspects of gender performance link to sexual harassment in the lived experiences of practitioners in public relations workplaces, especially young women and gay men. In exploring this theme, she investigates the clothes–body complex as a text to reveal hidden relations of power and sites of meaning. The chapter sheds light on the different forms of social sexuality that are promoted but can work against career advancement. In a similar way, Anne Surma and Christine Daymon (Chapter 2) disrupt the binaries of gender stereotypes when they examine the interrelationship of work and home in the lives of public relations practitioners, in particular the acute pressures for workers in public relations emanating from the neo-liberal project. They argue that this is evident in Western Australia where an economic boom is in full swing and which in turn dictates an uncritical approach from practitioners. Their chapter analyses the effects of this between men and women and in doing so they open up new ground for public relations practitioners as cultural intermediates to engage with the 'ethics of care' on two levels: first with their client and community stakeholder relationships, and second with their own lived experiences.

By delving into the personal, emotional and everyday experiences of individuals, as authors contributing to this book have done, we are able to come to a greater understanding of how social and organizational discourses, such as public relations, must change if women and men are to be freed from the discriminatory structures, social relations and meanings under which many of them, particularly women, suffer. We are also able to see – through the narratives of those involved in the production and consumption of public relations – how, in certain instances, public relations has already changed in order to provoke and rupture discrimination and bring about reformation.

As critical feminist public relations researchers, our interests do not align with the conventional contemplation of corporate discourse as a means of garnering consent. Instead, our responsibility is to illuminate the processes and assumptions through which public relations employs discourses to influence certain values, opinions, images and ways of speaking and acting, and take an interest in how and why these have become commonsense and ubiquitous (Rakow and Nastasia 2009). In concerning ourselves with the effects and consequences of public relations on and in individuals' lives, including women and excluded or marginalized groups, we might present, for example, accounts of how meanings can be disrupted through subversive accounts of individuals' experiences.

For example, in Chapter 4, Liz Yeomans explores what happens on 'the inside' and how public relations practitioners in consultancies experience, practise and understand work-based relationships as 'emotion work' and how this links to identity and empowerment. In particular, her work focuses on the ways in which workplaces work within a service culture socially to position women and men in hidden and inflexible ways. In an insightful chapter on corporate and personal identities, Jane Arthurs (Chapter 6) discusses the experiences of aging women TV presenters at the BBC. The exposure of their personal narratives led to the emergence of a social movement that subverted the discriminatory meanings, norms and professional practices of the BBC's organizational culture and internal communications. Arthurs' research highlights how public relations practices can be employed for domination – to reinforce masculinized corporate and professional norms – but also for reformation and liberation when used successfully by social movements and activist groups. Focusing on the notion of exclusion in public relations, Kate Fitch and Amanda Third (Chapter 11) examine the interplay of the competing discourses of feminization and professionalization in the historical context of the 1980s. They reveal how women in Australia responded to the hegemonic notions of professionalism that shaped their professional identities and disadvantaged their careers throughout their working lives.

Researching the transformative

Advocacy often seeks to overcome major structural (as opposed to individual or behavioural) barriers to reform. In bringing these activities to light, this book seeks to give voice to the communicative activities and campaigns, often by marginal groups, around gendered issues that are transforming people's lives. Not only does the book raise these as new issues of difference and inequality, but the ways in which these issues are described in relevant chapters opens up far more nuanced understandings of discourse and how it works through different modes and trajectories. From the margins, patterns of discourse begin to emerge that challenge the status quo and thus advocate more caring and equitable social and cultural relations. The transformative effects of public relations are thus canvassed for their empowering effects, disarticulating the discussion from the familiar corporate sites.

In Chapter 7, Ian Somerville and Sahla Aroussi discuss the effective lobbying strategies of a transnational advocacy network of women's and human rights non-governmental organizations (NGOs) in bringing about the passage of the United Nations Security Council (UNSC) Resolution 1325 in October 2000. As well as showing the communicative processes involved in pushing for policy change, and the complexities and assumptions entwined within various discourses, they explore what these have meant for women in war zones and in post-conflict reconstruction. Importantly, their study reveals how public relations enabled women's voices to be heard (and gendered norms to be reformed) at one of the most powerful and traditionally masculinized spaces in global politics. Continuing with the theme of transforming discourses, Marianne Sison (Chapter 8) draws on post-colonial theory to analyse the actions and reactions between the Catholic Church and the state and within women's groups in the passage of a Reproductive Health Bill in the Philippines. In studying loud and absent voices at the point where empowerment, politics, commerce and morality intersect, she focuses on a dynamic issue that has important ramifications for the health not only of individual women but Filipino society as a whole. In a similar vein, Kay Weaver (Chapter 5) investigates a provocative activist campaign in New Zealand which raises questions about how the female body can be a powerful site for domination and control – and, indeed, condemnation and censorship – when it is used to challenge dominant discursive framings of issues. In arguing that activist communication is gendered, she illustrates how the terms 'woman' and 'mother' are highly politicized and how challenging normative understandings of them is contextual, complex and socially contested.

The above chapters focus on social change and reform, and reveal something of the interplay between global actors and public relations in reshaping understandings of and interactions with community groups. The findings of these chapters indicate that social conditions of late modernity are changing and are distinct from those of early modernity, of which mainstream public relations literature, with its entrenched hostility towards activism, is an expression. The changes demonstrated by these empirical studies reveal that new relations between advocates for social change and state and business organizations are possible to achieve in ways that alter the relations of power and agency. Generated by multiple and diverse voices and experiences, which may include nationality, race, ethnicity, class, age, ableness and sexuality, studying people from their own experiences is important so that they can understand themselves and the worlds in which they exist.

Researching the gendered and political in public relations

In turning our gaze towards the shaping of understandings and meaning making, we are compelled to acknowledge the existence and effects of power which are manifest in the relations between individual women and men as well as in the structure of society. Powerful institutions produce and enforce meanings through public relations about the social order and the place of people within it (Rakow and Nastasia 2009). This, in turn, influences the self-image of individuals and publics and their various communicative relationships which are rarely unproblematic. As critical feminist public relations scholars, our research efforts focus on how public relations affects those who are subjected to its practices and discourses, whether they are publics or practitioners, individuals or organizations and societies. Our responsibility is to illuminate this process from the perspectives of those at the margins as well as the centre of power. This means taking note of voices that are excluded from institutional discourses, and illuminating injustice or inequity where it exists, especially where voices are suppressed or points of view are ignored.

Maree Keating's study of migrant women workers who have lost their jobs and subsequently their engagement from workers' rights (Chapter 9) reveals the distress and 'invisibility' felt by those whose voices are so overlooked that they could be described as 'beyond marginal' (Rakow and Nastasia 2009: 269). Keating claims that public relations carried out by trade unions has the transformatory potential to empower such marginalized stakeholder groups and thus assist in rectifying their position. She demonstrates this through a case study of a union campaign to build worker voice and visibility which raises issues of gender as it relates to both class and race. Her study stresses the responsibility of critical feminist public relations scholars to highlight the gendered domination, 'blindness' and/or liberation that public relations practices and various contexts inspire.

Consciousness of power hierarchies brings us back to a point we made earlier regarding the need to acknowledge that the terms 'woman' and 'femininity' are not homogeneous concepts. This is a common criticism of mainstream feminist research: that there are many differences among women and their experiences cannot be essentialized. Yet much research continues to be underpinned by false generalizations which imply that the same experiences, aspirations, emotions and values are common to all women. Unsurprisingly, this has 'reflected the situations of privileged white women: those with the power to have their voices heard' (Bowden and Mummery 2009: 99). Thus, whiteness is 'the unmarked but dominant term' (p. 104). In such cases, black women and those from ethnic groups are considered 'the Other' and thus their voices, experiences and contexts are excluded.

Two chapters in this book highlight this particular issue. Donnalyn Pompper's ten-year study of women and men working in public relations (Chapter 3) points to the way in which gendered disadvantage cross-cuts with race and age, thus further discrediting a generalized notion of gender and feminism in relation to public relations. She draws on Critical Race Theory to theorize about the embeddedness of both privilege and disadvantage in the public relations workplace, notably in relation to career (in)equalities linked to social identity intersectionalities. At the end of the chapter, she offers practical intervention strategies to inspire change in public relations theory building. In Chapter 10, Jennifer Vardeman-Winter, Hua Jiang and Natalie Tindall present a study of the implications of gendered health communications and policy making on the multiple, intersecting identities of publics. They argue that public relations is a gendered industry that aids the creation of policies which have inequitable consequences, and thus highlight how public relations plays into the consolidation of racial 'blindness' with gendered discrimination.

In summary, critical feminist public relations research seeks to illuminate or subvert public relations practices which are discriminatory, as well as motivate more equitable and caring public relations practices, education and research. The focus of this research is on the gendered 'self' leading towards the uncovering of multiple voices and narratives of personal, lived experiences which, in turn, illuminate public relations' powerful but less understood political role in meaning making and the shaping of social and global contexts and relations. Each chapter in this book has sought to situate itself in the lived experiences of its research participants. It has sought to examine the socially transformative cultural effects of public relations. And it has sought to reveal what this means in terms of the political and social investment in and implications of public relations. These various research trajectories outlined over the previous pages can be seen to overlap, intersect and mesh through the various chapters of this book.

Contours and futures

In this book, the contributors have concentrated primarily (although not exclusively) on the notion of gender as it has developed in the Western intellectual traditions. This is not surprising, given that all the writers have been schooled in Eurocentric systems of thought. To further critical feminist public relations research, we would encourage other researchers, especially those from different ethnic and cultural backgrounds, to develop research strategies, analytic techniques and gender-focused theories which are empirically grounded in and pertinent to *local* systems of thought, so that questions of gender are considered alongside questions of culture, sex, race and location.

An important area for future research which cross-cuts with gendered disadvantage and public relations is disability. For example, future work which builds on extant studies of hegemonic practices concerning gendered embodiment and adornment in public relations might question the pervasiveness of cultural norms concerning the physical and mental capabilities inherent in our notion of 'the body'. If, as Wendell (1996; cited in Bowden and Mummery 2009) states, the dominant societal culture is unable genuinely to understand and engage with disability, then surely there is a role for critical feminist public relations scholars to attempt some form of societal transformation in this regard.

Although a focus on gender, especially one that employs a critical feminist perspective, usually sets out to highlight women's oppression specifically in relation to men (Bowden and Mummery 2009), there is no reason why research should not take account of the ways in which public relations practices and contexts may also subjugate or empower men. The experiences of men alongside those of women are noted in a number of chapters in this collection. However, a lacuna in this book – and in public relations generally – is reflexive writing by men about men. Recently, Paul Elmer (2010) brought the masculine voice and identity to the fore in an amusing and provoking autoethnographic account of his encounters with professional expectations of physique, adornment and age in public relations consultancy. Gender research will be enriched by more of this type of writing.

In presenting this collection of international research writings, we are seeking to legitimize gender as a topic for exploration in public relations and further the agenda set in 2008 at the 'Radical Public Relations' roundtable. The upcoming chapters present empirically based studies with new, creative theorizing that concern the ways in which publics and public relations practitioners respond individually and collectively to the hegemonic processes and gendered consequences of public relations in its connection to society's 'ruling relations'. For those interested in understanding the complex interconnectedness of public relations with powerful social forces, this book opens a social space that deserves further exploration. By encouraging future researchers to focus on the gendered 'self' as central to research in public relations, the book offers a methodology for understanding the cultural effects and critical power relations in and between public relations and society. By deconstructing and rebuilding knowledge, it prepares the groundwork to locate and identify gender inequalities, disadvantage and abuse in public relations – as well as pursue its potential to empower and transform.

References

Aldoory, L. (2005) 'A (re)conceived feminist paradigm for public relations: A case for substantial improvement', *Journal of Communication*, 55(4): 668–84.

Aldoory, L. (2009) 'Feminist criticism in public relations: How gender can impact public relations texts and contexts', in R.L. Heath, E.L Toth and D. Waymer (eds), *Rhetorical and Critical Approaches to Public Relations II*, New York: Routledge: 110–123.

Aldoory, L., Reber, B.H., Berger, B.K. and Toth, E.L. (2008) 'Provocations in public relations: A study of gendered ideologies of power-influence in practice', *Journalism and Mass Communication Quarterly*, 85: 735–50.

Aldoory, L. and Toth, E.L. (2002) 'Gender discrepancies in a gendered profession: A developing theory for public relations', *Journal of Public Relations Research*, 14(2): 103–26.

Bowden, P. and Mummery, J. (2009) *Understanding Feminism*, Stocksfield: Acumen.

Calás, M. and Smircich, L. (1992) 'Rewriting gender into organizational theorizing: Directions from feminist perspectives', in M. Reed and M. Hughes (eds), *Rethinking Organization: New Directions in Organization Theory and Analysis*, London: Sage: 227–53.

Choi, Y. and Hon, L.C. (2002) 'The influence of gender composition in powerful positions on public relations practitioners' gender-related perceptions', *Journal of Public Relations Research*, 14(3): 229–63.

Cline, C.G. and Toth, E.L. (1993) 'Re-visioning women in public relations: Practitioner and feminist perspectives', in P.J. Creedon (ed.), *Women in Mass Communication* (2nd edition), Newbury Park, CA: Sage: 183–98.

Cline, C.G., Toth, E.L., Turk, J.V., Walters, L.M., Johnson, N. and Smith, H. (1986) *The Velvet Ghetto: The Impact of the Increasing Percentage of Women in Public Relations and Business Communication*, San Francisco, CA: IABC Foundation.

Coombs, W.T. and Holladay, S.J. (2007) *It's not Just PR: Public Relations in Society*, Malden, MA: Blackwell.

Creedon, P.J. (1991) 'Public relations and "women's work": Toward a feminist analysis of public relations roles', *Journal of Public Relations Research*, 3(1–4): 67–84.

Creedon, P.J. (1993) 'Acknowledging the infrasystem: A critical feminist analysis of systems theory', *Public Relations Review*, 19(2): 157–66.

Daymon, C. and Demetrious, K. (2010) 'Gender and public relations: Perspectives, applications and questions', *PRism* 7(4). Online. Available HTTP: <http://www.prismjournal.org/fileadmin/Praxis/Files/Gender/Daymon_Demetrious.pdf> (accessed 4 December 2012).

Daymon, C. and Surma, A. (2012) 'The mutable identities of women in public relations', *Public Relations Inquiry*, 1(2): 177–96.

Demetrious, K. (2008) 'The object of public relations and its ethical implications for late modern society – a Foucauldian analysis', *Ethical Space: The International Journal of Communication Ethics*, 5(4): 22–31.

Demetrious, K. (2012) 'Media effects: E-simulations and authentic "blended" learning', in D. Holt, S. Segrave and J.L. Cybluski (eds), *Professional Education Using E-simulations: Benefits of Blended Learning Design*, Hershey, PA: IGI Global: 255–70.

Demetrious, K. (2013) *Public Relations, Activism and Social Change: Speaking up*, New York: Routledge.

Elmer, P. (2010) 'Re-encountering the PR man', *PRism* 7(4). Online. Available HTTP: <http://www.prismjournal.org/fileadmin/Praxis/Files/Gender/Elmer.pdf> (accessed 29 November 2012).

Fröhlich, R. and Peters, S.B. (2007) 'PR bunnies caught in the agency ghetto? Gender stereotypes, organizational factors, and women's careers in PR agencies', *Journal of Public Relations Research*, 19(3): 229–54.

Grunig, L.A. (1988) 'Women in public relations: An overview', *Public Relations Review*, 14: 3–5.

Grunig, L.A. (2006) 'Feminist phase analysis in public relations: Where have we been? Where do we need to be?', *Journal of Public Relations Research*, 18(2): 115–40.

Grunig, L., Toth, E.L. and Hon, L.C. (2000) 'Feminist values in public relations', *Journal of Public Relations Research*, 12: 49–68.

Grunig, L.A., Toth, E.L. and Hon, L.C. (2001) *Women in Public Relations: How Gender Influences Practice*, New York: Guilford Press.

Harding, S. (1991) *Whose Science? Whose Knowledge? Thinking from Women's Lives*, New York: Cornell University Press.

Harding, S. (1998) *Is Science Multicultural? Postcolonialisms, Feminisms and Epistemologies*, Bloomington: Indiana University Press.

Harding, S. (2008) *Sciences from below: Feminisms, Postcolonialities, and Modernities*, Durham, NC, and London: Duke University Press.

Hon, L.C. (1995) 'Toward a feminist theory of public relations', *Journal of Public Relations Research*, 7(1): 27–88.

Hon, L.C., Grunig, L.A. and Dozier, D.M. (1992) 'Women in public relations: Problems and opportunities', in J. Grunig (ed.), *Excellence in Public Relations and Communication Management*, Hillsdale, NJ: Lawrence Erlbaum: 419–38.

Horsley, J.S. (2009) 'Women's contributions to American public relations, 1940–1970', *Journal of Communication Management*, 13(2): 100–15.

L'Etang, J. (1999) 'Public relations education in Britain: An historical review in the context of professionalisation', *Public Relations Review*, 25(3): 261–89.

MacKinnon, C.A. (1983) 'Excerpts from MacKinnon/Schlafly debate', *Law and Inequality*, 1(2): 341–53.

MacKinnon, C.A. (1987) *Feminism Unmodified: Discourses on Life and Law*, Cambridge, MA: Harvard University Press.

Martin, J. (2003) 'Feminist theory and critical theory: Unexplored synergies', in M. Alvesson and H. Willmott (eds), *Studying Management Critically*, London: Sage: 66–91.

O'Neil, J. (2003) 'An analysis of the relationships among structure, influence, and gender: Helping to build a feminist theory of public relations', *Journal of Public Relations Research*, 15(2): 151–79.

O'Neil, J. (2004) 'Effects of gender and power on PR managers' upward influence', *Journal of Managerial Issues*, 16: 127–44.

Pompper, D. (2007) 'The gender–ethnicity construct in public relations organizations: Using feminist standpoint theory to discover Latinas' realities', *Howard Journal of Communications*, 18: 291–311.

Pompper, D. (2011) 'Fifty years later: Mid-career women of color against the glass ceiling in communications organizations', *Journal of Organizational Change Management*, 24: 464–86.

Pompper, D. (2012) 'On social capital and diversity in a feminized industry: Further developing a theory of internal public relations', *Journal of Public Relations Research*, 24(1): 86–103.

Rakow, L.F. and Nastasia, D.I. (2009) 'On feminist theory of public relations: An example from Dorothy E. Smith', In Ø. Ihlen, B. van Ruler and M. Fredriksson (eds), *Public Relations and Social Theory: Key Figures and Concepts*, New York: Routledge: 252–77.

Reinharz, S. and Davidman, L. (1992) *Feminist Methods in Social Research*, Oxford and New York: Oxford University Press.

Russell-Loretz, T. (2008) 'Working the system: The evolution of feminist perspectives in public relations scholarship', in T.L. Hansen-Horn and B.D. Neff (eds), *Public Relations: From Theory to Practice*, Boston: Pearson: 317–42.

Smith, D. (1987) *The Everyday World as Problematic: A Feminist Sociology*, Boston: Northeastern University Press.

Toth, E.L. (2001) 'How feminist theory advanced the practice of public relations', in R.L. Heath (ed.), *The Handbook of Public Relations*, Thousand Oaks, CA: Sage: 237–46.

Toth, E.L. and Cline, C.G. (1991) 'Public relations practitioner attitudes towards gender issues: A benchmark study', *Public Relations Review*, 17(1): 161–74.

Toth, E.L. and Cline, C.G. (2007) 'Women in public relations: Success linked to organizational and societal cultures', in P.J. Creedon and J. Cramer (eds), *Women in Mass Communication* (3rd edition), Thousand Oaks, CA: Sage: 85–96.

Toth, E.L. and Grunig, L.A. (1993) 'The missing story of women in public relations', *Journal of Public Relations Research*, 5(3): 153–75.

Tsetsura, K. (2011) 'Is public relations a real job? How female practitioners construct the profession', *Journal of Public Relations Research*, 23(1): 1–23.

Tsetsura, K. (2012) 'A struggle for legitimacy: Russian women secure their professional identities in public relations in a hyper-sexualized patriarchal workplace', *Public Relations Journal*, 6(1). Online. Available HTTP: <http://www.prsa.org/Intelligence/PRJournal/Archives/> (accessed 19 February 2013).

Warner, J. (2006) 'She changed America', *New York Times*, 29 January. Online. Available HTTP: <http://www.nytimes.com/2006/01/29/books/review/29warner.html?pagewanted=all&_r=0> (accessed 30 December 2012).

Weaver, K., Motion, J. and Roper, J. (2006) 'From propaganda to discourse (and back again): Truth, power, the public interest and public relations', in J. L'Etang and M. Pieczka (eds), *Public Relations: Critical Debates and Contemporary Practice*, Mahwah, NJ: Lawrence Erlbaum Associates: 7–22.

Wrigley, B.J. (2002) 'Glass ceiling? What glass ceiling? A qualitative study of how women view the glass ceiling in public relations and communications management', *Journal of Public Relations Research*, 14(1): 27–55.

Wrigley, B.J. (2006) 'Bumping their heads: A study of how women public relations and communications management view variables contributing to the glass ceiling', *Journal of Human Subjectivity*, 4(1): 33–47.

1 Surface effects
Public relations and the politics of gender

Kristin Demetrious

Gender conformity embedded unquestioningly as 'common sense' is a powerful but often unseen force within social structure that has played a central role in shaping the politics, direction and practice of public relations. Despite this, public relations scholarship and education pay limited attention to questions of gender and power, where they intersect and how the effects are expressed. This chapter uses a socio-cultural lens to understand both the dominant as well as divergent and emergent ways in which public relations as a discourse – that is, as a specific formation of language articulated to history, institutional authority and normative practices – culturally configures 'gender'. It focuses on how socially constituted gendered identities are performed within contemporary public relations workplaces and how this anticipates cultural possibility (Butler 2008: xv). In particular, it focuses on how gender, power and sexual hierarchy are intertwined, and the ways in which fashion – as social practice – authorizes behaviour, rules and conventions to construct a set of dispositions that both imitates and promotes these cultures. These lines of inquiry engage theoretically with a view of gender, not just as a socially constructed category, but as a socially sexualized form of inequality.

According to Judith Butler: 'sexual hierarchy produces and consolidates gender' (2008: xii). For Catharine MacKinnon, an exploration of gender without this 'obscures and legitimizes the way gender is imposed by force' (MacKinnon 1987: 3). This nexus of the 'social' and 'sexuality' frames the discussion in two ways: first, in terms of the binding particularities of 'difference' between men and women in and through the construction of gender; and second, in terms of a wide cultural field of social processes articulated to this construction. Therefore, the ideals of gender promoted in public relations, and dynamic social processes and practices that create the ideals, will be explored *as an imposition* on subjects engaging with the politics of repression as a means of legitimizing and silencing discussion about sexual dominance and inequality. By questioning the configuration of women, men, bodies, representation and politics within public relations, gender is thus defined as a 'set of free-floating attributes ... performatively produced and compelled by the regulatory practices of gender coherence'

(Butler 2008: 34). Discarding fixed (essentialist) notions of 'men' and 'women', the research engages with ideas of subjects as individual 'agents' who interact within fluid and moving cultural fields of concealed relations of power linked to ideology and control. This trajectory allows for movement of, and the unlocking of, new understandings of public relations and its relationship to gender and the performance of social sexuality.

Contemporary workplaces appear normatively different from the male-dominated strongholds of the 1950s and 1960s: before the contraceptive pill became widely accepted, and before rights such as equal pay and equal opportunity were extensively progressed by second-wave feminists who mobilized in the 1970s to advocate 'more nuanced and marginalised forms of disadvantage' (Daymon and Demetrious 2010: 2). Indeed, MacKinnon argues that since the 1970s feminists have made visible a socially embedded pattern of abuse of women by men. She says, 'In fact, it is the woman who has not been sexually abused who deviates' (1987: 5). In accordance, MacKinnon discusses that 'The pervasiveness of male sexual violence against women is therefore not denied, minimized, trivialized, eroticized, or excepted as marginal or episodic or placed to one side while more important matters discussed' (1987: 5–6). Paradigmatically, and over time, views like these led to the challenging of long-held assumptions about women and men. They led to the creation of different meanings and knowledge bases and of shared understandings in society, some of which had significant and long-term legal, political, social and cultural implications. Based on this, these questions – how public relations discourse culturally constructs gendered identities, and how these are performed within diverse workplace settings – are contextually characterized by a general view that feminists have already done the 'main work' in relation to gender and inequality, and, as a result, today's workplaces are qualitatively different. This view is further buttressed because social relations within them appear to be more relaxed and informal than in the past. For this reason, the chapter explores if and in what ways the constitution of gender in today's public relations workplaces affects relations of power, and in particular if this produces and reinforces a sexualized relationship of inequality while at the same time discouraging diversity. Thus, the chapter will use an interdisciplinary lens to consider if, in recent times, gendered categories have been reconstituted by cultural conditions and what this means for hidden relations of power.

While not the only way of enforcing gender inequality, sexual harassment is a significant site for the production of meaning. According to Judith Butler, 'sexual harassment is the paradigmatic allegory for the production of gender. Not all discrimination can be understood as harassment. The act of harassment may be one in which a person is "made" into a certain gender' (2008: xiii).

Investigating gender, power and public relations, the study considers the public records and reporting of two cases of sexual harassment brought by public relations staff in Australia. The first occurred in 2010 when a female publicist for a major department store chain, David Jones, began civil action against its chief executive officer; the second took place in 2012 when a male parliamentary staffer in media relations made allegations against the Speaker of the House of Representatives. The testimony and the public reporting of these two cases contain descriptions of females and males and public relations workplaces that provide an opportunity to identify indicative patterns of gender construction for analysis. Hence the rights or wrongs of cases will not be analysed, but rather the media representation of them: what is signified, what absences occur and the public understandings of gender and public relations that might result from this. The powerful assumptions around gender in and towards 'PR' seen through these cases suggest ways sexual hierarchies are produced and reproduced that work against equality and diversity in public relations workplaces. In particular, these investigations open up the possibilities that, far from unbinding women from repressive regimes of the past, the normative boundaries in contemporary workplaces have been redrawn around gender and this category of inequality now includes gay men.

PR and the clothes–body complex

A little black dress, pencil skirt, blazer with patterned shirts, revealing cleavage, striped tie, tailored shirt, classic suit, luxury brand-name watch, accessorizing with technology, spray tan, manicured nails, teeth whitening, hair colour: what are the accepted norms of appearance for women and men in public relations workplaces? Interrelationships between the sexual harassment cases and the production of knowledge through the clothes–body complex or 'fashion' in public relations will also be investigated. The sexual harassment thesis is also understood through fashion as a culturally specific social practice in a 'complex' where sites of gender construction link to ideology, agency and rules of discourse. Jennifer Craik argues:

> [F]ashion constitutes the arrangement of clothes and the adornment of the body to display certain body techniques and to highlight relations between the body and its social habitus. The body is not a given, but actively constructed through how it is used and projected. Clothes are an index of codes of display, restraint, self-control, and affect-transformation.
>
> (Craik 1994: 10).

This view builds on Butler's thesis that:

> Gender ought not to be constructed as a stable identity or locus of agency from which various acts follow; rather, gender is an identity tenuously constituted in time, instituted in an exterior space through

a *stylized repetition of acts*. The effect of gender is produced through the stylization of the body and, hence, must be understood as the mundane way in which bodily gestures, movements, and styles of various kinds constitute the illusion of an abiding gendered self.

(Butler 2008: 191; italics in the original)

To explore the notion of gender as a sexualized relationship to inequality in public relations, an empirical component to the study will consider fashion as grammar or rules which direct the development of professional identities. 'Mundane' textual samples sourced from internet blogs and other sites will be analysed as part of the process of investigating gender in public relations; in particular, those providing fashion and style advice for potential public relations practitioners about what to wear at interviews and within the job. As texts, these samples provide valuable insights into the assumptions underpinning the gendered boundaries in public relations workplaces that link to sexual harassment. They not only reveal the way relations are being constructed, but whether these relations are marked by uneven power relations and forms of subordination, as well as ways these relations may be imposed.

In summary, these lines of investigation reveal normative understandings in public relations, what happens when transgressions occur, and how public discussion of these can become woven into a broader understanding of occupational practice and workplaces. Significantly it is argued that in public relations a self-contradictory reality exists, paradoxically both obvious and obscured: on the one hand, the career pleasure promoted in public relations links to a controlling sexual hierarchy but, on the other, these very practices contribute to the loss of career opportunity and the delegitimization of the occupation. For public relations, resolving this self-contradictory stance on gender and its flow-on effects such as anxiety and confusion about body and appearance is an important dynamic in occupational reform. The conclusion considers the implications of this for ethics and public relations practice.

Fashioning gender in modernity

Historically, public relations, like other manifestations of capitalism and modernity, was profoundly anchored to culturally constructed understandings of gender as heteronormativity and linked to a discourse which privileged masculinist positions to the exclusion of others. In relation to earlier periods of modernity Robert Nelson observes that:

> It was necessary ... for men to appear standardised, mechanical, predictable, rational, and regular: they are the responsible organisers of society. Women meanwhile would be encouraged to retain all the aspirations to frivolous hedonism, leggy fancies, extravagant and

irrationality, because these indulgences became signs of inferiority and powerlessness.

(Nelson 2011: 15)

Butler reveals other meanings in the complex power dynamic between men and women in modernity. The following quotation shows how 'sexuality' and 'gender' can be understood in two distinct ways: first, in a 'sexist' mode where an act of sexual submission, in effect, fulfils a woman; and second, in a 'feminist' mode where it is evidence of subordination.

> There is thus a difference between sexist and feminist views on the relation between gender and sexuality: the sexist claims that a woman only exhibits her womanness in the act of heterosexual coitus in which her subordination becomes her pleasure (an essence emanates and is confirmed in the sexualized subordination of women); a feminist view argues that gender should be overthrown, eliminated, or rendered fatally ambiguous precisely because it is always a sign of subordination of women. The latter accepts the power of the former's orthodox description, accepts that the former's description already operates as powerful ideology, but seeks to oppose it.
>
> (Butler 2008: xiv)

The views of Nelson and Butler suggest that the politics of repression, as social sexuality, manifests through a limited selection of options linked to powerful orthodoxies and gender conformity.

Is sexual submission essentialized and embedded within ideology in public relations thinking and practice? Edward Bernays' book *Propaganda* (originally published in 1928) is to an extent a justification of the commodification of the 'public' and the rise of public relations counsel within the "unworkable fiction" of democracy (Lippmann 2010: 22), but it is also embedded within the ideology of heteronormativity. In some ways his works could be interpreted as progressive in respect to the status of women, as he anticipated a shift in gendered power relations. However, his thinking was limited in its scope, which extended only to legitimizing women enhancing men's roles:

> Just as women supplement men in private life, so they will supplement men in public life by concentrating their organized efforts on those objects which men are likely to ignore. There is a tremendous field for women as active protagonists of new ideas and new methods of political and social housekeeping.
>
> (Bernays 2005: 133)

More broadly, Bernay's work is of interest for its gendered depiction of the 'crowd' as female while the propagandist's, or public relations counsel's, power was 'cool and manly' (Miller 2005: 21). Constructing a gendered metaphoric representation of the "public" as essentially female within a masculinist discourse provided public relations counsel with the means by which their domination and subordination of the public could be naturalized as common sense. This suggests that power relations of gender were hegemonically concealed and performed so that 'an expectation ends up producing the very phenomenon that it anticipates' (Butler 2008: xv). Arguably, these gendered interpretations continued to underpin and shape public relations thinking and practice over the twentieth century.

Hegemony takes many subtle and seemingly contradictory forms. In explicating this, Geoffrey Boucher (2006: 112–13) shows how two congruent strands of ideological domination may become intricately entwined, making it harder to detect, interpret and break its grip, a situation that can be applied to public relations. Drawing on Butler's conception of performativity, he argues that when personal and social identity fuse to produce culturally scripted subjects there is a particular (non-)response to the subversion of power. The sliding between the personal and social identity creates a level of ambiguity about individual agency that obscures the controlling hegemonic aspects. When this happens, Boucher argues that 'social identities are the permanently divided result of the ritualistic repetition of conventions, the possibility for subversion of the reigning social norms remains an ineradicable potential of all social relations' (p. 113). Therefore, contributing to hegemony in public relations is the embedded belief in individual rather than collective power. Accordingly, this may position public relations practitioners not to have an overt sense of actually being oppressed, even if they are, because they perceive that they have personal power and agency. In turn, public relations practitioners are less challenging than other occupational groups of the power relations that are oppressing them. As a result, workplace norms and controlling hegemonic aspects become almost impossible to remove.

Women and men in public relations workplaces may also ritualize and perform complex cultural structures of domination and subordination in other ways that reveal how meanings are naturalized as common sense. In particular, fashion, as a social ritual within public relations, shows how gendered understandings are performed, repeated and embedded. For Butler: 'This repetition is at once a re-enactment and re-experience of a set of meanings already socially established; and it is the mundane and ritualized form of their legitimation' (Butler 2008: 191). Craik's ideas shed light on how this repetition, re-enactment, re-experience and ritualization can take place. She suggests that an individual subject enters into an acculturation process through fashion or the clothes–body complex:

> Fashion is a technology of civility, that is, sanctioned codes of conduct in the practise of self-formation and self-presentation. The body is

trained to perform in socially acceptable ways by harnessing movement, gesture and demeanour until they become 'second nature'.

(Craik 1994: 5)

This suggests that performing sexualized social rituals in this way may not only naturalize but produce individual subjects that hegemonically perpetuate gender as inequality in changing social conditions. However, if gender is naturalized through the grammar of fashion, 'then the alteration of gender at the most fundamental epistemic level will be conducted, in part, through contesting the grammar in which gender is given' (Butler 2008: xx). For this reason, in public relations, the clothes–body complex is a powerful textual site which is inscribed by multiple, congruent hegemonies and readable in terms of its significance in maintaining, reinforcing and disrupting power relations in gender and shifting gendered boundaries.

The significance of clothes and accessories in workplaces can also be understood in relation to 'habitus', a concept of social space in which 'a set of dispositions ... incline agents to act and react in certain ways' (Bourdieu 1991: 248). For Craik, individuals and their self-presentation also reflect and relate to habitus: 'the clothes–body complex operates in ways appropriate to a particular habitus or milieu' (1994: 10). The concept of habitus provides context for understanding fashion on two levels: first, in terms of individual self-presentation and the projection of constructed meaning; and second, in terms of the social space in which the gendered self performs rituals of subordination. Applied to public relations practitioners and their workplaces, these ideas show how the individual subject and their workplace/space intersect. Practitioners are surrounded by other practitioners who dress, walk and speak and relate to each other, and in doing so produce a set of dispositions and project the values of the wider social context. Therefore, fashion systems and codes – that is, combinations of styles, accessories, repertoires of design and use of colour – can help identify the dominant codes in self-presentation constructing hegemony within workplace contexts. Orthodoxy in the clothes–body complex and the way norms in workplaces are enforced and policed provide a lens that contextualizes wider cultural milieux of public relations. It focuses attention on assumptions in workplaces that may not be obvious, but work to normalize sexual domination and hierarchy, while at the same time giving insight into lived experiences, the daily tensions, dilemmas and conflicts of real-life public relations practitioners. Therefore, it is argued that a highly gendered and socially sexualized role draws on and emphasizes a field of socially constructed and culturally scripted performances; for example, personal performances of sexual display such as the touching of hair, giggling, short skirts, a show of cleavage and flirtation. However, what happens when women themselves reinforce and construct these realities in the belief that they will progress their careers?

Working in public relations: BACI – boy am I confused

Katerina Tsetsura (2010) explores how public relations through gender can be used as a prism in which to understand social relations and the character of a society, especially in developing countries like those of Eastern Europe, the Middle East and Africa. Her article discusses the notion of 'a real job' and 'a woman's job' to help explain how socio-economic, professional and gender-defined contexts influence practitioners' perceptions of public relations. She argues: 'Work in public relations, according to interviewees, is often seen by outsiders as easy'. This is a job for 'young, pretty, stupid girls representing a company, showing up in right places' and 'circulating at the parties' (p. 11). Tsetsura also maintains that men and women fit into different modes of public relations:

> Corporate public relations could be defined as a woman's job because it is the most accessible area for women entering the profession, whereas political public relations is perceived as a man's job, a male-dominated area, because of both the number of men working in public relations and power these men have.
> (Tsetsura 2010: 15).

She found that young female practitioners were also asked to undertake ethically dubious work in technical roles: 'For instance, some employees of the political consulting agencies were once required to write blackmail reports about other candidates and supervise tabloids that are sponsored and published by a single candidate during elections' (p. 7).

The work of Tsetsura suggests that the extent to which public relations is sexualized could be an indicator of ethical behaviour in organizational cultures. Romy Fröhlich and Sonja Peters (2007: 242) discuss women in German public relations and a belief among female public relations practitioners that the 'PR bunny' stereotype is highly prevalent and associated with the agency sector. However, they argue that not all women see this as a disadvantage:

> There is also the opinion that the behaviour of a typical 'PR bunny', the use of 'women's natural weapons' as participants term it, might well be a legitimate and subtle strategy to outwit male dominance. One participant argues that image and show in public relations are quite simply part of professionalism itself: 'PR sluts! (laughs) We call ourselves that! And I don't have a problem with it. We are service-people. And you just have to play the game of service, don't you?'
> (Fröhlich and Peters 2007: 242)

Gender counts in public relations and so does sexuality. Unspoken fashion codes are culturally shared and interpreted. In turn, public relations workplaces, and the expectations set about what to wear or what people think they should wear, enforce and shape identity. This is apparent in early writings and in reflections on earlier periods of public relations workplaces. Forty-five years ago, an experienced Australian communications practitioner, R.R. Walker, wrote a book about public relations practice, but on the whole this is characterized by an absence of statements about women. One of the few references is to 'a week's work [which] can range from hiring girls in fish-net stockings to preparing a report on the economic implications of Japanese deep-sea fishing' (Walker 1967: 346). Susan O'Byrne recalls that when she 'first started working professionally in the early 1990s, the senior women in journalism and public relations had lived through the golden era of the shoulder pad in the 1980s and had survived in some tough, male-dominated environments' (O'Byrne 2010: 1). However, she writes that more recently younger women are 'dressing in a style that emphasises their body and leaves the overwhelming first impression of women as sexual beings' (p. 2). For Paul Elmer, the sexualization of labour is evident for both women and men:

> While sexualized labour has only begun to emerge into the margins of feminised discussions of public relations labour, it may be a mistake to restrict interest to the female experience. Men, too, may engage their sexuality to perform an occupational role, and within the labour process.
>
> (Elmer 2010: 4)

Elmer says sexual performances in occupational workplaces were also evident:

> Adopting techniques of the self that lead to the worker being judged as sexually attractive, and hinting at sexual availability, are not uniquely female concerns, especially within a labour contract that engages with the self as part of the service offered. Flirtatious behaviour, for example, emerged as one of the routines of practice enacted by male and female public relations workers alike. This does not imply public relations is sex work, only that the sexual aspects of the self that it engages could be acknowledged more fully and accounted for with more attention than at present.
>
> (Elmer 2010: 4)

Therefore, while fashion might seem like a surface effect of gender, in one sense it reveals political fault lines and social fractures that have flow-on effects for ethical behaviour and transparency as well as the tenor of the public communications produced. However, this is not a set of fixed relations. Shifting social conditions affect constraints and relations of power for women and men which intersect and are subject to change within different social contexts.

Twenty-first-century office: ideas, choice, fun and screens

Social spaces, while structured to protect and reinforce power relations, are subject to wider social change. In particular, the sexual aspect of gender performance in contemporary workplaces is very different from earlier forms; however, this is a shift rather than a substantive change. Late modernity is distinctive for the plethora of choices it offers individuals, such as the ability to adopt different identities, greater choice of gender in participation, and the ability to work flexible hours, increased mobility, and access to technology. In particular, information and digital technologies have transformed practices and concepts of work, especially in relation to time and space. New styles connote freedom and self-determination: for example, accessorizing with technology such as the latest laptop or mobile phone that links to other social spaces, culture jamming through vintage and retro styles, jeans, and tee-shirts bearing self-reflexive political slogans. However, these developments have not undermined authority, as might be implied; rather they have reorganized ways in which it is exercised. According to Zygmunt Bauman, the modality of authority has changed; it is less about 'command and control', and more about offering a suite of choices around identity that permeates through and fuses with public and private worlds.

> 'Heavy', Fordist-style capitalism was a world of legislators and supervisors. The world of goals fixed-by-others. For this reason it was also the world of authorities: of leaders who knew better and of teachers who told you how to be better. But 'light', postmodern and consumer friendly capitalism has not put paid to authorities. It has simply given birth to too many authorities for any one of them to stay in authority: 'numerous authorities' is a contradiction in terms. When there are many authorities, they tend to cancel each other; hence the authority remaining in the field is the one who has to choose between them. It is courtesy of the chooser that a would-be authority becomes an authority. Authorities no more command; they tempt and seduce.
>
> (Bauman 2000: 204)

Therefore, contemporary workplaces appear categorically different from those of the past in that they are more fluid and accepting of difference. But, while functionalism has changed its grammar, the grammar has not fundamentally changed functionalism. Rather, central tenets of functionalism underpin the colonization of authority by private discourses. The imperative to be non-conformist promotes the appearance of change, rather than creating deeper transformations. Public relations in its contemporary setting looks different from the past. In part this is because, to a greater degree than other industries, public relations must be forward looking, and must generate an appetite for consumerism as its core business is the promotion and positioning of new thinking and new products. Innovations in technology and changes in social milieux must be embodied by workers and performed in their workplaces. This suggests that, in public relations, privileged masculinist discourses have merely been re-fashioned within the frameworks of neo-liberalism, rather than fundamentally overturned their thinking. Difference, paradoxically, can be conformism.

Method(s) of data collection and analysis

To investigate the experiences of females and males in public relations workplaces, and the cultural conditions that produce gendered categories, I collected two interrelated sets of data. The first was the public records and reporting of two court cases of sexual harassment brought by public relations staff against their employers in Australia. First, the applicants', or text producers', statements of claims to the Court were analysed and then the public reporting of these claims. In particular, I analysed the public reporting and reception of the text producers' claims by the dominant Australian media stables Newscorp (*Herald Sun*) and Fairfax (*The Age* and *Sydney Morning Herald*), as well as various independent online sources such as the critical left *Crikey*. The online editions of these news sources often had blogs for readers to make comment over a defined period. I also analysed these. The data was first used to develop a list of key actors and their roles: for example, the key individuals, businesses and other sectors involved. Second, a set of criteria or major categories was utilized to organize and categorize all the data forms into a logical structure. These categories include gender representations, sexuality, power relations and social influence, ideology, values and beliefs, persuasive arguments and perceptions of rationality. In particular, this allowed understanding of how journalists positioned readers and how meanings were created. I used the analysis to explore absences and the process of selection and signification by the text producer in order to understand what has been omitted and why (Threadgold 1993).

For Babbie (2001: 326), to achieve accuracy in researching events, 'where possible, obtain data from a variety of sources representing different points of view'. Therefore, as a corollary – and to provide an understanding of the specific subjectivity of the journalists and their readers – general websites and blog conversations about fashion and public relations were surveyed. In particular, I appraised internet advice about how to get a job in public relations. Predominantly this involved internet searches using the phrases 'What should I wear to a public relations interview?' and 'Advice about public relations workplaces'. In terms of the clothes–body complex, the selection and signification process in dressing for a job interview was used to analyse an underlying logic. I regarded these unmediated documents or artefacts of discourse that were produced *in situ* within the period of the cases of sexual harassment studied as valuable, authentic representations of subjective responses to the social and political conditions of the time. As such, they assisted in my understanding of what statements were being made by clothes, colours, combinations of fashion; and their relationship to ideology, performance and habitus. In all, ten different internet sites were analysed from Australia, the UK and the US.

Intertextuality hybridizes and transforms textual meanings and in the investigation provided a theoretical bridge between both sets of data. For Fairclough (1999), intertextuality is a subtle effect where various discourses are often absorbed unconsciously by the reader. He argues that it comes in two forms: manifest intertextuality, where specific texts occur in a text such as a quote; and interdiscursivity, where orders of discourse are drawn on to constitute the text from discourse and text types or conventions such as genres, discourses and narratives. By studying the manifest and interdiscursive intertextuality in the public reporting – that is, looking for tropes and tracking their movement through the discourse as well as analysing the orders of discourse – I gauged and located hegemonic and gendered understandings in and towards public relations. This two-pronged approach to reception analysis provided me with insight into not just how readers are positioned by the text producers, but how meanings are created and circulated about gendered roles and relationships in public relations workplaces.

Behind the face of PR

> Prepare the night before. It's not just the outfit. It's the whole package. Start with your body. Dress for Success.
>
> (*Chique St.* 2009)

An analysis of internet sites (visual and textual) offering advice about working in public relations revealed intricate codes and meanings around male and females. In all of the sources, the central consuming subject was assumed to be female, although there was one instance where additional commentary was offered for males. Although overlap is to be expected, three key themes emerged from the data that locate different normative relations in public relations workplaces: classic, sexualized, and lifestyle.

'Classic public relations' was evident as the controlling discourse within the spectrum analysed. It was described in terms of both 'reliability and professionalism' and as 'conservative and traditional'. Negative associations were that of being boring, unimaginative and overdone. However, seeking work in these settings meant showing 'you take the job and your professional career seriously'. Tailored suits were recommended for these workplaces in solid 'black, navy and grey'. In client presentations, it was acceptable to pair a solid black pencil skirt with 'a patterned top, or a flattering A-line, full skirt with a pattern'. Low-key accessorizing was also acceptable: 'Unique accessories and an unexpected shoe colour or heel are also great ways to infuse a bit of personality into your look'. Advice about accessorizing also extended into stationery items:

> I use a white binder for my portfolio filled with plastic sleeves for clippings – as long as your items are clean and organized I think that's fine. I think carrying those in hand or having in a purse or messenger style bag works, just make sure to bring them! And something to write with!
>
> (McKinniss 2010)

However, 'classic' public relations also nudged boundaries with the notion of sexy communications. This setting led to extended discussion:

> Back in the day, dressing for a PR job work was easy – we all had to wear suits. Nowadays, it's tricky getting an outfit sorted. It has to be smart, but not too smart. It has to show some flair, but not be too wacky. My boss has this near obsession with power dressing – but for her this seems to mean looking almost asexual.
>
> (*PR Moment* 2011)

The overlap was also evident in a list of sartorial tips for men, which advised: 'the look du jour is smart jeans with a jacket' and 'Suits and ties still have a place, but only for boring clients, such as financial institutions'.

In the 'sexualized public relations' category, the 'PR girl' trope was highly represented and connoted a young, nubile female, unmarried, with a degree of sexual power and permission to display that power. Number one on the list of fashion recommendations was a 'well-tailored blazer'. 'Top Five Wardrobe Essentials for PR Girls' advises: 'the blazer is a key component to any PR girl's wardrobe. If you must have only one, go for black at first and work in navy and gray hues' (Mary Ann 2011). Like the classic mode, the dress code suggests that black, navy and greys as a foundation means that you fit in to the setting (KC You There 2012). However, in addition, the little black dress (LBD) signalled where boundaries blur between work and social activity. According to one blog, the LBD is 'versatile enough to hit the bar for drinks after a long day and not appear too stuffy' (Mary Ann 2011). Implied is that while the practitioner's day may be technically over, it is not really; rather, it is now time for some different type of work, entertaining and socializing. In a similar way the cross body purse is something to fuse the various modes of work, whether you're at the bar or at the desk: 'Work, play, day or night, cross body purses are essential for city living' (Mary Ann 2011). The sexualized nature of PR work and its complex normative setting was revealed in this tip: 'if legs are bare, make sure hemlines are not too short. If your boss is male he won't know where to look and if she's a female, despite what she says, she did notice and she doesn't like it' (*PR Moment* 2011). This theme of sexuality is picked up in another tip, which cautions: 'Too much cleavage is not a good idea. Some contacts will love this look of course, but it does beg the question, "where is this business relationship headed?"' (*PR Moment* 2011). Clearly there are danger zones for the uninitiated, especially when alcohol and the blurring of work and play are involved: 'when it comes to awards dinners, brave outfits are not always the way forward. You don't want to be the "girl in that dress"' (*PR Moment* 2011). The emphasis on 'that dress' indicates that it is a powerful text that draws attention to the wearer and her body. The suggestion is that choice of garment can advance but also brand individuals and ruin reputations well beyond the occasion. 'And remember you're almost bound to get drunk and then you'll decide that you're the best dancer in PR, so maybe veer on the side of caution' (*PR Moment* 2011). Along this border, the twin pillars of career respectability and sexualization sit uneasily.

'Lifestyle public relations' refers to an 'open' workplace that, *prima facie*, has relaxed the boundaries that encode status in 'social and fun' ways (Selter 2012). Website advice is to 'Follow the dress code. Many modern firms are moving to a more casual workplace environment. This includes permission to "dress down"' (eHow Contributor 2013). One example of this is the sanctioning of casual wear and work-appropriate jeans: 'Many PR firms have a pretty relaxed dress code', so if you stick with 'darker denim in a flattering style for casual days at the office' that should do the trick. Vintage was also deemed acceptable, 'so long as it fits well and is free of damage' (Mary Ann 2011). However, the extent of encoding within the clothes–body complex within lifestyle was holistic. Sites of meaning were revealed in a blog where advice extended to series of actions prior to the dressing in order to develop greater overall confidence and radiance. These included relaxing, exfoliating (removing dead skin), painting nails and toenails, hydrating by drinking green tea and taking vitamins for health, bronze tanning, and teeth whitening and dieting for glow:

> Take a bath and relax. Exfoliate (If you don't have a scrub, use a little sugar with some soap or body wash). Lotion up. Paint your nails and your toenails. (Why? It's not like they are going to see your toenails anyway? WRONG. Feeling good from head to toe boosts our confidence levels.)
>
> (*Chique St.* 2009)

Collectively, the advice in these websites suggests that these decisions construct an identity that positions the worker in relation to the cultural norms of the workplace and the esteem of their colleagues. Making the 'right' clothes choices, conforming to an expected body shape and style, or practising a smile is not an insignificant or frivolous activity but anticipates a complex presentational performance linked to sexual hierarchy, authoritarianism and capitalism.

PR workers, sexual harassment and media representation

In recent years two high-profile workplace sexual harassment cases in Australia have centred on public relations. The first occurred in 2010 and involved a female in-house publicist. It resulted in an out-of-court settlement. The second involved a male media relations parliamentary staffer for the Commonwealth of Australia employed by the Speaker of the House of Representatives.

The Kristy Fraser-Kirk case

The sexual harassment case that Kristy Fraser-Kirk brought against the David Jones department store chain is important for its portrayal of the public relations workplaces where norms supported highly sexualized, gendered relations linked to powerful hierarchies of power. First in this case study I report on the contents of Fraser-Kirk's application to the Federal Court on 2 August 2010. Following this, I draw on public reporting of the case, online sources of newspaper articles, discussion and blogs to develop an understanding of the different subjectivities surrounding the case.

Trading under the same name since 1838, David Jones is Australia's oldest department store. Known for the quality of its merchandise and service, as well as a penchant for designer fashions, the store has won accolades for setting high benchmarks in retailing and now has a strong national profile. According to her statement of claim (2010), having studied and worked previously in public relations, Kristy Fraser-Kirk applied for a job at David Jones. At her interview she was told 'the workforce consisted of largely women', that these women could be like a 'clique', but that 'once you get your head around that' she would be 'a fantastic fit' for David Jones. When employed with the retail chain, she moved between several roles in marketing and PR. However, Fraser-Kirk claims that at a function hosted by Mark McInnes, David Jones' chief executive officer, unwelcome comments of a sexual nature were made to her, in particular that she should try a dessert because it was like 'a fuck in the mouth'. He also made unwelcome sexual advances, groping her under her clothes, grabbing her and sending inappropriate texts suggesting that she accompany him to his home to have sex (p. 3). Significantly, she claimed that some of this behaviour took place within metres of David Jones' general manager of public relations, Anne-Maree Kelly (p. 4). According to Fraser-Kirk, when she raised the matter, her PR manager indicated that McInnes' behaviour was not a one-off and that she had personally dealt with other employees who had had similar experiences. 'Kelly told Fraser-Kirk "next time that happens, you just need to be very clear and say 'no Mark' and he'll back off"' (p. 4). Fraser-Kirk claimed, *inter alia*, that as a result of her experiences at David Jones she suffered offence, humiliation, distress and anxiety, loss of opportunity for promotion and advancement in her chosen career, and damage to her personal and professional reputation (p. 21). A claim was made for 5 per cent of David Jones' and McInnes' earnings over the period 2003 to 2010, 'during which McInnes served as Chief Executive Officer', and that he should also pay '5% of the total remuneration and benefits earned by him during his regime' (p. 22). According to Maguire (2010), this amounted to a 'staggering' A$37 million. She argued that 'Fraser-Kirk's strategy right from the beginning was to win the PR war'. Despite this, the case was settled out of court for a much lesser figure – a reported A$350,000 for Fraser-Kirk after legal and public relations representation fees were paid.

News reports of the case were mixed. Key media reports emphasized the salacious sexual conduct in the case. The descriptions of Fraser-Kirk centred on her youth, naivety and ambition: for example, it was said that she was 'working her way up the corporate ladder' (Fife-Yeomans 2010). The public relations workplace represented was a complex one, very busy and largely female and with a strong hierarchical element which was gender based: 'Even before she started work at David Jones, Kristy Fraser-Kirk was warned the mostly female workplace could be quite a "clique". But it wasn't the women she needed to worry about' (Kontominas and Mann 2010). Another aspect that attracted media attention was the fact that the unwelcome behaviour of McInnes was 'witnessed by two of her [Fraser-Kirk's] bosses including David Jones public relations general manager Anne-Maree Kelly' (Fife-Yeomans 2010).

The news reports pointed to a relaxed ethical culture in the public relations department where this type of behaviour was not just tolerated but expected. Reinforcing this view was reportage that despite Fraser-Kirk's concerns, and the fact that her manager witnessed her behaviour, she was still required to attend a further work function where McInnes would be present. Gome (2010) wrote: 'In her statement of claim she describes the workplace of my youth, a place where a woman could be groped and harassed in full view of others with no action taken.' The media reports showed that, within her workplace, Fraser-Kirk's claims appeared to be trivialized and to some extent viewed as her own fault, due to her youth, inexperience and misguidedness.

According to Campbell (2010), in the news reports, 'the 27 year old was constantly, monotonously identified as a "junior publicist", as if to underscore her general naïveté and poor judgement'. Reporting was also significantly hostile to Fraser-Kirk's ambit claim for a large financial compensation. In particular, the reader blog commentary exploded around this point, with derogatory insults levelled at Fraser-Kirk. Particularly prominent was the term 'gold-digger'. Similarly, a perception that she had reneged on a promise to give the compensation to charity also caused a furore:

> Kristy Farser Kirk [sic] is a crumb of a female. Greedy and pr hungry! She has gone back on her word about giving the money to charity.

What a pity she has done more harm for us females in the work place than good. Karma Miss Fraser Kirk

(Ang 2010)

According to public reports, Fraser-Kirk's 'sensational claim' for millions of dollars backfired, leading to 'a media campaign to discredit her' (Hinch and Jamal 2010):

> Yesterday Ms Fraser-Kirk said she had been forced to walk away from a career that she loved and a company she believed in due to the alleged sexual harassment. 'I believed I could have gone far if my career had been able to continue,' she said.
>
> (Kontominas and Mann 2010)

The James Ashby case

The James Ashby case of sexual harassment was the subject of much conjecture and public discussion in Australia. In part this was because Ashby's employer, Peter Slipper, the man accused of sexual harassment, was at the time the Speaker of the House of Representatives for the Commonwealth of Australia. Compounding interest in this case was the effect it may have had on the minority Australian Labor Party's (ALP) tenuous grip on power.

According to Ashby's originating application (hereafter referred to as statement of claims), in 2011 Peter Slipper offered Ashby the role of media adviser after establishing that he was homosexual. The job involved work in both the electoral office in Queensland and in Canberra, the nation's capital. After initially declining the offer, Ashby eventually accepted it. Once installed in the job, Ashby claimed that numerous sexually suggestive and/or ambiguous actions were directed at him. These included being asked to give Peter Slipper a massage, sharing accommodation with him and being pressurized to abandon modesty and shower with the door open (which Slipper himself practised). Text exchanges between the two men were also included as evidence in Ashby's claim. In particular, the following text history was tendered as evidence that Ashby was being pressurized by his employer to consent to an inappropriate and unprofessional working relationship. In this section the 'second respondent' refers to Slipper.[1]

10.38.32	SECOND RESPONDENT:	'If you interested we could be closer?'
10.43.25	SECOND RESPONDENT:	'?'
10.49.20	APPLICANT:	'I think we're good already. I'm happy seeing Tim being closest. I hate stepping on toes'
10.49.29	SECOND RESPONDENT:	':)'
10.51.26	SECOND RESPONDENT:	'Your call if u want to keep degrees of separation. No toes'

10.51.44 SECOND RESPONDENT:	'I told him positrion [sic] open'
10.54.38 SECOND RESPONDENT:	'But your call and no hard feelings in that you only want businesslike contact. In that event of the difficulty in our personal'
10.57.22 APPLICANT:	'I don't know what type of contact you expect Peter. Perhaps u should define that [sic] u would like and I can then be clearer on my position.'
10.58.14 SECOND RESPONDENT:	'U want something more? U brillianmt [sic] at massages'
10.59.57 APPLICANT:	'No I'm happy the way things are. I care for u Pete but the massage is as far as it goes. Life's a lot more simpler when it's business and a few drinks after work.'

By March 2012, after several other incidents of this nature, Ashby 'had formed the view that the Second Respondent had recruited the Applicant to his personal staff for the purpose of pursing a sexual relationship' (p. 11).

News reports of the case were complex and many involved greater focus on Slipper and the threat to the ALP's minority government than on the details of the case (Peatling 2012; Wright 2012). In relation to this it was speculated that Ashby was not just peddling lies, but was a puppet in a political game, being used opportunistically by the Coalition (opposition) frontbencher Christopher Pyne to make political points in the hung parliament. Therefore, in order to elicit meanings, I found it important to sift through the political commentary to find implications for public relations.

In a similar way to the Fraser-Kirk case, news reports of the 'highly salacious allegations' pointed to a 'languid' and ethically relaxed workplace setting (Higgins 2012). Overall, Ashby was portrayed as a man of dubious character, both untrustworthy and unreliable. Some of the focus concerned his personal history and the fact that in 2002, when working for Newcastle radio station as a DJ, Ashby had phoned a rival drivetime host and abused him while pretending to be a genuine radio talkback caller. Ashby claimed the threatening behaviour was a practical joke, but he was fined A$2000 and given a good-behaviour bond. Ashby's colourful past led to the media framing him as 'no stranger to controversy', and his relatively mature age of thirty-three at the time he made his sexual harassment claim against Mr Slipper was stressed (Silmalis and Clune 2012). While the public reports generally produced a respectful commentary around homosexuality and same-sex relationships, the following reader-blog commentary (now inactive) revealed deeper animosities:

> It could suggest conspiracy. Same se [sic] is not frowned upon but sex in work situations can be fraught with danger as it always has been!

perhaps the thirty three year old, of certain political persuasions and perhaps a mincing gait, was deeply involved with the oleaginous Pyne for a number of reasons, not all honourable.[2]

(Reply 91 2012)[3]

Social sexuality: double appearances and layers of reality

Gender, for MacKinnon (1987), is socially sexualized inequality. Butler discussed the process of sexual harassment by which individuals are 'made' into a 'certain gender' (2008: xiii). Performance through ritual and repetition can reinforce this. Boucher (2006) discussed some of the ramifications of performativity where the personal and social identities merge to produce shifting, ambiguous forms of hegemony. These themes are evident in the cases of sexual harassment examined in this chapter, which suggest that, in some public relations workplaces, a concealed set of social practices exist that pressure employees to display sexualized subordinance, and that these practices are reinforced within the workplace habitus and are highly resistant to change (Bourdieu 1991). The statements of claim by Fraser-Kirk and Ashby depict public relations workplaces that are highly stratified and in which status can exert enormous pressure to conform to a sexualized gender role. Fraser-Kirk and Ashby said that they feared discrimination and loss of opportunity when challenging these pressures. The blog advice for aspiring public relations practitioners showed how sexualized meanings were actively produced and proliferated through the construction of the clothes–body complex. These lines of inquiry point to a complex element of inequality through sexual hierarchy and gender construction.

In particular, the blog advice revealed that there is a range of competing discourses at play in public relations, and that for aspiring and even experienced practitioners these are difficult to navigate. Evidence of manifest intertextuality was found in both the public reporting of the case studies and the blog advice, in particular the notions of 'sexy coms' and 'PR girls' connoting servitude and blurred boundaries between work and play and sexual hierarchy. Despite this, the overwhelming tenor of the commentary was that aspiring young practitioners need to look sexually attractive in a PR job and prepare themselves for the work/play mode. Low-key accessorizing alluded to a sexual exchange both in the classic public relations context and in the more explicit 'sexy coms' context. For the subject, these discursive elements anticipate the ambiguous normative cultures in public relations workplaces that embed gender inequality. However, an analysis of the online advice also revealed that women who get to be bosses understand the complex play of sexuality and how this fits in workplaces, and are generally 'conservative' or 'asexual'. This points to a complex set of social relations in public relations workplaces that presents serious hazards and the danger of entrapment for practitioners at all levels.

The public response to sexual harassment cases was characterized by vehemence and strong positions on sexual relations in workplaces. On the one hand, audiences in the Fraser-Kirk case reinforced stereotypes of sexualized relations in media and communication jobs as a typical means of career advancement. For example, there was little sympathy for Fraser-Kirk in seeking redress: instead, she was accused of fanning a storm over something that 'was just flirting' and of being a 'gold digger', greedy and PR hungry, as well as manipulative. The term 'gold digger' draws on ideas that women will utilize sexual resources to gain unfair advantage. It is at once heteronormative and phallogocentric, and the trope reveals that there are deep forces at play that support these cultures (MacKinnon 1987; Butler 2008; Boucher 2006). A further complication and fuel for angst was Fraser-Kirk's appointment of a PR firm to manage the publicity around the case and to use her own skills in communication to further her self-interest. Absent from the public reporting and reader-blog commentary was the duty of care her workplace should demonstrate, particularly in light of the claims that much of the behaviour took place in front of her line managers. Indeed, the blogs revealed an entrenched belief that public relations is merely 'sexy coms'. Thus, for women, it is evident that part of the job in PR is to gauge what and how the company wants to be represented through the clothes–body complex as sexualized (Frohlich and Peters 2007). At the same time, succumbing to this pressure puts the employee in an invidious position as there is also evidence that this path limits career opportunity in the long term as women who take their careers seriously in public relations eschew these choices (Tsetsura 2010; O'Byrne 2010). This suggests that for a long time women were viewed as the 'face', the visible front, of PR, but tellingly were not considered the hands or the brains. Moreover, in some workplaces women were regarded as legitimate as a sexualized embodiment to display products that in a functionalist sense could be used in tactical ways to reach an audience and achieve the organizational objective of increasing market share and positioning. However, while it is argued that predominantly young females continue to be exposed to these practices, recent events suggest that this may also now extend to males (Elmer 2010).

The James Ashby case indicates that boundaries have been redrawn around gender and inequality. So while changes may be perceived in public relations – that is, it is more fluid and open to newer ideas – this is only partly true, because structurally the boundaries have been redrawn to sexualize gay men in a similar way to that in which women have been in the past.

> The two main differences between the Fraser-Kirk and Ashby cases are that Ashby risks being labelled a political stooge, rather than a gold digger, and that it is the most prominent example of a man bringing a case of sexual harassment against another man. But both highlight

the ferocity of the court of public opinion when people decide to take action in sexual harassment cases.

(Peatling 2012)

Lifestyle public relations is a mode intersecting with the social phenomena of post-Fordism and the overabundance of choices and mutability of roles as well as with the mode in which authority is exercised as an appeal rather than command (Bauman 2000). Taken together, findings show that functionalism is still the underlying, dominant perspective in public relations workplaces. Assumptions about gender, sexuality and hierarchy remain largely unquestioned. The higher level of differentiation in workplaces gives an appearance of change. But the classic, sexualized and lifestyle categories of public relations simply intersect with gender in ways that produce different subjects with similar problems and issues.

Taken together, the case studies and the analysis of internet sites about public relations workplaces indicate that while there is an emphasis on looks and clothes and an association of empowerment and status, these are deceptive and for the uninitiated have some dangerous pitfalls. Moreover, the research indicates that various sectors, both government and corporate, can be sexualized. At the heart of this is an inward focus in public relations on the promotion of 'self' as a sign of success or competitive advantage. This is intrinsically linked to the blurring of work and play, and an interpretation of the ambiguous behavioural and cultural norms at this level as a necessary requirement for fast job promotion and peer esteem. In the Fraser-Kirk case the disparaging blog commentary around sexualized relations in public relations contexts was particularly strong. It implied that women are not taking their careers 'seriously' because they are flippant, not really interested, distracted by sexual power. Bound up with this was the idea of servitude but also disdain. Therefore, this ill-defined and problematic area works against reform in the occupation, and fails to support practitioners who challenge the idea that success is linked to being sexually receptive and that a culture of sexual hierarchy and harassment must be tolerated for career longevity.

Conclusion

A powerful assumption underpinning the personal selection of clothes and accessories is that it is a creative expression of the individual with agency to make informed choices (Bourne 2009; McKinniss 2010; Mary Ann 2011). However, this study shows how the clothes–body complex can also do the opposite. It can construct a fixed identity that directs the subject and leads them towards a gendered self which is interdiscursively linked to controlling discourses that potentially disadvantage and discourage career choices. Hierarchical, sexualized and closed workplaces were evident in both the Fraser-Kirk and James Ashby case studies. If, as is argued in this chapter, some constructed categories for females and males within public relations workplaces are opaque and mask consequences such as unequal power relations that limit career choices, then further research could explore the relation of this blurring to unethical public relations practices and campaigns. Deploying public relations campaigns is a powerful discursive force that on many occasions is designed to intervene socially in political process and public debate. Hence an ethical approach towards practice involves providing high-quality advice and making informed judgements that lead to good decisions. But a preoccupation with 'self' informs a world view which is narrow and less considerate of wider social consequences.

Fashion – its embellishments, blandness and conformism – reveals behaviours, rules, values and beliefs in public relations and its imagined futures. Thus the choices that women and men in public relations make about their clothes and appearance can affect or indicate their career trajectories. For public relations, resolving this self-contradictory stance on gender and power relations and the flow-on effects such as anxiety about body and appearance is an important dynamic in reform. If the theoretical directions of performativity are applied to public relations, the suggestion that a nuanced form of hegemony through which complacency and oppression can coexist is valid. This study has exposed a highly ambiguous area of practice that presents an obstacle for the serious development of the communicative role. Curricula in public relations continue to be anchored to functionalist views focused on technical aspects of the job rather than cultures and embedded ideologies. Not only are stagnant ideas perpetuated within this framework, but the absences imply that gendered relations are unimportant.

Notes

1 The first respondent in the case was the Commonwealth of Australia.
2 On 28 September 2012, and in an out-of-court settlement, the federal government agreed to pay James Ashby '$50,000, ending legal action in which he claimed the commonwealth had failed to provide a safe workplace while working for Mr Slipper' (Shanahan 2012). However, further court action by Ashby against Slipper was not upheld. On 12 December 2012 the Federal Court dismissed the sexual harassment claim against the former Speaker, deciding it was a political attack, and ordered Ashby to pay costs (Hawley 2012). As of late December 2012, as well as appealing the Federal Court decision, Ashby and his legal team were intending to lodge a sexual harassment claim against Slipper with Fair Work Australia, the independent national workplace relations tribunal (Cullen 2012).
3 Downloaded copy of this now-inactive reader blog in possession of author.

References

Babbie, E., (2001) *The Practice of Social Research*, Australia: Wadsworth.
Bauman, Z. (2000) 'Shopping around for a place to stay', in J. Rutherford (ed.), *The Art of Life: On Living, Love and Death*, London: Lawrence and Wishart: 197–219.

Beck, U., Giddens, A. and Lash, S. (eds) (2000) *Reflexive Modernization Politics: Tradition and Aesthetics in the Modern Social Order*, Stanford, CA: Stanford University Press.
Beck, U. and Willms, J. (2004) *Conversations with Ulrich Beck*, Cambridge: Polity Press.
Bernays, E. (2005) *Propaganda*, Brooklyn, NY: IG Publishing.
Boucher, G. (2006) 'The politics of performativity: A critique of Judith Butler', *Parrhesia: A Journal of Critical Philosophy*, 1: 112–41.
Bourdieu, P. (1991) *Language and Symbolic Power*, Cambridge: Polity Press.
Butler, J. (2008) *Gender Trouble*, New York: Routledge.
Craik, J. (1994) *The Face of Fashion: Cultural Studies in Fashion*, London and New York: Routledge.
Daymon, C. and Demetrious, K. (2010) 'Gender and public relations: Perspectives, applications and questions', *PRism* 7(4). Online. Available HTTP: <http://www.prismjournal.org/fileadmin/Praxis/Files/Gender/Daymon_Demetrious.pdf> (accessed 11 January 2013).
Elmer, P. (2010) 'Re-encountering the PR man', *PRism* 7(4). Online. Available HTTP: <http://www.prismjournal.org/fileadmin/Praxis/Files/Gender/Elmer.pdf> (accessed 11 January 2013).
Fairclough, Norman (1999) *Discourse and Social Change*, Cambridge: Polity Press
Fraser-Kirk, Kristy Anne (2010) Statement of Claim Application (Form 5), filed in the Federal Court of Australia, New South Wales District Registry, 2 August.
Fröhlich, R. and Peters, S.B. (2007) 'PR bunnies caught in the agency ghetto? Gender stereotypes, organizational factors, and women's careers in PR agencies', *Journal of Public Relations Research*, 19(3): 229–54.
Holtzhausen, R.D. (2005) 'Public relations practice and political change in South Africa', *Public Relations Review*, 31: 407–19.
Lippmann, Walter (2010), *Public Opinion*, Blacksburg, VA: Wilder Publications, Inc.
MacKinnon, C.A. (1987) *Feminism Unmodified Discourses on Life and Law*, Cambridge, MA: Harvard University Press.
Miller, Mark C. (2005) 'Introduction', in Edward Bernays, *Propaganda*, Brooklyn, NY: IG Publishing: 9–33.
Nelson, R. (2011) 'A rich exploration of male sartorial splendour', *The Age*, 27 July. Online. Available HTTP: <http://www.theage.com.au/executive-style/style/in-search-of-sartorial-splendour-20110727-1hzhf.html> (accessed 11 January 2013).
O'Byrne, S. (2010) 'Clothing and gender in the workplace', *PRism* 7(4). Online. Available HTTP: <http://www.prismjournal.org/fileadmin/Praxis/Files/Gender/Obyrne.pdf> (accessed 11 January 2013).
Threadgold, Terry (1993) *Halliday's Language as a Social Semiotic: Forgotten Issues and Necessary Directions*, Geelong: Deakin University.
Tsetsura, K. (2010) 'Is public relations a real job? How female practitioners construct the profession', *Journal of Public Relations Research*, 23(1): 1–23.
Walker, R.R. (1967) *People, Practices, Philosophies in Australian Advertising, Media, Marketing*, Melbourne: Lansdowne Press.

Websites

Ang, Mary Lou (2010) Blog commentary, 19 October, in Derryn Hinch and Nadia Jamal (2010) 'Kristy Fraser-Kirk to keep money', 3AW 693 News Talk. Online.

Available HTTP: <http://www.3aw.com.au/blogs/3aw-generic-blog/kristy-fraserkirk-to-keep-money/20101018}16pmn.html> (accessed 14 January 2013).

Australian Associated Press (AAP) (2012) 'James Ashby "took no steps to resolve dispute" with Speaker Peter Slipper', *Herald Sun*, 17 May. Online. Available HTTP: <http://www.heraldsun.com.au/news/more-news/james-ashby-took-no-steps-to-resolve-dispute-with-speaker-peter-slipper/story-fn7x8me2-1226359300206> (accessed 11 January 2013).

Australian Associated Press (AAP) (Steve Lewis) (2012) 'Peter Slipper ambushed, subject to character assassination – lawyer', *Herald Sun*, 18 May. Online. Available HTTP: <http://www.heraldsun.com.au/news/more-news/getting-messy-by-the-minute/story-e6frf7l6-1226360217402> (accessed 11 January 2013).

Ashby, James Hunter (2012) Originating application under the Fair Work Act 2009 alleging discrimination, filed in the Federal Court of Australia, New South Wales Registry – Federal Court of Australia Fair Work Division No: NSD580/2012, 25 May.

Bourne, Leah (2009) 'What women should – and shouldn't – wear in the workplace', *Forbes*, 9 February. Online. Available HTTP: <http://www.forbes.com/2009/02/09/workplace-office-clothing-women-style_0209_suit.html> (accessed 11 January 2013).

Brett, Samantha (2010) 'Are women really too distracting for men?', *Sydney Morning Herald* 'Life and Style', 11 August. Online. Available HTTP: <http://www.smh.com.au/lifestyle/life/blogs/ask-sam/are-women-really-too-distracting-for-men-20100811-11yyp.html> (accessed 11 January 2013).

Campbell, Mel (2010) 'Were Kristy Fraser-Kirk's PR advisers snoozing on the job?', *Crikey*, 21 October. Online. Available HTTP: <http://www.crikey.com.au/2010/10/21/were-kristy-fraser-kirk%E2%80%99s-pr-advisers-snoozing-on-the-job/> (accessed 14/1/2013).

Chique St. (2009) 'Dress for success: What to wear to a media/PR/marketing interview', *Chique St.*, 22 September. Online. Available HTTP: <http://streetchique.wordpress.com/2009/09/22/dress-for-success-what-to-wear-to-a-mediaprmarketing-interview/> (accessed 5 January 2013).

Cullen, Simon (2012) 'Ashby to take Slipper case to Fair Work Australia', *ABC News*, 23 December. Online. Available HTTP: <http://www.abc.net.au/news/2012-12-21/ashby-to-take-case-to-fair-work-australia/4439832> (accessed 8 March 2013).

eHow Contributor (2013) 'How to dress for a public relations job', eHow.com. Online. Available HTTP: <http://www.ehow.com/how_2045234_dress-public-relations-job.html#ixzz2I0NQ8nQf. http://www.ehow.com/how_2045234_dress-public-relations-job.html> (accessed 15 January 2013).

Fife-Yeomans, J. (2010) 'David Jones CEO accused of harassing multiple staff members', *Herald Sun*, 3 August. Online. Available HTTP: <http://www.heraldsun.com.au/news/victoria/david-jones-ceo-accused-of-harassing-multiple-staff-members/story-e6frf7l6-1225900375741> (accessed 11 January 2013).

Freeney, Katherine (2010) 'The blonde, the brunette and the boss', *Sydney Morning Herald* 'Life and Style', 4 August. Online. Available HTTP: <http://www.brisbanetimes.com.au/lifestyle/life/blogs/citykat/the-blonde-the-brunette-and-the-boss-20100804-115qt.html> (accessed 11 January 2013).

Gome, Amanda (2010) 'Why didn't the DJs board act against McInnes sooner?', *Crikey*, 4 August. Online. Available HTTP: <http://www.crikey.com.au/2010/08/04/

gome-why-didnt-the-djs-board-act-against-mcinnes-sooner/> (accessed 14 January 2013).

Hawley, Samantha (2012) 'Slipper case thrown out', *PM with Mark Colvin*, 12 December. Online. Available HTTP: <http://www.abc.net.au/pm/content/2012/s3653232.htm> (accessed 8 March 2013).

Higgins, Ean (2012) 'James Ashby's accusations against Peter Slipper labelled an "ambush"', *The Australian*, 18 May. Online. Available HTTP: <http://www.theaustralian.com.au/national-affairs/in-depth/james-ashbys-accusations-against-peter-slipper-labelled-an-ambush/story-fndckad0-1226360123217> (accessed 11 January 2013).

Hinch, Derryn and Jamal, Nadia (2010) 'Kristy Fraser-Kirk to keep money', 3AW 693 News Talk, 18 October. Online. Available HTTP: <http://www.3aw.com.au/blogs/3aw-generic-blog/kristy-fraserkirk-to-keep-money/20101018-16pmn.html> (accessed 14 January 2013).

KC You There, LLC (2012) 'What to wear: PR internship interview', *KC You There: A Lifestyle Blog*, 16 April. Online. Available HTTP: <http://kcyouthere.wordpress.com/2012/04/16/what-to-wear-pr-internship-interview/> (accessed 11 January 2013).

Kohler, Alan (2010) 'The David Jones case shows middle managers need to be better trained: Kohler', *Smart Company*, 3 August. Online. Available HTTP: <http://www.smartcompany.com.au/legal/20100803-the-david-jones-case-shows-middle-> (accessed 11 January 2013).

Kontominas, Bellinda and Mann, Simon (2010) '"My life has been turned upside down": The sordid details behind the $37 million DJs sex claim', smh.com.au, 3 August. Online. Available HTTP: <http://www.smh.com.au/business/my-life-has-been-turned-upside-down-the-sordid-details-behind-the-37-million-djs-sex-claim-20100802-113d4.html#ixzz2Huk35Krx> (accessed 14 January 2013).

Lewis, S. (2012) 'More staff accuse Peter Slipper', *Herald Sun*, 16 May. Online. Available HTTP: <http://www.heraldsun.com.au/news/victoria/more-staff-accuse-peter-slipper/story-fn7x8me2-1226356724221> (accessed 11 January 2013).

Maguire, Tory (2010) 'Fraser-Kirk's confronting a monster of her own creation', *The Punch*, 28 September. Online. Available HTTP: <http://www.thepunch.com.au/articles/fraser-kirks-confronting-a-monster-of-her-own-creation/> (accessed 5 January 2013).

Mary Ann (2011) 'Top five wardrobe essentials for PR girls', *nyc pr girls*, 10 May. Online. Available HTTP: <http://nycprgirls.com/wardrobe-essentials-for-pr-girls/> (accessed 5 January 2013).

McKinniss, Sara (2010) 'What to wear to a PR interview', *Young Profashionable*, 7 April. Online. Available HTTP: <http://youngprofashionable.com/2010/04/07/what-to-wear-to-a-pr-interview-featuring-prcouture/> (accessed 5 January 2013).

Peatling, Stephanie (2012) 'Where is the sympathy for James Ashby?', *Daily Life*, 23 April. Online. Available HTTP: <http://www.dailylife.com.au/news-and-views/news-features/where-is-the-sympathy-for-james-ashby-20120423-1xghn.html> (accessed 20 February 2013).

PR Moment (2011) 'What not to wear: Hacked Off gives some tips for dressing appropriately at work', *PR Moment*, 9 May. Online. Available HTTP: <http://www.prmoment.com/648/what-not-to-wear-in-pr-hacked-off-gives-some-tips-for-dressing-appropriately-in-public-relations.aspx> (accessed 5 January 2013).

Reply 91 (2012) 'Topic Peter Slipper and sexual harassment claims', meganau. proboards.com. Formerly online at: <http://www.meganau.proboards.com/index. cgi?board=general&action=display& thread=8227&page=7> (accessed 31 May 2012; now inactive).

Selter, Emily (2012) 'Interviews with fashion insiders: PR pro Chrissy Sheahan', *College Fashion*, 18 March. Online. Available HTTP: <http://www.collegefashion. net/fashion-news/interviews-with-fashion-insiders-pr-pro-chrissy-sheahan/> (accessed 11 January 2013).

Shanahan, Leo (2012) 'Peter Slipper's accuser James Ashby now turns his legal sights on Nicola Roxon', *The Australian*, 28 September. Online. Available HTTP: <http://www.theaustralian.com.au/national-affairs/government-settles-in-james-ashby-case-after-staffer-sued-peter-slipper-and-commonwealth/story-fn59niix-1226483349747> (accessed 11 January 2013).

Silmalis, Linda and Clune, Richard (2012) 'Peter Slipper accuser James Ashby convicted over offensive phone calls to DJ', *Sunday Telegraph*, 22 April. Online. Available HTTP: <http://www.news.com.au/national-old/peter-slipper-accuser-james-ashby-convicted-over-offensive-phone-calls-to-dj/story-e6frfkvr-1226335352067> (accessed 11 January 2013).

Urban, Rebecca (2010) 'DJs case points to a company culture and a "corporate cancer"', *The Australian*, 7 August. Online. Available HTTP: <http://www. theaustralian.com.au/business/djs-case-points-to-a-company-culture-and-a-corporate-cancer/story-e6frg8zx-1225902280334> (accessed 11 January 2013).

Williams, Luke (2010) 'Why workplace sexual harassment may never be the same again', *Crikey*, 31 August. Online. Available HTTP: <http://www.crikey.com. au/2010/08/31/why-workplace-s-xual-harassment-may-never-be-the-same-again/> (accessed 11 January 2013).

Wright, Jessica (2012) 'Skipper accuser Ashby was secretly helping rival', smh.com. au, 5 May. Online. Available HTTP: <http://www.smh.com.au/national/slipper-accuser-ashby-was-secretly-helping-rival-20120504-1y4in.html> (accessed 14 January 2013).

2 Caring about public relations and the gendered cultural intermediary role

Anne Surma and Christine Daymon

This chapter explores the interaction between the occupation of public relations and the daily lives of those working in the field. How do men and women working in public relations negotiate the responsibilities and demands of their work and home commitments? And why do so many women practitioners feel a sense of guilt about their competing obligations? This study is based on interviews with women and men working in the thriving resource-boom economy of Western Australia. We enquire how public relations practitioners, whom we define as cultural intermediaries, articulate their gendered engagements with work- and home-life.

Public relations, as cultural intermediary work that involves the promotion and extension of a neo-liberal agenda, affects the lives and wellbeing of its practitioners. In effect, public relations practitioners engage with, resist and adapt to social and organizational discourses in diverse ways according to their gendered professional and personal orientations and attachments. Drawing on a feminist ethics of care, we suggest that a critical reappraisal of public relations approaches and practices is now both urgent and timely. Public relations, as a socially significant type of cultural intermediary work, is well placed to contribute to the reshaping of dominant discourses and to demonstrate the centrality of caring relationships in private and public life.

How best to deal with the interrelationship between work- and home-lives is an ongoing challenge faced by individuals and organizations in most industrialized societies, as illustrated in a range of studies conducted in the UK and Europe (Crompton and Lyonnette 2006), Hong Kong and Singapore (Thein *et al.* 2010), India (Rajadhyaksha 2012), North America (Kreiner *et al.* 2009) and Australia (Pocock *et al.* 2012). Highly skilled, professional women and men face acute pressures of time and competition from the globalizing forces of neo-liberalism. Those involved in professional roles are subject to workplace cultures and commercially oriented discourses that value very long hours, even during family formative years (Brooks 2011) and many are 'wilfully blind' (Heffernan 2011) to the toll on their emotional, physical and psychological health, as well as on the effectiveness of work itself. Public relations practitioners, as professional communicators, are not immune from these pressures and their consequences. Practitioners' immersion in globalizing flows, particularly those enabled by a range of advanced communication and media technologies on which they depend for their daily work, makes it much harder for them to resist work as an all-encompassing activity, as we found in an earlier study of women working in public relations (Daymon and Surma 2012). Despite this, we found that some women do achieve a satisfactory relationship between the professional and the private, by segmenting, blurring or overlapping the different spheres of their lives in order to achieve a meaningful self-identity.

It is the interplay between a satisfying and meaningful life and the discourses of globalization underpinned by a neo-liberal agenda that interests us in this chapter. We posit that in their role as cultural intermediaries, public relations practitioners necessarily engage with and are influenced by such discourses and may also reinforce or resist them, with implications not only for their own lives but for society as a whole. Thus, our research questions are:

- In what ways do public relations practitioners' interpretations of and responses to the confluence of work and home represent and/or challenge dominant neo-liberal discourses, and how do these influence (a) public relations as cultural intermediary work, and (b) practitioners' own lives and identities?
- Are there differences in the above interpretations and responses between men and women? If so, how is gender implicated in the privileging of certain discourses that serve to enable or inhibit the capacity for enjoying a sense of wellbeing, in terms of people's work- and home-lives and the diverse relationships that sustain them?
- Can a gender-based critique suggest alternative approaches to and practices of public relations that would facilitate a more authentic appreciation of the caring relationships which develop and sustain both professional and personal lives?

We address these questions through interviews with women and men in public relations based in Western Australia. This is a region undergoing rapid economic transformation, so it offers an interesting cultural site for investigation of how dominant social discourses play out in the daily lives of those who do public relations and how gendered identities are implicated in the privileging of certain discourses over others.

We pause for a moment in our narrative to define gender. We take both sex and gender to be contingent, provisional, discursive positions, and the relationship between them as uneven and discontinuous. In this view, gender is not the 'natural' expression of sex or the social manifestation of a biological given; and sex is not the prediscursive 'cause' of gender (Butler 1990). Understanding sex and gender in this way is not to suggest that binary categories of sex and gender, of men and women, can or should be abandoned. After all, these ways of identifying are (for some people) meaningful, empowering and reassuring ways to engage with, and represent themselves to, others and the world they inhabit. However, understanding sex and gender as discursively produced and institutionally (as well as individually and collectively) regulated helps us reflect on and critically evaluate the socially constituted and constituting nature of gendered attitudes and behaviours. It also encourages us to scrutinize how particular ways of being and behaving in the world are recognized, validated and even rewarded, while others are occluded, denigrated and perhaps even punished or prohibited. Moreover, it helps us consider the ways in which certain practices and attitudes might be challenged and transformed.

Before moving on to discuss our primary data, we give some consideration to the geographical, commercial and cultural context of our research, and then to the role of the cultural intermediary.

The research context: Western Australia – a transforming economy

Taking our cue from feminist scholars, our research is grounded in the everyday experiences and understandings of the social world of individuals. This enables us then to 'study up' in order critically to reveal the domination and marginalization inherent in broader discourses which are often evident at the level of gender. In the words of Dorothy Smith (1990: 51), this approach enables us to 'identify the "conceptual practices of power"'. Harriet Jacobs (1987 [1861]) demonstrated that the concrete lived experience is the core on which to build knowledge and foment social change. To this end, we interviewed forty-six men and women involved at various levels of seniority in public relations consultancies and in-house in private, government and not-for-profit organizations operating in Western Australia (see the Appendix at the end of this chapter for full methodological details).

Western Australia, with its transforming economy, provides a context which usefully brings into relief the pressures experienced by public relations practitioners in the face of the colonizing spread of neo-liberalism, with its normalizing of the distinction between the professional and the private, and its promotion of competition and consumerism. Asia's surging demand in 2000 for commodities such as iron ore and coal led to rapid economic growth over the following decade in Western Australia, where most of Australia's natural resources are situated. Major resource companies such as BHP Billiton, Rio Tinto, Argyle Diamonds and Alcoa are based in Western Australia's capital, Perth, which by 2012 had become the fastest-growing Australian city (Australian Bureau of Statistics 2012), with a regular influx of immigrants attracted by good living conditions and a strong labour market (BREE 2012). The opening of new luxury stores by international brands such as Gucci, Louis Vuitton and Tiffany's attested to the increasing affluence and materialistic tastes of Western

Australia's professional and skilled classes. When economies such as Western Australia's transform in accordance with the globalizing forces of neo-liberalism, a restructuring takes place in the traditional patterns and rhythms of work with consequences for how professionals, such as public relations practitioners, position themselves in the market and in relation to the various public and private spheres of their lives (e.g. Brooks 2011).

Public relations practitioners in Perth, where women practitioners outnumber their male counterparts by four to one (De Bussy and Wolf 2009), live in a city whose citizens wrestle with an identity that, on the one hand, embraces traditional notions of 'mateship', family values (Dixson 1999) and a relaxed, often outdoors lifestyle and, on the other, is in the thrall of the increasingly hegemonic and globalizing forces of neo-liberalism. Yet research has shown that neo-liberalism can be toxic: for example, the compulsion to acquire more goods drives consumers to a more frantic pace of life where 'people work harder and longer to purchase, maintain, replace, insure and constantly manage goods' (Lawrence 2011). This expends the energy necessary for living a fully satisfying life. Economies focused on consumption foster conditions that heighten psychological insecurities and in effect they end up fuelling themselves. To acquire the buying power to obtain more goods that a neo-liberal discourse has convinced them they and their families need, people work longer hours outside the home. Attention to children, intimate time with partners and friends, and other satisfactions such as having time for fun and enjoyment that cannot be bought are pushed to the periphery. Ryan and Dziurawiec (2001) have argued that such patterns of consumption now define Australia and a study by Rindfleisch *et al.* (1997) has pointed out that this is a gendered phenomenon, with men valuing such consumption and its associated self-centred behaviour more than women. Public relations practitioners who are citizens of Western Australia are not invulnerable to these global and neo-liberal influences in their lives and in their practice as cultural intermediaries; indeed, we argue that the neo-liberal agenda is often perpetuated through the public relations role of cultural intermediary.

Cultural intermediaries

To date, there has been no consideration of gender in discussions of the cultural intermediary role in public relations, nor investigation of the influence of cultural intermediary work on the lives of those who engage in public relations. Yet this is an area demanding scrutiny, given the capacity of public relations both to constitute and to be constituted by broader societal discourses. The ideological practices, values and attitudes promulgated by the neo-liberal agenda, in whose promotion and extension public relations is (to a greater or lesser extent) inevitably involved as an active participant circulating mainstream cultural, commercial and political discourses, will likely affect the lives and wellbeing of its practitioners as well as its publics (irrespective of whether they choose to accept, resist or subvert its prescriptions).

To understand the concept of the cultural intermediary, we turn to the work of Pierre Bourdieu, who drew attention to the rise of 'the new petite bourgeoisie', a social class evident in mid-twentieth-century France (and other Western countries) which manifests itself 'in all the occupations involving presentation and representation (sales, marketing, advertising, public relations, fashion, decoration and so forth) and in all the institutions providing symbolic goods and services' (1984: 359). Recently, scholars have tended to conflate cultural intermediaries with the new petite bourgeoisie in order to direct attention to questions of how production and consumption are made (Hesmondhalgh 2006). We follow this line in claiming that the role of cultural intermediaries, granted a certain cultural and commercial authority, is to contribute to the shaping of the attitudes, opinions and consumption patterns of the public to whom they promote symbolic goods and services, such as cultural products, ideas and knowledge.

After his introduction of the term in *Distinction* (1984), Bourdieu did not develop it in any great detail (Negus 1992). However, others have done so for the fields of advertising (Nixon 2003; Cronin 2004), music (Negus 1992) and public relations (Curtin and Gaither 2007; Edwards 2012; Hodges 2006). Negus (1992: 504) argues that the concept of the cultural intermediary is important for the way it encourages us to think about 'the reciprocal interrelationship of what are often thought of as discrete "cultural" and "economic" practices. Hence, Bourdieu's work is pivotal in the resurrection of or return to a "cultural economy" of social life.' The cultural intermediary is charged with articulating for publics and consumers the use value of, or what they might do with, a given product or service as well as its exchange value, or its worth on the market.

The resonances of this mission with the work of public relations are strong, and it is therefore apposite that Lee Edwards, in her 2012 paper, highlights how the ascendant contemporary role of public relations enables practitioners to 'lead rather than merely respond to the media agenda' (Edwards 2012: 2); and how public relations work represents a specific form of cultural intermediary, 'because it is grounded in discursive struggle and misrecognition ... public relations constitutes a form of symbolically violent cultural intermediation, ultimately designed to generate symbolic power for vested interests' (p. 2).[1]

Edwards' comments relating to public relations as cultural intermediary work are salutary, and we aim to draw on them below in order to highlight the cultural intermediary's embeddedness in a globalized environment. In particular, we take into specific account the complex relational and subjective processes involved in cultural intermediary work.[2] In doing so, what becomes evident is the gendered inflection of the cultural intermediary role, an issue not taken up by Bourdieu or (to date) other public relations scholars. However, as Nancy Fraser points out when discussing Bourdieu's distinctive culture of the petite bourgeoisie from whose ranks the cultural intermediary emerges:

> This process of distinction ... helps explain the exacerbation of the sexism characteristic of the [Habermasian] liberal public sphere; new gender norms enjoining feminine domesticity and a sharp separation of public and private spheres functioned as key signifiers of bourgeois difference from both higher and lower social strata. It is a measure of the eventual success of this bourgeois project that these norms later became hegemonic, sometimes imposed on, sometimes embraced by, broader segments of society.
>
> (Fraser 1990: 60)

Even though the exclusionary limits of the public sphere and the segregation of public and private domains have, in some respects, been progressively eroded in the late twentieth and early twenty-first centuries, there is no doubt that their relationship with traditional and entrenched gendered attitudes and practices in professional/public and domestic/private lives still lingers.[3] For example, Ann Brooks notes that Australia has one of the lowest maternal employment rates, which is consistent with the country's 'more traditional family models' (2011: 75). In the UK, although attitudes have shifted, with a minority of parents (29 per cent) no longer believing that childcare is the primary responsibility of the mother or that fathers are responsible for providing for the family (38 per cent), it appears that the arrangements families put in place for work and childcare continue to be constrained along traditional lines (Ellison *et al.* 2009). We thus examine closely the significance of cultural intermediary work as a gendered practice in the discussion that follows.

The sections below unfold by integrating key findings from the rich and varied data drawn from discussions with public relations practitioners in Perth, Western Australia, during 2010–12. The sub-headings relate to ideas and categories which emerged directly from the data, thus emphasizing the inductive strength of our analysis. We situate the personal and professional lives of these PR practitioners as cultural intermediaries in their local and global, cultural and economic contexts. The gendered nature of the neo-liberal discourses that shape the globalized landscape suggests the different positioning of women and men within and in relation to them.

We begin our analysis by examining how the engagements of cultural intermediaries with their work- and home-life commitments replicate and reinforce the dominant discourse. We follow this with an alternative reading of the data, whereby we draw on feminist theories of care to highlight how notions of care, attachment and relationship are regarded as pivotal to both men and women, though in quite different ways and with quite different implications.

Individualism and the 'respectable addiction'[4]

> On Australia Day [a public holiday] recently I got a call from the General Manager. I had to go and write something ... when I was meant to be doing something else [with the family] and you just do it ... I've never said 'no I won't do it because I've got a child'. I mean I just accept that I've got to go and do it. I've done lots of work travel, it's just part of the job so I just sort of get on and do it.
>
> (Female manager, in-house)

The notion that home, family and personal needs should be subservient to the interests of business is evident in this quotation from a single mother working in internal communications in the mining industry. Such a view is not uncommon among highly skilled, affluent professionals, such as public relations practitioners, whom Rhacel Salazar Parreñas has called the high-end 'servants of globalization' (2001). For these individuals, the forces of globalization have motivated a fundamental restructuring of the rhythms and patterns of work, as well as encouraged professionals to articulate their identities in relation to the free market, while relating instrumentally to the various public and private spheres of their lives. For example, a participant working in-house spoke about her life's ambition:

> I guess I really wanted just to be independent and self-sufficient: so that means financially independent and self-sufficient and not having to rely on people.
>
> (Female manager, in-house)

It was not uncommon for our participants to equate self-reliance and the achievement of materialistic goals with hard work at the cost of personal relationships. A consultant voiced his experience of working and living in a 'flexible', though predominantly work-oriented, market-driven environment as:

> I would say that I'm pretty much thinking about work most of the time and I respond to emails and those kinds of things when I'm not asleep pretty much, so any time from 6.00 in the morning 'til 10.30 at night.
>
> (Male consultant)

His experience was echoed by others, including a female participant in one of our focus groups, who said:

> Clients want and value availability. There is always in the back of your mind that you want to be available ... With what we do in PR, it is very

difficult to switch off. We are always sort of thinking about whatever project.

(Female consultant)

The 'economic capture of the social', as Subhabrata Bobby Banerjee (2007: 146) has described it, highlights the extent to which individualistic, instrumental and free market principles, as spread through globalizing flows, have become normalized and even normative in regulating and evaluating the quality of individual and social lives. For example, when success is based on an economic model of having 'it all including dogs and children, whether or not [professionals] have time to care for them' (Sassen, cited by Brooks 2011: 74), then the family or non-work sphere becomes commercialized and characterized by outsourced social and domestic arrangements (such as childcare, old-age care and domestic chores), which enable both men and women to benefit financially from participation in lucrative, demanding jobs that may involve extended working hours. A consultant whose wife works full time as a lawyer manages family responsibilities through 'a combination of my mum and day care ... If [my daughter] is sick and can't go to day care or has a doctor's appointment or an activity, we always just find a way to make it happen.' He does this by trading time, in other words making up for any absence from the office by 'returning the favour' and working at home at night – 'I still always check my emails and I'll talk to clients' – or going into the office on weekends. A female communications manager for a multinational mining company who has moved her family to three international locations in the course of her career stated that her extended hours were possible only because of paid childcare arrangements and a supportive husband with a less demanding job: 'Work has been my consuming focus for years and the sorts of roles I have had have been lots of after hours work, lots of travel.'

Other women delegated childcare responsibilities to parents or friends in order to enable them to achieve their career goals:

> If I go away for work, I'll organize for my kids to be dropped off and taken to day care or school by other school parents and that's who will support me.
>
> (Female consultant)

> I'm fortunate that my parents are here, so I rely on them very heavily and that enables me to travel for work. I can say 'Yes, I'll go' and they will always have [my daughter].
>
> (Female manager, in-house)

In extreme cases, the professional may be so enthralled by this 'respectable addiction' that, as Aldoory and colleagues (2008) have pointed out, they might opt out entirely from family obligations.

Gender inflections

Although the depersonalized discourse of globalization may claim a gender-neutral stance, as various theorists have noted (Connell 1998; Connell and Wood 2005; Elias 2008; and Elias and Beasley 2009, for example), it is heavily gender-inflected. Elias demonstrates that 'the global sphere cannot be regarded as a gender-neutral arena, but rather should be seen as a site for the production of gender identity' (2008: 409). For example, a female practitioner in her twenties, working in the mining sector, stated that 'there is a level of having to prove yourself as a young woman' if she were to be seen as credible as a public relations professional. The stereotype of the exemplary worker – the autonomous, rational, competitive, goal-driven and invulnerable individual who demonstrates self-sufficiency and self-containment as well as an attitude that embraces flexibility, mobility and change – may well reside in the aspirational rather than the real world. However, the positive masculinist associations in discourses that define 'successful' workers in the globalized economy are multiple and widespread in the popular cultural imagination. Indeed, several participants talked about their embrace of the 'flexibility' offered by their role, their enjoyment of being 'in control', their relishing of 'a challenge', their drive to 'hit the big goals' and 'to win', and their pleasure in work as 'an addictive thing of doing something really well and achieving something'.

The writing of David Harvey (2005) serves to highlight the ways in which most women's emotional, interpersonal and social connections with and dynamic interdependent positioning in the domestic and public spheres are likely to be occluded by the forces of globalization, underpinned by a neo-liberalist framework. For example, the sense of blameworthiness often experienced by professional women in their neo-liberal role of 'new entrepreneurs' is rarely publicly articulated (at least directly). Yet, in outsourcing their traditional family and care arrangements in order to participate in demanding professional work, these women are cast by a conservative rhetoric as 'selfish and irresponsible if they do not fulfil their mothering roles' (Marchand and Runyan, cited by Brooks 2011: 74). Further, as one female participant admitted, 'I would never mention children when I was working for an organization'. Such acquiescence to the perceived expectations of employers and clients is in sharp contrast to the way in which every man we interviewed expressed confidence about his ability to make autonomous choices, revealing a sense of control over his work environment and a separation of that from the home and personal life. For example, when we asked a communications director who works in-house how his family would view the relationship between his work and home endeavours, he said:

> They would probably say he works too hard. They would probably say he works long hours whereas in fact I work the hours I choose to.

So I have no-one to blame. If I don't get to my child's concert, I have no-one to blame except for myself. There are occasionally diary clashes but, look, I live my life according to the fact that you choose everything, every choice is yours ... there is nothing that anyone can make you do. So I don't feel constrained by my job or by my family even, or by anything. So I choose to live my life and my career the way I want to.

(Male director, in-house)

This self-assured ability to distance himself at will from work or home contrasts with the experiences of most women, for whom the different spheres of their lives were intrinsically interrelated. Furthermore, women's intimate investment in and privileging of non-economic modes of production and reproduction (through the 'free' labour of care-giving, bearing and raising children, for example) risk making them marginal to or invisible within a discourse of globalization. Such a perspective creates the mainstream 'fiction' (Harvey 2005) that individuals are *not* embedded in networks of social relations, are *not* bound by emotional and ethical ties of responsibility with others, and do *not* need these relational attachments to make their lives rich, meaningful and valuable. However, and as the comments indicate, while public relations practitioners as cultural intermediaries are regularly involved in perpetuating the circulation of globalization discourses in their professional lives, they represent the gendered, emotional and relational aspects of their experiences as being in dialectical tension with the individualist tenor of those mainstream public discourses. In other words, in a commercially driven environment, the aspects that make the lives of professional men and women valuable as shared, interdependent endeavours are sidelined. They can be made to seem trivial or irrelevant or out of step or 'unrealistic', or insufficiently focused on the imperatives of competition, individualism, acquisition, self-reliance, self-interest, independence, freedom and, of course, profit.

Care and interdependence: a critique of the neo-liberal model

Having argued that many public relations practitioners both embody and replicate the gender-inflected discourse of globalization through their cultural intermediary role, we turn now critically to interrogate the hegemonic neo-liberal motivations for such practices. We draw on the feminist ethics of care to illustrate how public relations practitioners might counter and modify the individualist, rationalist and competitive thrust of broader organizational and social discourses in their own lives, with consequences for how they do public relations.

Despite their supposed allegiance to the hegemonic practices and processes that embody the neo-liberal logic (including their financial dependence on the strong neo-liberal economy that characterizes the resource-industry juggernaut driving the state of Western Australia), women public relations professionals, and some (but not all) of their male counterparts, revealed in interviews that they perceive and/or identify themselves as fundamentally relational beings (in their professional and private lives). They also revealed that they are motivated by connections of care for, service to, and obligations towards others, whether clients, colleagues, family or friends: 'we actually care about what we do'; '[there's] the satisfaction of making a difference to my clients' work'; and 'we're a service, we're a service sector. So we're always putting someone else ahead of ourselves.'

In going about their daily lives at work and in the home, contemporary professional women, in particular (as well as some men), are habituated to straddling and juggling the often conflicting (practical, temporal, emotional) demands of the domestic and professional spheres, even if the mainstream discourse treats and validates these spheres as separate or separable. A feminist ethics of care highlights both the dissonance and tension between work and non-work commitments *and* draws attention to their necessary interdependence. This is highlighted in the following account by a senior public relations consultant:

> I remember standing in a queue in the Channel Seven canteen one day with Tom and for some reason we got onto talking about his kids ... and Tom said 'Yeah, I've got two daughters and one of them I know really, really well, the other I hardly know at all because I was never around.' It was amazing. He actually turned to me in this queue with all these people around, looked me in the eye, and – this is Tom, he's the most calm, the most non-aggressive person – basically put his fingers in my chest and said: 'Don't let that happen to you.' It's funny how you have those moments; it's really stuck in my head.
> (Male consultancy owner)

Following this episode, which caused this consultancy managing director to reflect on his lack of attention to his family responsibilities, he revised his career goals and subsequently accepted a less pressured, less high-profile role in another company in order to spend more time with his children and nurture his family relationships.

The activity of caring, as this man's actions exemplify, is not only central to human survival and flourishing, but, as feminist theories of care argue, inextricable from the relations of obligation and responsibility that bind human beings to one another, not only in intimate and familial relationships but in social and political ones as well. The work of feminist scholars such as Fiona Robinson (1999) and Virginia Held (2006), among others, compels us to interrogate the merit of neo-liberal values, and enables us to understand how this mainstream 'fiction', as described by Harvey (2005) in an earlier section of this chapter, misses so much in its account of 'the good life'. Feminist researchers also offer us an insight into the ways in which neo-liberal values are gendered, in that they favour a masculinist way of relating. For example, with a view endorsed by many of our male participants, a communications director for an international company articulated how he positioned the different (relational) facets of his identity:

> I think when you describe yourself, if you're writing a profile on Twitter or something and you describe yourself: 'PR professional, father, cyclist', you know that kind of thing, the PR part's always going to be first.
>
> (Male director, in-house)

A masculinist way of relating historically and typically positions the roles and identities of the professional and home spheres hierarchically, while obscuring the fundamental, nourishing roles of emotional labour and care, despite their connections to broader questions of power and the social and institutional networks that structure individual lives. For public relations practice, such privileging of public and objective over personal and subjective concerns and connections risks overlooking the pivotal role of relationships as these are understood in ethical and interdependent – and not simply in functionalist or instrumentalist – terms.

In contrast to the view in the previous quotation, another participant alluded to the importance of the personal and emotional as intrinsic to caring relationships, highlighting the inextricability of the private and the public, and the personal and professional:

> I have a small team and so it matters to me now a lot how they're going, how their career is tracking, how happy they are, how well they're progressing. The first thing I heard this morning was that one of my three people who work with me is resigning. She was tearful which was lovely, so I was delighted for her. It's going to cause a huge hassle but it makes me feel very good that she's found a job which is better paid, more advanced and yes, to be honest, those are the things that matter to me at the moment.
>
> (Male manager, in-house)

That individuals exist in a web of relationships where people are always and everywhere 'relational and interdependent' (Held 2006: 156) necessitates great care in human interactions. Held argues that an ethics of care helps highlight the connections between people as emotionally rich and mutually sustaining relations of interdependence, not as exclusively rationally based or as centred on the lone individual (or autonomous person or private organization or single society). It is the emotions, Held argues – such as empathy, sensitivity and responsiveness – that are better guides to what we should or should not do, in moral terms (p. 157).

Guilt, stress and the emotional struggle

The validation of the emotional in a feminist ethic of care draws our attention to the way in which the emotions act as an indicator of what individuals perceive to be right or wrong. It also highlights the particular struggles of public relations practitioners as they reconcile or resist the different obligations of the workplace and the home. At the same time as public relations practitioners derive significant satisfaction from their professional identities, their valorizing of and/or commitment to their identities as parents, partners, friends and as industry and community members are also salient. For many of the women whom we interviewed, the effort to straddle these sometimes competing roles and identities regularly brings about feelings of guilt, stress and frustration that neither role or identity is being properly fulfilled, or that one is being privileged over the other.

> I always suffered awful guilt at times when I felt I should be home with my daughter, particularly as she got older around 11 and 12 and of course at that age kids are saying 'I'm alright Mum, I can do this Mum, I can do that Mum'. So you go off to work thinking, 'Yes, that's ok'. And then you get to work and you just feel horrendously guilty. And then, of course, you're home and not so much feeling guilty about the work that needs to be done, but the pressure of it. I don't think I ever actually when I was with my daughter felt guilty about that time with her, but I always worried about how I was going to catch up with what needed to be done work-wise.
>
> (Female PR manager)

> I stressed during meetings that everything was ok with [the child]. So, I'd be in the meeting but all these other thoughts were going through my head. I once had no choice, I had to take her to a meeting, and breastfed whilst taking notes, and the client was very family-friendly and said no [to rescheduling the meeting]. They were fine with it, but I felt very uncomfortable, because I couldn't focus.
>
> (Female consultant)

Whether or not women had parental or other family obligations, were childless, solo or married, the majority expressed a sense of guilt and/or stress about their endeavours to resolve their competing obligations harmoniously. The notion of 'guilt' was commonly raised by women in interviews, but, by contrast, not once when we spoke with men. Indeed, the men whom we interviewed (to a man) said that while they experienced the tension between their different identities, they did not feel guilt about the pull between their roles as PR practitioners and as partners, parents or friends. Indeed, most chose consciously and autonomously to privilege one sphere of their lives over another, thus living the different aspects of their identities in sequence rather than concurrently. Even when working from home, a single father explained how he could distance himself psychologically and physically from his children by 'locking myself in my car at home so that I could give radio interviews'.

Only a minority of women were able – or wished – to privilege the personal, the family and the home over the professional. In doing so, they experienced relatively little conflict (although simultaneously greater disconnectedness) between the demands and different temporalities of the public and private spheres. The majority found it difficult to resist work as an all-encompassing activity, or indeed consciously chose to prioritize work over other life spheres and identities. The interdependence of their various relationships extended beyond the specific place of work into their dealings with clients and publics, as highlighted in this description of the ubiquity of emotional connections in cultural intermediary work:

> In community relations, meeting with wonderful people doing amazing things, every now and again I do feel like you just get quite emotional with some of the situations you find yourself in, whereas previously when I was lobbying government, I would just get angry. Now you actually do feel a bit heartbroken with a lot of what you are engaging in and also the inability to help everyone.
>
> (Female manager, in-house)

Through this quotation, and others presented in this section, we see that an ethics of care treats human beings 'not as autonomous subjects, but as ... embedded in networks and relationships of care' (Robinson 2009) which determinedly situates discussions about relations between self and other at the centre of what might be imagined as valuable, thus sustaining the home lives, work lives and, by extension, civic, professional and political lives of women and men working in public relations.

The implications for public relations

Our investigation into the role of the PR practitioner as a cultural intermediary in the transforming economy of Western Australia has revealed how gendered behaviours expose and highlight the pervasiveness and significance of care across private and public domains. In our study, women and men articulated, and responded differently to, relations of care at home and at work, but for them all, whether explicitly acknowledged or not, the quality of relationships is the foundation for and the basis of their personal and professional lives.

Thus, relational ties and responsibilities appear to be central to experiencing, nurturing and helping to shape mutually enriching personal and professional lives. This might be alternatively understood as caring, or an ethics of care. In turn, this has spurred us to reconsider the artificial and forced – even if unspoken or taken-for-granted – distinction between caring both as a private, domestic endeavour and as a public/professional practice, and to reflect on what it might mean to evaluate and revise public relations approaches and practices through a care perspective. Recognizing the value of care calls into question the structure of values in a globalized society. Care is not a parochial concern of women, a type of secondary moral question, or the work of the least well off in society. Care is a central concern of human life, and feminists such as Virginia Held (2006) urge us that it is time to change our political and social institutions to reflect this truth.

For public relations, this has significant implications for helping us reconsider an ethical orientation to the profession and the potential for its critique and transformation. Critical approaches to public relations have already alerted us to the need to interrogate public relations' pivotal role in serving powerful interests and, accordingly, in developing and negotiating relationships by means of specific discursive practices that aim to influence publics' attitudes and behaviours. An ethics of care can extend the critical agenda by making visible the relational dynamics integral to public relations practice and by facilitating a questioning of approaches that merely serve to bolster existing power inequities, particularly through marginalizing the significance of caring/relational responsibilities, which necessarily affect the subjective, emotional and gendered identities of individuals and communities in all areas of their lives.

Given the neo-liberal environment in which much public relations work is practised today and through which it is legitimized, we think it is timely – indeed urgent – that a care perspective be brought to bear on developing, reviewing and potentially transforming public relations practices. The public relations practitioner's role as cultural intermediary, given its often ready access to diverse local and global communicative platforms and the capacity to contribute to the discursive and material shaping of culture, is presented with specific opportunities and obligations. Not least of the latter, we believe, is, first, the responsibility of public relations professionals to probe and reflect on the patterns and relations of care and interdependence – both personal and professional, domestic and professional – that obtain in any issue, crisis, campaign, or strategy, and in any discursive account of or response to those which public relations professionals might make.

Second is the cultural intermediary's responsibility to admit or make visible, rather than obscure or marginalize, the existence of other, alternative, subjective ways of being in the world beyond the instrumental, the economically expedient. As soon as public relations professionals accept this responsibility, then thay accept others as full relational beings whose lives and experiences are meaningful and important *apart from* our commercial or strategic interest in or use for them. This could work to temper the risks of doing symbolic violence or of misrepresenting the 'reality' and the 'real value' of contemporary existence in a context of globalization, too often ruthlessly rationalized and justified by neo-liberal measures. In other words, public relations practitioners might thus consider using their status as cultural intermediaries not to distort or inhibit (including by means of entrenched gendered practices) but to enhance the possibility of less powerful others engaging and contributing actively in shaping the personal, social and professional lives they (wish to) lead.

Our hope is that a future research agenda that advances an ethics of care will begin with the assumption that the everyday lived experiences of practitioners and publics – as they engage with, modify or resist public relations discourses – are in need of articulation. Such research will focus on public relations not for its strategic or economic effectiveness, and not necessarily to demonize its role as a promulgator of discourses that bolster the powerful. Instead, it will have a care for the practices and consequences of public relations on personal, professional and community relationships in their temporal and material contexts. And it will use the same care in the process of research itself, with researchers paying heed to the potential implications of their own research methodologies and outputs. Researchers investigating public relations practices or issues and crises, for example, will widen their research horizons to document the relational, emotional and interdependent dimensions of professional and personal lives as they intersect with public relations-related activity. In so doing, they will seek to enhance the intellectual and political awareness of their readers, providing them with new frameworks for making sense of and challenging the public relations-influenced realities they encounter in their own lives.

Acknowledgement

We would like to thank Karen Kerlin and Susan O'Byrne for research support.

Notes

1 Bourdieu's notion of 'symbolic violence', for Edwards, describes the ways in which PR harnesses language – a key source of symbolic violence: 'it expresses the space of possibles available to individuals through field-specific connotations that create the limits of legitimate discussion' (2012: 441). Edwards also talks about the way in which public relations' use of language intends to create 'misrecognition'. These notions – symbolic violence, misrecognition, manipulation, etc. – all (misguidedly in our view) assume, as Judith Butler (1997) points out, a deterministic role for language and the speech act, and significantly underestimate the role of language as constitutive and contingent, as well as the agency of interlocutors to intervene and resist particular symbolic versions of the world. They thus also ignore the ways in which 'dominant norms may be appropriated and subverted by marginal groups' (McNay 2008: 205).
2 Further, we would argue that the work of public relations practitioners as cultural intermediaries is complex, interactive and contested, particularly in

a contemporary new media environment in which the opportunities for the direct intervention of diverse interlocutors into the communication process are significantly enhanced.
3 In writing about public relations in the 1980s, Lana Rakow (1989) likened the notion of a dominant public sphere and a less powerful private sphere to the distinction between the values traditionally assigned to masculinity (rationality, competition and individualism) and femininity (emotionality, cooperation and community). Public relations, she posited, may have coopted a feminine discourse (such as corporate social responsibility) in order to make the masculine more palatable, thus solidifying an organization's vested interests.
4 In her book on workaholism, Killinger (1997) described this as the 'respectable addiction', where individuals take a perverse pride in toiling for long hours and sleeping for too few.

References

Aldoory, L., Jiang, H., Toth, E.L. and Sha, B.-L. (2008) 'Is it still just a women's issue? A study of work–life balance among men and women in public relations', *Public Relations Journal* 2(4). Online. Available HTTP: <http://www.prsa.org/Intelligence/PRJournal/Fall_08/> (accessed 30 May 2011).
Australian Bureau of Statistics (2012) *Australian Social Trends*, March. Online. Available HTTP: <http://www.abs.gov.au> (accessed 19 September 2012).
Australian Government (2012) National Accounts June Quarter 2012. Online. Available HTTP: < http://www.treasurer.gov.au> (accessed 19 September 2012).
Bourdieu, P. (1984) *Distinction: A Social Critique of the Judgement of Taste*, (trans. Richard Nice), London, Melbourne and Henley: Routledge & Kegan Paul.
Boyar, S.L., Maertz, C.P. Jnr, Pearson A.W. and Krough, S. (2003) 'Work–family conflict: A model of linkages between work and family domain variables and turnover intentions', *Journal of Managerial Issues*, 15: 175–91.
BREE [Australian Government Bureau of Resources and Energy Economics] (2012) *Resources and Energy Quarterly 2012*. Online. Available HTTP: <http://www.bree.gov.au> (accessed 20 February 2013).
Brooks, A. (2011) 'Women executives and emotional labour: The work–life balance of professional women in the Asia–Pacific and the US', in A. Brooks and T. Devasahayam (eds), *Gender, Emotions and Labour Markets*, Abingdon: Routledge: 73–84.
Butler, J. (1990) *Gender Trouble: Feminism and the Subversion of Identity*, New York: Routledge.
Butler, J. (1997) *Excitable Speech: A Politics of the Performative*, New York: Routledge.
Casper, W.J. and Martin, J.A. (2002) 'Work–family conflict, perceived organizational support, and organizational commitment among employed mothers', *Journal of Occupational Health Psychology*, 7: 99–108.
Connell, R.W. (1998) 'Masculinities and globalization', *Men and Masculinities*, 1(1): 3–23.
Connell, R.W. and Wood, J. (2005) 'Globalization and business masculinities', *Men and Masculinities*, 7(4): 347–64.
Crompton, R. and Lyonette, C. (2006) 'Work-Life "balance" in Europe', *Acta Sociologicica*, 49(4): 379–93.

Cronin, A.M. (2004) 'Regimes of mediation: Advertising practitioners as cultural intermediaries?', *Consumption, Markets and Culture*, 7(4): 349–69.
Crouter, A.C., Bumpus, M.F., Head, M.R. and McHale, S.M. (2001) 'Implications of overwork and overload for the quality of men's family relationships', *Journal of Marriage and Family*, 62: 404–16.
Curtin, P. and Gaither, K. (2007) *International Public Relations: Negotiating Culture, Identity and Power*, Thousand Oaks, CA: Sage.
Daymon, C. and Holloway, I. (2011) *Qualitative Research Methods in Public Relations and Marketing Communications* (2nd edition), Abingdon: Routledge.
Daymon, C. and Surma, A. (2012) 'The mutable identities of women in public relations', *Public Relations Inquiry*, 1(2): 177–96.
De Bussy, N. and Wolf, K. (2009) 'The state of Australian public relations: Professionalization and paradox', *Public Relations Review*, 35(4): 376–81.
Dixson, M. (1999) *The Imaginary Australian: Anglo-Celts and Identity, 1788 to the Present*, Sydney: University of New South Wales Press.
Edwards, L. (2012) 'Exploring the role of public relations as a cultural intermediary occupation', *Cultural Sociology*, 6(4): 438–54.
Elias, J. (2008) 'Hegemonic masculinities, the multinational corporation, and the developmental state: Constructing gender in "progressive" firms', *Men and Masculinities*, 10(4): 405–21.
Elias, J. and Beasley, C. (2009). 'Hegemonic masculinity and globalization: "Transnational business masculinities" and beyond', *Globalizations*, 6(2): 281–96.
Ellison, E., Barker, A. and Kulasuriya, T. (2009) *Work and Care: A Study of Modern Parents*, London: Equality and Human Rights Commission.
Fraser, N. (1990) 'Rethinking the public sphere: A contribution to the critique of actually existing democracy', *Social Text*, 25–26: 56–80.
Gilligan, C. (1982) *In a Different Voice: Psychological Theory and Women's Development*, Cambridge, MA: Harvard University Press.
Government of Western Australia Department of Mines and Petroleum (2012) 'Western Australian resources industry delivers a record $107 billion in sales in 2011'. Online. Available HTTP: <http://www.dmp.wa.gov.au/1525.aspx> (accessed 20 February 2013).
Greenhaus, J.H. and Beutell, N.J. (1985) 'Sources of conflict between work and family roles', *Academy of Management Review*, 10: 76–88.
Haar, J.M. (2006) 'The downside of coping: Work–family conflict, employee burnout and the moderating effects of coping strategies', *Journal of Management and Organization*, 12: 146–59.
Harvey, D. (2005) *A Brief History of Neoliberalism*, New York: Oxford University Press.
Hefferman, M. (2011) *Wilful Blindness*, London: Simon and Schuster.
Held, V. (2006) *The Ethics of Care: Personal, Political, and Global*, Oxford: Oxford University Press.
Hesmondhalgh, D. (2006) 'Bourdieu, the media, and cultural production', *Media, Culture and Society*, 28(2): 211–31.
Hochschild, A.R. (2003) *The Commercialization of Intimate Life*, Berkeley: The University of California Press.
Hodges, C. (2006) 'PRP culture: A framework for understanding public relations practitioners as cultural intermediaries', *Journal of Communication Management*, 10(1): 80–93.

Hoobler, J.M., Hu, J. and Wilson, M. (2010) 'Impact on career progression: Do workers who experience conflict between the work and family domains hit a "glass ceiling?": A meta-analytic examination', *Journal of Vocational Behavior*, 77: 481–94.
Ireland, J. (2011) 'Workaholic nation', *Sydney Morning Herald* News Review, 7–8 May: 22.
Jacobs, H.A. (1987 [originally published 1861]) *Incidents in the Life of a Slave Girl, Written by Herself*, Cambridge, MA: Harvard University Press.
Killinger, B. (1997) *Workaholics: The Respectable Addicts*, Buffalo, NY: Firefly Books.
Kirby, E.L., Wieland, S.M. and McBride, M.C. (2006) 'Work/life conflict', in J. G. Oetzel and S. Ting-Toomey (eds), *The SAGE Handbook of Conflict Communication*, Thousand Oaks, CA: Sage: 327–57.
Kreiner, G.E., Hollensbe, E.C. and Sheep, M.L. (2009) 'Balancing borders and bridges: Negotiating the work–home interface via boundary work tactics', *Academy of Management Journal*, 52(4): 704–30.
Lawrence, C. (2011) *Economic Growth and Human Wellbeing (Part One)*. Online. Available HTTP: <http://www.shapingtomorrowsworld.org/lawrence_growth_wellbeing_1.html> (accessed 19 September 2012).
Lero, D.S., Richardson, J. and Korabick, K. (2009) *Cost–Benefit Review of Work–Life Balance Practices – 2009*, Gatineau: Canadian Association of Administrators of Labour Legislation (CAALL).
Macnamara, J. and Crawford, R. (2010) 'Reconceptualising public relations in Australia: A historical and social re-analysis', *Asia Pacific Public Relations Journal*, 11(2). Online. Available HTTP: <http://www.deakin.edu.au/arts-ed/apprj/vol11no2.php#3> (accessed 20 February 2013).
McNay, L. (2008) *Against Recognition*, Cambridge and Malden, MA: Polity Press.
Negus, K. (1992) *Producing Pop*, London: Edward Arnold.
Nixon, S. (2003) *Advertising Cultures: Gender, Commerce, Creativity*, London: Sage.
Pocock, B., Skinner, N. and Williams, P. (2012) *Time Bomb: Work, Rest and Play in Australia Today*, Sydney: University of New South Wales Press.
Rakow, L. (1989) 'From the feminization of public relations to the promise of feminism', in E.L. Toth and C.G. Cline (eds), *Beyond the Velvet Ghetto*, San Francisco, CA: IABC Research Foundation: 287–98.
Rajadhyaksha, U. (2012) 'Work–life balance in South-East Asia: The Indian experience', *South Asian Journal of Global Business Research*, 1(1): 108–27.
Rindfleisch, A., Burroughs, J.E. and Denton, F. (1997) 'Family structure, materialism, and compulsive consumption', *Journal of Consumer Research* 23: 312–25.
Robinson, F. (1999) *Globalizing Care: Ethics, Feminist Theory and International Relations*, Boulder, CO, and Oxford: Westview Press.
Robinson, F. (2009) EIA interview: 'Fiona Robinson on the ethics of care', Carnegie Council. Online. Available HTTP: <http://www.carnegiecouncil.org/studio/multimedia/20090305/index.html> (accessed 14 January 2013).
Ryan, L. and S. Dziurawiec (2001) 'Materialism and its relationship to life satisfaction', *Social Indicators Research*, 55(2): 185–97.
Salazar Parreñas, R. (2001) *Servants of Globalization: Women, Migration and Domestic Work*, Stanford, CA: Stanford University Press.
Salazar Parreñas, R. (2005) *Children of Global Migration: Transnational Families and Gendered Woes*, Stanford, CA: Stanford University Press.

Smith, D.E. (1990) *The Conceptual Practices of Power: A Feminist Sociology of Knowledge*, Boston: Northeastern University Press.

Subhabrata, B.B. (2007) *Corporate Social Responsibility: The Good, the Bad and the Ugly*, Cheltenham and Northampton, MA: Edward Elgar.

Thein, H.H., Austen, S., Currie, J. and Lewin, E. (2010) 'The impact of cultural context on the perception of work/family balance by professional women in Singapore and Hong Kong', *Cross Cultural Management*, 10(3): 303–20.

Appendix

Our study is based on a purposive sample of forty-six Western Australian public relations practitioners aged from early twenties to sixties: unmarried, married, with and without children, in junior and senior roles, working in consultancy, as freelancers, and in-house for government, corporations, not-for-profits and small businesses. We collected and analysed the data iteratively, beginning with an exploratory phase of interviews with women working in-house that sensitized us to provisional themes. These eventually led to a working hypothesis about the way in which gendered practices, as manifestations of broader discourses, reinforced the tensions between the personal and the professional.

We approached participants through our own professional contact lists, from information about members of the Public Relations Institute of Australia in Perth, via the professional contact list of the public relations events manager whom we employed to schedule the first rounds of interviews and focus groups, and through the lists of names provided to us by other participants. In the first phases of the study, we concentrated on female practitioners because of women's propensity to shoulder the majority of childcaring and domestic responsibilities while also having an increasing presence in the paid workforce. We considered that the ways in which women deal with the competing demands of different cultural spheres such as home and profession would offer us an entry into understanding how public relations practitioners embody the cultural intermediary role. Following interviews, focus groups and feedback presentations with thirty-five women (see Daymon and Surma 2012 for more detail), we interviewed male public relations practitioners, comparing and contrasting their views and experiences with those of the women. During interviews, it was apparent that men did not engage as wholeheartedly with our questions as the women, who, in the main, were more proficient at reflecting on their lives and more able to articulate their emotions. However, the responses of all our participants showed us that all public relations practitioners experience some degree of pressure at the point where work and home lives intersect, although strategies to deal with that depend on gender. After eleven interviews, we stopped collecting data, as we found no further new information of relevance and therefore our data had reached saturation (Daymon and Holloway 2011).

Through presentations first of our nascent findings to a group of participants and then of our completed research to a wider industry forum, we were able to validate our study and gain further new insights.

We recorded all interviews and focus groups, transcribing and analysing immediately. By conducting the interviews jointly, we were able to discuss our reflections immediately after interviewing, and then in more detail after we had read the transcriptions. Working iteratively, we modified our interview questions in light of these discussions, with the themes emerging from our analysis of the data and our ongoing reading. This also helped us to make informed choices about the selection of participants for the following stages of data collection.

We analysed our data both inductively and deductively, coding according to themes in the literature and also from the words of participants themselves. On completion of the final phase of interviews with men, we re-analysed the full data set in order to focus specifically on what had now emerged as key ideas associated with 'care', 'service', 'guilt' and 'addiction'. Each quotation introduced in this chapter represents multiple, similar statements and views around these themes.

Elsewhere, we have reflected on how our personal subjectivities as teachers, researchers and former PR executives influenced our engagement with the research (Daymon and Surma 2012). We have already noted our emotional attachment to the project through hearing the many personal accounts of lives and careers that were told to us, and how we were saddened or uplifted when learning about the choices that public relations practitioners made or were forced to make which had affected their families or careers. However, after each interview and also when interpreting the data, we conversed reflectively with each other and other academic colleagues in order to maintain a critical subjectivity that would ensure our account is an honest (and therefore authentic) illustration of the experiences and perceptions of women and men working in public relations.

3 Interrogating inequalities perpetuated in a feminized field
Using Critical Race Theory and the intersectionality lens to render visible that which should not be disaggregated

Donnalyn Pompper

This chapter is about the ways in which advantage is maximized and privilege is resisted and negotiated in the feminized field of public relations. The intent is to apply Critical Race theory (CRT) and intersectionality to expose the effects of workplace inequalities on career growth in the United States and then to present accounts of how such outcomes are navigated, according to lived experiences drawn from in-depth interviews and focus group sessions with over 150 female and male African-American, Asian-American, Caucasian/white, and Latina/o practitioners of various ages over the past decade (2001–11). The study probes ways that privilege and disadvantage are reinforced according to social identity dimensions. These are salient phenomena given that the public relations field now has a majority of Caucasian/white women at mid- and lower levels, but with most senior roles held by older Caucasian/white men. Propositions are offered for new directions in public relations to explain, predict, and eradicate underlying forces that promote career inequalities linked to social identity intersectionalities.

Broad social problems steeped in intolerance and disrespect have implications for the career growth of women and men of various ages and ethnicities who practice public relations. Past efforts to understand organizational inequalities have failed to embrace fully the richness of each individual's unique identity, resulting in uninspired policies. Various metaphors qualify this shortcoming, including 'single-axis analysis' and 'silo-oriented thinking' (African American Policy Forum n.d.: 2). It is well established that women of color encounter sexism in a context of racism (Bell and Nkomo 2001), with similar experiences among various groups. Pompper (2005) found that decades of shortsighted reductionist thinking produced research negatively framing 'difference' in public relations in terms of black/white, violence, and conflict. This chapter is a clarion call for embraced social identity intersectionalities, for the purpose of exposing power dynamics and inspiring meaningful interventions for real change.

Themes among literatures serving as foundation for this chapter are:

1 Critical Race Theory and the intersectionality lens;
2 public relations as a feminized field;
3 gender identities and organizational leadership; and
4 age and ethnic identity leadership in public relations.

Critical Race Theory and the intersectionality lens

The CRT framework challenges scholars to re-examine paradigms, theories and practices whose effects subordinate certain social identity groups. By naming discrimination and identifying its origins, CRT supports research driven by a sense of moral activism (Ladson-Billings and Donner 2005). CRT originated in legal studies, yet applying this critical framework to public relations promotes a transformative worldview (Pompper 2005). CRT critique emphasizes that US employers still normatively pursue workplace homogeneity which protects the status quo (Appold, Siengthai and Kasarda 1998). In policy terms, diversity is about carefully including people who 'look different' (Puwar 2004: 1), so human resources departments strategically manage heterogeneity and reward 'nonwhite' employees who assimilate (Carbado and Gulati 2003: 1762). Ultimately, organizations use diversity as a marketing ploy to generate the 'right image' while obscuring a dominant white culture and core inequalities (Ahmed 2009: 45).

Applying CRT to public relations unmasks the requisite variety concept for its homophily thesis roots. Excellence Theory (Grunig, Grunig and Dozier 2002), public relations' dominant paradigm, qualifies diversity according to Weick's (1979) notion of requisite variety by suggesting that organizations have as much multiplicity internally as exists among external stakeholders. There has been a dearth of empirical diversity research in public relations, albeit with some exceptions (Hon and Brunner 2000). Instead, researchers have focused on status of minorities in the profession so that Caucasian/whites' circumstances serve as benchmark (e.g., Kern-Foxworth Gandy, Hines and Miller 1994). Because a control impulse (McKie and Munshi 2005) undergirds requisite variety, workforce homogeneity should be passé. Aldoory (2006: 674) opined that eradicating 'norms in dominant-culture organizations' created by Caucasian/white males is needed to reverse homogeneity trends.

Intersectionality is a critical lens attributed to formative CRT scholar Kimberlé Crenshaw (African American Policy Forum n.d.), and used to explore interconnections of multiple and overlapping social identities to ensure that rich complexity is not diluted and that dimensions are not considered as separate, unrelated categories. Intersectionality is used to study institutionalized inequalities through lived experiences (Dill and Zambrana 2009). It is a social justice intervention tool for 'promot[ing] more inclusive coalitional advocacy' (African American Policy Forum n.d.: 3), discerning groups within groups, and recognizing that social problems are neither exclusive to any one set of people nor separately defined. Conversely, disaggregating organizational dynamics into distinct issues distorts experiences, rendering them invisible.

In sum, the CRT framework and the intersectionality lens enable critique of public relations' limited notion of requisite variety and its implied benchmarks that support ongoing binary dualisms (black/white, female/male, young/old), reinforce neglect of social identity intersectionalities and promote lip service to diversity management within homophilic systems.

Public relations as a feminized field

A new body of scholarship was established when public relations salary disparity was attributed to gender (Broom and Dozier 1986) and the field was proclaimed feminized with publication of the first comprehensive gender study (Cline, Toth, Turk, Walters, Johnson and Smith 1986). Findings suggested that a profession's salary ranges and status are negatively affected when a field goes from male- to female-dominated, and that socialization forces work against women who lack salary negotiation skills, undervalue their own worth, and experience private–public sphere conflict. Ten years later, the feminization trend had escalated (Dozier, Grunig and Grunig 1995), and *PR Week* (2010) suggests it continues.

Seventy percent of female practitioners work below the glass ceiling (PRSA 2000), while Caucasian/white males still dominate public relations executive suites and out-earn women (Dozier and Sha 2010). Women and ethnic minorities can see those executive offices above their ranks, but work in vain to join them. The US Department of Labor (1991) defined 'glass ceiling' as an artificial barrier that prevents qualified individuals from advancing upward to management where the largest salaries and rewards abound; effects are linked to gender and ethnicity (Hwang 2007). Empowered by the Federal Glass Ceiling Act of 1991 in the United States, the Glass Ceiling Commission in 1995 investigated why advancement in management was slow for ethnic groups and women. Findings suggested that women's lack of managerial preparedness exacerbates glass ceiling effects (Woo 2000). Feminist critics fault ongoing gender inequities wherein women are 'devalued overtly and subtly' (Buzzanell 1995: 333).

Public relations researchers consistently fail to critique vestiges of patriarchy by instead emphasizing that women (somehow) are better communicators anyway. Rakow (1989) stands alone as an early critic of feminization in public relations by calling it a crisis fueled by conflicting gender ideologies – a field where women are paid less than men. In the *Encyclopedia of Public Relations*, Feminization Theory offers themes resolving that 'the field is healthier because of this feminist bias' (Papinchak 2005: 323). Also, Aldoory (2003) applauded the feminist paradigm's promise to empower women, and Sha (1996) argued that feminization makes public relations more ethical. Other researchers have examined ways the feminization trend affects field credibility as perceived by clients (Grunig, Toth and Hon 2000).

Little has been published about the effects on male public relations practitioners' job-related satisfaction levels as a gender minority. Lesly (1988) prophesied that growing numbers of women in public relations might dissuade young men from considering it as a career option. Employees' attachment to an organization is linked to willingness to work with people who are demographically different from them, with men exhibiting most resistance and minorities feeling the adverse effects of workplace heterogeneity (Tsui, Egan and O'Reilly 1992). Furthermore, anti-affirmative action sentiments have gained momentum, with Caucasian/white men charging that under-represented groups gain advantages at their expense (Greenberg 1990). In the words of L. Grunig (1988: 3), 'heterogeneity also lends texture to the history of our field', so we are compelled to discover more about practitioners' social identity intersectionalities and ways to eliminate barriers that prohibit some from achieving the most senior leadership positions.

Gender identities and organizational leadership

To contextualize this chapter's inquiry of ways privilege is maximized and disadvantage is resisted and negotiated further, it is useful to link feminization trend and organizational leadership literatures. Women's sluggish ascendance into management ranks since the 1980s has been attributed to deficiencies in their leadership potential and offered as explanation for why men still dominate public relations' senior management even though women significantly outnumber men in the lower ranks. Whether people actually exhibit gender-specific traits or communication styles remains a hotly debated issue, with some positing that organizational leaders are evaluated differently according to a gendered lens (Eisenberg, Goodall and Tretheway 2007) and others finding that gender matters in organizations if men and women have 'differential access to influencing meanings, discourses and practices' (Marshall 2007: 176).

Perceived communication-style differences reinforce stereotypes of women as passive, or supportive, and men as active, or authoritative. Tannen (1990) opined that men are active and set a normative standard that passive women are encouraged to reach. Attributes linked to female public relations consultants are preference for building relationships, cooperation, consideration, transformational and interactive approaches, group work, intuition, rational thinking, focus on long-term goals, and a win–win outlook in conflict resolution (Rosener 1994). Attributes linked to male practitioners are preference for competition, individualism, short-term goals, and a win–lose conflict resolution perspective (Loden 1986). A 'gendered nature of leadership in public relations' has been refuted (Mang, Berger, Gower and Heyman 2012: 32), but Aldoory and Toth (2004) said women make better public relations leaders due to empathy and collaboration traits even though leadership styles are situational. Some researchers have focused on dynamics among women competing for leadership opportunities. Wrigley (2002) investigated the 'queen bee' syndrome, a symptom of institutionalized patriarchy wherein women advance their careers by sabotaging the careers and work of other women, and Pompper (2012) said these effects short-circuit strong internal public relations.

Age and ethnic identity leadership in public relations

Social identity intersectionalities of age and ethnicity pose specific challenges that have eluded public relations researchers as important sites for power/conflict critique. Public relations is a field lacking in diverse ethnic identities, with 94.3 percent of all public relations managers in the United States being Caucasian/white (US Department of Labor 2010). This finding suggests that non-whites are unable to achieve leadership ranks. Everyday practices in US public relations reinforce Caucasian/white, male and youthful-but-experienced power hierarchies (Pompper 2012), meaning that fifty years of social change is not as complete as some might wish to believe.

Positioning public relations as a mere function obscures a broader view that organizations 'exclude the social world' as context for decision- and policy-making (Edwards and Hodges 2011: 2). In the United States, Latina public relations practitioners resist an institutionalized gender–ethnicity construct that fuels discrimination and thwarts career growth (Pompper 2007), and CRT in public relations helps to interrogate such constructs, expose affirmative action backlash and color-blind racism, and render meritocracy a myth (Pompper 2005). Beyond the United States, Munshi and McKie (2001) used a post-colonial lens to examine public relations in Australia, and Edwards (2011) offered critical 'race' perspectives of EU experiences. Munshi and Edwards (2011) further opined that a dominant Western managerial frame emphasizes 'race' as a variable of diversity management rather than a social category.

When US affirmative action was launched with the Civil Rights Act of 1964 and Title VII to 'protect individuals against employment discrimination on the bases of race and color, as well as national origin, sex, and religion' (US Equal Opportunity Commission 2004), legislation was expected to eliminate discrimination so that all could compete fairly. However, a Caucasian/white identity is perceived as a prototypical, benchmark attribute of business leadership (Rosette, Leonardelli and Phillips 2008), while in public relations leadership, being African-American/black is not (Logan 2011). A popular trade magazine found Caucasian/whiteness still dominates the field (*PR Week* 2010). Caucasian/whites' communication patterns and experiences become 'the norm from which Others are marked' (Nakayama and Krizek 1995: 293), with mindsets bolstered by business case practices endorsing color-blindness and 'happy diversity' (Ahmed 2009). Aldoory (2006: 674) opined that eradicating 'norms in dominant-culture organizations' created by Caucasian/white males means removing organizational barriers that reinforce homogeneity.

Age discrimination in employment is as much a part of the stratification process as is 'race', gender or class, so that overlapping social identity dimensions increasingly make certain people more susceptible to workplace discrimination (Roscigno, Mong, Byron and Tester 2007). Age is a social identity dimension less researched, but it may be the most salient among social membership categories, with reports of ageism on the rise in the United States (Fiske 2002). Employers benefit from ageist stereotypes, given that policies maintain preference for youth and stand for reduced overhead costs. The Age Discrimination in Employment Act of 1965 mandates protection for workers starting at age forty (US Department of Labor 1965), with none for those under forty (Greenberg and Pasternack 1998). Perceived age discrimination is high in the twenties, dips in the thirties, and peaks in the fifties (Gee, Pavalko and Long 2007). Nearly five decades of studies chronicle age discrimination among older workers who suffer pay inequities, barriers to new jobs, and reduced economic opportunities (Chan and Stevens 2001). Young adults are an understudied social class (Maguire and Maguire 1997), but Thompson (1997) found that they endure negative stereotypes for lacking experience and knowledge.

Age/gender intersectionalities suggest uniquely negative workplace outcomes. A gender gap in top corporate jobs in the United States means that women are, on average, younger, have less seniority, and are paid 45 percent less than male counterparts (Bertrand and Hallock 2001). While women in corporate management may benefit from federal legislation, their comparative age can work against them. Young women report high awareness levels of discrimination and strategically decide to establish careers before childbearing, believing that it will be more difficult for them to enter the workforce and excel as they age (Kurland 2001), and older women report more negative health effects associated with workplace discrimination (Pavalko, Mossakowski and Hamilton 2003). In public relations, age combines with gender and ethnic social identity for severe, negative effects. Midlife upper-management women (African-American, Asian-American, Latina, Caucasian/white) underscored ways they resist and accept master narratives of 'less than' in striving to break public relations' glass ceiling and change organizations from the inside out (Pompper 2011).

This review of literature on theoretical frameworks of Critical Race Theory and the intersectionality lens, public relations as a feminized field, gender identities and organizational leadership, and ethnicity and age identity leadership in public relations logically leads to two research questions. Too much research in public relations about social identity advances prescriptive goals rather than critical perspectives on why senior management levels remain dominated by older Caucasian/white males. Also, studies have been grossly inattentive to formation and perpetuation of discrimination linked to social identity dimensions that are intrinsic to heterogeneity outcomes and exclude some from leadership positions. Also lacking are employees' perspectives on ways they navigate challenges.

Two research questions informed this study. In what ways might a practitioner's social identity reinforce and perpetuate privilege and/or disadvantage in the public relations workplace? And in what ways do practitioners negotiate barriers associated with social identity intersectionalities in the public relations workplace?

A ten-year study

In-depth interviews and focus group sessions were conducted with over 150 female and male African-American, Asian-American, Caucasian/white, and Latina/o practitioners of various ages between 2001 and 2011. Research participants represented a variety of geographic locations across the United States. They worked in corporate, public relations agency, and not-for-profit organizations (including government, military, state college/university), and the interviews and focus groups generated nearly a thousand pages of transcripts. Both methods are well suited to:

1 gaining a simultaneously wide and sharp view of a phenomenon in context;
2 capturing data on perceptions 'from the inside' (Miles and Huberman 1994: 6);
3 collecting rich, textured data consisting of in-depth responses;
4 facilitating deep probes of participants' comments; and
5 serving as an initial phase in developing a hypothesis to be tested in subsequent research.

Noteworthy were public relations practitioners' stories about age, ethnicity, and gender barriers – which emerged from probes about workplace diversity, relationships among co-workers and managers and clients, leadership and growth opportunities, social identity manifestations at work, and coping–resistance techniques.

Next, a hermeneutic phenomenological theme analysis was performed on transcript data, a qualitative research method used to reveal 'lived experience' in context via practitioners' voices as unit of analysis (Van Manen 1990). Inspired by Glaser and Strauss's (1967) grounded theory approach, data analysis involved several steps taken by the author, a third-year doctoral student, and a public relations practitioner. First, the data analysis team read transcripts to get a sense of the data. Formal research questions served to navigate readings of transcripts. Inductively, notes were made on index cards that were categorized in piles and reshuffled as needed; comments from transcripts then were thematically arranged, with anomalies noted (Glaser and Strauss 1967). Deductively, the data analysis team worked from the larger body of scholarship to contextualize participants' voices and experiences. Throughout both steps, the vast amount of text was consolidated through selectively considering statements that seemed particularly revealing, essential, or remarkable. This technique promotes identification of patterns of meaning embedded among participants' voices (Van Manen 1990). Multiple readings were conducted until the analysis team members agreed 100 percent that the data were adequately organized.

Pseudonyms protect participants' confidentiality. Identifying comments via their self-described ethnic identity, a generic job title, and public relations practice site are in no way meant to suggest universally that all people of those groups hold such opinions. Also, no findings presented here may be generalized, but they offer a foundation for later hypothesis testing.

Three themes provide an answer to the first research question: in what ways might a practitioner's social identity reinforce and perpetuate privilege and/or disadvantage in the public relations workplace?

Advantage and privilege: who has it?

The first theme underscores perceptions that men remain doubly advantaged as a unique commodity in the feminized field of public relations at both lower and upper levels, in their minority numbers, while women experience disadvantaged status in their majority numbers. Such dynamics foment discontent within and solidify a glass ceiling for women. What follows are public relations practitioners' anecdotes about ways that one's social identity reinforces and perpetuates privilege and/or disadvantage.

Undermining federal equal opportunity laws and internal policies' promise of equal footing is an ongoing acknowledgement that men are more valuable in public relations than women. Ryan, an African-American/black man in an entry-level position at a New Jersey agency confidently anticipates a shorter management climb as compared to a female counterpart: 'As a male in this, you already stand out just because of your gender.' Similarly, John, an Asian-American man who heads a San Francisco agency, opined that it is essential to impress clients by having men in meetings to lend credibility to campaign pitches: when men are in the room, people perk up and say, 'Well, there's a guy talking and it's kind of rare.'

Participants raised the higher status of men issue, especially in regard to leadership. Louis, a Caucasian/white man who works in a Midwest corporation's public relations department, said that he has little respect for most women in public relations since they lack the ability and assurance to lead: '*If* a female is able to hold her own *and* prove her confidence in what she knows with professionalism, I find no problem working for her.'

Angelique, an African-American/black woman who heads a Los Angeles not-for-profit organization, explained that enduring socialized gender roles esteem men as business leaders, with women as support staff: '[N]ow that there's a corporate emphasis on reputation management, men are more attracted to it [public relations], and they get paid better for it.'

Although women recognize the feminization/minority-in-leadership paradox and lament a perpetual salary gap, some explain the contradiction by consoling themselves into accepting that women are inherently better at communication and relationship building. Rather than naming discrimination as the underlying cause of men's higher organizational status, Gloria, an African-American woman at an Atlanta not-for-profit organization, rationalized that women are better in the trenches than their male counterparts:

> A guy once asked me why there are so few men in public relations' lower ranks. I said it's because men have a tough time taking low and women don't have a problem with that. Even if I'm talking to a grouchy, grumpy reporter, I put the ego aside – not like a male co-worker who I once heard say to a reporter: 'Well to hell with you, then'!

Likewise, Andrea, an Asian-American woman at a Philadelphia corporation said that women perform better in support roles: 'Females are better suited to assuage and make every situation calmer and make it nice for everyone ... I completely can see why there would be more women in it.' Bethany, a Caucasian/white woman at mid-management in a New York agency, spoke of women's gender advantage when it comes to serving clients, but failed to link this argument to gender–salary disparity: '[W]e have an advantage because we understand men and we understand women. I think we understand men better than they understand themselves. And men rarely understand women as well as we [do]. So, we have a total advantage.'

The 'advantage and privilege: who has it?' theme explains that men validate their privilege despite being a minority in the feminized field of public relations, and women use defense mechanisms to accept a disadvantaged status.

Negative effects of gender identity: between- and within-gender issues

This second theme crystallizes public relations practitioners' perceptions about ways that social identity traits can foster within- and between-gender workplace challenges that may result in privilege and disadvantage effects. Describing between-gender issues, Greg, a Caucasian/white man who works for a Seattle-area corporation, told of department meetings where women have stormed out in tears, causing him to prefer working for a male boss since men are 'less sensitive'. Lorena, a Latina who works at a San Diego public relations agency, explained how traditional gender roles keep women down:

> They [men] feel threatened because we [women] can be assertive ... We can take care of a lot of things at once, where they cannot if they're focused on their career ... They're intimidated by us and try to keep us in our place. Men don't want to see us advance and will do everything they can to keep us out of client meetings.

Both women and men also spoke of within-gender challenges in public relations work. Women shared painful outcomes of operating within patriarchal structures that pit women against one another. Josefina, a Latina who works with a Miami-area for-profit organization, explained: 'I notice that a lot of women who own their own PR firms or are very up there are cut throat ... I was going to leave PR altogether because they were so horrible.' Also, James, a North Florida Caucasian/white man at a not-for-profit organization, opined about male versus male rivalry: 'I feel almost more at ease working with a female protégé than I would a male protégé because there is a lot less competition there; the dynamics are better.'

As the 'negative effects of gender identity' theme suggests, conflicts associated with working in same-gender and cross-gender dyads illustrate a specific set of social-identity-and-power effects in the field of public relations. The next theme suggests that social identity dimensions beyond only gender further exacerbate negative effects.

Age, ethnicity and gender intersectionalities

Finally, public relations practitioners stressed how social identity dimensions, beyond gender alone, intersect and overlap to reinforce and perpetuate privilege and disadvantage. Women across ethnic identities lamented that they are not only discriminated against by older men at the top but defied by younger men at entry levels. Also, young female practitioners worry that they are disadvantaged by their social identity intersectionalities. While younger men fear privilege loss in association with the feminization trend and attempt to restore the male status quo beyond executive suites, they also develop strategies for maximizing their commodity status.

To begin, practitioners agreed that diversity training and EEOC policies are impotent in the face of socialization that 'trains' people from formative years to consider age, ethnicity, and gender in ways that perpetuate disadvantage. Lourdes, a Los Angeles Cuban-American not-for-profit practitioner, told of an exchange with a former boss. Here, her overlapping gender and ethnic identities became visible in light of discriminatory treatment:

I knocked on [the boss's] door and said, 'Everyone else got an invitation to a barbecue at your house, but I haven't seen or received one – and I wonder why?' His pasty white face got very, very red and he said, 'Well, I've got to tell you that I'm from North Carolina and in my state, I was brought up to never socialize with people of your ilk ... Oh, I think you're a fantastic professional. I have the highest respect for you. But I was taught just not to associate with women – with *people* like you.' I said, 'I'm so glad that it's only your childhood phobias that keep you from inviting me to dinner.'

Similarly, Patricia, a Mexican-American New York agency executive, regrets having to attend sexual harassment and diversity 'political correctness workshops' because Latinos there 'have lived a lifetime of failing to take women seriously ... considering it [the workshop] the biggest joke imaginable'.

Several practitioners spoke to the point about how men guard against relinquishing privilege (or try to restore it) in the feminized field of public relations; one that is further complicated by general failure to accept intersecting social identity dimensions of ethnicity and age – along with gender. Isabella, a Caucasian/white woman at a Los Angeles not-for-profit agency, said: 'We've had a couple of young males express interest in public affairs and I've encountered a problem with them taking instruction ... these are white guys and Latinos. They just don't respect white women.' Similarly, Joyce, an African-American/black woman, told how her gender–ethnic social identity is a significant obstacle among young Caucasian/white males at the Chicago-based corporation where she works:

I have a young white male who is very smart; in his mid-twenties. He graduated number one in his class. I just know he's swallowing a whole lot of stuff because I'm the boss ... especially since he used to report to a white male.

Even though public relations is dominated by women at lower and mid-levels, practitioners admit that it is males at the top who still call the shots. Maria, who works at a New York agency, explained that it's not only Caucasian/white males who discriminate against women: 'It's much easier to be a Latina working in PR in a general market environment than in a Hispanic firm. We're [older women] just not taken seriously there.' Joy, a Taiwanese-American at a New York corporation, said her dream is for a future of 'increase[d] tolerance, appreciation for diversity ... and destruction of old paradigms and cultures of the past – especially all-old-white-men at the top who don't want to give up or give in to [older] women or people of color'.

In the lower ranks, young men may not be socialized to work with and for more experienced women. Dave, a Caucasian/white male who works for a

West Coast corporation, said he shares this advice with young male public relations interns who may resist a female superior:

> Check your macho at the door because that's going to get you in trouble ... Being a largely female-dominated field at the moment, nine times out of ten you're probably going to have a female boss. If you're the type of guy that feels like, 'Oh, man. I'm not paying her any attention and she doesn't know what she's talking about,' you're not going to last long. Be prepared to take criticism.

Speaking indirectly about restoring male dominance in the lower ranks, Adrian, a male African-American entry-level practitioner at a Southwest-based public relations agency, said: 'Many women feel as if they have something to prove and have a tendency to micromanage. Most men leave you alone and let you do your job. I prefer that because men understand each other.' George, a middle-aged Caucasian/white male who works for a Midwest public relations agency, attributed his preference for more men in public relations to clients: 'They think [female consultants'] objectives are too soft and not well connected to business goals. That makes all of us look bad.' Acknowledging the intersections of his African-American–male social identity, Phil, who works at a New York agency, relishes his commodity status:

> There are few African-American men who are in the field ... Our command of whatever the topic and subject matter is helps to raise our stock in terms of a client's confidence in our ability to deliver on the job ... I'm not a quota hire, but now that I'm here, I'm proving myself.

Also, young female practitioners worry that their age–gender attributes fuel inequitable treatment. Tanya, an African-American/black lower-level practitioner working at a Philadelphia-area university, explained how her overlapping age, ethnicity, and gender social identities are used by managers to restrain her ambitions:

> While I've experienced racial and gender bias in work settings, what most surprised me was the age discrimination I faced at my last job ... My younger colleagues and I were ambitious and looked for ways to share our energy and fresh ideas in hopes of advancing up the ladder ... When mid-level employment opportunities opened up, we were passed over for individuals in their thirties with similar skills and experiences.

Tracey, a Caucasian/white entry-level public relations specialist at a Mid-Atlantic region software company, explained:

My male, foreign manager would even go so far as to say that because I was a young woman, I was a good fit for [secretarial] types of tasks ... I was often not given the raise amounts I was promised and was told that I didn't receive as much of a bonus payment because the nature of my work was not as valued ... I was treated differently simply for the fact that I was young and I was a woman.

To summarize, the three themes of 'advantage and privilege: who has it?', 'negative effects of gender identity: between- and within-gender issues', and 'age, ethnicity and gender intersectionalities' undergird public relations practitioners' experiences with bias and inequalities that perpetuate privilege and disadvantage in public relations.

Just one theme emerged among public relations practitioners' responses to the second research question: in what ways do practitioners negotiate barriers associated with social identity intersectionalities in the public relations workplace?

Strategically navigating one's career

This theme emphasizes the effect of strategic thinking in public relations for oneself when resisting or navigating socially imposed biases attached to a social identity. Women, chiefly, respond to barriers by leaving to launch their own independent consultancies; others develop techniques for staying the course.

Some practitioners said that using the term 'feminization' serves as a barrier, too, by diverting attention away from 'more important issues' in public relations – a perception that ignores enduring patriarchal effects and suggests a slower liberal feminist approach of waiting for change. Mabel, an older Caucasian/white female who heads her own New Jersey agency, said feminization semantically aggravates gender disparity: 'I think if we continue to perpetuate this, we become a self-fulfilling prophecy.' Bill, an older Caucasian/white man at a Midwest-based corporation, also disapproves of the feminization term, but perhaps for a different reason: 'I refuse to discuss this issue! What does that mean, anyway? We follow equal opportunity laws about gender and diversity and all that. I hire the best people. Period.' Yet, most practitioners spoke of systematic unfairness linked to social identity and offered advice on navigating barriers.

A pattern of 'out-spiraling career moves' (Bell and Nkomo 2001: 161) has marked the public relations field since the 1980s – especially among women who start their own consultancies after failing to break through the glass ceiling where they can see Caucasian/white men in senior management positions, work hard to prove their worth, but are repeatedly denied advancement. Gloria, a Latina, became an independent entrepreneur twenty years ago after she continually was refused promotions at a Houston corporation because she was 'not management material'. Among men, the entrepreneurial impulse has been less prevalent – perhaps because men have not felt the glass ceiling effects that women have. However, age and gender social identity intersectionalities convinced Lou, a Caucasian/white man, that the timing was right for taking early retirement from mid-management at a Southern California agency: 'I felt like a dinosaur, so I decided to go out on my own. Women work for less and I'm just not willing to do that.' A gender salary gap reflecting women's devalued status in public relations affects everyone.

On the other hand, some women across age and ethnic identities prefer to resist workplace inequalities by sticking it out in one organization or by routinely changing jobs in search of greener pastures. Claudia, a Latina who works at a Miami agency, said that beyond using legal recourse, women must learn how to combat workplace discrimination:

> You have to stand your ground … You have to have enough confidence in yourself – whether you're super young, whether you're a woman, whether you're a person of color, or whatever – I think in general to have enough confidence in yourself and in your work to say, 'You know what, this is bullshit.'

This story is especially powerful given popular, trade, and academic literatures concluding that women possess softer, non-aggressive leadership qualities. Claudia offered a more radical approach to confronting and breaking down organizations' patriarchal boundaries.

Men encouraged younger counterparts simply to do a good job so that rewards would follow 'naturally'. They did not mention career advancement barriers at all, even among men of color. Meanwhile, women's advice (especially from women of color and older women) focused on preparing younger counterparts to encounter discriminatory forces. They stressed that skill sets are not enough since gender biases (further complicated by ethnic and older-age identities) are institutionalized – and shared strategies for enhancing others' perceptions of intersectional social identities. Emphasized was networking among 'the right people', those who influence organizational leaders who make hiring and promotion decisions, and gaining visibility as valuable employees rather than remaining a stowed-away 'token' hire. Mid-life-aged women of color also encouraged affecting change from within by providing opportunities to other 'different' employees; working from the inside out to amend organizations' infrastructures. Among Caucasian/white men and women, advice focused primarily on 'fixing yourself' by taking additional coursework, enhancing technology skills, and volunteering for high-profile charities.

The 'strategically navigating one's career' theme underscores how some people are constrained in public relations along social identity dimensions, with women recognizing their particularly diminished status that requires navigation of normalized Caucasian/white–maleness, while men assume that a level playing field exists and that they merely need to work hard to ascend the management ladder and join older counterparts in executive office suites above the glass ceiling.

Power at the heart of workplace inequalities

Deep knowledge about power structures undergirding the occupational field of public relations emerges when listening to women and men of various ages and ethnicities sharing their work experiences. Investigating ways that meanings are imposed upon social identity intersectionalities offers a departure point for understanding enduring patriarchal effects on ability to achieve maximum potential as a public relations leader. The four themes that shape answers to research questions underscore a zero-sum gain wherein one person's privilege usually means another's disadvantage. Moreover, findings emphasize that systematic inequalities are large, complex issues not just about gender alone and not just between social identity groups but within them. Organizational leaders affix lesser status to those who are 'different' from Caucasian/white males at the top.

To theorize about the paradox of Caucasian/white males dominating senior positions in public relations while females dominate mid- and lower ranks, findings attest to the transformative worldview impulse of CRT in conjunction with social identity intersectionality thinking to shed new light on an old, enduring problem. CRT in public relations challenges scholars and practitioners to unearth institutionalized infrastructures and socialization outcomes that remain at the heart of workplace inequities, biases, and discrimination. Until the upper-most levels of public relations leadership are as diverse as our global population, the hard work will remain incomplete and organizational commitments will remain empty promises. Indeed, new paradigmatic thinking – such as emphasizing the relevance of pondering social identity intersectionalities along with gender – is required to adjust public relations theory and to catapult it into present, global realities.

Below are five propositions to inspire real change in public relations theory building.

1 Excellence Theory's reliance on less politically charged words of 'diversity', 'multiculturalism', and 'minorities' must be supplanted by more meaning-filled concepts like 'power' and 'discrimination' which more directly interrogate root causes and outcomes of multifaceted issues.
2 Use of Weick's (1979) requisite variety concept, the basis for Excellence Theory's operationalization of 'diversity', has failed to abolish patriarchal infrastructures that continue to hold women and people of color below the glass ceiling. Requisite variety is mired in a homophily thesis which underpins preservation of the status quo by concluding

falsely that there is less conflict when people are the 'same', and implies a qualitative judgement of degree but is unclear about who makes such a determination. The requisite variety concept is turning in upon itself with discrimination against older mid-management males being paid less on par with their female counterparts. Furthermore, liberal feminism reproduces Caucasian/white privilege by encouraging patience for eventual workplace equality that somehow might emerge without radical, infrastructural change.

3 Practitioners and applied public relations research that consider 'diversity' in terms of image, marketing appeal, and business case, because organizations want to look good and/or think that hiring window-dressing tokens to represent expertise associated with specific social identity groups, disingenuously represent public relations' normative function (Holtzhausen and Voto 2002). Such effects obscure a dominant Caucasian/white worldview at the center with organizational inequalities invisible (but deeply felt) at the margins.

4 Social identity dimensions cannot be divorced from political and cultural intersections which produce and maintain them. Using the intersectionality concept helps in avoiding essentializing tendencies, especially in terms of black/white, male/female, young/old. We must avoid disaggregating intersectionalities by focusing on *just* age, ethnicity, gender, 'race', sexual orientation, or any other single social identity dimension – for doing so oversimplifies the intensity and breadth of individual experiences.

5 Encourage organizations to invest resources in reality checks, such as inviting scrutiny of ways work spheres impact constituents across social identity intersectionalities. Likewise, trade groups such as the Public Relations Society of America (PRSA) must use their member-supplied resources to monitor salary gaps carefully by routinely and consistently investigating via surveys (more frequently than once per decade), publishing results, and naming offenders.

These five propositions apply to public relations contexts, but should prove useful in other contexts as well, particularly as compass points for navigating theory building and for inspiring more radical, long-overdue change that redefines and redistributes organizational power, breaks down infrastructures and systems, and dismantles ongoing workplace inequalities.

References

African American Policy Forum (n.d.) *A Primer on Intersectionality*, New York: Columbia Law School. Online. Available HTTP: <http://www.scribd.com/AAPFdocs/d/59819079-Intersectionality-Primer> (accessed 22 February 2013).

Ahmed, S. (2009) 'Embodying diversity: Problems and paradoxes for black feminists', *Race, Ethnicity and Education*, 12: 41–52.

Aldoory, L. (2003) 'The empowerment of feminist scholarship in public relations and the building of a feminist paradigm', *Communication Yearbook*, 27: 221–55.
Aldoory, L. (2006) 'A (re)conceived feminist paradigm for public relations: A case for substantial improvement', *Journal of Communication*, 55: 668–84.
Aldoory, L. and Toth, E. (2004) 'Leadership and gender in public relations: Perceived effectiveness of transformational and transactional leadership styles', *Journal of Public Relations Research*, 16: 157–83.
Appold, S. J., Siengthai, S. and Kasarda, J. D. (1998) 'The employment of women managers and professionals in an emerging economy: Gender inequality as an organizational practice', *Administrative Science Quarterly*, 43: 538–65.
Bell, E. L. J. E. and Nkomo, S. M. (2001) *Our Separate Ways: Black and White Women and the Struggle for Professional Identity*, Boston, MA: Harvard Business School Press.
Bertrand, M. and Hallock, K. F. (2001) 'The gender gap in top corporate jobs', *Industrial and Labor Relations Review*, 55: 3–21.
Broom, G. M. and Dozier, D. M. (1986) 'Advancement for public relations role models', *Public Relations Review*, 12: 37–56.
Buzzanell, P. M. (1995) 'Reframing the glass ceiling as a socially constructed process: Implications for understanding and change', *Communication Monographs*, 62: 327–54.
Carbado, D. W. and Gulati, M. (2003) 'The law and economics of critical race theory', *Yale Law Journal*, 112: 1757–828.
Chan, S. and Stevens, A. H. (2001) 'Job loss and employment patterns of older workers', *Journal of Labor Economics*, 19: 484–521.
Cline, C. G., Toth, E. L., Turk, J. V., Walters, L. M., Johnson, N. and Smith, H. (1986) *The Velvet Ghetto: The Impact of the Increasing Percentage of Women in Public Relations and Business Communication*, San Francisco, CA: IABC Foundation.
Dill, B. T. and Zambrana, R. E. (2009) 'Critical thinking about inequality: An emerging lens', in B. T. Dill and R. E. Zambrana (eds), *Emerging Intersections: Race, Class, and Gender in Theory, Policy, and Practice*, New Brunswick, NJ: Rutgers University Press: 1–21.
Dozier, D. M., Grunig, L. A. and Grunig, J. E. (1995) *Manager's Guide to Excellence in Public Relations and Communication Management*, Mahwah, NJ: Lawrence Erlbaum Associates.
Dozier, D. M. and Sha, B.-L. (2010) 'Delusions vs. data: Longitudinal analysis of research on gendered income disparities in public relations', paper presented at Association for Education in Journalism and Mass Communication, Denver, CO, 5 August.
Edwards, L. (2011) 'Critical perspectives in global public relations: Theorizing power', in N. Bardhan and C. K. Weaver (eds), *Public Relations in Global Cultural Contexts: Multi-paradigmatic Perspectives*, New York: Routledge: 29–49.
Edwards, L., and Hodges, E. M. (2011) 'Introduction', in L. Edwards and C. E. Hodges (eds), *Public Relations, Society & Culture*, London: Routledge: 1–14.
Eisenberg, E., Goodall, H. L. J. and Trethewey, A. (2007) *Organizational Communication: Balancing Creativity and Constraint* (5th edition), Boston, MA: Bedford/St. Martin's.
Fiske, S. T. (2002) 'What we know now about bias and intergroup conflict, the problem of the century', *Current Directions in Sociological Science*, 11: 123–28.

Gee, G. C., Pavalko, E. K. and Long, J. S. (2007). 'Age, cohort and perceived age discrimination: Using the life course to assess self-reported age discrimination', *Social Forces*, 86: 265–90.

Glaser, B. G. and Strauss, A. L. (1967) *The Discovery of Grounded Theory: Strategies for Quantitative Research*, Chicago: Aldine Publishing Company.

Greenberg, D. H. and Pasternack, J. (1998) 'Age discrimination', *The Successful Accountant*. Online. Available HTTP: <http://www.discriminationattoryen.com/article-age.html> (accessed 22 February 2013).

Greenberg, J. (1990) 'Organizational justice: Yesterday, today, and tomorrow', *Journal of Management*,16: 399–432.

Grunig, L. A. (1988) 'Women in public relations: An overview', *Public Relations Review*, 14: 3–5.

Grunig, L. A., Grunig, J. E. and Dozier, D. (2002) *Excellent Public Relations and Effective Organizations: A Study of Communication Management in Three Countries*, Mahwah, NJ: Lawrence Erlbaum Associates.

Grunig, L., Toth, E. L. and Hon, L. C. (2000) 'Feminist values in public relations', *Journal of Public Relations Research*, 12: 49–68.

Grunig, L., Toth, E. L. and Hon, L. C. (2001) *Women in Public Relations: How Gender Influences Practice*, New York: The Guilford Press.

Holtzhausen, D. and Voto, R. (2002). 'Resistance from the margins: The postmodern public relations practitioner as organizational activist', *Journal of Public Relations Research*, 14: 57–84.

Hon, L. C. and Brunner, B. (2000) 'Diversity issues and public relations', *Journal of Public Relations Research*, 12: 309–40.

Hwang, M. J. (2007) 'Asian social workers' perceptions of glass ceiling, organizational fairness and career prospects', *Journal of Social Service Research*, 33: 13–24.

Kern-Foxworth, M., Gandy, O., Hines, B. and Miller, D. A. (1994) 'Assessing the managerial roles of black female public relations practitioners using individual and organizational discriminants', *Journal of Black Studies*, 24: 416–34.

Kurland, N. B. (2001) 'The impact of legal age discrimination on women in professional occupations', *Business Ethics Quarterly*, 11, 331–48.

Ladson-Billings, G. and Donnor, J. (2005) 'The moral activist role of Critical Race Theory', in N. Denzin and Y. Lincoln (eds), *Handbook of Qualitative Research* (3rd edition), Thousand Oaks, CA: Sage Publications: 279–301.

Lesly, P. (1988) 'Public relations numbers are up but stature is down', *Public Relations Review*, 14: 3–7.

Loden, M. (1986) 'Feminine leadership: It can make your business more profitable', *Vital Speeches of the Day*, 2: 472–75.

Logan, N. (2011) 'The white leader prototype: A critical analysis of race in public relations', *Journal of Public Relations Research*, 23: 442–57.

Maguire, M. and Maguire, S. (1997) 'Young people and the labour market', in R. MacDonald (ed.), *Youth, the Underclass and Social Exclusion*, London: Routledge: 26–38.

Mang, J., Berger, B. K., Gower, K. K. and Heyman, W. C. (2012) 'A test of excellent leadership in public relations: Key qualities, valuable sources, and distinctive leadership perceptions', *Journal of Public Relations Research*, 24: 18–36.

Marshall, J. (2007) 'The gendering of leadership in corporate social responsibility', *Journal of Organizational Change Management*, 20: 165–81.

McKie, D. and Munshi, D. (2005) 'Tracking trends: Peripheral visions and public relations', *Public Relations Review*, 31: 453–57.

Miles, M.B. and Huberman, A.M. (1994) *Qualitative Data Analysis* (2nd edition), Thousand Oaks, CA: Sage.

Munshi, D. and Edwards, L. (2011) 'Understanding "race" in/and public relations: Where do we start and where should we go?', *Journal of Public Relations Research*, 23: 349–67.

Munshi, D. and McKie, D. (2001) 'Different bodies of knowledge: Diversity and diversification in public relations', *Australian Journal of Communication*, 28: 11–22.

Nakayama, T. K. and Krizek, R. L. (1995) 'Whiteness: A strategic rhetoric', *Quarterly Journal of Speech*, 81: 291–301.

Papinchak, K. M. (2005) 'Feminization Trend', in R. L. Heath (ed.), *Encyclopedia of Public Relations*, Thousand Oaks, CA, Sage Publications: vol. 1, 323–6.

Pavalko, E. K., Mossakowski, K. N. and Hamilton, V. J. (2003) 'Does perceived discrimination affect health? Longitudinal relationships between work discrimination and women's physical and emotional health', *Journal of Health and Social Behavior*, 44: 18–33.

Pompper, D. (2005) 'Difference in public relations research: A case for introducing Critical Race Theory', *Journal of Public Relations Research*, 17: 139–69.

Pompper, D. (2007) 'The gender–ethnicity construct in public relations organizations: Using feminist standpoint theory to discover Latinas' realities', *Howard Journal of Communications*, 18: 291–311.

Pompper, D. (2011) 'Fifty years later: Mid-career women of color against the glass ceiling in communications organizations', *Journal of Organizational Change Management*, 24: 464–86.

Pompper, D. (2012) 'On social capital and diversity in a feminized industry: Further developing a theory of internal public relations', *Journal of Public Relations Research*, 24: 86–103.

PR Week (2010) *Power list 2010*. Online. Available HTTP: <http://www.prweekus.com/power-list-2010/section/1641/> (accessed 1 October 2011).

Public Relations Society of America (PRSA) (2000) *PRSA/IABC Salary Survey 2000*. Online. Available HTTP: <http://www.prsa.org./salser/secure/tempfile/index.html> (accessed 23 February 2001).

Puwar, N. (2004) *Space Invaders: Race, Gender and Bodies Out of Place*, Oxford: Berg.

Rakow, L. F. (1989) 'From the feminization of public relations to the promise of feminism', in E. L. Toth and C. G. Cline (eds), *Beyond the Velvet Ghetto*, San Francisco, CA: International Association of Business Communicators: 287–98.

Roscigno, V. J., Mong, S., Byron, R. and Tester, G. (2007) 'Age discrimination, social closure and employment', *Social Forces*, 86: 313–34.

Rosener, J. B. (1994) 'Ways women lead', *Harvard Business Review*, 68: 3–10.

Rosette, A. S., Leonardelli, G. J. and Phillips, K. W. (2008) 'The white standard: Racial bias in leader categorization', *Journal of Applied Psychology*, 94: 758–77.

Sha, B.-L. (1996) 'Does feminization of the field make public relations more ethical?', paper presented at the International Communication Association, Chicago, May.

Tannen, D. (1990) *You Just Don't Understand: Women and Men in Conversation*, New York: Ballantine.

Thompson, N. (1997) 'Children, death and ageism', *Child and Family Social Work*, 2: 59–65.

Tsui, A., Egan, T. and O'Reilly, C. (1992) 'Being different: Relational demography and organizational attachment', *Administrative Science Quarterly*, 37: 549–79.

US Department of Labor (1965) 'The older American worker: Age discrimination in employment,' report of the Secretary of Labor to the Congress under Section 715 of the Civil Rights Act of 1964.

USDepartment of Labor (1991) 'A report on the Glass Ceiling Initiative', Washington, DC: US Government Printing Office.

US Department of Labor (2010) *Labor Force Characteristics by Race and Ethnicity, 2009 (Report No. 1026)*. Online. Available HTTP: <http://www.bls.gov/cps/cpsrace2009.pdf> (accessed 31 October 2011).

US Equal Employment Opportunity Commission (2004) 'Celebrating the 40th anniversary of Title VII'. Online. Available HTTP: <http://www.eeoc.gov/eeoc/history/40th/panel/index.html> (accessed 1 October 2011)

Van Manen, M. (1990) *Researching Lived Experience: Human Science for an Action Sensitive Pedagogy* (2nd edition), Albany: State University of New York Press.

Weick, K. E. (1979) *The Social Psychology of Organizing* (2nd edition), Reading, MA: Addison-Wesley.

Woo, D. (2000). *Glass Ceilings and Asian Americans: The New Face of Workplace Barriers*, New York: Alta Mira Press.

Wrigley, B. (2002) 'Glass ceiling? *What* glass ceiling? A qualitative study of how women view the glass ceiling in public relations and communications management', *Journal of Public Relations Research*, 14: 27–55.

4 Gendered performance and identity work in PR consulting relationships
A UK perspective

Liz Yeomans

This chapter, which examines identity work in UK public relations (PR) consulting relationships, seeks to provoke students and researchers to think about gender as it is performed in everyday PR practices and how these practices might relate to the broader context of a numerically 'feminized' profession where women occupy the lower and middle ranks, and men occupy the upper echelons (CIPR 2011).

'Diversity' issues in PR have only recently become the subject for discussion and policy-making by the UK's professional bodies (*PR Week* 2012), yet the so-called 'debate' surrounding gender remains muted within the industry and largely unexamined from an academic perspective. Drawing on original research with agency practitioners, as well as literature from PR, gender studies and emotional labour, this chapter takes a critical-interpretive stance that raises questions about whose interests are served by gender segregation in PR, including the 'professional project' itself.

Few scholars have explored gender and identity in PR consulting relationships (with the exception of Krider and Ross 1997; Fröhlich and Peters 2007; Tsetsura 2010 and 2011) and none has explored these themes through the theoretical lens of emotional labour (Hochschild 1983). Emotional labour theory highlights the role of gendered performance in managing the feelings of self and others in service-orientated occupations. This chapter draws on empirical work to explore, from accounts of their everyday relationships with agency managers, colleagues, clients and journalists, how female and male PR consultants negotiate identity in the process of doing 'emotion work' (Hochschild 1983: 220).

The chapter begins by outlining the concepts of 'gender' and 'gender identity' in social theory. It moves on to describe the concept of gendered emotional labour in regard to PR work, and reflects on how it applies specifically to consultants. The literature on gender identity construction is explored for social and interactional features that explain practitioners doing 'emotion' work in agency relationships. Six PR consultants' experiences illustrate how identity is produced through gendered performances, often in response to stereotypical images of PR as well as its 'professional project'. The conclusion considers the research implications in the wider debates of professionalization and the feminization of PR.

Gender and gender identity

The term 'gender' is widely understood as relating to the biological category of male or female. However, its meaning in social theory has developed since the term was first used in the 1970s (Howard *et al.* 1999; Dow and Wood 2006). The challenge of constructivist social theory has been most starkly put by Judith Butler in her ground-breaking work on gender, *Gender Trouble* (1990), in which she conceptualizes gender as an aspect of identity which is repeatedly performed and embodied; gender is what people *do*, not what they *have*. Butler stretches the concept of gender to a postmodern notion of identity, something that is fluid, unstable and dependent upon social context. According to Butler (2004: 1), gender has 'no single author': it is dependent upon social interaction and is collaboratively or socially accomplished.

Further to Butler's notion of gender, Alvesson and Billing (2009) argue that gender is often complex and nuanced: 'gender identity' is an *ongoing project of the self*, 'prompted by social interaction' (p. 98) and is subject to flux and change, hence the term 'identity work' (Alvesson and Willmott 2002). 'Identity work' refers to people routinely engaging in a process that achieves 'a feeling of a reasonably coherent and positive sense of self, necessary for coping with the ambiguities of existence, work task and social relations' (Alvesson and Billing 2009: 98). Gender identities are not only fluid, but multiple (de Bruin and Ross 2004), which allows for differently gendered performances to be enacted according to different social situations. These *social* and *interactive* definitions of gender and gender identity, and how they are drawn upon in the professional role and professional identity in PR, inform the analysis and discussion in this chapter.

Gendered emotional labour in professional occupations

Recent research (e.g. Smith and Gray 2000; Mann 2004; Mastracci, Newman and Guy 2006) suggests that those occupying semi-professional and professional occupations fulfil the tenets of Hochschild's 'emotional labour' thesis, requiring: face-to-face or voice-to-voice contact with the public; workers managing their own emotions and displays of feelings to elicit a desired emotional response in other people; and, finally, allowing the employer, through 'training and supervision to exercise a degree of control over the emotional activities of employees' (Hochschild 1983: 147).

The 'feeling rules' (Hochschild 1983: 57), or the social and cultural demands and expectations of professionals, are not as highly 'routinized' or 'scripted' (Leidner 1993) as those applied to service workers in low-pay areas of the economy. However, there is still a pressure for professionals to adhere to the implicit feeling rules embedded in the professional ethics, norms and expectations of their own sphere of public interaction, including direct clients (Anleu and Mack 2005; Bolton 2005).

Such expectations may place demands on the professional to perform differential emotional tasks according to ascribed gender roles (Hochschild 1983) while aligning their performances with the gendered (i.e. masculine) notion of 'a profession'. Bolton and Muzio (2008: 291) argue that professional projects as 'masculine cultural projects' are typified by their claim on specific knowledge and skills which ultimately serve to undermine 'feminine work'. Thus professional work becomes segregated along gender lines, with men occupying the more senior, high-status positions, and women typically acting in support roles. Echoing this analysis, Fitch and Third (2010: 9) argue that the dual processes of feminization and professionalization in PR have inadvertently led to gender segregation in PR 'that privileges masculinity'.

Marsh (2009: 279) identifies two competing discourses in the management consulting profession: 'the objective professional' which relates to masculine discourse of rationality and impartiality 'offering transferable knowledge and expertise focused on measurable outcomes'; and the 'trusted adviser' which relates to feminine discourse, where 'relational practices' (as defined by Fletcher 1994 and 1998), processes, social purposes and emotions are valued. Although PR consultancy work is not the same as management consulting, my own research, discussed later in the chapter, suggests that similar competing discourses do exist.

This suggests a tacit requirement for PR consultants to work on their own identities in performing relational work with clients, journalists, colleagues and agency managers within the contexts of a masculine 'professional project' and a numerically 'feminized' profession (Fitch and Third 2010) where women occupy the lower ranks and men the upper echelons of agency structures (CIPR 2011). This 'hierarchical binary' (Dow and Wood 2006) may compel actors to perform 'gender displays' (Reskin and Padavic 1994) in their relational practice according to cultural norms both external to and within the workplace, thus raising questions concerning feminine and masculine relational styles, and whose styles are taken seriously (Holmes 2006).

Gender identity in non-PR and PR occupations

Few studies have examined women's gender identity in PR consulting relationships (e.g. Krider and Ross 1997; Fröhlich and Peters 2007; Tsetsura 2010), and it would appear that no studies relating to men's gender identity in PR have been undertaken. However, numerous occupational studies within the broader literature on gender identity are fruitful areas to explore in understanding male experience and male identity in female-intensive occupations other than PR (e.g. Leidner 1991 and 1993; Williams 1993; Alvesson 1998; Lupton 2000; Chalmers 2001; Simpson 2004). The literature discussed here provides not only the basis for illuminating the identity constructions of the male PR consultants in this chapter but also the development of a framework for understanding the social and cultural processes that structure male identity within the wider PR occupational context.

Men's identity in non-PR occupations

Simpson (2004), in a UK study of masculine identity in four occupations – nursing, primary school teaching, library work and cabin crew – found that men adopted three strategies to help them combat discomfort with the female image of the job. Two of these strategies bore similarities to Lupton's (2000) findings in a study of masculine identity among men who had entered, or were about to enter, traditionally female occupations. These two strategies included: *re-labelling the job* (for example, the label 'librarian' with its associated 'dowdy female' image was re-labelled 'information scientist' or 'researcher'); and, similar to Leidner's earlier (1993) study of North American insurance sales agents, *re-casting the job as male* to emphasize masculine qualities (for example, cabin crew emphasizing the health and safety role over the service role). A third strategy for combating discomfort with the female image of the job involved *men distancing themselves* from its 'feminine' aspects (Simpson 2004). 'Distancing' was practised in a number of ways: for example, librarians cast female colleagues as non-career orientated (so-called 'second-income' earners). Closer to the occupational context of PR, Chalmers (2001) found that male marketing managers invoked gendered discursive strategies to construct 'strategic/business' and 'service/support' areas of marketing work differentially as masculine and feminine in order to support marketing's claim to legitimacy as an aspiring management function.

Thus, 'feminization' (Reskin and Roos 1990) cannot merely be seen as a phenomenon that describes a larger proportion of women than men entering a profession. Men who enter an occupational culture where the feminine, or relational, characteristics of the job, such as rapport-building, empathy and communication, are emphasized (e.g. to provide a client service) may find that this kind of work presents a lack of reinforcement to masculine identity, and indeed may present threats if men have concerns about the external image of the profession and the way they are perceived among friends and potential partners. Therefore, it is reasonable to infer from the work of Leidner (1993), Lupton (2000), and Simpson (2004) that similar discursive strategies may be found in PR practice to legitimize the work of male PR consultants, as well as to legitimize the profession itself (Fitch and Third 2010). Further, Chalmers' (2001) study may help to explain male PR consultants' interactions with their male client contacts.

Women's identities in PR firms

Three qualitative studies offer insights into the construction of women's identities within PR firms. Qualitative, small-scale studies reveal the subtle features of gendering through actors' social interactions, including the contradictions and conflicts that arise from these interactions, which, in turn, respond to broader social and cultural contexts.

A 1997 North American study, involving seven female participants within a PR firm, exposed the conflicts between the ascribed roles (being a woman and a daughter) and the achieved role (being a PR practitioner) of women PR practitioners (Krider and Ross 1997). More recent studies demonstrate that women in PR firms continue to be challenged by their gender roles and identities.

Research undertaken in Germany, where 69 per cent of PR agency employees are female, addressed the issue of gender stereotypes among women agency practitioners (Fröhlich and Peters 2007). Agency practitioners strongly described women's superior communication skills as the key factor behind the female majority in PR, and yet they subjected female agency practitioners to stereotyping through terms such as 'PR slut', 'PR bunny' or 'PR girly'. At the same time, the study participants distanced their own identities from these stereotypes.

Tsetsura's (2007) study of Russian female PR agency practitioners found that within the Russian cultural context, the 'professional PR practitioner' identity was emphasized by women (specifically through clothing) and the 'female PR professional' was minimized as a defence against sexual harassment and sexual stereotyping. Women strongly constructed PR as a service profession, which in turn influenced their negotiating strategies, such as 'saving face' and 'compromise' with clients (Tsetsura 2010: 79). This culture-specific understanding of PR as a 'service' may well suggest a struggle between the roles of offering 'professional' (that is, impartial, objective) advice and providing a service whereby the PR consultant does not seek to challenge the client directly but seeks a more subtle way to accommodate their ideas.

Viewed from a critical perspective, the gendered negotiating strategies used by Russian female agency practitioners reinforce the 'hierarchical binary' (Dow and Wood 2006: xvii), forcing women into performing their ascribed role of doing 'deferential' emotion work (Hochschild 1983:165). Equally, however, playing with the 'PR bunny' stereotype as recognition of women's exceptional communication skills in agency work means that German female practitioners risk becoming victims of self-stereotyping and are assigned, or assign themselves, to gender roles that reinforce the status quo.

Much of the feminist literature in PR provides considerable knowledge about structural inequalities within the profession (e.g. Toth and Cline 1989; Grunig, Toth and Hon 2001). It also offers strategies to practitioners and educators on how to overcome these inequalities (e.g. Hon 1995). The focus of the research is liberal feminist with an agenda for achieving equity rather than understanding how the social processes of feminization and professionalization in PR, together with the rise in Western service economies, might influence and reinforce patriarchal gender relations in the workplace.

Constructionist studies of women in PR serve to deepen understanding of the feminization of the profession by examining gender stereotypes and women's identity in PR agency work. However, these studies are few and do not examine how workplace relationships are experienced, practised and understood by female *and* male PR consultants, using emotional labour theory as a frame of reference, nor how gender identity is made visible through day-to-day professional interactions.

Using phenomenology to examine gender and PR

I adopted an empirical phenomenological approach (Aspers 2006 and 2009) to examine how PR consultants experienced, practised and understood professional relationships with their clients, journalists and colleagues. Phenomenological research is characterized by small samples of between three and twenty-five participants (Creswell 2007). I interviewed six participants, comprising four female and two male practitioners. Four practitioners were accessed via academic contacts and two through agency contacts. I held semi-structured, face-to-face, hour-long interviews with each participant in order to elicit descriptions of their 'lifeworld' as PR consultants from their own perspectives (Kvale and Brinkmann 2009). Interviews were followed up with a second round of interviews lasting between twenty and forty-five minutes, which helped me to develop a richer understanding of the participant's perspective, using the first interview transcript, as well as the participant's online diary entries and CV information, as the basis for further discussion.

Participants represented different levels within the agency hierarchy, from a female senior account executive at the lower end through to a male account director at the top end, and were aged between twenty-three and thirty-four. This age grouping approximates the age grouping that represents the largest proportion of PR consultants in the UK (CIPR 2010). All were educated to degree level, with four out of the six possessing either a first degree or masters in PR. All participants had enjoyed relatively rapid advancement within their careers.

To validate the research, I sent a 'descriptive account of practice' to participants as part of the 'member checking' process (Creswell 2007). Analysis involved a process of coding, categorization and thematic analysis

(Richards 2005). Within this chapter, the relevant theories for analysis are emotional labour and gender identity applied to the professional context of PR. All the names of participants have been changed to preserve anonymity.

Gendered emotional labour: how PR consultants negotiate identity with agency managers, clients and journalists

This section discusses PR consultants' constructions of everyday interactions with agency managers, clients and journalists, from the perspectives of emotional labour, gender and identity.

Relationships in agency life

While the statistics tell one story of PR agencies, I now turn to the everyday story of relationships in regional PR agencies where consistent as well as contradictory depictions of agency life emerged. Pamela and Alison characterized their two different agencies as having 'a friendly, family atmosphere', owing to the relatively small number of colleagues and the informal, sometimes close relationships. John described his working environment as a 'quite masculine, quite ladsy kind of culture' and 'totally open plan, run almost like a newsroom, people shouting upstairs and downstairs'. The working culture for PR consultants was 'friendly' and 'relaxed', you could 'be yourself', but it was also 'stressful' and 'competitive'. Casual clothing reinforced the 'relaxed' environment, unless there was a client meeting to attend. Colleagues in agencies were understood to be mainly, if not all, women. However, John, an account director, managed an all-male team, while Graham, another account manager, reported to other men occupying account-handling and director roles.

Relationships with agency managers: anticipating and 'responding to the way they think'

Typically, the most senior people in agencies were men, although Emma's managing director was female and Pamela reported to a female director. Agency bosses, as small business entrepreneurs, appeared to hold little regard for supporting the career development of their staff through structured business or PR training, yet were often seen as supportive managers and mentors in 'learning on the job' – particularly in regard to handling professional relationships: 'it's all from the people above me really and watching how they do it, and, yeah, doing the same thing. It's all on the job' (Emma, interview 2).

Agency directors were often regarded as mentors, so the skill of 'managing upwards' was understood to be important to influence the people who could sponsor or support young practitioners in their early careers.

Part of the work of PR consultants was to build strong relationships with their agency directors and not just their line managers who occupied the lower rankings. At the start of his agency career, Graham's line manager, for example, took time to explain carefully how he should respond to two agency directors:

> And she pulled out two pieces of paper and said: 'Ways to impress X' and 'Ways to impress Y'. X: Be enthusiastic, talk about ideas, talk about money. Make him coffee in the morning, that sort of thing. Y: Lots of blogging, high standards on grammar, expertise, and try and learn, do as much reading as you can.
>
> (Graham, interview 2)

Gill's competitive work environment meant she had to think about 'what you look like to senior management, because you know that they're watching you and what you're doing and how you're acting and it will come into your appraisal' (Gill, interview 2). Much of Gill's effort was directed towards 'profiling' herself among the many female contenders for promotion within her agency. Alison forcefully asserted her flexibility and adaptability to different social situations in that: 'you are always trying to be ... what your director on that particular account wants you to be'. This ultimately meant adapting herself to suit the demands of different clients.

Where a significant level of trust was established with their agency directors, however, two consultants, Emma and John, felt 'empowered' to manage accounts without interference from senior people: 'it's very much we do the work and get the results, how we go about it is very much up to us ... she doesn't check up on people' (Emma, interview 1).

For these young practitioners, senior agency directors played a highly influential role as mentors and guides in developing their professional practice. Therefore, anticipating and 'responding to the way they think' (Graham, interview 1) meant that the implicit 'feeling rules' (Bolton 2005) or emotional norms of agency directors carried a special significance, more so than formal training. Although some agency directors were perceived as lacking openness and trust in their account handlers (for example, in the case of Pamela), these directors' implicit emotional cues were nevertheless deferred to in order to enable practitioners to thrive in their careers. Within the relatively intimate agency environment, agency directors had the perceived power and authority to limit or support a practitioner's aspirations for promotion within the agency or to another agency by virtue of their own social capital (Ihlen 2009) as agency heads.

Agency directors, as business entrepreneurs, were in turn driven by their own idea of professional practice in meeting the needs of clients and journalists to ensure that the agency was profitable: this could be summed up as 'making the client happy', a 'commercial' feeling rule (Bolton 2005), which meant performing identity work in response to whatever the situation demanded (de Bruin and Ross 2004), including 'gender displays' (Reskin and Padavic 1994) or performances that suited the client's preference.

Relationships with clients: managing their expectations and earning their trust

The client contacts of PR firms were typically male chief executives, managing directors or partners of small firms; and then marketing or PR managers of larger organizations, who could be male or female. 'Business-to-business' (B2B) consulting characterized much of regional PR work, typically with law firms. B2B consulting means that practitioners help their clients to promote their services to other businesses (as opposed to directly to the consumer, known as B2C). For practitioners, this implied the more 'serious' side of PR. Indeed, both Emma and Alison had consciously avoided working in consumer PR as they felt it did not reflect their more serious interests or social concerns. Graham, who worked for an online PR consultancy, talked of working in 'progressive PR', thus setting apart his practice from what he referred to as 'traditional' PR, by which he meant those agencies that relied on the traditional press release in dealing with the processes of print media and print journalists.

At the same time, however, some clients expected their PR contacts to be 'quite bubbly, creative, a happy person' (Emma, interview 1), so it was important 'to know when to be a lot more friendly' (Alison, interview 2) and 'fashion the way you are and the way you communicate with people' (Graham, interview 2). Therefore, knowing when to turn on the charm (and when to turn it off) was essential to the job.

The externally held, popular image of the PR industry, epitomized in television satires, was never far from the minds of practitioners, and as a consequence they dissociated themselves from what they considered to be unprofessional practice in some agencies. Young, typically female and inexperienced junior account executives were sometimes caricatured as socializing too much with clients and phoning journalists 'from a call sheet' (John, interview 1) with worthless stories. Both John and Pamela used a high-pitched, feminine tone of voice to imitate an inexperienced practitioner phoning an influential journalist.

Thus, while it was important to 'be yourself', which meant being friendly, informal and approachable with clients, it was equally important for practitioners to be mindful of how they presented themselves, even with colleagues with whom they might share jokes, offload frustrations, swear, or talk about their social lives. Senior colleagues needed to know 'that they could take you into a kind of really high-level pitch or difficult client meeting ... [and] that you'd perform' (Alison, interview 2). For Alison, 'being 100 per cent professional' with clients in a pitch situation was associated with being formal and businesslike and, importantly, not 'fluffy'.

Being professional for John involved 'providing best advice' and for Graham 'offering counsel based on expertise, not being afraid to challenge a client, not being a Yes man'. As a senior male practitioner, preserving self-respect as a professional meant, for John, not just withholding or controlling his frustrations and anger, but 'matching' the confrontational styles of clients in some situations.

A common relational strategy for dealing with clients, including 'difficult' clients, was 'educating' them about how PR worked to demonstrate its value to their business. This process could take place during a pitch for new business, after winning new business, or when there was a problem on the account. Educating the client in Graham's experience took place 'pretty much every day' because of his need to explain how social media was used in a PR campaign. Demonstrating the value of PR to a new client – or a 'reluctant' client – involved showing them examples of other client work and 'talking through' the process of how media coverage is obtained, as illustrated here:

> Nurturing them, nurturing *him* ... gave him time, gave him examples of what other departments in the law firm had done and showing him the results so that he started to come round ... and then end up getting to the stage where he was more comfortable with us ... got his comments on the front cover of [name omitted] magazine ... and from then on he was willing to work with us on everything.
>
> (Pamela, interview 1)

The 'educating' process is well illustrated in Pamela's account, where the value of PR work, rather than being couched in business terms as financial benefits (for example, 'return on investment'; advertising value equivalents), is instead a careful exercise in the status enhancement of her 'reluctant' client (Hochschild 1983).

Typically, new clients were unaware of the agency practitioner's effort behind any media coverage and often had unrealistic expectations – and demands – of what could be achieved. Client demands sometimes led to the PR agency being blamed for a lack of 'results' that, in turn, led to a continuous process of explanation or 'talking it through' by the PR consultant in order to maintain the client's confidence. 'Managing the client's expectations' meant knowing when to be upbeat about the possibility of media coverage and when to be low key, while remembering that the client was paying a monthly retainer fee for 'results' that could never be guaranteed.

Some agency directors expected their account handlers to spend time focusing on the 'little touches' that made a difference to relationships, such as building rapport with the client at an early stage of the relationship. Rapport-building approaches could involve entertaining the client in relaxed surroundings, remembering the details of clients' personal lives and celebrating clients' own special events through sending flowers or organizing a special lunch. These situations sometimes involved playing on traditional gender roles:

> his wife had just given birth so we decided to send some flowers. He gets on really, really well with everyone in the agency, so it was a genuine touch. But at the same time we know that he sits on an open floor plan with other people high up from [his company].
> (Graham, interview 2)

> I know that colleagues do play on being the woman, and ... my boss is always telling me, 'Use the charm and you can get away with things if you're a woman,' and it works for her. Clients really like that because she's kind of flirty and lighthearted but that doesn't really suit my personality so I don't play on it at all, really.
> (Emma, interview 1)

> I have another client who prefers to deal with women in the office and actually if he has a problem he would never, like, come to me or any of the other females working on the account ... he would maybe go to one of the guys and maybe even shout at them but he would never, ever, shout at a woman. [Laughs.] So it can work in your favour, I suppose. [Laughs.]
> (Pamela, interview 1)

Some performances or gestures (such as sending flowers to a client's wife) may be seen as examples of 'surface acting' (Hochschild 1983: 33) to elicit a desired response. Bolton (2005: 120) regards these performances as 'cynical' when there is little emotional cost to the social actor in fulfilling an instrumental role; however, not all agency interactions involved limited emotional effort.

The implicit feeling rules of agency directors (in response to their clients' preferences) suggested that expectations of performance could present challenges to the agency practitioner in managing emotions in different directions. For example, the flirtatious client handling encouraged by Emma's female managing director suggested that the otherwise sober law and engineering clients enjoyed the 'bubbly', 'creative' and 'happy' aspect of PR when it suited their needs, yet they expected a professional service to achieve the media coverage to promote their business. Emma, however, did not 'play on being the woman' with her clients as this conflicted with her 'serious' self-identity. This suggested, perhaps, that the role of 'playing the woman' could be reallocated to her managing director if and when the situation arose.

In the case of Pamela, however, her authority as a professional could be undermined if her work with a male client was re-allocated to a male colleague so that the client might express his anger. Hochschild refers to the 'fictional re-distribution of authority' where male flight attendants were assumed by passengers to hold more seniority (by virtue of their maleness) even though they were less likely to hold these positions in reality. Both male and female workers adapt to this 'fiction', although this may be understood by workers as 'merely a difference of style' (Hochschild 1983: 178): hence, in this study, it was possible for PR consultants to rationalize client preferences in terms of different *styles* or *personalities*, rather than gender.

An important emotion management strategy with clients involved 'empathizing' (John) or 'putting yourself in their shoes' (Alison). This meant understanding clients' daily pressures and sometimes, as illustrated below, changing personal attitudes towards that client to achieve results:

> And so I went away and learned a bit about what actually is it that she has to cover off in her job? ... And these things must be really time-consuming, and I know she is always really busy, she is always on the road ... So now I've got a brilliant relationship with her ... because I've invested quite a lot of time in making sure that, for example, I don't blame her if we don't get information through.
>
> (Alison, interview 2)

Hochschild (1983: 113) would claim that this is an example of 'deep acting' where, to rid oneself of anger towards someone, 'the recommended strategy is to focus on what the other person might be thinking and feeling: imagine a reason that excuses his or her behaviour'. Alison's statement suggests a complex navigation around the client's own identity and status within her company, and the need to find routes or channels to ensure that the work gets done and the client is happy without the client's direct help in the process.

Such instances of 'going the extra mile' to exceed a client's expectations enabled practitioners to win the client's confidence so that they were routinely consulted as a trusted source of information and advice on PR matters. A good client relationship involved being trusted by the client to run an account with a free hand to generate media coverage. The demands of this work meant that there was continuous pressure on PR consultants to draw on their 'presentational selves' or 'socialised selves' (Bolton 2005: 133) as friendly, approachable people to manage and indeed manipulate their own feelings and the feelings of others, according to what the situated demanded.

Agency directors also expected PR consultants to challenge clients. 'Challenging' the client could take the form of friendly banter in terms of 'bouncing' ideas and providing 'pure PR consultancy'; however, both John and Graham gave instances of using a 'take it or leave it' approach 'that I'll pull out of the bag so many times' (John, interview 1) when a client rejected professional PR advice.

John cited particularly confrontational encounters with male managing directors of software and IT companies: 'In some respects it almost became a threatening exchange. And bizarrely I gained some respect out of that' (John, interview 2). One of Graham's main clients was a financial services organization where he dealt with an all-male marketing team. The 'marketing guys' were not 'receptive' to his agency's ideas and 'didn't like being educated on what they thought they knew was their territory' (Graham, interview 2) – that is, social media campaigning.

Challenging (and sometimes rejecting) a client's ideas, however, was sometimes hard to handle, and a 'softly-softly approach' to challenging a client, which meant being honest, direct and giving your reasons for 'doing it our way' (Pamela), was a typical course of action:

> 'cause your instinct is to please and say 'yes' to everything and er, yeah, sometimes it is quite difficult to say 'no'. 'Cause I do get quite a lot of, you know, 'we've got a new software system, can we get it in *The Times*?' [Laughs.] You have to explain why you can't and why it's not a story.
>
> (Emma, interview 1)

The gendered performances that involved managing the expectations of clients, including 'empathizing', 'educating' and the 'softly-softly approach' to rejecting a client's ideas, well illustrate what Marsh (2009) refers to as the feminine discourse of the 'trusted adviser' in management consulting. Crucially, as Marsh (p. 269) asserts, the 'trusted adviser' discourse is more than 'embracing the emotional dimension of apparently objective work': it is a feminine discourse that privileges the processes of 'relational practice' in their own right. However, much of the work of male and female PR consultants constitutes 'relational practice' (Fletcher 1994 and 1998) and this raises questions about whether PR is regarded as women's work and therefore not a 'real job' (Tsetsura 2011).

Relationships with journalists: understanding what they want ... and supplying it

Journalists were understood to be male if they worked for a regional newspaper, particularly on the business desk, or if they were editors of business magazines. Trade press journalists were often female, although this varied from sector to sector. The goal of gaining results and 'making the client happy' involved relational strategies that could anticipate as well as respond to journalists' specific requirements.

A typical interaction with a journalist is 'selling-in', whereby a journalist contact is phoned with a news story. The story is quickly summarized and an email sent through with the story attached. PR consultants learned to avoid appearing 'too desperate' when selling-in, so a common opening line was: 'I thought you might be interested in this.' Quite often journalists did not want to talk over the phone and were 'rude or short with you' (Gill), but if they were willing to talk, the PR 'pitch' had to be straight to the point: 'he says "pitch to me in ten seconds or the phone's going down" and he'll count down from ten. [Laughs.] So ... yeah, scary' (Graham, interview 1).

John, Graham and Alison forcefully asserted that their gender did not make a difference to journalists: 'they don't care whether you are a man or woman ... all they care about is, is it relevant to them? Can it help their job? Is it going to help them write up the story?' (Alison, interview 2). However, a more complex picture emerged when practitioners discussed the types of journalists with whom they dealt. De Bruin (2000: 232) noted a similar phenomenon in discussing the professional identities of journalists: 'Sometimes journalists define situations as gender-neutral while at the same time indicating that gender does play a significant role, and in doing so, they seem to make contradictory statements.'

Women PR consultants were wary of some older, male business editors on regional newspapers because 'you do worry about the perception of "PR girls" ringing them up' (Alison) and so they had to 'work that bit harder to get that respect' (Pamela, interview 1). 'Working that bit harder' meant being well briefed and informed about the client's policies and announcements because 'they try and catch us out' (Gill, interview 1). The 'PR girl' image was evoked by Pamela in describing how she responded to a particular type of male business editor:

> so if we're phoning about a management buy-out, we know how to explain to them, we're not just phoning them with [adopts a quiet, high-pitched voice] 'Can you do this story?', we know the ins and outs and know exactly what ... yeah, what we're talking about basically.
>
> (Pamela, interview 1)

Gill and Alison emphasized they had learned not to 'take it personally' if a journalist did not want their story, but it was important to 'persist' (John) by asking the journalist for their opinion or guidance on improving the story, in case the client needed an explanation for why their story did not appear in print. Emma, who tried not to 'pester' journalists too much for fear of irritating them, felt particularly frustrated by the lack of response from journalists, mentioning the same example more than once: '[I] sent her loads of information ... And she kind of went into a black hole after that. There are only so many times you can push' (Emma, interview 1).

Getting into a publication that mattered to the client often meant months of 'plugging away' (Alison) to secure an interview with a particular journalist. If a journalist responded positively on a story, however, it could mean asking the client to 'drop everything' to help the journalist meet a deadline.

The gendered, sensitive performances required of agency practitioners in understanding the needs and navigating the identities of some journalists (e.g. as autonomous news-gatherers), however inaccurate these may be in fact (de Bruin 2000; Davies 2008), indicate that they tread a fine line between 'persisting' and 'pestering' in their journalist interactions. Unless there is a trusting relationship, irritating a journalist may result in losing that journalist's respect, losing the client's trust (in the practitioner's ability to tap into media channels) and, ultimately, in a loss of status for the practitioner.

Identity work in PR consulting

Bolton (2005) asserts that identity work is intertwined with the image of a particular profession; therefore, emotional effort will be put into conforming to implicit 'feeling rules' to live up to that image. As the following discussion demonstrates, the implicit feeling rules that influence the preferred image of a PR professional (i.e. not 'fluffy') are aligned discursively with the 'masculine' notion of a profession by both female and male practitioners.

Women's identity work in PR consulting

Women participants emphasized their 'professional' attributes (Tsetsura 2007) and aligned their performances with a 'masculine' notion of a profession (Davies 1996; Bolton and Muzio 2008; Marsh 2009; Fitch and Third 2010). Gill and Alison claimed that they 'did not take it personally' when clients and journalists were difficult or rude. For Pamela, it was important to come across as well informed when calling a (male) business editor about a client's management buy-out; for Emma, it was a matter of ensuring that her 'serious' side was emphasized when dealing with engineering and legal clients. For Alison, it was imperative to come across to senior colleagues and clients in a pitch situation as '100 per cent professional' (meaning formal and businesslike); for Gill, it was important to self-monitor and 'profile' herself in the presence of agency directors to enhance her promotion prospects.

These aspects of identity were carefully worked on, it would appear, in order to counter the stereotypical image of the 'PR girl' (Fröhlich and Peters 2007; Tsetsura 2007 and 2011) but were also motivated by women practitioners' claims to professional status and rewards (Bolton 2005). The apparent denial of gender in this study, discussed earlier, may be symptomatic of a post-feminist era in which it is assumed that gender equality has been achieved and that explicit consideration of gender 'is no longer necessary' (Fitch and Third 2010: 8).

Men's identity work in PR consulting

John's professional identity as a PR practitioner was preserved by working with an all-male team and asserting his professional and masculine identity during sometimes 'confrontational' encounters with clients, claiming that this earned him the (male) client's respect (Leidner 1993). Some male clients were small business owners who, perhaps, encapsulated 'entrepreneurial ideologies and discourses' of capital accumulation and traditional ideas of male and female roles (Mulholland 1996: 149) and this consideration of clients' demands could be regarded as a pressure on the male PR consultant to perform the masculine role of asserting his authority and status (Hochschild 1983). Therefore, John used a 'take it or leave it' brinkmanship strategy (Henderson 1963) to force the client into accepting or rejecting PR advice.

Graham's interactions with male marketing managers also called upon him and his senior male colleagues to 'challenge' the client using a brinkmanship strategy; therefore, consciously or not, both John and Graham (and the latter's male bosses) were playing on 'being a man' to protect their professional status and their masculinity as well as to achieve the desired outcome with the client. In addition to adhering to the feeling rule of 'not being a Yes man' in a similar way to John, Graham further defined his PR role as masculine (Simpson 2004) by emphasizing his online PR specialism, which, it may be argued, implicitly possessed the gendered attributes of technology (Keller 1985). However, the claim to online 'expertise' was contested in Graham's agency's client relationship and indeed may have got in the way of his clients' claim to corporate power and status as online marketing strategists (Chalmers 2001).

Conclusion and implications

Williams (1993, cited in Abbott, Wallace and Tyler 2005: 256) argues that there is a tendency for both men and women to be rewarded for distancing themselves from femininity. From this, it would appear that both John and Graham had, in rather different ways, constructed a masculine version of PR that both distanced their work from the predominantly 'feminized' agencies and acted as a defence against any possible perceptions of doing 'women's work' (Lupton 2000; Simpson 2004). The women, on the other hand, practised 'distancing' by dissociating themselves from the 'PR girl' stereotype and aligning their identities with the masculine discourse of the 'objective professional' (Marsh 2009). Paradoxically, however, much relational work in agency PR, performed by both men and women, employed the strategies of 'empathizing'; 'educating' and 'managing expectations' which, in turn, could be said to be closely aligned with an element of the feminine discourse: the 'trusted adviser' (Yeomans 2010).

The perspectives of emotional labour (Hochschild 1983) and gender identity (Butler 1990 and 2004) highlight the centrality of gendered performance and identity work in PR. As skilled emotion managers (Bolton 2005), practitioners are highly attuned to anticipating and responding to the different expectations and emotional cues of different agency directors;

managing the expectations of different clients and earning their trust; and understanding what different journalists want and supplying it. In response to these different expectations and demands, practitioners engage in different levels of performativity (Butler 1990), which may be viewed along a continuum, ranging from instrumental, 'surface acting' to empathetic 'deep acting', that re-image the agency director, client or journalist to achieve a positive sense of self for the PR practitioner in their own identity work (Alvesson and Billing 2009). Performances may include 'fictionalized' (Hochschild 1983) gender displays (Reskin and Padavic 1994) that are adapted according to different relational requirements. Identity work for the women agency practitioners involves adopting different discursive strategies that emphasize their professionalism and their suitability for career advancement while distancing themselves from female PR stereotypes (Fröhlich and Peters 2007). Identity work for men also involves a discursive 'distancing' from the notion of doing 'women's work' (Lupton 2000; Simpson 2004) while differently constructing the PR role as masculine in order to advance their own careers. Finally, practitioners' gendered performances in managing their professional relationships may be understood as contributing to the structuring of the PR profession, which is understood as a gendered construct (Fitch and Third 2010).

This chapter drew on empirical work to explore how PR consultants negotiate identity through their relationships with their agency managers, colleagues, clients and journalists, using emotional labour and gender identity perspectives as analytical frameworks. Data gathered from interviews with four female PR consultants and two male PR consultants revealed the complex, gendered nature of emotion work in UK regional PR firms.

This analysis shows that identity in PR is not 'fixed' and that PR consultants become skilled in negotiating different identities, through specific relational performances, in response to the social and cultural expectations of agencies and clients. The strategies that both female and male PR consultants use could be characterized as largely 'feminine' while having an instrumental goal in achieving 'results' and earning the client's trust. Importantly, however, gendered performances in everyday agency practice do not respond solely to the situational demands of agency relationships: they respond to the broader context of a feminized industry and the PR 'professionalization project'. From this study, I argue that feminization should be understood not only in terms of a female majority in the profession but also in terms of the relational characteristics of the job, and how male PR practitioners negotiate identity through their interactions to preserve their masculinity and professional status.

This chapter also highlights the discursive strategies that reinforce gender segregation in the PR firm, where the few men who do enter the profession are more likely to reach the upper echelons of agency life by perhaps adopting a more confrontational style and re-defining their practice discursively as masculine. Further, I argue that professionalization in PR should be understood as a masculine cultural project to which both aspirant male and female practitioners respond by emphasizing their professional (or masculine) attributes, and in doing so reject the 'fluffy' PR stereotype.

It would appear, then, that gendered emotional practices in the PR firm serve the interests of the professional project in PR and its claim to legitimacy and status in corporate boardrooms.

The conclusions of this study are limited to regional agency PR practitioners in the UK. Therefore, more research is required to investigate the theory I have outlined in larger agencies and in-house departments. However, the findings raise a number of questions for educators and researchers:

- Is PR education to some extent marginal when so much of the work that is valued by agency directors is situational and 'learned on the job'?
- How is gender taught in PR courses?
- If it is taught, is a performative definition of gender used?
- If gender is not taught in PR courses, is there an assumption, perhaps, that 'gender equality has been achieved'?
- In investigating masculine identities in PR, how do gay men in PR negotiate their own identities in professional relationships?

Finally, PR practitioners' emotional labour raises ethical questions. For example:

- What are the personal consequences for those working at the most junior levels of PR firms, specifically young women working as unpaid interns?
- And what are the consequences for those practitioners who lack the necessary personal skills to become successful 'emotion managers' and 'identity workers' in the process of negotiating different social demands?

Acknowledgements

I wish to thank the two anonymous reviewers for their helpful critique at an early draft stage; Dr Neil Washbourne, Senior Lecturer in Media Studies, Leeds Metropolitan University, for his constructive comments; and, finally, the editors for their rigorous critique, encouragement and support throughout the preparation of this chapter.

References

Abbott, C., Wallace, P. and Tyler, M. (2005) *An Introduction to Sociology: Feminist Perspectives* (3rd edition), London and New York: Routledge.

Alvesson, M. (1998) 'Gender and identity: Masculinities and femininities at work in an advertising agency', *Human Relations*, 51(8): 969–1005.
Alvesson, M. and Billing, Y. D. (2009) *Understanding Gender and Organizations* (2nd edition), Los Angeles, London, New Delhi, Singapore and Washington, DC: Sage.
Alvesson, M. and Willmott, H. (2002) 'Producing the appropriate individual: identity regulation as organizational control', *Journal of Management Studies*, 39(5): 619–44.
Anleu, S. R. and Mack, K. (2005) 'Magistrates' everyday work and emotional labour', *Journal of Law and Society*, 32(4): 590–614.
Aspers, P. (2006) *Markets in Fashion: A Phenomenological Approach*, London and New York: Routledge.
Aspers, P. (2009) 'Empirical phenomenology: A qualitative research approach (the Cologne seminars)', *Indo-Pacific Journal of Phenomenology*, 9(2): 1–12.
Bolton, S. C. (2005) *Emotion Management in the Workplace*, Houndsmills: Palgrave Macmillan.
Bolton, S. C. and Muzio, D. (2008) 'The paradoxical processes of feminization in the professions: The case of established, aspiring and semi-professions', *Work, Employment and Society*, 22(2): 281–99.
Butler, J. (1990) *Gender Trouble*, New York and London: Routledge.
Butler, J. (2004) *Undoing Gender*, New York: Routledge.
Centre for Economic and Business Research/Chartered Institute of Public Relations (2005) '48,000 professionals; £6.5 billion turnover: The economic significance of public relations', London: Centre for Economics and Business Research.
Chalmers, L. (2001) *Marketing Masculinities: Gender and Management Politics in Marketing Work*, Westport, CT: Greenwood Press.
Chartered Institute of Public Relations (CIPR) (2010) '2010 CIPR membership survey: The state of the PR profession', London: ComRes/CIPR.
Chartered Institute of Public Relations (CIPR) (2011) '2011 CIPR membership survey: The state of the PR profession', London: ComRes/CIPR.
Creswell, J. W. (2007) *Qualitative Inquiry and Research Design: Choosing among Five Approaches*, Thousand Oaks, CA, London and New Delhi: Sage.
Davies, C. (1996) 'The sociology of professions and the profession of gender', *Sociology*, 30(4): 661–78.
Davies, N. (2008) *Flat Earth News: An Award-Winning Reporter Exposes Falsehood, Distortion and Propaganda in the Global Media*, London: Vintage.
de Bruin, M. (2000) 'Gender, organizational and professional identities in journalism', *Journalism*, 1(2): 217–38.
de Bruin, M. and Ross, K. (2004) 'Introduction: Beyond the body count', in M. de Bruin and K. Ross (eds), *Gender and Newsroom Cultures: Identities at Work*, Cresskill, NJ: Hampton Press: vii–xii.
Dow, B. J. and Wood, J. T. (2006) 'The evolution of gender and communication research: Intersections of theory, politics, and scholarship', in B. J. Dow and J. T. Wood (eds), *The Sage Handbook of Gender and Communication*, Thousand Oaks, CA, London and New Delhi: Sage Publications: ix–xxiv.
Fitch, K. and Third, A. (2010) 'Working girls: Revisiting the gendering of public relations', *PRism* 7(4). Online. Available HTTP: <http://www.prismjournal.org/fileadmin/Praxis/Files/Gender/Fitch_Third.pdf > (accessed 5 October 2011).

Fletcher, J. (1998) 'Relational practice: A feminist re-construction of work', *Journal of Management Inquiry*, 7(2): 168–86.

Fletcher, J. K. (1994) 'Toward a theory of relational practice in the workplace: A feminist reconstruction of "real" work', doctoral dissertation, Boston University.

Fröhlich, R. and Peters, S. B. (2007) 'PR bunnies caught in the agency ghetto? Gender stereotypes, organizational factors, and women's careers in PR agencies', *Journal of Public Relations Research*, 19(3): 229–54.

Grunig, L. A., Toth, E.L. and Hon, L. C. (2001) *Women in Public Relations: How Gender Influences Practice*, New York: The Guilford Press.

Henderson, B. (1963) 'Brinkmanship in business'. Online. Available HTTP: <http://www.managementplace.com/fr/bcg/brink.pdf> (accessed 28 February 2012).

Hochschild, A.R. (1983) *The Managed Heart: Commercialization of Human Feeling*, Berkeley: University of California Press.

Holmes, J. (2006) *Gendered Talk at Work: Constructing Gender Identity through Workplace Discourse*, Malden, MA, and Oxford, Victoria: Blackwell.

Hon, L. C. (1995) 'Toward a feminist theory of public relations', *Journal of Public Relations Research*, 7(1): 27–88.

Howard, J. A., Risman, B., Romero, M. and Sprague, J. (1999) 'Series editors' introduction', in M. M. Ferree, J. Lorber and B. B. Hess (eds), *Revisioning Gender*, Thousand Oaks, CA, London and New Delhi: Sage: xi–xiv.

Ihlen, Ø. (2009) 'On Bourdieu: Public relations in field struggles', in Ø. Ihlen, B. van Ruler and M. Fredriksson (eds), *Public Relations and Social Theory: Key Figures and Concepts*, New York and London: Routledge: 62–81.

Keller, E. F. (1985) *Reflections on Gender and Science*, New Haven, CT: Yale University Press.

Krider, D. S. and Ross, P. G. (1997) 'The experiences of women in a public relations firm: A phenomenological explication', *Journal of Business Communication*, 34 (4): 437–54.

Kvale, S. and Brinkmann, S. (2009) *Interviews: Learning the Craft of Qualitative Research Interviewing* (2nd edition), Los Angeles, London, New Delhi and Singapore: Sage.

Leidner, R. (1991) 'Serving hamburgers and selling insurance: Gender, work and identity in interactive service jobs', *Gender and Society*, 5: 154–77.

Leidner, R. (1993) *Fast Food, Fast Talk: Service Work and the Routinization of Everyday Life*, Berkeley: University of California Press.

Lupton, B. (2000) 'Maintaining masculinity: Men who do "women's work"', *British Journal of Management*, 11(special issue): S33–S48.

Mann, S. (2004) 'People work: Emotion management stress and coping', *British Journal of Guidance and Counselling*, 32(2): 205–22.

Marsh, S. (2009) *The Feminine in Management Consulting: Power, Emotion and Values in Consulting Interactions*, Basingstoke: Palgrave Macmillan.

Mastracci, S. H., Newman, M. A. and Guy, M. E. (2006) 'Appraising emotion work: Determining whether emotional labor is valued in government jobs', *American Review of Public Administration*, 36(2): 123–38.

Mulholland, K. (1996) 'Entrepreneurialism, masculinities and the self-made man', in D. L. Collinson and J. Hearn (eds), *Men as Managers, Managers as Men: Critical Perspectives on Men, Masculinities and Managements*, London, Thousand Oaks, CA, and New Delhi: Sage: 123–49.

PR Week (2012) 'Diversity: five ways to break the barriers', 4 April. Online. Available HTTP: <http://www.prweek.com/uk/features/1125741/diversity-five-ways-break-barriers/> (accessed 17 April 2012).

Reskin, B. and Padavic, I. (1994) *Women and Men at Work*, Thousand Oaks, CA: Pine Forge Press.

Reskin, B. F. and Roos, P. A. (1990) 'Queuing and changing occupational composition', in B. F. Reskin and P. A. Roos (eds), *Job Queues, Gender Queues: Explaining Women's Inroads into Male Occupations*, Philadelphia, PA: Temple University Press: 29–68.

Richards, L. (2005) *Handling Qualitative Data: A Practical Guide*, London, Thousand Oaks, CA, and New Delhi: Sage.

Simpson, R. (2004) 'Masculinities at work: The experiences of men in female dominated occupations', *Work, Employment and Society*, 18(2): 349–68.

Smith, P. and Gray, B. (2000) 'The emotional labour of nursing: How students and qualified nurses learn to care', London: South Bank University.

Toth, E. L. and Cline, C. G. (1989) *Beyond the Velvet Ghetto*, San Francisco, CA: IABC Research Foundation.

Tsetsura, K. (2007) 'Discipline and control in negotiating female and professional identities in public relations', paper presented at the International Communication Association Conference, San Francisco, May.

Tsetsura, K. (2010) 'How female practitioners in Moscow view their profession: A pilot study', *Public Relations Review*, 36: 78–80.

Tsetsura, K. (2011) 'Is public relations a real job? How female practitioners construct the profession', *Journal of Public Relations Research*, 23(1): 1–23.

Williams, C. (ed.) (1993) *Doing 'Women's Work': Men in Nontraditional Occupations*, London: Sage.

Yeomans, L. (2010) 'Soft sell? Gendered experience of emotional labour in UK public relations firms', *PRism* 7(4). Online. Available HTTP: <http://www.prismjournal.org/fileadmin/Praxis/Files/Gender/Yeomans.pdf> (accessed 2 October 2011).

5 Mothers, bodies, and breasts
Organizing strategies and tactics in women's activism

C. Kay Weaver

There is an increasing trend in public relations scholarship to consider how activist groups use strategic communication to achieve their goals, and yet the discipline pays no attention to how activist communication is gendered. This chapter draws on the themes of voice, image, and identity to explore how the New Zealand group Mother's Against Genetic Engineering (MAdGE) campaigned against the use of genetically engineered (GE) products in food and the environment. The chapter examines MAdGE's use of motherhood, the female body, and nudity in their protest campaign, and how groups of New Zealanders responded to some of these tactics. The investigation highlights how women activists can creatively and symbolically attempt to influence social, political, and cultural meaning-making processes, and also the challenges they face in promoting new and unorthodox ways of thinking about social issues.

Public relations is most commonly researched as an activity conducted by commercial corporations and other forms of organizations such as not-for-profits, governments, political parties, and the education and health sectors. It is less commonly analysed and theorized as a practice of social movement and activist groups. According to Edwards, this reflects the 'continued dominance of empirical work based on commercial or government organizations and the relative lack of attention paid to activist groups, community groups, and non-government organizations' (2011: 30). Yet activist groups clearly do strategically manage communication in order to increase their public visibility and support, in fundraising, and in engaging with stakeholders (Bob 2005; Hansen 2000; Henderson 2005; Kavada 2005; Motion and Weaver 2005; Reber and Berger 2005).

Recently there have been increased calls to examine how activists use strategic communication and to explore how this can contribute to the body of public relations knowledge (Coombs and Holladay 2012a; Demetrious 2006; Derville 2005; Weaver 2010). Some of the attention given to activism in the public relations literature has focused on how corporate and commercial organizations should best respond to criticism and attack by activist groups (Grunig 1992; Smith and Ferguson 2001). Other researchers have argued that through the investigation of activist groups and their communication practices, we can widen the 'conceptualisation of public relations communication' (Weaver 2010: 35) and diversify public relations theory to take on board notions of resistance and difference (Derville 2005; Dozier and Lauzen 2000). However, while the past decade has seen more attention given to activism and activist groups in public relations literature, there has been no specific exploration of women as activists and women activist groups within public relations research, or, indeed, how activism is gendered. This is despite women's activism having a vast history of scholarly literature devoted to its analysis in disciplines such as women and gender studies, sociology, and cultural studies (e.g. Naples 1998; Ricciutelli, Miles and McFadden 2004; Miethe 2009). The importance of considering how activism and its communication are gendered is further underlined when we consider that 'all struggles for social change, not just women's movements, are highly gendered' (Motta *et al.* 2011: 2)

In this chapter I discuss how women's activist groups have specifically used their identity as mothers to communicate about social causes and how groups have deployed quite specific communication strategies which mark them out as maternal and, at times, unruly, as they challenge established ideologies, ethics, and patriarchal ways of governing the word. I also explore how groups have used the naked female body as a site through which to communicate their concerns. Such use of the female body and nudity raises interesting questions in terms of what this is designed to achieve. Is it a tactic that plays into the media's thirst for spectacle and controversy, or does it work to communicate meaningful messages to audiences?

In the second half of the chapter I focus on one New Zealand-based activist group – Mothers Against Genetic Engineering – in an assessment of the communication strategies that this group used to mobilize the public, and particularly mothers, against the introduction of legislation to allow the commercialization of GE technologies in New Zealand. As well as exploring how the group used motherhood as a strategic focus for its campaign, I examine its use of a controversial billboard depicting a naked genetically engineered woman, its censorship by the New Zealand Advertising Standards Authority, and interpretative responses to this representation by selected groups of New Zealanders.

Activism and public relations

What the terms 'activism' and 'activist' exactly refer to is a matter of some definitional debate. In the public relations literature Laurisa Grunig (1992: 504) defined activism as 'a group of two or more individuals who organize in order to influence another public or publics through action that may include education, compromise, persuasion, pressure tactics, or force'. As Kim and Sriramesh (2009) note, in some contexts (such as the US) and academic fields (such as political science), the term 'public interest group' is preferred over the term 'activist group'. Yet, as Ganesh and Zoller argue in their exploration of definitions of activism, 'Across perspectives and disciplines ... one finds an emphasis ... on contestation as a core aspect of activist communication, and key concepts such as advocacy, conflict, and transgression do appear to be central to activism' (2012: 69). This points to some crucial tensions between definitions of activism and definitions of public relations. Indeed, some might argue that activism and activist communication (contestation, protest, conflict, and transgression) do not fit at all with dominant definitions of public relations which emphasize it as, for example, a 'strategic communication process that builds mutually beneficial relationships between organizations and their publics' (Public Relations Society of America 2012). Equally problematic in attempting to claim a space for consideration of activism within the public relations field are dialogic definitions that promote best-practice public relations as two-way symmetrical communication (Coombs and Holladay 2012a; Grunig and Hunt 1984). As Ganesh and Zoller (2012) identify, activism and dialogue are often cast in oppositional terms by public relations and communication theorists. Additionally, there is the issue that 'many activists fail to identify their public communication activities as "public relations" simply because of its association with big business, manipulation, and undemocratic practice' (Demetrious 2006: 104).

Part of the difficulty of positioning activist work as public relations comes from the 'inescapable understanding of PR as an organizational function' (Edwards 2012: 12), and one overwhelmingly associated with business. Edwards sums up the arguments of several key contributors to the public relations field in calling for the definition of public relations to shift to a more all-encompassing one, such as 'the flow of purposive communication produced on behalf of individuals, formally constituted and informally constituted groups, through their continuous trans-actions with other social entities' (p. 21). Under this broader definition, the communication tactics of activist groups become a subject with which public relations research should concern itself. Further, researching activist campaigns brings the opportunity to explore the challenges faced by marginalized groups and voices – women as a case in point – in trying to change public policy, opinion, and dominant social, cultural, and or/economic practices.

Women activists organizing through motherhood

There is a long and complex history of activism that has been driven by, and aimed at, improving the lives of women. More accurately, these are histor*ies* (the problems of wording are obvious and deeply ironic) of women's activism*s*, as within and across nations, race and class divisions, there have been many and varied attempts by women to campaign on issues of women's and human rights, some of which are feminist in orientation, while others are not. Indeed, it cannot be assumed that women who organize in social movements necessarily have common interests, politics, or lived experiences, or that they support gender equality. As Motta *et al.* have stated: 'Women in movement ... are not *necessarily* emancipatory or progressive; we have to look more closely at what women are talking about, which movements, at the specific context in which mobilisation takes place and organisational practices' (2011: 18; emphasis in original). The involvement of women in the Ku Klux Klan (Ferguson 2008), as well as groups such as the US Independent Women's Forum and Concerned Women for America (which both support traditional family roles and have been critiqued as anti-feminist), attests to the fact that some women activists support what most feminists decry as racist and patriarchal agendas (Schreiber 2002).

While complex sexual, racial, class, national politics and ideologies prevent any generalizing about women's activism, it is notable that women activists have frequently used 'their motherhood as a lever in establishing rights and fomenting social change' (Woyshner 2002: 66). In the early years of the twentieth century in the US, both white and black women (though under very different conditions of organizing) strategically mobilized around motherhood because it was an acceptable identity platform on which 'women of this era were able to enter the public world, despite the widely held belief that they belonged at home, by arguing the community, city, or town was an extension of the walls of their home' (Woyshner 2002: 66). During the Depression, housewives and mothers from across the class and racial boundaries in the US organized and campaigned against excessively high costs of food, using consumer boycotts, strikes, and government lobbying with the result that they 'politicized the home, the family and motherhood in important and unprecedented ways' (Orleck 2004: 208).

The use of motherhood as an identity strategy for activism became a matter of division within the so-called 'second wave of feminism' as debates pitted mothers against non-mothers and working mothers against stay-at-home mothers (Woyshner 2002). However, Ferguson's extensive review of research and writing on women and grassroots organizing identifies 'nearly all of the women [as] guided by anxiety about their children and their communities' (2008: 111). Developing the analysis of motherhood and activism in the Million Mom March – which protested for tighter restrictions on firearms ownership – Hayden argues that there is a particular 'rhetorical power of the maternal metaphor' (2003: 201) encompassing a 'feminine discourse' that empowers those 'who might otherwise see themselves as powerless' (p. 205). She further states that the 'Nurturant Parent morality ... poses a significant challenge to dominant power structures' (p. 208) as it celebrates the interconnectedness of mothers with their children, and encourages mothers to see themselves as members of larger empathetic communities that can effect change.

It can be argued that the strategic use of motherhood as a subjectivity for mobilization reinforces essentialist stereotypes of women as carers

(Motta *et al.* 2011). However, it can equally be contested that what Hayden (2003) terms a 'motherist politics of care' and its performance, by its very presence in the public sphere, creates a 'disruptive space', where the empathetic emotions of self-care and self-sacrifice and their expression challenge and resist dominant individualist, competitive, rationalist ideologies. This idea that women activists can create such a disruptive space also connects with a history of the representation of women protesters as hysterical and 'unruly'. The Greenham Common women's peace camps in England, which began in the early 1980s and disbanded only in 2000, provide an example of such depictions. Protesting against nuclear cruise missiles based at RAF Greenham Common, living in homemade tents in unsanitary conditions and suffering almost daily eviction by the police, the women flaunted social expectations of gender through how they dressed and protested, using symbols of fire, menstruation and weaving to communicate their antinuclear stance (Laware 2004). Stallybrass and White theorize these women as 'matter out of place' and 'drawing (in some cases self-consciously) on historical and political resources of mythopoetic transgression' (1986: 24). From a Bakhtian perspective of the carnivalesque – which has been influential in theorizing social movements' use of performance (Bogad 2010; Boje 2001; Bruner 2005; Shepard 2011) – these women created a grotesque and taboo corporeal discursive space at the entrance of the otherwise rigid, sterile, and highly masculine military base.

Bakhtin's writings about the ideologically disruptive, carnivalesque, and grotesque potential of the female body and its corporeal evocation of the physical and material aspects of life are valuable in theorizing activist protests in which women deliberately make a spectacle of their bodies. He states:

> woman is essentially related to the material body lower stratum; she is the incarnation of this stratum that degrades and regenerates simultaneously. She is ambivalent. She debases, brings down to earth, lends a bodily substance to things, and destroys; but, first of all, she is the principle that gives birth.
>
> (Bakhtin 1984: 240)

Bakhtin could be accused of misogynistic essentializing of women in these assertions. However, understanding female flesh as having the strategic potential to shock and challenge when flaunted for political purposes – rather than for the socially accepted purpose of attracting male attention – also provides a framework for understanding the increasing significance of the part-naked and naked female body in women's activist protest.

Activism and naked materiality

A complex relationship exists between the social and maternal respectability which motherhood can bring to women's activism and the unspoken taboos around the physical needs, pleasures, and materiality of the female body. Perhaps it is not surprising, then, that the female body has come increasingly to the fore in women's activism. Motta *et al.* (2011: 24) have argued:

> for women in movement, the body is not merely a site of pain, pleasure for others and exhaustion, but can also be an element in the articulation of ability to create and defend life. Its use against the oppressive and coercive elements of the state in protests, and as a means to protect the community, turns the body into a site of resistance and pride ... the body can also be accompanied by an emphasis on corporeal care and pleasure in movement contexts.

Naked protest performance is not confined only to women or feminist action. Groups such as Bare Witness (campaigning for peace and sense in the world), Greenpeace (environmental), PETA and AnimaNaturalis (animal rights), and Liberate Tate (against oil industry sponsorship of the arts), which have no explicit gender focus, have all staged high-profile naked demonstrations. A common concern of such protests is said to be 'a desire to extend the parameters of the political domain by seeking an ethical recognition of vulnerable, interdependent, interwoven, human and non-human flesh' (Alaimo 2010: 15). Naked bodies feature in several of these campaigns, spelling out words such as 'PEACE', 'NO GM' (genetic modification), or 'NO WAR', and are not represented in any sexualized way. In a campaign against Chevron Texaco's pollution of Nigerian Delta land in 2002–3, women's organizations used their nakedness as a weapon. It is said of this campaign that:

> women throw off their clothes in an ultimate protest to say 'this is where life comes from. I hereby revoke your life' ... Women wielding the weapon of the exposed vagina could be killed or raped. It is therefore with knowledge of the act's life and death implications that women enter in such protest and implicitly state that they will get their demands met or die in the process of trying.
> (Turner and Brownhill 2004: 169)

A number of campaigns specifically involving women protesters have adopted a more sexual approach in their use of nudity. For example, since 2008, a group of Ukrainian 'neo-feminist' activists, FEMEN, have held deliberately provocative and erotic topless protests campaigning against sex tourism, prostitution, and other issues such as the price of gas and lack of public toilet amenities in the Ukraine (Bidder 2011). FEMEN's leader declared: 'If sexuality is used to sell cars and cookies, why not use it for social and political projects? ... Sometimes you need to show your breasts for ideological reasons' (Hutsul, quoted in Danilova 2010).

Naked protests, and especially those that sexualize women's bodies, do raise significant issues given that the trivialization, objectification, and sexualization of women are key concerns of feminist critique. Media representations of women's objectification are critiqued for sustaining male domination of women and inequalities in gendered power relations, as well as supporting cultures of violence against women (Carter and Weaver 2003). Consequently, Alaimo (2010: 17) asks:

> How then are we to understand the significance of the naked body in recent protests? Are activist women simply capitalizing on the cultural currency of female flesh, or are they – quite literally – employing another sort of ethics, another sort of politics?

Drawing on feminist theories of the corporeal and introducing the concept of the trans-corporeal – in which humans are not only connected with each other and animals but with 'the material flows of substances and places' (Alaimo 2010: 24) – Alaimo argues that naked protest represents *more* than strategically performed spectacle. She claims that such activists 'perform vulnerability as ... a trans-corporeal condition in which material interchanges between human bodies, geographical places and vast networks of power, provoke ethical and political actions' (p. 32).

Women's pro-creative possibilities, their identities as mothers, and women's bodies have featured significantly in activist protest. Motherhood has functioned as both an organizing force and a force of disrupting resistance and power in the public arena. It could be argued that this organizing identity is essentializing because it reduces women's subjectivity to caring and nurturing roles, and that it is heterosexist in that it fails to acknowledge the wide variety of women's sexual identities and relationships. Nevertheless, motherhood has provided a significant subjective strategic dimension to protest for women, and activist use of the female body and the exposure of its flesh have been theorized as challenging individualistic, autonomous, rationalist, and disembodied discourses and their associated ethics.

In the second half of this chapter, I explore how one of New Zealand's highest-profile women's activist groups, Mothers Against Genetic Engineering, used both motherhood and the representation of the naked female in its campaign against the commercial release of GE crops and organisms. I also explore the extent to which the New Zealand public was motivated to think about the ethics of this science in response to the group's most controversial campaign representation – a naked genetically engineered woman.

Mothers Against Genetic Engineering – politicizing the personal

During the period 1999 to 2003 New Zealand was in the throes of deciding whether it would pass legislation permitting the release of GE products within its national boundaries, or whether GE science would be confined to the laboratory. Corporate, government, science, non-profit organizations, and activist groups all participated in debating this contested issue, which was positioned not only as about new science, but about New Zealand's image as a clean, green nation (Henderson 2005; Henderson, Weaver and Cheney 2007; Kurian and Munshi 2006). One of the highest-profile activist groups involved in attempting to engage the New Zealand public in this debate was Mothers Against Genetic Engineering – otherwise known as MAdGE.

MAdGE described itself as a 'network of politically-aligned women who have decided to actively resist the use of genetically engineered organisms in our food and in our land' (Mothers Against Genetic Engineering 2003a: 1). The initiative for the group came from Alannah Currie, well known as a member of the 1980s pop band the Thompson Twins, who was living in Auckland with her husband and two children at the time. While neither Currie nor MAdGE was ever positioned as a feminist group, its *raison d'être* was a classic example of the feminist slogan 'the personal is political' and the refusal to accept distinctions between the public sphere (of community and political reason) and the private sphere (of the family and emotional sentiment) (Elshtain 1998; Pardo 1998).

Currie's concerns about GE organisms came about as a direct and very personal experience of what at first appeared to be food safety issues. In 2000 her sister died of Creutzfeld–Jakob disease (CJD). Initially it was thought she suffered the new variant 'mad cow disease' type of CJD caused by eating contaminated beef. Although an autopsy identified her as having the naturally occurring classical human form of the disease, Currie was said to 'suspect [the autopsy] did not reveal the full truth' (Wong 2004). It was through Currie's continued investigations into her sister's death that she discovered that some foods on sale in New Zealand contained GE ingredients (Starrenberg 2003). Currie then attended a public lecture in Auckland by Professor Arpad Pusztai, who was in New Zealand giving evidence to a Royal Commission on Genetic Modification that had been established by the then Labour–Green Party coalition government (Weaver and Motion 2002). There Pusztai reported his research finding that feeding rats GE food had negatively affected their immune systems. Currie explained to a current affairs reporter at the time that the lecture disturbed her because she was 'unwittingly feeding my own children food containing GE ingredients and that was unlabeled' (quoted in Starrenberg 2003). After further research Currie concluded that GE was 'a new science, it's an experiment and as such should be contained to safe secure laboratories and not allowed out in the wild' (quoted in Starrenberg 2003).

In response to the Royal Commission's (2001) decision that New Zealand should, under regulatory approval, allow GE field trials and the commercial release of GE crops, Currie became involved in the campaign to confine GE research to laboratories and have foods containing GE ingredients labelled.

Her first foray into anti-GE activism, in September 2001, saw her credited as 'pushing GE into the mainstream political debate with the 20,000 strong march she organised up Auckland's Queen Street' (*One News* 2002). In March 2002, Currie, along with ten other Auckland-based artists and businesswomen, launched MAdGE.

MAdGE's objective was to create awareness, educate all New Zealanders about GE, and stop the lifting of a moratorium on the commercialization of GE crops that was to expire on 30 October 2003 (Weaver 2010). However, the campaign particularly targeted mothers, whom research had identified as purchasing 80 per cent of the food bought in New Zealand (*One News* 2002). In constructing and appealing to mothers as playing a vital role in protecting children's health, and promoting that role as politically significant in the context of the GE debate, MAdGE's message was that 'GE foods must be proven to be 100% safe before we will feed them to our families' (Mothers Against Genetic Engineering 2003a: 1). Further, in attempting to mobilize public support for its 'GE-free in food and environment' message, the group's strategy was to present activism as stylish and fashionable (Wong 2004).

The materiality and emotion of food

Developing a dialogue with 'mainstream New Zealanders' and gaining their funding support was an important part of MAdGE's strategy. Many of its activities were pitched at this group, not least its – albeit rather exclusive – inaugural appearance on the New Zealand stage. On 31 March 2002, MAdGE was launched with a six-course, $200-per-head fundraising banquet for 200 people at St Matthew's in the Auckland City Church. Created by celebrated chefs, and including performances from high-profile artists, the event was billed as a 'wild, stylish, highly creative celebration of New Zealand food and wine ... highlighting the need for our country to retain its clean green image in the world and keep out genetically engineered food' (GE-Free New Zealand in Food and Environment 2002). News reporting of the launch credited it as drawing 'dozens of volunteers from chefs to florists offering their services for free' (*One News* 2002), indicative of a cultural kudos brought by association with the event.

Whether intended or not, MAdGE's launch banquet bore considerable similarities to literary representations of feudal feasting theorized by Bakhtin (1984) as emphasizing the materiality and emotionality of the human experience of eating. MAdGE's launch proffered food – specifically GE-free food – as a source of both material and emotional bodily sustenance just as Bakhtin theorized the medieval banquet 'as a triumphal celebration ... [which] often fulfils the function of completion. It is the equivalent to nuptials (an act of procreation)' (1984: 283). Similarly, Currie promoted an understanding of food as 'more than just a combination of vitamins and minerals. It's about taste, smell, love, sex, tradition and memory' (*Waitrose Food Illustrated* 2003). Here the experience of eating was discursively framed as highly emotive, sensory, and life sustaining. This was compared with MAdGE's discursive positioning of GE foods as bringing unknown risks to consumers. It was these risks that became focus of the group's campaign.

Purse Power and the mother's breast

One of MAdGE's goals was to force corporate supermarket retailers to label foods containing GE ingredients. A consumer activist campaign entitled 'Purse Power' was used in efforts to achieve this (*One News* 2002). To develop women's awareness of and participation in Purse Power, 120,000 educational toolkits comprising pink and black credit-card-size leaflets were distributed outside supermarkets (*The Age* 2003). Designed to be kept in women's purses and referred to when shopping, these provided details of food brands committed to being GE free as well as those that used GE ingredients, and encouraged women to write to the latter companies explaining why they would not purchase their products and demand that they be labelled. Positioning this consumer activism as that of caring, concerned, and responsible mothers, Hilary Ord, a fashionable Auckland restaurant owner and prominent MAdGE spokesperson, stated:

> For thousands of years women have knowingly and intuitively and instinctively known what to feed their children. There's something about this product, this development, this technology, the very core of my being says 'No. Wrong' ... To be able to read a food label is the most powerful way to shop right now, so you don't become a victim and we refuse to be victims.
>
> (Quoted in *One News* 2002)

Here Ord represents food as a product that humankind should have consumptive power over, rather than a commodity that benefits the wealth of corporations and threatens the health of the consumer, and especially vulnerable children.

The mother's breast also featured as a focal point of MAdGE's consumer campaign message with women protesting outside supermarkets and handing out the educational toolkits dressed in magenta and pink bras to attract public interest and hilarity, as well as media attention. This was a provocative tactic emphasizing the part of the female anatomy that is most usually sexualized. Yet the group re-presented the breast as basic to all human relations, stating on its website: 'What is the first thing a mother does when she gives birth? She puts her baby to the breast and feeds it. It is the most profound and intimate of relationships. It is the way we bond with our children' (Edmond 2002).

It could be argued that MAdGE's focus on the breast was a mere publicity stunt. Yet, in centring its campaign on the breast in what was clearly intended to be a humorous and provocative way, MAdGE focused the GE debate on subjective identity, material, and bodily levels of concern. This was in opposition to the abstract, economic, and highly 'rational' and 'objective' rhetorical approaches favoured by scientists and politicians. Similar humour drawing attention to the female body and women's subjectivities featured in MAdGE's newsletter and website campaign materials, with headlines such as 'Ladies in Waiting Lunch Protest' (Mothers Against Genetic Engineering 2003b), 'News from the MAdGE Mothership' (Mothers Against Genetic Engineering 2003c), and 'Bra-vo Madge' (Mothers Against Genetic Engineering 2003d).

While MAdGE's consumer campaign brought a uniquely domestic, emotional, humorous, and accessible perspective to New Zealand's GE debate, the group can be accused, as have other women's movements, of 'privileg[ing] a partial, white, bourgeois, liberal perspective' (Motta *et al.* 2011: 2) in their activism. Certainly, their campaign was largely targeted at, and expressed the voice of, middle-class, white mothers, and it addressed these women primarily as consumers. In the context of neo-liberalism, consumer activism hardly represents a fundamental challenge or disruption to the political economic system. However, one of MAdGE's final campaign efforts to promote debate about GE certainly proved more controversial, to the extent that it was censored.

The controversy of the cowgirl

On 1 October 2003, four weeks prior to the anticipated lifting of the moratorium on GE field trials and the commercialization of GE crops, MAdGE posted seven billboards at key sites throughout Auckland and Wellington. These depicted a naked four-breasted woman on her hands and knees with a milking machine attached to her breasts and 'GE' branded on one of her buttocks. Pictured on a plain white background, the 'cowgirl' reproachfully looks directly into the camera. The only text on the billboard was MAdGE's website address in black in the top left-hand corner. MAdGE explained that the image was designed 'to provoke public debate about the social and cultural ethics of genetic engineering in New Zealand' (Mothers Against Genetic Engineering 2003e).

Although there was nothing to indicate it, the billboard image made reference to laboratory research being conducted by one of New Zealand's Crown Research Institutes, AgResearch, to generate a herd of transgenic cattle. The cattle were created by inserting human genes into calf embryos and it was claimed they would produce pharmaceutical milk to aid sufferers of multiple sclerosis (Collins 2002). While this transgenic research had been approved by the Environmental Risk Management Authority (ERMA), MAdGE challenged ERMA's approval process and AgResearch's

GE experiments in a case that went to the High Court in June 2003 (Weaver 2010). It was after MAdGE lost that case that the group launched the cowgirl billboard campaign.

The highly provocative cowgirl image mocked transgenic research and typical claims of the pro-GE lobby that this controversial science could 'improve and even perfect nature in the name of humanity' (Didur 2003: 100). The billboard depicted a chimera–cyborg-type creature, and while it could be said that the cowgirl represented a kind of beauty in that she possessed the typical attributes of a youthful slender model (with some additions), she was far from the disease-cured 'completed' being that AgResearch claimed was the objective of its GE research. It was this fusing of stereotypical beauty with the grotesque representation of a woman with an 'udder' attached to a milking machine that made this cyborg image so potentially transgressive. Indeed, Hitchcock has written 'the cyborg image is an image of the pleasure of the confused bodily boundaries, a cyborg body politic stresses responsibility in the articulation of such transgression' (1998: 84). In these terms, the cowgirl poster appeared to appeal for a careful examination and discussion of the ethics of transgenic GE science and the trans-corporeal 'in which the skin of the human extends to the skin of the animal' (Alaimo 2010: 24).

However, while MAdGE claimed that the cowgirl billboard was designed to promote debate about the *ethics* of GE science, it was the actual controversy around the image – whether it was a literal representation of possible GE outcomes, and its depiction of a modified naked woman – that became the subject of media coverage. For example, the vice-chancellor of Wellington's Victoria University expressed concern that the billboard implied 'that women might be genetically modified to have four breasts' (quoted in Collins 2003). Others described it as 'offensive' (*Weekend Herald* 2003; Alley 2004), a sentiment echoed by the chairman of the pro-GE lobby group the Life Sciences Network, William Rolleston, in his statement that 'the billboards denigrate women' (quoted in Tankersley 2003). The Advertising Standards Authority (ASA) lent its support to this view by upholding a complaint against the billboard in which the complainant, whose gender was not specified, stated:

> Whilst I am an ardent supporter of the anti-GE campaign, I found the depiction of a female body in this manner totally disgusting. For many years it has been a common insult to refer to a woman as a 'Silly Cow', and the blatant image of this concept is denigrating to women. For those people who do not understand what may be a highbrow attempt to stir debate on a subject, it is bordering on the pornographic and has no place in general public view. For myself, I find it offensive, and the fact that any child of any age can be exposed to such images in a public place is intolerable.
> (Gonsalves, quoted in Advertising Standards Authority 2003)

The ASA (2003) reported that opinions similar to those quoted above were 'expressed by ... approximately 30 duplicate complaints'. Ruling that the billboard should be withdrawn from public display, and thereby effectively banning it, because it breached the Advertising Code of Ethics, the ASA (2003) stated, 'the depiction had indeed caused both serious and widespread offence in the light of generally prevailing community standards, distorting the debate on genetic engineering and implying a deformation of women'. In these terms, the self-regulating advertising industry failed to agree that MAdGE was employing any sort of ethics other than using female nudity to attract attention to its cause. In light of the extensive sexist and, indeed, semi-pornographic imagery found in a vast range of advertisements (Carter and Weaver 2003), this decision was somewhat surprising and motivated me to explore how New Zealanders from a range of backgrounds really engaged with this image.

Accessing public responses to the cowgirl billboard

Public responses to the MAdGE cowgirl billboard were collected as part of a larger project conducted just after the 2003 lifting of the GE moratorium which asked: 'How do the public respond to the communication of GE by advocacy groups?' Twelve focus groups were recruited for the research: six groups of Pākehā[1] men and women, and six groups of Māori men and women. Within each ethnic group, two groups comprised people of 50 years and over, two groups were between 25 and 49 years, and two groups were between 18 and 24 years of age. The groups were constituted this way to capture, on the one hand, the target audiences for the majority of activist communication – that is Pākehā of different ages – and, on the other hand, Māori, who, while not a specifically targeted audience of anti-GE activist campaigns, had raised a range of concerns about the development of GE in New Zealand (Hutchings 2004). It was of interest to examine whether and how Māori related to anti-GE campaigns organized by predominantly Pākehā activists, of which MAdGE was a typical example. Groups were between six and eight members in size and were asked to engage with a range of activist campaign materials. A total of eighty-seven interviewees participated in the research.

The focus groups were shown a selection of MAdGE's campaign materials – from press releases to newspaper reporting, newsletters, and the Purse Power educational toolkit. However, the cowgirl poster invariably drew most comment and discussion. This is perhaps not surprising given the media attention and public controversy that the billboard had attracted when originally displayed in Auckland and Wellington and when it was banned. In all groups at least one member was able to recall the controversy around the billboard. Yet the extent to which the groups homed in on the poster in their discussions also demonstrates just how powerful and controversial an image of a naked woman can be. In the next section I explore the dominant themes in the discussions about the billboard, and also how the gender and ethnicity of participants influenced their responses.

Responding to the shocking, provocative, and strange

Invariably one of the first responses to the cowgirl image in the focus groups was that it constituted a deliberate attempt to shock. For example, the following exchange occurred in a Pākehā group of 18–24-year-olds:

RESPONDENT 1, FEMALE: It's obviously going for shock value. To try and get a response out of people. But the response may be just against the poster, rather than towards whatever they're trying to promote.
RESPONDENT 2, FEMALE: The first reaction is to have a laugh I guess.
RESPONDENT 3, MALE: It gets the point across pretty well.
INTERVIEWER, FEMALE: What point does it get across?
RESPONDENT 3, MALE: It just draws attention to the issue. The issue being putting genes into cows.

Most respondents, like those above, viewed the billboard as designed to provoke an emotional reaction. As one Pākehā woman over 50 years old commented, 'I think it was meant to shock, wasn't it? Also ... well you couldn't see it without having some view about it. You wouldn't ignore it.' While there was an understanding of how MAdGE attempted to engage the public through a transgressive image in these responses, there was little indication that interviewees were provoked to think about how vulnerable the corporeal body might be to the risks of GE technologies.

For some respondents, the cowgirl image went too far in its transgressions because they felt it constituted unnecessary use of female nudity. It is also notable that concern about the naked representation was frequently expressed in the Māori focus groups and especially strongly by women. For example, one 18–24-year-old Māori female said:

> I agree with what they've all said that it does bring across that thing like a shock tactic, but why do they always have to use a sexual image? Why the sexual image, [why does that] imagery always have to be used? It really hurts me because I know it's sort of like an inch away from porn really.

In another Māori group of 25–49-year-olds, participants explained why they found the image offensive, relating this to their belief in bodily modesty and a concern around the representation of transgenics. Interestingly, in this exchange one woman indicated a mistrust of a male group participant's expression of disgust at the image, and an implied view that he adopted that position because he was in women's company:[2]

RESPONDENT 1, FEMALE: As a Māori, showing things like that is quite rude.
RESPONDENT 2, MALE: It's a bit offensive.
RESPONDENT 1, FEMALE: It is. And ... from a woman's perspective sort of thing, you know, because we were taught, well, I have been taught to keep myself covered and sit like that [cross-legged]. That's the weird side of it, the funny side.
RESPONDENT 3, FEMALE: I think it is disgusting. I'm offended.
RESPONDENT 4, MALE: I found it quite disgusting.
INTERVIEWER, FEMALE: Why?
RESPONDENT 3, FEMALE: Tell the truth. [Group laughter.]
RESPONDENT 4, MALE: The quality of the extra set of tits there, ... having cups coming from there. I mean at the end of the day we are human beings, we are not cows and the cups obviously indicated that intention. I mean, the head's alright. [Laughs.]

In Māori culture humbleness and modesty (*whakaiti*) are highly valued characteristics (Holmes 2007), and proudly displaying one's mental or physical attributes is not considered appropriate. *Whakapapa*, or genealogy, is also a critical component of Māori culture as it identifies who you are and where you come from (Hutchings 2004). For this reason, transgenic GE research has been especially controversial for Māori as it mixes up the genealogy of species and significantly complicates how a genealogical line can be understood and referred to. In the exchange quoted above, the interviewees were objecting to the ethics of the cowgirl *representation*. However, in another group of Māori 25–49-year-olds one interviewee suggested that the ethics of GE should be the focus of concern, rather than the cowgirl image. This followed a male participant's statement that the image was 'disrespectful to women', to which a second female participant asked, 'But then don't you think that GE is disrespectful to animals?' The male group member replied, 'I just think there is better ways of telling you things.'

A further concern – albeit for a minority of participants – around the female nudity in the cowgirl poster was that the billboard was on very public display. One woman in the youngest Pākehā group (18–24-year-olds) explained, 'I think it's the sort of thing that I'd find amusing but I ... wouldn't want my six-year-old little brother seeing [it].' However, in most focus groups at least one participant argued that in order to engage the public in the GE debate, controversial tactics were necessary, such as these two 18–24-year-old Māori women:

RESPONDENT 1, FEMALE: I like it. I think it humanizes the issue and makes it relevant to us rather than corn in a field or cows in a paddock.

RESPONDENT 2, FEMALE: And I don't … feel like it's sexual. I mean the fact is we've all got bodies and some of them are … everyone is different obviously, but I think … they've had to resort to things like shock tactics … because the message just doesn't seem to be getting through to a lot people. At the very least, what MAdGE did was shock people, and people remember that. And it probably encouraged a lot of discussion.

In the group where this statement was made, the participants came to a consensus that the billboard had value in promoting debate about GE. However, this view did not prevail across the groups. Indeed, whether the image succeeded in communicating any message was a matter of considerable discussion. For example, in the oldest Pākehā group (50 years and over) the following exchange took place:

RESPONDENT 1, FEMALE: I don't think it gets the message across at all. I think it's flippant and you look at that and say … 'GE won't do this'. So instead of really carrying a message of 'we have to be cautious about GE', it's flippant and it's silly …

RESPONDENT 2, FEMALE: Sorry, I disagree because I think an image like that has impact when words will go in one ear and out the other.

A significant number of participants' views were aligned with the first of the interviewees quoted above. As a Māori man (50 years and over group) stated, 'I think most people … they'd just look at it and you'd have a laugh, and wouldn't want to know anything about it.' Indeed, the billboard did attract a number of jokes in the focus groups, such as: 'I wish my Mrs had done that' (Māori male, 50 years and over); 'I wished I had a figure like that without the extra [cups hands to chest]' (Pākehā female, 50 years and over); and, in response to the question 'What kind of message do you think MAdGE were trying to get across?', the comment, 'Well, if you genetically modified her you could get twice the production!' (Pākehā female, 50 years and over).

Also evident from the focus group interviews was that a small minority of participants viewed the cowgirl image as a literal representation of the possibilities of GE science – an interpretation that was of concern to the Advertising Standards Authority in its decision to ban the billboard. For example:

Well, for me, that picture, it just pretty confirms what genetic modifying can, is possible, of doing. That could be a reality. If somebody makes a mistake and accidentally puts … you know. That could happen.

That's why I'm saying, well, 'whoa', you know, it's possible with the science that's going on today. Anything's possible and because it's not natural you don't want that happening.

(Māori female, 25–49 years old)

For some other participants, there was a concern that in using the cowgirl image MAdGE was deliberately – and unethically – scaremongering about GE:

This is what they're trying to say: 'This is what's going to happen in the future' ... That's the message it's giving and it doesn't work with me. It's just a scare tactic. Yeah, that's all it is. They want people to be scared of this GE and, you know, 'Please vote against it, this is what's going to happen. You will end up with four breasts.' That's what it says to me.

(Pākehā female, 25–49 years old)

While the use of nudity in activist campaigns has been theorized as able to 'provoke ethical and political actions' (Alaimo 2010: 32), focus group responses to MAdGE's cowgirl poster indicate that it was mostly viewed as a deliberately shocking representation, and, for some, an unnecessarily sexual one. Although some interviewees argued that such tactics were necessary to attract public attention and encourage debate, none expressed viewing the representation of the female body in terms of a trans-corporeal ethics and very few even mentioned being provoked to think about the ethical questions that GE transgenic research might pose. Ironically, for the vast majority of interviewees, the only time that concern was expressed about such species transgressions was in relation to MAdGE's representation of this, and not in reference to the GE research that had prompted MAdGE's campaign. However, unlike the Advertising Standards Authority, none of the interviewees declared that the cowgirl image should have been banned. Certainly some, most notably Māori women of various ages, were offended by it, and some worried about the consequences of children seeing it; but there was not a sense that it caused widespread offence in terms of 'prevailing community standards', as had been suggested by the ASA, or that it was generally perceived as 'implying a deformation of women' (Advertising Standards Authority 2003).

Epilogue to MAdGE

The controversy around the cowgirl billboard marked one of MAdGE's final contributions to the GE debate in New Zealand. In response to the Advertising Standards Authority's decision to ban the billboard, Currie (quoted in Alley 2004) declared:

I think it is fantastic we got busted. It was supposed to be provocative. I've tried every other means, ... but basically one image just wiped the floor. It shows you how powerful protest art can be when it's done properly and there's a real sense of passion behind it.

Lending considerable support to Currie's view that the billboards had increased public engagement with the GE debate, in the week that they were erected, visits to MAdGE's website 'skyrocketed' (*Scoop Independent News* 2003). In the same week, other anti-GE groups, such as Greenpeace New Zealand and Physicians and Scientists for Responsible Genetics, also experienced a marked rise in visits to their websites. It is difficult to attribute this increased interest in anti-GE groups entirely to MAdGE's billboard campaign, yet it was the most significant news event related to the GE debate that week (Weaver 2010). This suggests that controversial protest tactics, such as female nudity, are able to stimulate public interest and have an impact on engagement with controversial issues.

Further evidence that MAdGE (along with other groups) succeeded in rousing public support for anti-GE perspectives came in the group's final public appearance on the New Zealand stage. On 11 October 2003, along with Greenpeace and the Auckland GE-Free Coalition, the group organized a march in Auckland protesting against the lifting of the GE moratorium. One of the largest demonstrations ever held in New Zealand (Dye 2003), police estimated attendance was around 15,000, though organizers claimed it was up to 35,000. Public opinion polling at this time also found that 68.6 per cent of New Zealanders wanted the moratorium to be extended (Fisher 2003).

On 30 October 2003, the New Zealand government lifted the moratorium on applications for field trials and the commercial development of GE. However, while government policy signalled the adoption of a pro-GE position, some corporate businesses aligned themselves with public concern about GE foods. The *New Zealand Herald* (2003) reported: 'A week after the moratorium on the commercial release of genetically modified organisms was lifted, supermarket chains are falling over themselves to claim the most anti-GM stance.' Within the next month over ten supermarket chains had declared a commitment to the sale of GE-free foods (*Waikato Times* 2003). Many activist groups, in addition to MAdGE, had campaigned for this, and the adoption of the GE-free foods policy by companies was testimony to what can be achieved through contestation, advocacy, and transgressive protest.

Subsequent to the lifting of the GE moratorium, MAdGE disappeared from New Zealand's political landscape, and in 2004 it vacated its website. Two key factors contributed to this: the group's unwillingness to fundraise $24,000 that the High Court had ordered it to pay AgResearch for costs incurred defending the case MAdGE had brought against its transgenic cattle research; and Alannah Currie's relocation to Britain in early 2004 (Carter 2004; Wong 2004). Many of MAdGE's protest artefacts, including its cowgirl billboard, Purse Power card, fundraising t-shirts, umbrellas, and lapel badges are now housed in a permanent collection at Te Papa, the Museum of New Zealand. This collection contributes to the record of items of historical and national significance that have a strong link to New Zealand's cultural heritage (Te Papa 2012). Te Papa reportedly requested a copy of the cowgirl poster and other MAdGE artefacts for its collection prior to the ASA's decision to ban the billboard (Advertising Standards Authority 2003).

Conclusion

The MAdGE case demonstrates some of the important questions that the public relations discipline should be asking about how it can better engage with, understand, and theorize activists' use of strategic communication, and the specific challenges that activists may face in communicating their interests and concerns. As Coombs and Holladay (2012b) have outlined, public relations has seriously failed to consider how its history was built on the campaigning work of activists, and how activists continue to pioneer forms and uses of new media and communication opportunities to advance public relations objectives. In the context of public relations research we also need to consider further how social movements and their interests are gendered, and how women's identities and voices are represented in activism, as well as how such identities and voices are interpreted and evaluated by the constituencies with which they attempt to engage.

Women activists have commonly used motherhood as a strategic mobilizing identity and one that brings social, cultural, and political legitimacy to their concerns. Motherhood can provide an important identity platform on which the personal and familial interests and concerns of mothers can be coordinated for political effect. Yet there is a need to investigate how constrained, or free, women are to engage other identities and voices in activism, and what drives their decisions to mobilize around particular identities, as well as how this affects public and political responses and the achievement of campaign goals. While the tactical use of the naked female body has been theorized as having symbolic power to effect change, we need to consider further how such use of the body impacts on perceptions of activists and the issues on which they campaign. As the analysis of responses to MAdGE's cowgirl billboard demonstrated, members of the public may be limited in their interpretations of activists' use of nudity and simply view it as an attempt to shock and attract attention because they have not encountered alternative discursive ways of making sense of such protest acts.

Furthermore, for many groups, strong cultural prescriptions equate exposure of flesh, and especially areas of the body associated with eroticism and sexual activity, with immodesty and inappropriate behaviour. As was the case for a number of Māori participants in my research, this diverted attention away from the cause about which activists were campaigning, and the activists themselves became the subjects of criticism.

In the MAdGE case, 'official' responses to the use of a naked representation also demonstrate how the female body can become a powerful site for domination and control and, indeed, condemnation and censorship when it is used to challenge dominant discursive framings of issues. The case also demonstrates how socially powerful voices and institutions, such as 'expert' commentators sought out for quotes by the media, and the Advertising Standards Authority, resisted and repressed the use of unorthodox challenges to what were claimed to be prevailing social and ethical standards and values.

At the very least, we should be excited by the potential for continued exploration of these and other issues around women's activism under the umbrella of public relations research.

Notes

1 The term 'Pākehā' refers to non-indigenous New Zealanders, most commonly those of European descent.
2 Focus group research is open to the criticism that due to factors such as rules of social politeness, participants censor their opinions and/or adopt and vocalize positions that align to the predominant group viewpoint (Zorn *et al.* 2006).

References

Advertising Standards Authority (2003) Decision, complaint 03/304, 24 November. Online. Available HTTP: <http://203.152.114.11/decisions/03/03304.rtf> (accessed 1 September 2008).
Age, The (2003) 'NZ mums campaign against GE', 30 October. Online. Available HTTP: <http://www.theage.com.au/articles/2003/10/30/1067233300167.html> (accessed 27 March 2004).
Alaimo, S. (2010) 'The naked world: The trans-corporeal ethics of the protesting body', *Women and Performance: A Journal of Feminist Theory*, 20(1): 15–36.
Alley, O. (2004) 'Currie delights as campaign milks the issue', *Sunday Star Times*, 15 February: A5.
Bakhtin, M. (1984) *Rabelais and His World*, trans. H. Iswolsky, Bloomington: Indiana University Press.
Bidder, B. (2011) 'The entire Ukraine is a brothel', *Spiegel Online*, 5 May. Online. Available HTTP: <http://www.spiegel.de/international/europe/kiev-s-topless-protestors-the-entire-ukraine-is-a-brothel-a-760697.html.> (accessed 3 August 2012).
Bob, C. (2005) *The Marketing of Rebellion*, New York: Cambridge University Press.
Bogad, L.M. (2010) 'Carnivals against capital: Radical clowning and the global justice movement', *Social Identities: Journal for the Study of Race, Nation and Culture*, 16(4): 537–57.
Boje, D. M. (2001) 'Carnivalesque resistance to global spectacle: A critical postmodern theory of public administration', *Administrative Theory and Praxis*, 23(3): 431–58.
Bruner, M. L. (2005) 'Carnivalesque protest and the humourless state', *Text and Performance Quarterly*, 25(2): 136–55.

Carter, B. (2004) 'Breakup ends role in Madge', *Weekend Herald*, 31 January–1 February: 1.

Carter, C. and Weaver, C. K. (2003) *Violence and the Media*, Buckingham and Philadelphia, PA: Open University Press.

Collins, S. (2002) 'Cash cow, or mad cow?', *Weekend Herald*, 5–6 October: B3.

Collins, S. (2003) 'Fear GM is creating anti-science nation', *New Zealand Herald*, 14 October: A6.

Coombs, T. W. and Holladay S. J. (2012a) 'Fringe public relations: How activism moves critical PR towards the mainstream', *Public Relations Review*. Online. Available HTTP: <http://www.sciencedirect.com/science/article/pii/S03638111110 01913> (accessed 24 April 2012)

Coombs, T. W. and Holladay S. J. (2012b) 'Privileging an activist vs. a corporate view of public relations history in the US', *Public Relations Review*, 38: 347–53.

Danilova, M. (2010) 'Topless protesters gain fame in Ukraine', *Guardian*, 19 November. Online. Available HTTP: <http://www.guardian.co.uk/world/feedarticle/9369293> (accessed 3 August 2012).

Demetrious, K. (2006) 'Active voices', in J. L'Etang and M. Pieczka (eds), *Public Relations: Critical Debates and Contemporary Practice*, London: Lawrence Erlbaum Associates: 93–107.

Derville, T. (2005) 'Radical activist tactics: Overturning public relations conceptualizations', *Public Relations Review*, 31: 527–33.

Didur, J. (2003) 'Re-embodying technoscientific fantasies: Posthumanis, genetically modified foods, and the colonization of life', *Cultural Critique*, 53: 98–115.

Dommisse, E. (2003) 'Risks still outweigh benefits', *New Zealand Herald*, 29 October. Online. Available HTTP: <http://www.nzherald.co.nz.storydisplay.cfm?storyID=3531189&thesection=news... > (accessed 7 November 2003).

Dozier, D. M. and Lauzen, M. M. (2000) 'Liberating the intellectual domain from the practice: Public relations, activism, and the role of the scholar', *Journal of Public Relations Research*, 12(1): 3–22.

Dye, S. (2003) 'Putting their foot down', *New Zealand Herald*, 13 October: A18.

Edmond, F. (2002) 'Mothers, milk and cows: Mothers Against Genetic Engineering'. Online. Available HTTP: <http://www.madge.net.nz/news/prel/pr_1oct.asp> (accessed 24 November 2004).

Edwards, L. (2011) 'Critical perspectives in global public relations: Theorising power', in N. Bardhan and C. K. Weaver (eds), *Public Relations in Global Contexts: Multi-Paradigmatic Perspectives*, New York and London: Routledge: 29–49.

Edwards, L. (2012) 'Defining the "object" of public relations research: A new starting point', *Public relations Inquiry*, 1(1): 7–30.

Elshtain, J. B. (1998) 'Antigone's daughters', in A. Phillips (ed.), *Feminism & Politics*, Oxford: Oxford University Press.

Ferguson K. E. (2008) 'Women and grassroots organizing', *Women and Politics*, 22(1): 97–111.

Fisher, D. (2003) 'Money talks for pro-GE spin machine', *Sunday Star Times*, 16 November: A13.

Ganesh, S. and Zoller, H. M. (2012) 'Dialogue, activism, and democratic social change', *Communication Theory*, 22(1): 66–91.

GE-Free New Zealand in Food and Environment (2002) 'Madge launch party on Friday 31 May', media release, 31 May.

Grunig, J. and Hunt, T. (1984) *Managing Public Relations*, New York: Holt, Rinehart & Winston.

Grunig, L. A. (1992) 'Activism: How it limits the effectiveness of organizations and how excellent public relations departments respond', in J. E. Grunig (ed.), *Excellence in Public Relations and Communication Management*, Hillsdale, NJ: Lawrence Erlbaum Associates: 503–30.

Hansen, H. (2000) 'Claims making and framing in British newspapers of the Brent Spar controversy', in S. Allan, B. Adam and C. Carter (eds), *Environmental Risks and the Media*, London and New York: Routledge: 55–72.

Hayden, S. (2003) 'Family metaphors and the nation: Promoting a politics of care through the Million Mom March', *Quarterly Journal of Speech*, 89(3): 196–215.

Henderson, A. (2005) 'Activism in "paradise": Identity management in a public relations campaign against genetic engineering', *Journal of Public Relations Research*, 17(2): 117–37.

Henderson, A., Weaver, C. K., and Cheney, G. (2007) 'Talking "facts": Identity and rationality in industry perspectives on genetic modification', *Discourse Studies*, 9(1): 9–41.

Hitchcock, P. (1998) 'The grotesque of the body electric', in M. Mayerfeld Bell and M. Gardiner (eds), *Bakhtin and the Human Sciences*, Thousand Oaks, CA: Sage: 78–94.

Holmes, J. (2007) 'Humour and the construction of Maori leadership at work', *Leadership*, 3(1): 5–27.

Hutchings, J. (2004) 'Tradition and test tubes: Maori and GM', in R. Hindmarsh, and G. Lawrence (eds), *Recoding Nature: Critical Perspectives on Genetic Engineering*, Sydney: UNSW Press: 179–91.

Kavada, A. (2005) 'Civil society organisations and the Internet: The case of Amnesty Internal, Oxfam and the World Development Movement', in W. de Jong, M. Shaw and N. Stammers (eds), *Global Activism, Global Media*, London and Ann Arbor, MI: Pluto Press: 208–22.

Kim, J.-N. and Sriramesh, K. (2009) 'A descriptive model of activism in global public relations research and practice', in K. Sriramesh and D. Vercic (eds), *The Global Public Relations Handbook* (revised edition), New York: Routledge: 79–97.

Kurian, P. and Munshi, D. (2006) 'Tense borders: Culture, identity, and anxiety in New Zealand's interweaving discourses of immigration and genetic modification', *Cultural Politics*, 2(3): 359–80.

Laware, M. L. (2004) 'Circling the missiles and staining them red: Feminist rhetorical invention and strategies of resistance at the women's peace camp at Greenham Common', *NWSA Journal*, 16(3): 18–41.

Miethe, I. (2009) 'Frames, framing, and keying: Biographical perspectives on social movement participation', in H. Johnston (ed.), *Culture, Social Movements, and Protest*, Cornwall: MPG Books: 135–56.

Mothers Against Genetic Engineering (2003a) 'Who is MAdGE?', *MAdGE Newsletter*, 10 April: 1.

Mothers Against Genetic Engineering (2003b) 'Ladies in Waiting Lunch Protest', *MAdGE Newsletter*, 28 June: 1.

Mothers Against Genetic Engineering (2003c) 'News from the MAdGE Mothership', *MAdGE Newsletter*, 28 June: 3.

Mothers Against Genetic Engineering (2003d) 'Bra-vo Madge'. Online. Available HTTP: <http://www.madge.net/news/prel/bravomadge.asp> (accessed 24 November 2003).

Mothers Against Genetic Engineering (2003e) 'Why not just genetically engineer women for milk?', media release, 1 October. Online. Available HTTP: <http://www.madge.net.nz/news/prel/pr_1oct.asp> (accessed 24 November 2003).

Motion, J. and Weaver, C. K. (2005) 'The epistemic struggle for credibility: Rethinking media relations for non-profit organisations', *Journal of Communication Management*, 9(3): 246–54.

Motta, S., Fominaya, C., Eschle, C. and Cox, L. (2011) 'Feminism, women's movements and women in movement', *Interface: A Journal for and about Social Movements*, 3(4): 1–30.

Naples, N. A. (ed.) (1998) *Community Activism and Feminist Politics: Organising across Race, Class, and Gender*, New York and London: Routledge.

New Zealand Herald (2003) 'Supermarket giants battle to be the most anti-GM', 7 November: A5.

One News (2002) 'Mothers unite against GE', 23 June. Online. Available HTTP: <http://onenews.nzoom.com_detail/0,1227,11057-1-8,00.html> (accessed 27 March 2004).

Orleck, A. (2004) 'We are that mythical thing called the public', in L. Ricciutelli, A. Miles and M. H. McFadden (eds), *Feminist Politics, Activism and Vision: Local and Global Challenges*, London and New York: Zed Books: 192–211.

Pardo, M. (1998) 'Creating community: Mexican American Women in Eastside Los Angeles', in N. A. Naples (ed.), *Community Activism and Feminist Politics: Organising across Race, Class, and Gender*, New York and London: Routledge: 275–300.

Public Relations Society of America (2012) *Public Relations Defined: A Modern Definition for the New Era of Public Relations*. Online. Available HTTP: <http://prdefinition.prsa.org/> (accessed 24 April 2012).

Reber, B. H. and Berger, B. K. (2005) 'Framing analysis of activist rhetoric: How the Sierra Club succeeds or fails at creating salient messages', *Public Relations Review*, 31: 185–95.

Ricciutelli, L., Miles, A. and McFadden, M. H. (2004) *Feminist Politics, Activism and Vision: Local and Global Challenges*, London and New York: Zed Books.

Royal Commission on Genetic Modification (2001) *Report of the Royal Commission on Genetic Modification*, Wellington, New Zealand: Royal Commission on Genetic Modification.

Schreiber, R. (2002) 'Injecting a woman's voice: Conservative women's organizations, gender consciousness, and the expression of women's policy preferences', *Sex Roles*, 47(7–8): 331–42.

Scoop Independent News (2003) 'Genetic engineering sends websites through the roof', 6 October. Online. Available HTTP: <http://www.scoop.co.nz/stories/BU310?S00056.htm> (accessed 9 October 2009).

Shepard, B. (2011) *Play, Creativity, and Social Movements: If I Can't Dance, It's Not My Revolution*, New York: Routledge.

Smith, M. F. and Ferguson, D. (2001) 'Activism', in R. L. Heath (ed.), *Handbook of Public Relations*, London: Sage: 291–300.

Stallybrass, P. and White, A. (1986) *The Politics and Poetics of Transgression*, Ithaca, NY: Cornell University Press.

Starrenberg, C. (2003) 'Alannah Currie: Anti GM', *Investigate Magazine*, January. Online. Available HTTP: <http://investigatemagazine.com/jan3ge.htm> (accessed 13 April 2007).

Tankersley, E. (2003) 'Pull the other one MAdGE', *Rural News*, 7 October. Online. Available HTTP: <http://www.ruralnews.co.nz/article.asp? channelid=32&articleid =4807> (accessed 22 June 2004).

Te Papa Museum of New Zealand (2012) 'Acquisition process'. Online. Available HTTP: <http://tepapa.govt.nz/ResearchAtTePapa/CollectionCareAndAccess/AcquisitionProcess/Pages/Overview.aspx> (accessed 3 August 2012).

Turner, T. E. and Brownhill, L. S. (2004) 'The curse of nakedness', in L. Ricciutelli, A. Miles and M. H. McFadden (eds), *Feminist Politics, Activism and Vision: Local and Global Challenges*, London and New York: Zed Books: 169–91.

Waikato Times (2003) 'Food giant goes GE-free', 26 November: 11.

Waitrose Food Illustrated (2003) 'GM foods'. Online. Available HTTP: <http://www.waitrose.com/food_drink/wfi/foodissues/campaigns/0304030> (accessed 27 March 2004).

Weaver, C. K. (2010) 'Carnivalesque activism as a public relations genre: A case study of the New Zealand group Mothers Against Genetic Engineering', *Public Relations Review*, 36(1): 35–41.

Weaver, C. K. and Motion, J. (2002) 'Sabotage and subterfuge: Public relations, democracy and genetic engineering in New Zealand', *Media, Culture and Society*, 24(3): 325–43.

Weekend Herald (2003) 'All in a slather', 4–5 October: A4.

Wong. G. (2004) 'Hear me now', *Sunday Age*, 11 January. Online. Available HTTP: <http://web.ebscohost.com/ehost/detail?vid=1&hid=103&sid=112f3ce-fce0-4c2e-b55b-8> (accessed 11 April 2007).

Woyshner, C. (2002) 'Motherhood, activism, and social reform', *USA Today*, March: 66–7.

Zorn, T., Roper, J., Broadfoot, K. and Weaver, C. K. (2006) 'Focus groups as sites of influential interaction: Building communicative self-efficacy and effecting attitudinal change in discussing controversial topics', *Journal of Applied Communication Research*, 34(2): 115–40.

6 Celebrity, gender and reputation management at the BBC

Jane Arthurs

The BBC is prone to reputational crises that arise from the tensions between bureaucratic control and creative innovation that underpin its brand identity. The strategic importance of public relations for the management of corporate reputations is in its influence on how the organization's activities are perceived by key stakeholders. Broadcast companies negotiate a range of often contradictory interests, values, contexts and expectations which make them especially prone to public conflicts. The BBC occupies a very particular position within the ecology of UK broadcasting as a guardian of the public sphere. This poses specific dilemmas for managing its public relations in that higher standards of editorial judgement and management ethics are expected in comparison to its commercial rivals. Consequently, its approach to public relations has to be highly sensitive to changes in the socio-cultural and political environment, given the greater risk of its attracting negative publicity than other media companies. At the same time, celebrity branding is an increasingly important dimension in creating and maintaining the BBC's reputation in an era of increased competition for viewers in a crowded media environment dominated by global commercial companies. It follows that the BBC's legitimacy increasingly depends on how it handles any difficulties that arise between the corporation and its celebrities.

This was demonstrated most starkly in the crisis that was unfolding at the time of writing (at the end of 2012) over the BBC's handling of revelations about Jimmy Savile, who died in 2011 after a lifetime as a BBC celebrity presenter. The failure of the BBC to broadcast an investigation into allegations that he sexually assaulted possibly hundreds of under-age girls led to a serious crisis of trust in the organization and the forced resignation of the newly appointed Director General, George Entwhistle, after only fifty-four days in office. Savile's posthumous reputation was destroyed by what was widely regarded as the worst possible sexual crime.[1] In contrast, the two case studies focused on in this chapter show that, in less extreme cases, celebrity careers can prosper from the increased levels of visibility for their personal brands that public relations controversies provide in an individualized enterprise culture.

These two cases studies were chosen from the period 2007–12 to exemplify the corporate risks and blind spots in the BBC's handling of public relations crises arising from its strategic commitment to diversity. This commitment is partly a response to maintaining the legitimacy of the universal licence fee which funds the BBC and requires that it provides for a diversity of audience tastes. It is also a response to the legal and cultural changes brought about by social movements campaigning for recognition and equality. Diversity in gender is just one of a range of characteristics protected within UK employment law that also include ethnicity, sexuality, disability and age.

The first case looks at how, in reaching out to younger audiences, charismatic forms of masculine sexualized performance carried a risk of scandalized responses from the press that threatened the BBC's reputation as a responsible broadcaster upholding normative standards of taste and decency in sexual behaviour and speech. The crisis erupted when the lewd behaviour of BBC presenters Jonathan Ross and Russell Brand sparked a press campaign accusing the corporation of moral degeneracy. Academic analyses have already focused on what this crisis can tell us about the cultural politics of offensive humour (Hunt 2010) and the gender politics of scandals (Kelly 2010), while James Bennet (2010) has rightly positioned it as a skirmish in the twenty-five-year battle between the defenders of public service broadcasting and a hostile commercial and political lobby.

In the second case, damage to the BBC's reputation as an exemplary employer arose from a successful legal challenge to an editorial decision to displace older women in a prime-time programme. The case was pursued by *Countryfile* presenter Miriam O'Reilly, who accused the BBC of perpetuating an institutional culture in which women's charismatic value as performers devalued as they aged as a result of a perceived decline in their sexual appeal. The issue had been brewing for some time in relation to other female performers and had been linked to wider concerns over the low political and cultural status of older women (Ross and Carter 2012; Dolan and Tincknell 2012).

I will be using these two crises to highlight the BBC's public relations approach to managing its reputation and the different kinds of risk embodied by the sexualization of male and female celebrities in relation to a gendered corporate and media culture.

Before turning to these case studies, the next two sections introduce the analytic approaches through which their significance will be read and demonstrate how conflicting moral and ideological discourses about gender, age and sexualization framed the ways in which events were understood and communicated. First I will consider reputation management and the role of public relations in protecting the BBC's core brand values in the face of a hostile political environment in which 'free market' rhetoric seeks to undermine its legitimacy. Then I will look at the concept of gendered professionalism and how contemporary forms of gendered self-presentation are manifest in personal celebrity brands. The case studies will examine how each of the crises emerged and were managed, and the consequences for public perceptions of the BBC and the celebrity presenters involved. In conclusion, I will argue that the success of the BBC's strategic commitment to creative risk taking and diversity depends on its ability to understand and navigate the complex politics of gender, age and sexualization in the environment in which it operates.

Branding and reputation management at the BBC

Branding originated in the communicative activities of private companies promoting goods and services but now extends to the ways in which public as well as private organizations establish their legitimacy among multiple stakeholders and the techniques of self-promotion and impression management undertaken by private individuals in order to achieve celebrity (Aronczyk and Powers 2010: 4). Branding has also become much more important to maintaining visibility in the fragmented, competitive markets of the global digital era where consumers have multiple calls on their attention (Johnson 2012). Corporate branding seeks to encapsulate and communicate what the organization stands for, using symbolic imagery to capture its distinctive identity and expressing its purposes and moral values in idealized narratives rooted in its history, while remaining open to adaptation in order to remain relevant. Sub-brands within that umbrella are designed to appeal to divergent markets and taste cultures that develop from changes in the commercial and cultural environment (Lair, Sullivan and Cheney 2005; Davenport and Beck 2001).

The BBC's multiple channels enable it to serve a diversity of audience tastes (Arthurs 2004), with each channel having a distinct brand identity that is partly communicated through its high-profile presenters, such as the popular appeal of light entertainment presenter Jonathan Ross on BBC1, or the youthful appeal of DJ and comedian Russell Brand on the niche digital channel Radio 6. Women presenters have had lower public profiles with none communicating brand values in quite the same way, especially in radio, where currently only 15 per cent of presenters are women on Radio 1 and 25 per cent on Radio 2, the corporation's two most popular radio channels (Skillset/Soundwomen 2011).

Reputation management is designed to secure the organization's legitimacy by maintaining public trust in its core brand identity. The BBC represents an historical ideal of public service premised on high moral and professional standards which underpins a conviction that it is the 'best broadcaster in the world'. The financing of the BBC through a universal licence fee is fundamental to its corporate identity and reputation. Despite the political hegemony of neo-liberal discourses of the free market, people respond as citizens, not just as consumers, to their whole experience of the organization and what it stands for: its purposes, values, policies, and standards of behaviour, as well as its products and services (Davies *et al.* 2003: 47–8).

The BBC's strategic priorities focus its internal activities on the areas that are central to its core brand values and ongoing legitimacy. In the current period, these are: to deliver value for money to the licence fee payer; to maintain the highest editorial standards; to produce distinctive, high-quality outputs through creative risk taking; and to serve all audiences through the diversity of both its workforce and its programmes (BBC 2012a). This means that the corporation's bureaucratic competence in delivering on these strategic priorities is essential to maintaining its brand reputation (Davies *et al.* 2003: 150–8) but so is the courting of risk in the creative innovation that delivers quality programming. It is therefore in the balance between bureaucratic control and creative freedom that the reputational risks to the BBC's core brand values are managed.

The BBC has multiple internal and external stakeholders whose perceptions matter when it comes to managing its reputation: the media industry, the government, BBC employees, and its audiences (Davies *et al.* 2003: 38–9). To enhance these relationships, the BBC uses a wide range of communications which involve human resources and marketing functions as well as public relations. Its media relations, which impact on all stakeholders, are managed through a large press office. Direct relations with the government are conducted through regular appearances at the Department of Media, Culture and Sport Select Committee, where executives are grilled on current controversies. Internal communications are governed by extensive editorial guidelines (BBC 2012b) and a compliance procedure famous for its 'referral up' to higher levels in the hierarchy to manage potential risks. Communications with the industry are conducted via the specialist press, such as the weekly *Broadcast* magazine, and at industry events such as the annual Edinburgh Television Festival. Regular research is undertaken to understand how output is perceived by the organization's audiences, in the knowledge that the public's trust in the BBC brand is the last court of appeal when the going gets tough politically (BBC 2005).

Reputational damage can be caused by blunders and by failure to adapt to changes in the environment to maintain relevance and legitimacy as new ideas, values and lifestyles emerge (Demetrious 2008; Dukerich and Carter 2000). Both are relevant to the crises that developed at the BBC in the period 2006–11. Bureaucratic failures in compliance within areas of strategic priority were exacerbated by a hostile environment in the period up to 2010. The BBC's monopoly on state funding was under siege from the neo-liberal ideologies of the regulator Ofcom (Currie 2006), relations with the Labour government had been dented by a bitter row over the reporting of the events leading up to the invasion of Iraq in 2003 (Arthurs 2010), and News International was campaigning against the BBC to boost its commercial ambitions for Sky (Murdoch 2009). The right-wing press made the most of this situation by amplifying any negative news they could find. In a speech at the 2010 Edinburgh Television Festival, the Director General commented: 'Systematic press attacks on broadcasters, and especially the BBC, are nothing new, of course – the first organised hostile campaign began in John Reith's day[2] – but the scale and intensity of the current assaults does feel different' (Thompson 2010).

These external factors were exacerbated by a series of blunders in 2006–8 which undermined trust in the core values of the BBC's brand, which dropped below 50 per cent. Compliance to editorial standards had been compromised by the deceiving of audiences of phone-in competitions and in the editing of a documentary about the Queen (BBC Trust 2008a). These scandals undermined the BBC's perceived role as a 'moral compass'. Value for money for the licence fee payer had been compromised by reports of a three-year £18-million pay deal for Jonathan Ross which fuelled a more general concern about the BBC's inflated salaries for presenters and its top executives which had risen in line with commercial rates as the BBC sought to secure its market position in the global expansion of television (BBC Trust 2008b).

At the same time the BBC's commitment to diversity was being undermined by senior management's failure to respond to a series of public complaints of discrimination from older women presenters. Arguably, it was their long-term blindness to the gendered power relations of celebrity in relation to sexuality and age that contributed to both the cases examined in detail here. In the Savile case (noted at the start of this chapter), sexual assaults were 'hidden in full view', as one YouTube clip now shows (YouTube 2012).

Once a crisis has developed, it needs to be managed through the deployment of image repair strategies (Benoit 1997; Xifra 2012). These include denial and shifting the blame to evade responsibility, or seeking to mitigate the seriousness of the offence. We will see that these strategies were used ineffectively by the BBC in its initial responses to the two cases examined here, which is why they intensified. In evaluations of Mark Thompson's term of office as Director General from 2004 to 2012, press commentary judged his handling of these crises as too slow in recognizing the serious reputational risks they posed and indecisive in taking action to resolve them (*Guardian* 2012b). Only when he moved to taking corrective action and admitting the lessons learned, accompanied by mortification and public apologies, did the flow of negative publicity abate. In the Savile crisis in 2012, the slowness of the Director General (by then George Entwhistle) to realize the seriousness of the situation sealed his fate. It seems that no one else at board level had overall responsibility for crisis management in an era where Twitter sets a challenging pace (Richard Sambrook, when a guest on BBC 2012c). This slowness to 'get a grip' was seen as evidence of his being too passive, 'a prisoner of bureaucracy'.[3]

Gendered professionalism and celebrity brands

Institutional legitimacy and brand values at the BBC are converted into conventions of self-presentation (Ytreberg 2002: 759) not only by celebrity performers but also in the public appearances of the BBC executive and board, and its Director General in particular (Boyle and Kelly 2010). These performances require professional skill to achieve the right style and appearance and forms of social interaction. Norms of gendered professionalism discipline such performances, which historically have been premised on the bureaucratic ideal embodied in white, male, middle-aged and middle-class modes of self-presentation whose restraint and formality express rationality, authority and control (Ytreberg 2002: 763–4; Weber 2007). At the BBC this mode of presentation emerged out of the dominant discourses of early public service broadcasting and is therefore integral to its historical sense of its brand identity, especially in news, documentary and current affairs, where the BBC's role as impartial mediator of political stories was foundational to its statutory purposes. Compliance with bureaucratic ideals also governs the rule-bound procedures laid down in the BBC's editorial standards; although, as previously noted, this is held in tension with artistic ideals of creative autonomy that allow producers the freedom to innovate in programming and presentation styles.

Women have had a difficult time negotiating this hegemonic style of self-presentation, so it is unsurprising that there has yet to be a female Director General. While they can work to achieve the technical skills required, their feminine attributes of style, appearance and social interaction alongside a lack of social acceptance into professional male networks have been barriers to success (Lair, Sullivan and Cheney 2005; Nadesan and Trethewey 2009; Seabrook 2012). In modern Western cultures the association of female embodiment with emotional expressiveness and as objects of sexual desire positions women in a binary opposition to rational masculine authority and power. But on-air, the bureaucratic ideal has largely been replaced by charismatic modes of self-presentation, a more feminine code of social interaction relying on the presenter's ability to simulate intimacy, immediacy and emotional rapport with the audience through gestural expressiveness and conversational informality (Sennet 1992; Ytreberg 2002).

Charismatic norms have arisen from the transformation of broadcasting into a global entertainment medium where popular tastes challenge the values of an elite male-dominated establishment. Entertainment genres in pursuit of new markets are more open to the development of individuated personal brands for celebrity presenters which redefine gendered performance. In comedy, for example, carnivalesque disruptions of gender in ambivalent forms of feminized masculinity or unruly female appropriations of masculine power signify the genre's licensed transgression of institutionalized authority. This transgressive mode of gender performance is more often a preserve of the male comedians who dominate the genre (Arthurs

1999, 2004). We can see this gender ambiguity in Russell Brand's avant-garde style, which attracts a cult following among young fans in which self-reflexive modes of performance incorporate a deliberately provocative mode of address marked by ' a high level of uncertainty and social aggression' and 'an atmosphere saturated with risk' (Ytreberg 2002: 770). The experimental nature of this style legitimates the BBC's claim to creative risk-taking as well as its commitment to serving audiences at the margin as well as the centre, on which its universal licence fee depends (pp. 770–1). Nevertheless, the risks of reputational damage are real, given the potential of these sub-cultural styles to cause offence to the wider audience.

The interplay between institutional, professional and gender norms in journalism varies around the world and across different professional contexts (Van Zoonen 1998; de Bruin 2000). At the BBC, although news and factual programming genres have over time developed a more informal style, there still remains a hierarchy of status in which male presenters occupy the most prestigious roles that embody the BBC's public service brand, such as prime-time current affairs or special events such as elections and royal occasions (there was widespread criticism when a more charismatic style was used for the Queen's Diamond Jubilee in 2012). Despite equal numbers of women now presenting the news, they are often the younger half of a pairing in which the male presenter does the 'serious stuff' while the woman presents lower-status 'infotainment' centred on celebrity and light-hearted human interest stories with popular appeal (Ross and Carter 2012: 1157). In these roles a restrained female glamour is the norm, requiring a bodily discipline designed to maintain their charismatic value as women, especially the aesthetic appeal of their youthful sexual allure, but in a style that maintains the veneer of bureaucratic authority on which the legitimacy of the news depends (Bennet 2010). The norms of gendered professionalism structure the way that women's charismatic value declines as they age, with their professional skills as presenters failing to compensate. Nor do they have equal access to prime-time slots, which are more often allocated to higher-status male celebrities. These gendered norms put the BBC's reputation for meeting its strategic commitment to diversity at risk.

Presenters also pose a risk as a result of the rise of enterprise culture and the emergence of the self-promoting entrepreneur as an ideal and mode of career advancement (du Gay 1996). The BBC has a value-for-money commitment to support the wider creative economy by outsourcing 25 per cent of its programmes to independent production companies. Celebrity talent increasingly set up their own companies to protect the intellectual property from the development of new programme ideas, and also employ public relations agencies – which lie beyond the BBC's control of its public communications – to promote their careers. As such, they are both a new source of creative innovation and an increased reputational risk to the BBC. Bureaucratic control over these performers and their production teams is loosened by the semi-autonomous contractual arrangements and by the absence of the carefully trained disciplines of the in-house staffer (BBC Trust 2008a). Even directly employed presenters like Jonathan Ross and Miriam O'Reilly rely on personal branding to survive in a fluctuating and insecure job market (Lair, Sullivan and Cheney 2005).

Neo-liberal adaptations of the broadcasting environment that emphasize market relations have had an ambivalent effect on the gender politics of celebrity identity. Celebrity can be short lived. The entrepreneurial celebrity adapts to changing environments by responding to signs of diminishing attention by refashioning their personal brand to adapt to prevailing values in the performance of gender and sexuality (Lair, Sullivan and Cheney 2005: 335–6; Cosentino and Doyle 2010). In O'Reilly's case, her personal brand was enhanced as a champion of women's equality; while in Brand's case, scandalous revelations renewed media interest in his private life in a culture where sexual confessions have become a staple of celebrity public relations. Public relations intermediaries ensure that these celebrity news stories circulate swiftly across different media platforms in the knowledge that the brand value of the commodified self is accumulated through circulation (Featherstone 1991; Lury 1996; Lury and Moor 2010). Presenters have something to gain from scandalous as well as promotional publicity: Brand's notoriety is as effective in reviving his charisma as positive stories of O'Reilly's heroic deeds on women's behalf are in reviving hers (Rojek 2001: 143, 180). The psychodynamics of celebrity idealization depends on a complex mix of desire and identification. Celebrities are both the object of our desiring gaze and a means to identify with their extraordinary deeds. We may project our own transgressive sexual impulses and narcissistic need for attention on to the celebrity but then disavow these pleasures in the condemnatory processes of media scandals (Rose 2003). It is an unstable and unpredictable dynamic to manage in public relation terms, especially where contradictory media messages about the sexualization of young women and girls creates a fuzzy boundary of acceptability.

Sachsgate

The shocked reaction to Jonathan Ross and Russell Brand's lewd joking behaviour during Brand's BBC Radio 2 late night Saturday show after they left a series of messages on *Fawlty Towers* actor Andrew Sachs' answering machine has come to be known as 'Sachsgate'. What could have emerged in playful innuendo or subtext in a phone conversation was instead shouted out by Ross in an obscenity – 'He fucked your granddaughter' – followed by the two presenters giggling like naughty children as they left a series of jokey messages in mock-apology for their bad behaviour.

All of this might have passed unnoticed – none of the audience complained when it was first broadcast – if Andrew Sachs' agent had not gone to the *Daily Mail* a week later, after receiving no response to his own complaint to the BBC. Instead, the press publicity subsequently generated 55,000 complaints, and the ensuing crisis was pored over by commentators in the press, by Ofcom regulators, by the BBC Trust, and by consultants brought in by the BBC to reassess its talent strategy. It has frequently been cited as a reputational nadir for the BBC and its Director General, Mark Thompson, in reflections on his eight-year period of office (which ended shortly before the Savile case erupted).

What do these events reveal about the management of the risks posed to the BBC brand by male celebrity presenters?

The moral outrage was provoked by the politically right-wing *Sunday Mail* and *Daily Mail* in fifty different articles over the course of a single week. The two newspapers framed it within a discourse of moral decline – a once great British institution had been brought low by a gutter culture that had destroyed the BBC's higher public service purposes in pursuit of populism. Any justification for the licence fee was therefore forfeited. The BBC brand had been debased by unchecked obscenity in its style of interaction with its audience, a judgement which is summed up in this characteristic quotation:

Gloating cruelty, foul vulgarity and a BBC that has lost all sense of shame
Long, long ago the BBC was a noble institution, supposed to have a mission to inform, educate and entertain. Now its mission appears to be to degrade, coarsen and brutalise.
(Phillips 2008)

The *Guardian*'s liberal editorial line also condemned the phone call as misjudged, albeit in less extreme terms. It shared the *Mail*'s view that the BBC had been seriously damaged but was critical that it had not protected the brand more effectively. It identified the problem not as moral decline but as a bureaucratic failure that could be fixed by better internal editorial controls and an improved public relations strategy. It was exasperated that managerial incompetence had put the BBC's future at risk in the run-up to the next licence fee settlement, which was due to be agreed in 2010. One of its leader commentaries summed up the paper's assessment of this mismanagement:

The BBC: Branded by abuse
Unfortunately, the BBC has responded with characteristic flat footed incompetence. It could have avoided much of the hysteria had its editorial and management processes worked properly. They should, after all, have stopped the hoax calls from being aired in the first place ... By first shrugging off the story, and then, belatedly, suspending the Radio 2 pair, while its bosses still stay silent, the BBC has behaved

with a haughty lack of awareness. It has also given its media detractors, who do not like it for commercial reasons, a target.

(*Guardian* 2008).

Despite these mistakes, within a month corrective action to repair the BBC's brand image had begun. The Chair of the BBC Trust, the board that holds the executive to account, held a press conference to announce that lessons had been learned about managing its public voice at times of crisis, and publicly appealed to its on-screen talent to reflect on what had happened (Lyons 2008). In order to restore public trust in the organization's bureaucratic competence, additional training was put in place in the interpretation of editorial guidelines, including the limits of acceptability in comedy, and tougher penalties for failure to comply were developed. Executive control would be strengthened over independently produced programmes owned or managed by the featured performer and a new register was to be kept of high-risk programmes (BBC Trust 2008a).

The dramatizing of the BBC's mortification in its Annual Report included a concerned-looking Director General, Mark Thompson, photographed with furrowed brow alongside a narrative expressing regret that the organization had breached the 'strong values of dignity, honesty and trust' that the BBC stands for in a year 'which showed what can happen if, even for a few thoughtless minutes, the BBC forgets it values or the people who own it and pay for it, the British public' (BBC 2009a: 11). In mitigation of the offence, the BBC repeatedly drew attention to the inherent risks in the organization's creative activities. BBC research had shown that 'the public did not want the BBC to lose its nerve' or its willingness to take creative risks (p. 11). Indeed, the BBC brand depended on such risk-taking, as the Chair of the Trust explained:

> Creative risk taking is an essential part of what the BBC is here to do. Every news story, every new show, every performance involves a risk. The BBC simply cannot justify receiving its licence fee if it is unwilling to take those risks. Indeed the Trust continues to argue that the BBC should take more risks with new talent, new ideas and new formats – constantly seeking to bring that something special and different to radio, television and online services. And it must continue to serve all audiences.
>
> (Lyons 2008)

But the Director of BBC Vision had already warned that creative risk should not be confused with judgements about what 'crosses the line' (Bennet 2008).

Despite the negative publicity and the fines that were imposed by the regulator, Ofcom, the longer-term effects of these events on the BBC's reputation were less than might have been expected because of the radical changes that occurred in the organization's political environment. From 2010, the News International phone hacking scandal dominated political attention and news headlines after a murdered girl was revealed as one of the victims. In times of national crisis the BBC comes into its own. Shocking revelations at the Leveson Inquiry about the collusion of senior police officers and politicians made the BBC appear a paragon of moral virtue in comparison (Leveson Inquiry 2012). It took the heat off press attacks and seriously weakened the political lobbying pursued by its commercial rivals. In 2012 there was a recalibration of risk when the newly appointed Director General, George Entwhistle, announced a relaxation in excessive bureaucratic controls in order to revive the BBC's creative energy (*Guardian* 2012b). However, in the aftermath of his resignation less than two months later, with public trust in BBC management having fallen below 25 per cent, this period of relative calm might well be seen as no more than a temporary respite.

Risky masculine performance

What was the role played by Russell Brand's gendered celebrity in this public relations crisis? As a performer he operates on the edges of popular boundaries of taste and can easily cross those boundaries in a live or as-live situation that is characterized by a charismatic performance of informality, authenticity and excitement through spontaneity.

Russell Brand connotes risky behaviour as a core component of his celebrity brand. His expertise emerged out of a strand of youth entertainment which generated conscious experimentation with forms of address in order to capture new young audiences using provocative tactics that are unsettling in their effects. He began his television career on MTV when still a self-confessed crack and heroin junkie. After being sacked for impersonating Osama Bin Laden on the day after 9/11, he returned to his stand-up comedy act, dried out, and got his next big break presenting a cult reality show hit – *Big Brother's Big Mouth* – on Channel 4's new digital youth channel E4. His transition to the BBC came when Lesley Douglas, whose position as Controller of BBC Radio was subsequently ended by Sachsgate, invited him to DJ a show on the niche digital radio channel BBC 6 Music, where in his own estimation Brand became 'Britain's first digital star' (Brand 2010: 58). His transition to the mainstream Radio 2 was marked in 2006 by appearing on BBC 1's flagship chat show *Friday Night with Jonathan Ross*, after which Ross became Brand's mentor, having himself achieved a mature style of bohemian celebrity attuned to the constraints of working for the BBC.

Brand's more avant-garde style was legitimated for the BBC by its public service commitment to innovation. His 'subcultural sophistication' (Ytreberg 2002) met public service claims to 'quality' but was distanced from the corporation's previously elite connotations in his mixing of popular with more intellectual references in his quick-thinking improvisational comedy. He courts danger, mostly staying just this side of uncontrolled chaos and transgression of the boundaries of taste. Formation of his own production company, Vanity Productions, and his entourage of trusted collaborators, minders and agents, many of whom shared his roots in working-class Essex culture, enabled the kind of semi-detached relationship with corporate BBC culture that suited him. His carnivalesque mixing of masculine and feminine signifiers in his rock star style of demeanour and dress – backcombed hair, eye make-up, tight black jeans and studded leather belts – put him in a different category from Jonathan Ross, who in his designer suits is a much more conventional television light entertainment personality. Brand's full-on bohemianism and uninhibited approach to intellectual and sexual discourse challenges the norms of British masculinity through a sub-cultural celebrity style associated with the global success of the UK's rock music industry.[4] He enthusiastically courted tabloid notoriety after a brief sexual encounter with the superstar model Kate Moss had launched him as a regular feature in front-page reports about his brazenly promiscuous lifestyle (Brand 2010).

Rebellion against the masculine norms of bureaucratic conformity is invested with heroism 'for daring to release the emotions of blocked aggression and sexuality that civilised society seeks to repress', argues Chris Rojek (2001: 15). Brand describes his Radio 2 show as 'a shameless, late night boys club, cool and stupid yet sometimes esoteric and tender' (Brand 2010: 240). The show on the night of Sachsgate was a risky combination of male celebrities lured into ludic competitive banter in which swearing and intimate revelations displayed the authenticity of their friendship and a consolidation of their intimacy with the audience who overheard their encounter (Butler and Fitzgerald 2011). Their roles were also reversed, with Brand, as host, the BBC's institutional representative and Ross the guest eager to make his mark. Ross's 'gaffe' (Goffman 1981) momentarily breached BBC institutional norms but instead of repairing the situation with a sincere apology the two celebrities egged each other on to further transgressions in a series of mock-apologies culminating in a scurrilous improvised song.

In the aftermath, Ross wanted to keep it off the air (the programme was pre-recorded, and was eventually broadcast 'as-live', despite Ross's reservations). As a seasoned broadcaster whose celebrity was dependent on the BBC he was right in thinking that it could damage his reputation. His BBC contract was terminated and his career has yet to recover fully.

Brand, on the other hand, was able to use the scandal to promote his career as an entrepreneurial celebrity brand whose loyalties and future success were tied to Vanity Productions rather than the BBC. The name of the company is a reflexive commentary on how different his own narcissistic purposes are from the public service values that define the BBC brand. The culture of personal branding has been described as involving 'looking at themselves in the mirror as well as over the shoulder of others while they strive to fashion and refashion themselves without concern for values, deep satisfactions or contributions to society' (Lair, Sullivan and Cheney 2005: 336). Although Brand later reflected regretfully in his autobiography on his lack of concern for Sachs and his granddaughter – Georgina Baillie – whose privacy he had breached, and for the damage his behaviour caused the BBC (Brand 2010), he nevertheless revealed even more details about his sexual exploits with Baillie, a member of burlesque troupe the Satanic Slut, who has been described as 'a minor player in another story of male power, celebrity and privilege', along with the sacked BBC Radio Controller Lesley Douglas (Kelly 2010: 117).

Brand immediately severed his relationship with the BBC to pursue a successful Hollywood career, and subsequently used the events as material for his Scandalous tour, which played to record audiences at London's O2 Arena (Brand 2009). The public relations value of branding 'transgressive' male sexuality for youthful audiences can be seen in this enhancement of Brand's career success, and at the same time serves to reinforce very traditional discourses about male sexuality as beyond rational control.

Ageing women

Gender identities are structured in binary relationship to each other: the celebrity power of Russell Brand's youthful sexuality is positioned in contrast to the loss of power experienced by ageing women performers as their sexual allure declines. The hyper-visibility of Brand's individualistic personal brand is in stark contrast to the marginalization and invisibility of older women presenters on daytime television. This second case study, about the public relations crisis at the BBC caused by Miriam O'Reilly's legal case against her removal from presenting a television show when it moved to prime time, is best understood within the long-term campaign to improve the situation of all women in broadcasting.

Pressure for change in the treatment of women within television has been pursued at regular intervals over the past thirty-five years, since the Sex Discrimination Act of 1975 opened up many jobs in the industry to women for the first time (Benton 1975). The first women newsreaders – Angela Rippon (BBC) and Anna Ford (ITN) – attracted a lot of commentary when they were appointed in the late 1970s (Root 1986; Holland 1987). The BBC has undertaken numerous initiatives, including positive action following the Sims Report in the 1980s, which highlighted the 'macho culture' at the BBC as a reason for the low proportion of women in management (Sims 1985; Arthurs 1989), as well as portrayal monitoring and research on the role of women in production cultures (Arthurs 1991, 1994; Coyle and Bhavnani 1991).

The issue of discrimination against older women came to a head because of a further change in the legislative environment: the Age Discrimination

Act 2006 and the Equality Act 2010, which changed the legal protections for ageing employees. Compulsory retirement ages were removed and age was added to the list of 'protected characteristics', alongside disability, ethnicity, sexuality and gender, that had to be taken into account in the decision-making of public bodies. The first signs of brewing trouble came in 2006 when newsreader Anna Ford (sixty-two at the time) resigned with the widely reported comment that she was pre-empting being 'shovelled off into News 24' – to the 'graveyard shift' – because of her age (BBC 2006).

What blinded the BBC management to the potential reputational risks of this issue was their conviction that their choice of presenters was a matter of creative judgement rather than bureaucratic compliance, a view widely held across the industry (Skillset 2012). Over the next four years recurring public accusations of sexism and ageism in the press were met with a strategy of denials and rebuttals by the BBC because managers were so convinced that they were above reproach. When Moira Stuart was dropped (aged fifty-eight) after a similarly long career as a newsreader with the BBC, 'Senior broadcasters, both inside and outside the corporation, joined forces with pressure groups and MPs to condemn her removal which they say highlights the inherent prejudice against older women in the television industry' (Alleyne 2007). Officially denying it had anything to do with ageism or sexism, the BBC sought to refute the accusation by shifting attention away from gender and age to the changing professional skills that multi-tasking journalism now required (Holmwood 2007a). When, in 2009, choreographer Arlene Phillips (sixty-six) was replaced on the judges' panel of the popular Saturday night dance competition *Strictly Come Dancing* by a previous winner of the competition, Alesha Dixon (thirty), the public outcry was enormous, but the BBC again claimed it was Phillips' professional skills that were the issue. In this case they wanted a judge on the team who could empathize with the contestants. (Dixon's mixed-race identity was probably another factor, given the BBC's pursuit of diversity.) A hesitant and defensive Mark Thompson was berated about the case on *Today*, BBC Radio 4's influential daily news and current affairs breakfast show, by the famous female crime writer and ex-Governor of the BBC P. D. James (aged eighty-nine), and from this point onwards accusations about the BBC's ageist attitude to women intensified (BBC 2009c).[5]

The issue came to a head when fifty-one-year-old Miriam O'Reilly took the BBC to an employment tribunal on the grounds of age and sex discrimination after being dropped from presenting *Countryfile* (along with three other women in their forties or fifties) on the grounds that she didn't have the right journalistic skill or prime-time profile when it moved from a daytime to an evening slot. John Craven, a higher-profile male presenter well into his sixties, was kept on. The judgement against the BBC of age discrimination and victimization was announced in early 2011 after a series of damaging revelations from internal emails were heard in court, including one detailing the corporation's public relations strategy to pre-empt any accusations of ageism by foregrounding its retention of Craven (Plunkett 2011). It was the lack of formal procedures that led to judicial condemnation of the BBC's 'complacent attitude to hiring and firing' and failure to meet its legal obligations to equality and diversity (Neilan 2011). This was a serious challenge to core brand values: the BBC's reputation for bureaucratic competence and moral leadership.

Thereafter, the BBC's public relations strategy for image repair moved from denial and reactive counter-arguments to an acceptance of culpability, mortification and proactive attempts to take the sting out of the accusations through an ongoing series of corrective actions. Mark Thompson, the Director General, quickly apologized and offered to re-deploy O'Reilly. As Chair of the Creative Diversity Network for 2011–12, he commissioned a report on audience and expert perception of age portrayal and representation in the media to inform future policy. When *Serving All Ages* was published it reported that, although age was not a priority for audiences, a significant minority felt that older women were 'invisible' (White et al. 2012). Thompson held a press conference to apologize again, saying that the O'Reilly judgement had been a 'turning point' and an 'important wake-up call' for the broadcaster:

> First, that there is an underlying problem, that – whatever the individual success stories – there are manifestly too few older women broadcasting on the BBC, especially in iconic roles and on iconic topical programmes. Second that, as the national broadcaster and one which is paid for by the public, the BBC is in a different class from everyone else, and that the public have every right to expect it to deliver to a higher standard of fairness and open-mindedness in its treatment both of its broadcasters and its audiences. If the BBC isn't prepared to take this issue more seriously, what hope is there that others will start to do so? I accept both of these arguments in full.
> (Thompson 2012)

In this statement Thompson accepts that the BBC's previous public relations strategy of citing individual success stories to mitigate the more general accusation of ageism against older women had been mistaken. By referring to 'iconic roles' he commits the BBC to using older women to communicate its corporate brand values. He uses the opportunity to reposition the BBC as setting the moral standard on the issue, not just for the industry but for the nation as a whole. *PR Week* reported that the BBC's strategy was to 'do the work to encourage more older women to be on TV and then talk about it once things have changed. This way we avoid the danger of making empty promises and damaging our reputation' (Luker 2012).

The BBC's Annual Report details the corrective actions taken: a new face-to-face and online training programme for managers across the BBC called

Fair Selection of Presenters; a mentoring scheme for women in radio in partnership with campaigning group Soundwomen; and the publication of a new equality and diversity strategy: *Everyone Has a Story* (BBC 2011). The report reassures stakeholders that 'Diversity in the workforce provides the opportunity to enhance the BBC's originality and distinctiveness and drive creativity and innovation' (BBC 2012a) as a means to reconcile the tensions between bureaucratic control and creative innovation that underpin its brand identity.

Risky female embodiment

This series of events can be understood through the previously examined concept of gendered professionalism. It was argued that, in order to be successful, women in broadcasting have to negotiate an established hierarchy of taste in which feminine styles of charismatic glamour and informality that characterize entertainment genres are lower in status than the masculine styles of bureaucratic authority that, historically, have been the mark of 'quality' programmes. It was also argued that the charismatic value placed on women's youthful sexual allure means that they are devalued as they age, making it much harder for women presenters to maintain their television careers, especially in the high-profile slots of prime time. This is a factor for women newsreaders who have been chosen for their sexual appeal as much as their expertise, while the gravitas of male news presenters simply accumulates.

The impact of this discursive environment can also be seen in the Arlene Phillips case. To maintain the BBC's brand reputation, *Strictly Come Dancing* had to negotiate a delicate balance between competing cultural values in offering popular Saturday night entertainment marked as quality programming to avoid its denigration as 'trash TV'. These contradictory values are embodied in the judging panel, the celebrity hosts, and the professional dancers paired with celebrities competing to win. The programme is double-coded as both popular entertainment in its carnivalesque display of glamorous camp sexuality and exuberant emotional expressiveness *and* quality programming in its educative emphasis on serious hard work to master technical expertise and controlled performance. When BBC 1 Controller Jay Hunt agreed to replace a professional choreographer on the judges' panel with a celebrity dancer the balance tipped towards the charismatic appeal of sexual glamour and emotion while the claim to seriousness that is embodied in the expertise and experience of the judges was undermined. That it was the one female expert who was deemed dispensable rather than any of the three equally ageing men conforms to the historical exclusion of women from positions of authority.

The complex demands made on women's performance of gendered professionalism is also evident in the *Daily Mail*'s response to these events. It is important for setting the public agenda as it has the second-widest newspaper circulation in the UK as well as a high percentage of female readers. Its editorial approach on women is a mix of solicitation and misogyny, with a high proportion of female-oriented content but also frequent subjection of female celebrities to scrutiny and public shaming for the many ways in which their bodies fall short of a youthful, decorous sexual 'ideal'. Visible signs of ageing, such as wrinkles and weight gain, are condemned alongside any overt effort to look younger (Watson and Railton 2012). But in reporting these ageism controversies, the paper's approach was modified in order to maintain its overriding narrative of political hostility to the BBC. It criticizes the 'BBC boss' who told O'Reilly, 'You'll have to be careful about those wrinkles when HDTV comes in' (Andrews 2010), and quotes her, alongside a smiling picture, saying: 'There's nothing offensive about wrinkles' (Sanderson 2011).

Instead, the *Mail* focused its misogyny on Jay Hunt (aged forty-three), the relatively youthful female Controller of BBC 1 during the period of these controversies, in a narrative about the BBC's moral decline that is explicitly linked to the feminization of its workforce. The writer dramatizes Hunt as the villain: 'Lean-lipped, humourless, the killer kitten who is steering Auntie on to the rocks. If you want to get ahead in telly, it's worth keeping in with blonde bobbed Jay', read the headline of an article in which she is portrayed as a feminist careerist who is 'dumbing down' the BBC by pursuing a populist agenda. Her 'killer' ambition and unwomanly power is associatively linked to her unfeminine 'thin lips', and her propensity to low-status populism to her feminine blonde good looks and kitten-heel shoes (Letts 2009). A more concise expression of the contradictions of gendered professionalism for women in television would be hard to imagine.

O'Reilly's tribunal victory substantially enhanced her status and the visibility of her personal celebrity, which she has used to give political leverage to a range of ongoing equality campaigns for women in broadcasting and to set up a network to support women facing discrimination at work (Women's Equality Network 2012). The industry response has been divided, with significant resistance from those who saw the judgement as a constraint on the creative freedom of producers (Neilan 2011; Sabbagh and Plunkett 2012; Skillset 2012). But several industry organizations are now collaborating to create widespread cultural change within broadcasting after Skillset's report on *Women in the Creative Media Industries* (2010) found a disproportionate number of women leaving the industry after the age of thirty-five, and with further research commissioned to find out why (Skillset 2012). Women in Film and Television (WFTV) set up a Working Party on Ageism which included Skillset, the UK Film Council, and trade associations BECTU, Equity and the NUJ (WFTV 2012). WFTV contributes its experience of running mentoring schemes, raising women's public profile through awards, and helping to develop women's professional networks (WFTV 2012). The weekly trade magazine *Broadcast*, which condemned the

BBC's condescending and inconsistent evidence at the tribunal, is continuing its campaign after publishing over fifty articles in support of the issue in the previous three years. Further political pressure on the BBC has been exerted through parliamentary debate, where the O'Reilly case, backed up by Skillset's statistics, was used to highlight women's inequality as media employees (*Guardian* 2012a; *Telegraph* 2012). In this case we can see how public relations campaigns can be successfully mounted by loose collaborations of individual employees and groups within civil society to take on entrenched gender inequalities within powerful organizations.

Conclusion

The purposive communications of public relations is always in a dialectical relationship with the changing norms and values of the environment (Edwards 2012). These case studies demonstrate how the BBC's survival depends on maintaining trust in its core brand values through fulfilling its historic purposes as a public service. But since the 1980s this has had to be pursued through a negotiation of the tensions created by the rise of entrepreneurial values and the commercial imperatives of free market ideologies. It has also had to adapt to generational differences in the cultural politics of sexualization, with changing codes of taste and decency governing celebrity culture and the increased political resistance of older women to their marginalization, bringing challenges to the norms governing the professional performances and identities of its male and female celebrities.

In reading the management of these public relations crises in relation to these ideological struggles within the political economy and the sociocultural environment, we have seen how the BBC's obligation to commission independent producers created a risk from the competing values and entrepreneurial autonomy of celebrity brands. This risk is now more fully recognized and its bureaucratic management strengthened. Less obviously, in gendered terms, two very different ideals of masculine performance were brought into conflict: the performance of bureaucratic responsibility conferring authority and legitimacy on the BBC leadership, as opposed to the transgressive charisma of Brand's celebrity appeal. Celebrity idealization creates an unstable situation to manage in public relation terms in that high media visibility thrives on scandalous revelations. Paradoxically, media scandals work to reinstate the cultural norms that are temporarily transgressed by drawing attention to the boundary which has been crossed. Although initially damaging, this ambivalent process enabled both a reassertion of the BBC's commitment to traditional codes of responsible restraint in public sexual discourse while the publicity enhanced Brand's appeal to a younger generation attuned to the emergence of more confessional norms in a commercialized celebrity culture that thrives on sexual scandal. However, the more recent Savile case is at a different level of seriousness and, at the time of writing, it is too early to say what impact it will have on the gendered cultures of the BBC.

In contrast, the second case study demonstrates the potential for the communicative processes of public relations to transform gendered discourses within organizations in response to social movements (Demetrious 2008). Promoting diversity is now a public relations priority at the BBC. The older women who exposed their career disappointment to public scrutiny risked a potential public shaming for falling short of professional standards rather than being judged as victims of age discrimination. But the media publicity for their personal stories proved to be an especially powerful means by which their private experience could be transferred into public knowledge where it could exert a political effect (Fraser 1995). Their individual stories were used to capture public support, build an informal campaign and collectively challenge the norms of gendered professionalism within the BBC's corporate culture. More stringent formal processes for selection of on-air presenters are now proudly presented in the corporate narrative guiding the BBC's strategic focus on diversity (BBC 2011; Younge 2012). Rather than being seen as a bureaucratic constraint on creative freedom, compliance with equality legislation is being presented as a means to strengthen creative innovation through enhancing workforce diversity.

Notes

1 The timing of this latest crisis at the BBC precludes its full consideration here, but I have briefly signalled its relevance to the argument presented.
2 John Reith was the first Director General of the BBC, from 1927 to 1938, when the commercial British Broadcasting Company Ltd, which he managed, was transformed into a public organization by Royal Charter to become the British Broadcasting Corporation. He laid the foundations of its public service ethos to educate, inform and entertain free from direct state control or commercial pressures.
3 The quoted phrases are from Steve Hewlett, host of *The Media Show* on Radio 4, a programme whose 7 November 2012 edition was particularly revealing in gender terms. A guest on the show declared, 'George is not an alpha male – he's a thoughtful, reflective man and actually in order to lead the BBC with everything that comes with it, you know, you need. [Hewlett interjects, 'Careful.'] ... Um, you need a proper alpha person. [Hewlett whispers, 'Well done.'] Ha ha – it's OK, I steered round that' (BBC 2012c).
4 These connotations of Brand's celebrity persona were reinforced by his inclusion in the closing ceremony of the London Olympics in August 2012, where he sang a Beatles song as part of a concert performed by illustrious UK rock and pop stars.
5 A similarly hesitant performance by George Entwhistle on the same programme led to his resignation the same day. Its regular presenter, John Humphrys, was astounded that, in the aftermath of the Savile revelations, Entwhistle had not known in advance about a *Newsnight* broadcast alleging paedophilia by a conservative peer, Lord McAlpine, nor had he seen a subsequent newspaper report identifying it as an error. This public exposure of 'lack of grip' gave credence to the on-air call for his resignation.

References

Alleyne, R. (2007) 'BBC accused of ageism and sexism after Stuart is axed', *Telegraph*, 4 April. Online. Available HTTP: <http://www.telegraph.co.uk/news/worldnews/1547538/BBC-accused-of-ageism-and-sexism-after-Stuart-is-axed.html> (accessed 4 April 2012).

Andrews, E. (2010) '"Ousted" *Countryfile* presenter, 53, claims BBC boss told her: "You'll have to be careful about those wrinkles when HDTV comes in"', *Mail Online*. Online. Available HTTP: <http://www.dailymail.co.uk/news/article-1326630/BBC-presenter-Miriam-OReilly-claims-boss-told-Be-careful-HDTV-comes-in.html> (accessed 5 January 2012).

Aronczyk, M. and Powers, D. (eds) (2010) *Blowing up the Brand: Critical Perspectives on Promotional Culture*, New York: Peter Lang.

Arthurs, J. (1989) 'Technology and gender: Women and the television industry,' *Screen*, 30(1 and 2): 81–96.

—— (1991) 'Spot the difference: BBC Conference on women in television,' *Screen*, 32(4): 447–51.

—— (1994) 'Women and television,' in S. Hood (ed.), *Behind the Screens: Broadcasting in the Nineties*, London: Lawrence and Wishart: 82–101.

——(1999) 'Revolting women: The body in comic performance', in J. Arthurs and J. Grimshaw (eds), *Women's Bodies: Discipline and Transgression*, London and New York: Cassell: 137–64.

—— (2003) '*Sex and the City* and consumer culture: Remediating post-feminist drama', *Feminist Media Studies*, 3(1): 81–96.

—— (2004) *Television and Sexuality: Regulation and the Politics of Taste*, Maidenhead and New York: Open University Press.

—— (2010) 'Contemporary British television,' in C. Smith and J. Storey (eds), *Cambridge Companion to Modern British Culture*, Cambridge: Cambridge University Press: 171–88.

BBC (2005) *Building Public Value*. Online. Available HTTP: <http://downloads.bbc.co.uk/aboutthebbc/insidethebbc/howwework/reports/pdf/bpv.html> (accessed 6 January 2012).

—— (2006) 'Anna Ford talks tough on ageism,' *BBC News*, 9 April. Online. Available HTTP: <http://news.bbc.co.uk/1/hi/programmes/panorama/4892178.stm> (accessed 8 January 2012).

—— (2009a) *Annual Report*. Online. Available HTTP: <http://downloads.bbc.co.uk/annualreport/pdf/bbc_trust_2008_09.pdf > (accessed 6 January 2012).

—— (2009b) 'Taste, standards and the BBC: Public attitudes to morality, values and behaviour in UK broadcasting', *Inside the BBC*. Online. Available HTTP: <http://www.bbc.co.uk/aboutthebbc/insidethebbc/howwework/reports/taste_standards2009.html> (accessed 6 January 2012)

—— (2009c) *The Today Programme*, Radio 4, 31 December.

—— (2011) *Everyone Has a Story: Equality and Diversity Strategy 2011–15*. Online. Available HTTP: <http://downloads.bbc.co.uk/diversity/pdf/Diversity_strategy_110523.pdf> (accessed 15 July 2012).

—— (2012a) *Annual Report*. Online. Available HTTP: <http://downloads.bbc.co.uk/annualreport/pdf/bbc_trust_2011 12.pdf> (accessed 15 July 2012).

—— (2012b) *Editorial Guidelines*. Online. Available HTTP: <http://www.bbc.co.uk/editorialguidelines/guidelines/> (accessed 15 July 2012).

—— (2012c) *The Media Show*, Radio 4, 7 November.
BBC Trust (2008a) *Editorial Controls and Compliance*. Online. Available HTTP: <http://i.telegraph.co.uk/multimedia/archive/00669/The_BBC_report_pdf_669927a.pdf> (accessed 10 July 2012).
—— (2008b) *On-Screen and On-Air Talent*. Online. Available HTTP: <http://downloads.bbc.co.uk/bbctrust/assets/files/pdf/review_report_research/talent_costs/report.pdf> (accessed 10 January 2012).
Bennet, Jana (2008) 'Enhancing and encouraging creativity in large organisations', speech at Manchester Media Festival, 27 November. Online. Available HTTP: <http://www.bbc.co.uk/mediacentre/speeches/2008/bennet_jana.html> (accessed 12 January 2012).
Bennet, James (2010) *Television Personalities, Stardom and the Small Screen*, London and New York: Routledge.
Benoit, W. L. (1997) 'Image repair discourse and crisis communication', *Public Relations Review*, 23(2): 177–86.
Benton, S. (1975) *Patterns of Discrimination against Women in the Film and Television Industry*, London: ACCT.
Boyle, R. and Kelly, L. (2010) 'The celebrity entrepreneur on television: Profile, politics and power', *Celebrity Studies*, 1(3): 334–50.
Brand, R. (2009) *Scandalous: Live at the O2*, DVD, Channel 4.
—— (2010) *Booky Wook 2: This Time It's Personal*, New York: HarperCollins.
Butler, C. and Fitzgerald, R. (2011) 'My f***ing personality": Swearing as slips and gaffes in live television broadcasts', *Text & Talk*, 31(5): 525–51.
Cosentino, S. and Doyle, W. (2010) 'Silvio Berlusconi, One Man Brand', in M. Aronczyk and D. Powers (eds), *Blowing up the Brand: Critical Perspectives on Promotional Culture*, New York: Peter Lang: 219–40.
Coyle, A. and Bhavnani, R. (1991) 'Watching the Crimewatchers: Women, Gender and Difference in the BBC', paper presented to Spot the Difference Conference, BBC.
Currie, D. (2006) 'Ofcom Annual Lecture', 1 November. Online. Available HTPP: <http://www.ofcom.org.uk/media/speeches/2006/11/annual_lecture> (accessed 12 November 2006).
Davenport, T. H. and Beck, J. C. (2001) *The Attention Economy*, Boston, MA: Harvard Business School Press.
Davies, G. with Chun, R., Vinhas Da Silva, R. and Roper, S. (2003) *Corporate Reputation and Competitiveness*, London: Routledge.
de Bruin, M. (2000) 'Gender, organizational and professional identities in journalism', *Journalism*, 1(2): 217–38.
Demetrious, K. (2008) 'The object of public relations and its ethical implications for late modern society – a Foucauldian analysis', *Ethical Space: The International Journal of Communication Ethics*, 5(4): 22–31.
Dolan, J. and Tincknell, E. (eds) (2012) *Aging Femininities: Troubling Representations*, Newcastle upon Tyne: Cambridge Scholars Publishing.
du Gay, P. (1996) *Consumption and Identity at Work*, London: Sage.
Dukerich, J. and Carter, S. (2000) 'Distorted images and reputational repair', in M. Schultz, M. Hatch and M. H. Larsen (eds), *The Expressive Organisation*, Oxford: Oxford University Press: 97–112.
Edwards, L. (2012) 'Defining the "object" of public relations research: A new starting point', *Public Relations Inquiry*, 1(1): 17–30.

Featherstone, M. (1991) 'The body in consumer culture', in M. Featherstone, M. Hepworth and S. Turner (eds), *The Body: Social Processes and Cultural Theory*. London: Sage: 170–96.
Fraser, N. (1995) 'Politics, culture and the public sphere: Towards a postmodern conception', in L. Nicolson and S. Seidman (eds), *Social Postmodernism: Beyond Identity Politics,* Cambridge: Cambridge University Press: 287–312.
Fredriksson, M. (2009) 'On Beck: Risk and subpolitics in reflexive modernity', in Ø. Ihlen, B. van Ruler and M. Fredriksson (eds), *Public Relations and Social Theory: Key Figures and Concepts*, London and New York: Routledge: 21–42.
Goffman, E. (1981) *Forms of Talk*, Philadelphia: University of Pennsylvania Press.
Guardian (2008) 'The BBC: Branded by abuse', editorial, 30 October. Online. Available HTTP: <http://www.guardian.co.uk/commentisfree/2008/oct/30/bbc-radio-russell-brand-jonathan-ross> (accessed 15 January 2013).
—— (2012a) 'Nadine Dorries on gender balance in broadcasting', extract from *Hansard* on House of Commons debate, 25 January. Online. Available HTTP: <http://www.guardian.co.uk/media/2012/jan/25/nadine-dorries-gender-balance-bbc> (accessed 31 March 2012).
—— (2012b) 'The BBC: Safeguarding the nation's values', editorial, 20 March. Online. Available HTTP: <http://www.guardian.co.uk/commentisfree/2012/mar/20/bbc-safeguarding-nations-values-editorial> (accessed 21 March 2012).
Holland, P. (1987) 'When a woman reads the news,' in H. Baehr and G. Dyer (eds), Boxed in: Women and Television, London: Pandora Press: 133–51.
Holmwood, L. (2007a) 'Newsreaders' role dying out, says Thompson', *Guardian*, 24 April. Online. Available HTTP: <http://www.guardian.co.uk/media/2007/apr/24/bbc.tvnews?INTCMP=ILCNETTXT3487> (accessed 15 January).
—— (2007b) 'Moira Stuart leaves BBC news amid allegations of ageism', *Guardian*, 4 October. Online. Available HTTP: <http://www.guardian.co.uk/media/2007/oct/04/1> (accessed 4 April 2012).
Hunt, L. (2010) 'Near the knuckle? It nearly took my arm off! British comedy and the new offensiveness', *Comedy Studies*, 1(2): 181–90.
Johnson, C. (2012) *Branding Television*, London and New York: Routledge.
Kelly, L. (2010) 'Public personas, private lives and the power of the celebrity comedian: A consideration of the Ross and Brand "Sachsgate" affair', *Celebrity Studies*, 1(1): 115–17.
Lair, D. J., Sullivan, K. and Cheney, G. (2005) 'Marketization and the recasting of the professional self: The rhetoric and ethics of personal branding', *Management Communication Quarterly*, 18: 307–43.
Letts, Q. (2009) 'Lean-lipped, humourless, the killer kitten who is steering Auntie on to the rocks', *Mail Online*, 5 August. Online. Available HTTP: <http://www.dailymail.co.uk/debate/article-1203899/Lean-lipped-humourless-killer-kitten-steering-Auntie-rocks.html> (accessed 5 April 2012).
Leveson Inquiry (2012) Report. Online. Available HTTP: <http://www.levesoninquiry.org.uk/> (accessed 16 July 2012).
Luker, S. (2012) 'BBC takes strategy of silence over Anna Ford's "token" older females criticism', *PR Week*, 19 March. Online. Available HTTP: <http://www.prweek.com/uk/go/news/article/1122805/bbc-takes-strategy-silence-anna-fords-token-older-females-criticism/> (accessed 5 April 2012).
Lury, C. (1996) *Consumer Culture*, Cambridge: Polity Press.
—— (2004) *Brands: The Logic of the Global Economy*, Abingdon: Routledge.

Lury, C. and Moor, L. (2010) 'Brand valuation and topological consumption', in M. Aronczyk and D. Powers (eds), *Blowing Up the Brand: Critical Perspectives on Promotional Culture*, New York: Peter Lang: 29–52.

Lyons, M. (2008) 'Opening statement by Sir Michael Lyons, Chairman of the BBC Trust', press conference, 21 November. Online. Available HTTP: <http://www.lexisnexis.com/uk/nexis/delivery/printDoc.do?jobHanlde=1825%3A3391> (accessed 8 January 2012).

Murdoch, J. (2009) 'McTaggart Lecture', speech at the Edinburgh Television Festival, 28 August.

Nadesan, M. and Trethewey, A. (2009) 'Performing the enterprising subject: Gendered strategies for success(?)', *Text and Performance Quarterly*, 20(3): 223–50.

Neilan, C. (2010) 'Trust in BBC drops by a third, study shows', *Broadcast*, 13 December. Online. Available HTTP: <http://www.broadcastnow.co.uk/news/broadcasters/trust-in-bbc-drops-by-a-third-study-shows/5021557.article> (accessed 5 April 2012).

—— (2011) 'O'Reilly fallout hits home', *Broadcast*, 13 January. Online. Available HTTP: <http://www.broadcastnow.co.uk/news/people/oreilly-fallout-hits-home/5022271.article#> (accessed 5 April 2012).

Phillips, M. (2008) 'Gloating cruelty, foul vulgarity and a BBC that has lost all sense of shame', *Daily Mail*, 27 October. Online. Available HTTP: <http://www.dailymail.co.uk/news/article-1080823/MELANIE-PHILLIPS-Gloating-cruelty-foul-vulgarity-shameful-BBC.html> (accessed 3 December 2011).

Plunkett, J. (2011) 'Miriam O'Reilly case: What the emails tell us', *Guardian*, 12 January. Online. Available HTTP: <http://www.guardian.co.uk/media/2011/jan/12/miriam-oreilly-emails> (accessed 15 July 2012).

Rojek, C (2001) 'Celebrity and transgression', in C. Rojek, *Celebrity*, London: Reaktion: 143–79.

Root, J. (1986) *Open the Box: About Television*, London: Channel 4 and Comedia.

Rose, J. (2003) 'The cult of celebrity', in J. Rose, *On Not Being Able to Sleep: Psychoanalysis and the Modern World*, London: Chatto and Windus: 201–15.

Ross, K. and Carter, C. (2012) 'Women and news: A long and winding road', *Media, Culture and Society*, 33(8): 1148–65.

Sabbagh, D. and Plunkett, J. (2012) 'Rowan Atkinson: BBC should have been allowed to drop Miriam O'Reilly', *Guardian*, 22 February. Online. Available HTTP: <http://www.guardian.co.uk/media/2012/feb/22/rowan-atkinson-miriam-o-reilly> (accessed 6 April 2012).

Sanderson, E. (2011) 'There's nothing offensive about wrinkles, says *Countryfile*'s Miriam O'Reilly after ageism victory', *Mail Online*, 17 January. Online. Available HTTP: <http://www.dailymail.co.uk/femail/article-1347627/Countryfiles-Miriam-OReilly-says-theres-offensive-wrinkles.html> (accessed 4 April 2012).

Seabrook, P. (2012) *The War of the Sexes: How Conflict and Cooperation Have Shaped Men and Women from Prehistory to the Present*, Princeton, NJ, and Oxford: Princeton University Press.

Sennet, R. (1992) *The Fall of Public Man*, New York: Norton.

Sims, M. (1985) *Women in BBC Management*, London: BBC.

Skillset (2010) *Women in the Creative Media Industries*. Online. Available HTTP: <http://www.skillset.org/uploads/pdf/asset_15343.pdf?3> (accessed 27 March 2012).

—— (2012) Personal interview with Kate O'Connor, Executive Director – Policy and Development, Deputy CEO, 10 May, London.
Skillset/Soundwomen (2011) *Tuning out: Women in the UK Radio Industry*. Online. Available HTTP: <http://www.creativeskillset.org/uploads/pdf/asset_16924.pdf?1> (accessed 15 July 2012).
Telegraph (2012) 'BBC should be scrutinised for sexism and ageism, says MP', 26 January. Online. Available HTTP: <http://www.telegraph.co.uk/culture/tvandradio/bbc/9042280/BBC-should-be-scutinised-for-sexism-and-ageism-says-MP.html> (accessed 21 March 2012).
Thompson, J. (2000) *Political Scandals: Power and Visibility in the Media Age*, Cambridge: Polity Press.
Thompson, M. (2010) 'James MacTaggart Memorial Lecture', speech at the *Media Guardian* Edinburgh International Television Festival, 27 August. Online. Available HTTP: <http://www.bbc.co.uk/mediacentre/speeches/2010/thompson_mark_mactaggart.html> (accessed 3 December 2012).
—— (2012) 'The BBC must change – older women should no longer feel they are invisible', *Mail Online*, 9 February. Available HTTP: <http://www.dailymail.co.uk/debate/article-2098490/The-BBC-change-older-women-longer-feel-invisible.html> (accessed 21 March 2012).
Thumim, J. (2004) *Inventing Television Culture: Men, Women and the Box*, Oxford: Oxford University Press.
Van Zoonen, L. (1998) 'A professional, unreliable, heroic marionette M/F: Structure, agency and subjectivity in contemporary journalisms', *European Journal of Cultural Studies*, 1: 123–43.
Watson, D. and Railton, P. (2012) '"She's so vein": Madonna and the drag of aging', in J. Dolan and E. Tincknell (eds), *Aging Femininities: Troubling Representations*, Newcastle upon Tyne: Cambridge Scholars Publishing: 195–207.
Weber, M. (2007) 'The nature of charismatic domination', in S. Redmond and S. Holmes (eds), *Stardom and Celebrity: A Reader*, London: Sage: 17–33.
White, C., Morrell, G., Luke, C. and Young, P., with Bunker, D. (2012) *Serving All Ages: The Views of the Audience and Experts*, London: Creative Diversity Network/BBC. Online. Available HTTP: <http://downloads.bbc.co.uk/diversity/pdf/serving_all_ages01022012.pdf> (accessed 4 April 2012).
Women in Film and Television (WFTV) (2012) Personal interview with Kate Kinninmont, Chief Executive, 29 May, London.
Women's Equality Network (2012) Online. Available HTTP: <http://www.womensequalitynetwork.org.uk> (accessed 15 July 2012).
Xifra, J. (2012) 'Sex, lies and post-trial publicity: The reputation repair strategies of Dominique Strauss-Kahn', *Public Relations Review*, 38: 477–83.
Younge, P. (2012) 'Keynote speech', at BBC Talent Ticket Event, 22 March, University of the West of England, Bristol. Online. Available HTTP: <http://info.uwe.ac.uk/news/uwenews/news.aspx?id=2227> (accessed 20 July 2012).
Ytreberg, E. (2002) 'Ideal types in public service television: Paternalists and bureaucrats, charismatics and avant-gardists', *Media, Culture and Society*, 24: 759–74.
YouTube (2012) 'Jimmy Savile molests girl live on *Top of the Pops* 1976'. Online. Available HTPP: http://www.youtube.com/watch?v=oxy1Lyw7U20 (accessed 24 November 2012).

7 Campaigning for 'women, peace and security'
Transnational advocacy networks at the United Nations Security Council

Ian Somerville and Sahla Aroussi

Women's organizations have had significant success over the past decade campaigning at the United Nations Security Council (UNSC). A series of important UNSC Resolutions on women, peace and security have been passed in the last twelve years, the most important of which is Resolution 1325, adopted in October 2000 to address three key issues: the protection of women from sexual violence in armed conflict; women's participation in peace negotiations; and gender consideration in peacemaking, peacebuilding and post-conflict reconstruction (Shepherd 2008; Anderlini 2007).

This chapter examines the public relations and lobbying strategies used by a transnational advocacy network made up of women's and human rights NGOs to push the issue of women's rights to the top of the UNSC's agenda and achieve transformational change which has had an impact at several important levels, including consciousness building, policy development and legal accountability. We argue that the approach of the women's movement in this campaign provides a model for other groups in how to use communication strategies to push for change in the area of justice and human rights. Our chapter engages with the key issues of this book by focusing on how a coalition of women's organizations successfully gave women a voice at one of the most powerful – and traditionally masculinized – spaces in global politics. Using innovative communicative strategies, the women's NGOs transformed the discourse surrounding gender issues in conflict situations by successfully reframing 'women's human rights' as 'peace and security' issues, and in doing so successfully pressed for the adoption of new norms at the UNSC.

Women and conflict

Armed conflicts undoubtedly have devastating effects on both women and men, but women's experiences of conflict are considerably different from those of men. This dissimilarity is due to sexual violence, to women's reproductive abilities, to their roles as the primary caretaker of the household, and to their second-class status in most conflict zones (Cahn 2006). During conflicts, women, like men, are murdered, tortured, displaced, imprisoned, dispossessed, starved and forced into slave labour. Yet, in addition to these crimes, women and girls are particularly targeted for sexual violence (Askin 2003; Brownmiller 1994). Sexual violence, and particularly rape, is used systematically, methodically and strategically as a weapon of war to terrorize, humiliate, demoralise, displace and annihilate the enemy as well as to re-energize soldiers (Askin 2003). Brownmiller (1994) observed how women's bodies in conflict often become the battleground on which the war is fought. Sexual violence, though often associated primarily with rape, encompasses a wide array of other forms of attacks, including, but not limited to, sexual assaults, sexual slavery, sexual torture; forced nudity, forced prostitution, forced impregnation, forced sterilization, forced marriage and sexual mutilation (Askin 2003; Ní Aoláin 2000). But while sexual crimes are widespread in conflicts, historically they have been met with indifference and hardly ever prosecuted. Despite evidence of the systematic occurrence of rape during the Second World War, the work and statutes of the International Military Tribunal (IMT) at Nuremberg and the International Military Tribunal for the Far East (IMTFE) were almost silent on the issue (Lippman 2000; Campanaro 2001). During transitional justice processes, due to the trivialization of women's concerns and the taboos surrounding sexual crimes, female victims typically become invisible and they are systematically denied access to justice and reparation (Nowrojee 2005).

However, women's experience of conflicts is not only that of victimhood. The victimization of women in wartime should not overshadow their agency in building peace but also in waging war. In many conflicts around the world, women have been active participants, if not leaders, at family, grassroots and national levels in community support strategies, peace-building, humanitarian relief and conflict itself. Women's peacemaking efforts, particularly at grassroots and community levels, are well documented within feminist literature (e.g. Anderlini 2007: 34–56). Women also play a very important role in the survival of conflict communities, assuming jobs and responsibilities that may have been prohibited to them in the past. As a result of political mobilization and of being heads of households, they acquire new skills and new status. Meintjes (2001: 64) argues:

> As men and women are drawn into war, the relations between them inevitably shift. Women become soldiers, labourers for the war effort, national political actors, refugees, and survivors of violence assuming roles previously reserved for men. It is in these role changes that opportunities emerge to forge new social relationships and identities including those of gender.

Thus, women may also contribute to the war machinery as political leaders, soldiers or combatants. Gonzalez-Perez (2006) and Alison (2004) have argued that many women seek participation in liberatory anti-state movements and domestic guerrilla movements as this changes their status and opens a greater ideological and practical emancipatory space. Women in some of these groups have occupied high leadership positions, including as commanders in Uruguay, El Salvador, Nicaragua, Peru, Colombia, Mexico, Sri Lanka, Nepal and Northern Ireland.

However, for women, often the return to peace entails a return to the previous gender status quo (Machanda 2001). Their considerable contributions to peace, their role in managing the survival of communities and their combat roles are devalued and they are pushed from the public sphere back to the private one (Meintjes 2001). Despite their significant peace-making efforts 'on the ground', women have historically seldom been included in the formal peace negotiations, and the lack of gender awareness during formal peace negotiations has often led to gender-blind peace agreements that marginalize women's rights, needs and interests during the reconstruction phase (Chinkin 2003; Aroussi 2011).

The result of all this is that violence against women and gender-based discrimination become even more entrenched in the post-conflict phase. This double victimization of women, during the war and later, during the peace and reconstruction process, has in recent years been successfully challenged by an innovative transnational advocacy campaign conducted by an alliance of women's rights and human rights groups – the NGO Working Group[1] – which came together in 1999 to focus on pushing for change at the most powerful organ of the UN, the Security Council.

Women's rights and the United Nations

Attention to women's rights within the UN dates back to the beginning of the organization in 1945. The UN Charter of that year reaffirms the equal rights of men and women and establishes as one of the organization's main purposes the promotion of and respect for the human rights and fundamental freedoms of all without distinction on the basis of sex. The Universal Declaration of Human Rights of 1948, and the UN Bill of Rights, comprised of the International Covenant on Civil and Political Rights (ICCPR; 1966) and the International Covenant on Economic, Social and Cultural Rights (ICESCR; 1976), reiterated numerous commitments to the equal rights of men and women to the full enjoyment of all the rights and freedoms contained therein. But perhaps most important of all, in respect to the promotion of women's rights, was the adoption by the UN General Assembly of the Declaration on the Elimination of Discrimination against Women (DEDAW) in 1967 and the Convention on the Elimination of All Forms of Discrimination against Women (CEDAW) in 1979. CEDAW was the first legally binding instrument specifically dedicated to women's rights. However, it must be noted that none of these instruments paid attention to the specific situation of women living in conflict societies. It was not until 1995, at the Fourth UN World Conference on Women in Beijing, that the issue of the endemic nature of sexual violence as a weapon of war and women's exclusion from formal peace processes was focused on substantively.

The Beijing conference was held following the conflicts in Rwanda and the former Yugoslavia, where widespread abuse and victimization of women had commanded the world's attention. As a result, the conference served as a platform to echo international concerns regarding the situation of women in armed conflict. The Beijing Declaration and Platform for Action, which were adopted during the conference, underlined the fact that women were still under-represented in decision-making forums related to armed conflicts and conflict resolution and demanded a policy of inclusion and of gender mainstreaming (Otto 2006). However, while important in drawing attention to systematic gender-based violence during conflicts and the exclusion of women from formal peace forums, these two documents ultimately had no legal force or strong normative significance, which meant that they were unlikely to lead to real progress. There was, therefore, a common recognition across the women's movement that a commitment stronger than the Beijing Declaration was needed. The call for the adoption of a UNSC Resolution on the issue began in May 1999 when a group of NGOs led by the Women's International League for Peace and Freedom (WILPF), International Alert and Amnesty International launched a global campaign demanding an end to violence against women in conflict and the participation of women in formal forums of peacemaking and peace-building to ensure women's security in the post-conflict phase (Porter 2007). It was principally the combined efforts of this diverse network of transnational women's groups and human rights organizations, helped by the UN inter-agency network of women's advocates and several governments that supported the initiative, that made the UNSC Resolution on Women, Peace and Security a reality.

The adoption of Resolution 1325 by the Security Council was hailed by women's groups as a watershed and a remarkable institutional achievement that had the potential to revolutionize the established patriarchal ways of peacemaking, peacekeeping and peace-building (Anderlini 2007; Cockburn 2007; Cohn, Gibbings and Kinsella 2004). The Resolution was perceived as the political framework that would allow for women's participation in peacemaking and for gender considerations in armed conflicts as well as in peace-building and post-conflict reconstruction (Shepherd 2008; Anderlini 2007). Most importantly, Resolution 1325 was passed by the Security Council, the most powerful organ within the UN (Cohn, Gibbings and Kinsella 2004). Unlike the UN General Assembly, the Security Council has the power to pass legally binding Resolutions, impose sanctions and order peace missions and humanitarian interventions. Cockburn (2007) noted that while the policy of gender mainstreaming had been officially adopted by the UN since 1997, the Security Council remained 'masculinist' in character and behaviour. Resolution 1325, represents the first instance in the history of the UN in which the Security Council has acknowledged the relevance of gender to peace and security, has recognized 'women' as an autonomous group, not only as victims but also as actors, and has dedicated an entire Resolution to them (Cohn, Gibbings and Kinsella 2004). During our interview with her, Special Representative of the Secretary General Radhika Coomaraswamy stated, 'Resolution 1325 was a big breakthrough in introducing new norms on women, peace and security to an arena which was a hundred per cent male.'

Being an initiative of civil society organizations, Resolution 1325 also effectively marks a turning point in the nature of the relationships between civil society and the UN Security Council. As Anderlini (2007: 72) argues, Resolution 1325 is a 'bridge ... between the grassroots communities in war-torn countries and the New York Skyline'. Since its adoption, attention to the protection of women from sexual violence in conflict, to women's participation in transitional governments and to addressing women's needs during peace negotiations and post-conflict reconstruction has noticeably increased (Aroussi 2011).

Resolution 1325 has a yearly anniversary in which the Security Council debates its implementation, reviews the progress achieved and identifies any actions to be taken. The global constituency behind the Resolution has continued to build up support and call for its effective implementation. Importantly, Resolution 1325 also paved the way for the adoption of a number of other important UN Security Council Resolutions. Resolutions 1820 (2008), 1888 (2009) and 1960 (2010) focus almost exclusively on the use of sexual violence as a weapon of war. Resolution 1889 (2009) focuses on increasing women's participation in all stages of the peace process. The adoption of Resolution 1325 has also helped advance the Security Council's adoption of other thematic Resolutions particularly dealing with issues related to human security in conflict, most notably Resolutions 1612 (2005), 1674 (2006), 1882 (2009) and 1894 (2009) on children in armed conflict (see True-Frost 2007). All of these UNSC Resolutions were the result of interactions between the 'third UN', comprising NGOs, independent commissions, academics, consultants and experts, with the 'first UN', member states, and the 'second UN', the UN Secretariat (Weiss, Carayannis and Jolly 2009). It is the communicative nature of these interactions in the process that led to the adoption of the groundbreaking Resolution 1325 that this study investigates.

Theoretically, this chapter is underpinned by a multidisciplinary framework drawn from a diverse range of academic fields, including public relations (PR), political communication, feminism and international relations (IR). Our review of the literature in these areas assisted in the development of the key themes of our project and the identification of our research questions.

For our study the following research questions were formulated:

- What were the key PR strategies utilized by the NGO Working Group?

- What were the key lobbying strategies adopted by the NGO Working Group?
- Who were the key 'norm entrepreneurs' involved in the campaign for Resolution 1325?
- Is the NGO Working Group's communication management surrounding Resolution 1325 a useful model for other activist groups?

The structure of the remainder of the chapter is as follows: in the next section our data-gathering method is outlined; then three sections analyse the communication management strategies of the NGO Working Group; finally, there is a concluding section.

Interviewing key activists

This research project uses desk research triangulated with primary data from semi-structured interviews with representatives from the women's NGOs who participated in the campaign. It should be noted that there is already an excellent archive of published data on the Resolution 1325 campaign and this material was of great value in conducting this project. For example, six key activist/academic participants in the campaign were involved in a roundtable discussion in 2003 – a transcript of which was published in the *International Journal of Feminist Politics* (see Cohn, Gibbings and Kinsella 2004) – in which they reflected on the struggle for Resolution 1325. Most of these participants and many others have also published memoirs or scholarly works on the campaign and we have drawn on this material to contextualize the present study. What tends to be absent from this work, however, is an analysis and critical reflection upon the actual communication management strategies and techniques deployed by the NGO Working Group to ensure the passing of the Resolution and to manage the issue of women, peace and security over the subsequent decade so that it remained sufficiently prominent to generate the subsequent Resolutions. Our primary data was gathered from interviews with elites within the transnational advocacy network that largely focus on the participant's reflections upon, and explanation of, the tactics and strategies they used in campaigning for Resolution 1325.

This research project has an international focus and the participants were geographically very dispersed (being located in Europe, Northern America and Oceania), which rendered conducting face-to-face interviews logistically and financially both impractical and unrealistic. For this reason, the researchers used telephone interviewing, a proven methodological tool to obtain important data from a geographically dispersed sample (Arksey and Knight 1999; Stephens 2007). This research aimed to gather the viewpoints of elites working within the area and to this end the researchers relied on the method of purposive sampling to target people who are relevant to the research questions (Bryman 2012), with a combination of snowball technique to facilitate access to elite participants. Details of our elite interviewees are set out below, with their role at the time of the campaign and their current affiliation in brackets:

- Sheri Gibbings – Women's International League for Peace and Freedom WILPF (currently Assistant Professor, University of Toronto).
- Maha Muna – Women's Commission for Refugee Women and Children (currently UN Women).
- Sanam Anderlini – International Alert (currently Senior Fellow, MIT Center for International Studies, and Senior Expert in Gender, Peace and Security, UN Mediation Standby Team).
- Cora Weiss – Hague Appeal for Peace (currently President, International Peace Bureau).
- Radhika Coomaraswamy – UN Special Rapporteur for Violence against Women (currently UN Special Representative of the Secretary General for Children and Armed Conflict).

In addition to the data gathered above, we utilized the transcripts from the 2003 roundtable discussion between key NGO Working Group representatives (Cohn, Gibbings and Kinsella 2004), which, as well as Maha Muna and Sheri Gibbings, included: Felicity Hill (WILPF), Isha Dyfan (WILPF), Helen Kinsella (University of Minnesota) and Carol Cohn (Centre for Gender in Organizations).

The NGO Working Group at the UNSC

In the Resolution 1325 campaign, the NGO Working Group proved itself adept at using traditional media relations and events management and also embraced what was at that time an embryonic internet capability, developing very effective online communications. Sheri Gibbings suggests that the provision of 'information subsidies' (Olasky 1987) to the Security Council members was a vitally important factor in pushing the Working Group's agenda forward:

> The NGO Working Group created information packs and sheets with key talking points and they would give these to different member states and they would have meetings with them and say, 'These are the kinds of talking points for this,' essentially doing the work for them. The NGO Working Group were able to strategically say, 'OK, member states want it easy in a sense, they don't have a lot of time or resources, they are dealing with a lot of issues, we are gonna make it easy for them, here's the talking points, here's the things you need to know, we have done the work for you.'

Organizing press conferences and disseminating press releases meant that the mass media were also kept up to date with the campaign and its progress at the UN. Gibbings recalls that the NGO Working Group was 'constantly formulating press releases ... and there was very much an attempt to make this an issue that would have a presence in the media'. It would be possible to analyse these communication efforts from what may be loosely described as a 'functionalist' perspective (L'Etang 2007), focusing on the technocratic expertise deployed in promoting and publicizing the issue. Indeed, the importance of traditional PR practices, such as the media relations activity noted above, cannot be underestimated; but, while necessary, such PR efforts would not have been sufficient to force change at the UN. Our approach draws more from the 'critical paradigm' (L'Etang 2007) in PR research and in our analysis we focus on the role of communication management strategies in the hegemonic struggle (Motion and Weaver 2005) over the discursive constructions of 'women', 'human rights' and 'security' at the UN. What is required to push an issue on to the agenda of the most powerful organ of the UN is not just 'good' communication but a more fundamental change at the level of the discourse surrounding women, peace and security, and this is what we endeavour to analyse below.

Coalitions, alliances and networks

Most studies of public affairs and lobbying, and much of the international relations literature, adopt a 'neo-liberal' position on political advocacy, which means there is a focus, at times almost exclusively, on state-level actors. Joachim (2003: 249) notes that liberal theories focus on the national level, 'treating the domestic level as the exclusive site of agency and interest formation ... [and] defining institutions too narrowly, equating them with the formal political apparatus only'. Public affairs and political communication research on coalitions and political alliances in the policy sphere reflects this tendency, with much of the research focused on analysing how public policy is developed, and legislation produced, at the state/national level. Public affairs research has largely ignored transnational lobbying work at organizations like the UN, the work of Martens (2009) on Amnesty International being an honourable exception.

However, there is no logical reason why studies of public affairs and lobbying work should largely ignore the transnational level. Indeed, it is clear from the Resolution 1325 campaign that Fleisher's (2003: 373) observation that, 'through well-conceived coalitions with other allied interests, various groups have been able to achieve important public policy successes' can apply at the transnational level as much as at the state level. This is an area which has been researched by IR scholars, who have in several important studies specifically focused on the strategies of transnational alliances. For example, Keck and Sikkink (1998), in a groundbreaking text, discuss the effectiveness of various transnational strategies, including the 'boomerang' model (see also Somerville 2011) in human rights lobbying, where 'domestic NGOs bypass their state and directly search out international allies to try and bring pressure on their states from outside' (Keck and Sikkink 1998: 12). This is a useful model, to some extent, in understanding the NGO Working Group that was pressing for the adoption of Resolution 1325 in order to bring pressure on state governments because domestic lobbying had largely failed in the past.

The NGO Working Group was, however, a unique strategic alliance because although transnational advocacy networks have existed for a long period of time, this was the first time a coalition of civil society organizations had organized formally to pressurize the UN Security Council. Maha Muna and Felicity Hill, key figures in organizing the NGO Working Group at the UN, note that developing and consolidating the coalition unsurprisingly took time. There was, after all, no model or template to copy. Muna points out that 'the network was very, very informal initially', while Hill notes:

> The NGO network began to appear informally at the 1998 meeting of the UN Commission on the Status of Women (CSW) ... [I]t was here that the idea to advocate for a Security Council Resolution was first raised ... In March 2000, at the CSW meeting, an NGO network was formalized and began to strategically organize around the goal of a Security Council Resolution.
> (Cited in Cohn, Gibbings and Kinsella 2004: 131).

Several of our participants make the point that developing and maintaining a campaign built upon a coalition of NGOs which usually campaigned autonomously was not always easy. Cora Weiss suggests that, 'compared with any other Resolutions passed by the Security Council, this Resolution has more civil society ownership' but she also notes that this meant it involved developing 'a process that required compromise to keep everybody at the table'. For several of the more radical NGOs, compromise was not always easy. Grant (2000: 16), in his study of pressure group politics, noted that an important distinction can be made between 'insider' and 'outsider' groups, with the former seeking and attaining legitimacy with governmental actors and being consulted on a regular basis while the latter 'does not wish to become involved in a consultative relationship with public policy-makers or is unable to gain recognition'. It is clear that some NGO Working Group members were uncomfortable with 'insider' status in relation to the UN Security Council, an organization which they regarded as requiring a fundamental redesign in order to become less of a 'boys' club', as Sheri Gibbings puts it. Gibbings agrees that with such a diverse network, certain frictions emerged at times and that, in particular, 'there was tension between WILPF and Amnesty', with the latter's human rights focus meaning it did not always see eye-to-eye with WILPF's anti-military agenda. Gibbings argues, 'Within the coalition there were different agendas. So they had to come up with solutions within the coalition.' But she also notes that the various members of the Working Group were ultimately able to focus on that which united them and, as we shall see below, effectively utilized the different strengths they brought to the alliance. There was eventually a compromise between those groups like WILPF whose agenda is to oppose militarism in all its forms (so, for example, they are against women's involvement in the military, even if the role is a peacekeeping one) and groups like Amnesty International which saw greater female involvement in these roles as potentially helping to guarantee greater rights and more security for women. The compromise ultimately favoured the Amnesty position, with the adopted version of Resolution 1325 emphasizing an increased involvement for women in the military and policing as an important component of peace agreements. Showlater and Fleisher (2005) point out that alliances and coalitions in the policy sphere are frequently fraught with difficulties, but groups can work together, even sometimes those with fundamentally different perspectives, if they can agree on what each should bring to the alliance and what the strength of each partner is.

Framing the discourse: the role of norm entrepreneurs

Entman (1993: 52) explains that the process of framing is, in essence, 'to select some aspects of a perceived reality and make them more salient in a communicating text, in such a way as to promote a particular problem definition, causal interpretation, moral evaluation and/or treatment recommendations for the item described'. In a similar vein, Campbell (1998: 381) argues that framing is at the centre of rhetorical battles in the policy sphere and suggests that 'actors deliberately package and frame policy ideas to convince each other as well as the general public that certain policy proposals constitute acceptable solutions to pressing problems'. There has been a great deal of debate in international relations literature on how NGOs frame 'problems' and 'solutions' for decision-makers within the policy process. Keck and Sikkink (1998:17) argue that NGOs use 'framing processes to render events or occurrences meaningful', while Joachim (2003: 247), in her analysis of how NGOs work to change state and intra-state institutions and policies, suggests 'that NGOs attempt to influence state interests by framing problems, solutions, and justifications for political action'. Their success, she notes, depends upon the interplay of different factors, including access to institutions and the presence of influential allies, but of crucial importance is 'the mobilizing structures that NGOs have at their disposal, including organizational entrepreneurs, a heterogeneous international constituency, and experts' (p. 247). She also suggests that normally

> in the beginning of the agenda-setting process, the influence of NGOs is rather limited, their frames are highly contested, and structural obstacles outweigh organizational resources. As they establish their own

mobilizing structures, they become capable of altering the political opportunity in their favour, and their frames gain in acceptance and legitimacy.

(Joachim 2003: 247)

We shall examine the relevance of Joachim's analysis to the Resolution 1325 campaign below, but first it is worth noting that the theoretical debate within the IR literature overlaps here conceptually with the position of critical public relations scholars who wish to emphasize the centrality of hegemonic struggles at the level of 'discourse' in the practice of public relations. For example, Motion and Weaver (2005: 52) suggest that in public relations work 'discourse is deployed as a political resource to influence public opinion and achieve political, economic and socio-cultural transformation'. On this view, 'discourse' is the vehicle by which public relations practitioners attempt to 'establish, maintain, or transform hegemonic power [because] public relations discourse strategies are deployed to circulate ideas, establish advantageous relationships, and privilege certain truths and interests' (pp. 52–3). We would suggest that not only public relations practitioners but lobbyists and campaigners of all kinds can be 'theorised as working to (strategically) privilege particular discourses over others, in an attempt to construct what they hope will be accepted as in the public interest and legitimated as policy' (Weaver *et al.* 2006: 18).

We suggest that 'discourses' can be expressed through 'norms' which are accepted and adopted in the global public policy process. We utilize the concept of the 'norm entrepreneur' from IR literature because it helps explain the significance of those actors who, as Carpenter observes, successfully create and diffuse new norms (ultimately through international treaties), such as 'an international criminal court' or 'the ban on landmines' (2007: 101). 'Norm entrepreneurs', notes True-Frost, 'might come from civil society, other international organizations that have internalized the norm, and even states, all of which could seek to further promote the norm' (2007: 118).

The participants in our study repeatedly emphasized the importance of the struggle to promote particular frames and thereby change the discourse surrounding women and peace and security issues. However, before we discuss the role of NGOs as 'norm entrepreneurs' in the Resolution 1325 campaign, it is worth noting that important changes in what Joachim (2003) refers to as the 'political opportunity structure' were significant in opening up spaces for the NGOs at the UN. Carol Cohn argues that the formation of the Human Security Network in 1999 by several UN member states reflected the beginning of a change of institutional thinking in the UN which the women's movement could eventually exploit. During the 2003 roundtable discussions she suggested:

Before the Human Security Network existed, so-called 'human security' concerns were seen as analytically and organizationally separate from

the Security Council ... The Human Security Network legitimized the inclusion of human security into the conceptualization of the Security Council's work; I have been told that without that step, the thematic resolutions (children and armed conflict; civilians and armed conflict; and 1325) could not have happened ... an organizational entity – in this case, the Human Security Network – is necessary to transform a concept, or new discourse, into an institutional force.
(Cohn, Gibbings and Kinsella 2004: 135–6)

Cohn's statement highlights the interlinked nature of policy processes and makes clear that changes in UN structures impacted on the adoption of the Resolution 1325 campaign just as the passing of the Resolution changed structures at the UN. This, to an extent, contradicts Joachim's assertion that it is through the establishment of mobilizing structures (such as the NGO Working Group) that political opportunity can be shifted in the direction of the NGOs' agenda. The political opportunity space was altered by a combination of state actors and other agencies at the UN before the NGOs mobilized around Resolution 1325. The NGO Working Group, of course, had to take advantage of this shift and at the heart of this was the battle to change the perception of women at the UNSC, which, along with attempting to enshrine the principles of protection and participation for women, was one of the key aims of the Resolution 1325 campaign. One of the areas keenly debated by the participants in the roundtable discussion in 2003 (Cohn, Gibbings and Kinsella 2004) was the issue of how 'women' were represented in Resolution 1325 and whether these representations advanced the cause of women or were politically problematic. Felicity Hill suggested that 'The strategy was to shift the focus from women as victims (without losing this aspect of conflict) to women as effective actors in peace and peace building' (Cohn, Gibbings and Kinsella 2004: 132). Helen Kinsella agreed that 'it is crucially important to consider how 1325 shapes and/or conceptualizes "women" and "gender"', but she noted, 'what troubles me is the reintroduction of women, or the justification of women's participation, on the basis of peacemaking ... why does it need to be qualified in regards to the "use value" of women?' (Cohn, Gibbings and Kinsella 2004: 136). Maha Muna suggested that 'Those arguments have a lot of selling power because they highlight the systems' advantages if women are included [as peacemakers/peace-builders] if the discourse is rights-based, then the advocacy is focused on more than not excluding women' (Cohn, Gibbings and Kinsella 2004: 136). This debate raises the important issue of how 'women' were framed in the communication strategy of the NGO Working Group, why they were framed in this way, and whether the strategy was successful, not just from a communication management point of view, but also from the perspective of whether it was ultimately beneficial to women. The risk of overemphasizing women as peacemakers in Resolution 1325 was highlighted by Helen Kinsella, who argued that presenting them in that way may not ultimately serve the cause of women's rights. She stated, 'I think it is politically unwise not to recognize that the construction of women as peace-makers and as pacificistic has not exactly "liberated" women as equal participants in policy processes' (Cohn, Gibbings and Kinsella 2004: 137).

All of our interviewees emphasize the importance of framing the issue of women, peace and security in ways which would resonate with the UNSC members. Sheri Gibbings notes that they had to be careful to avoid

> speaking in ways that were not acceptable in UN spaces ... [T]he discourses that are allowed are positive, uplifting ... so a lot of women activists that are brought in to speak to the UN have to fit into very well-defined pre-existing narratives ... [T]here is a fight to mould what's possible and not possible to talk about.

This approach arguably involved the adoption of what Spivak (1988: 25) termed 'strategic essentialism'. Spivak, while recognizing that there is no shared essential reality of women, argued that nevertheless some form of essentialism is not only legitimate but required in the field of feminism and women's rights to help assert group rights or attain a specific political goal. From this perspective, presenting women as mothers, as peacemakers, as victims – the traditional images recognized in the masculinized Security Council arena – is legitimate if it attains certain political goals. It is effectively a utilitarian, ends-justify-the-means, approach.

Thus, the strategic communication employed by women's rights activists revolved around the adoption and promotion (and, arguably, exploitation) of all too familiar images of women as victims, vulnerable mothers and girls, on the one hand, and peacemakers and peace-builders, on the other. These images of women should be understood both as accurate representations and rhetorical constructs which were deployed (at times) as techniques of persuasion to influence male decision-makers who, as noted above, perceived the world, and in particular war and conflict, from within a masculinized discourse. Sanam Anderlini notes that presenting women as victims and peacebuilders gave a 'human face' to conflict and she also suggests that 'women as peacebuilders was a positive message which could be seen as not threatening to the status quo'. However, other interviewees emphasized that while such a frame may help gain access to male decision-makers, they were anxious to promote other views of women – not just as peacemakers and peace-builders but as equal partners in the post-conflict transitional phase. Therefore, while the reality and the representation of women as victims of conflict was important, Maha Muna reminds us that there was a battle to make sure other representations of women were recognized. A key issue Muna acknowledges is 'articulation'. She notes of the NGO Working Group that people were not sure how to articulate it, we kept fighting against the vulnerability, you know, 'poor women and the Security Council has to protect poor women', and we had to be very careful about the way we constructed the discussion, you know, from a rights-based approach and I think that is where Florence Martin [Amnesty International] really came in strong and gave us clear arguments.

In respect to the strategy deployed by the NGO Working Group, it may be helpful to consider the process that Fairclough (1992: 93) describes as the 'articulation, disarticulation and re-articulation of elements of a discourse'. Much in the same way as the debate on 'female circumcision', which had traditionally been articulated within a 'cultural values' discourse, was disarticulated from this discourse by feminists in the 1970s and rearticulated within a 'human rights' discourse when it was framed as 'female genital mutilation' (Somerville 2011), framing women as natural peacemakers, while not abandoned by the campaigners, was rearticulated in important ways. Indeed, we would argue that the NGO Working Group transformed the discourse surrounding women, peace and security. As True-Frost notes, this group of NGOs played the role of 'norm entrepreneurs' (2007: 145) by pressing the UNSC through various activities to absorb new human security norms and to reconsider its responsibilities with regards to women in armed conflicts. While the notion of women's inherent peacefulness justifies and naturalizes their engagement in peace-related activities, it also has been seen as problematic because it can allow for women's exclusion and marginalization at the political level (Cockburn 2007). Thus, a key task for the NGO Working Group was to build on the readiness of the UNSC to accept women as peace-builders and push for the full participation of women in all aspects of post-conflict transitional justice mechanisms as well.

While the NGOs, as a group, can be characterized as norm entrepreneurs, our respondents point to certain figures who played key roles in rearticulating the 'problem' and the 'solution' of women, peace and security at the UNSC. Maha Muna recalls:

As with all groups you have people who are very strong leaders and I remember Florence Martin from Amnesty International being really strong in terms of her ability to express Security Council language in a way that was progressive ... [S]he was really a core figure in terms of articulating a position that was new, that was fresh, that was relevant to the Security Council ... And other people I saw there who were significant were Sanam Anderlini, Felicity Hill and Isha Dyfan. Felicity Hill was the most articulate among us in speaking and conceptualizing but I think Florence Martin as a quiet member of the group was the best in terms of putting it down on paper in a way that could be digested by the Security Council ... Cora Weiss was much more outspoken but knew the system really well, she guided us.

The use of the 'essentialist' argument, emphasizing women as natural peacemakers, was clearly important, as was the reality of women as victims in conflict and post-conflict contexts. However, it is also very clear that the NGO Working Group had to move the discourse beyond these conceptualizations of women and to emphasize that women should be included in post-conflict transitional justice mechanisms and participate in peace negotiations and treaties on the basis that it is their right to do so as equal human beings. As we have noted, to move the agenda forward required that they introduce UNSC members to new ways of thinking about women and, in particular, rearticulate the issue of women, peace and security within a human rights discourse. A key element in this strategy was to gain access to decision-makers and present this message to them directly through face-to-face lobbying.

Framing the discourse: access and face-to-face lobbying

McGrath (2007: 269) notes that face-to-face lobbying still determines the success or failure of lobbying activity in many public policy processes, and that in these encounters the lobbyist uses 'language consciously to frame policy issues in such a way as to position their organization and its policy preferences to greatest effect'. He also suggests that 'public policy issues tend to be complex, involving an array of both factors and alternatives; framing is an attempt by lobbyists to set the boundaries of debate on a given issue' (p. 271).

Of course, in order to present your case to key decision-makers face to face, you must meet them, so negotiating access is of vital importance. In fact, as Joachim (2003: 251) notes,

> access is probably the most important resource for NGOs with respect to influence ... Access is vital because it enhances the chances for winning influential allies ... Influential allies can amplify and legitimize the frames of NGOs because they possess resources that these non-state actors themselves lack, such as money, institutional privileges, or prestige. Three types of actors appear particularly crucial: individual states, UN offices ... and the media.

We have already discussed the media relations of the NGO Working Group, so the remainder of this section focuses on the lobbying tactics used to engage with and persuade state actors and UN offices.

The women's network strategically targeted the Namibian presidency of the UNSC (October–December 2000) to introduce the Resolution proposal. They avoided approaching the five permanent members because of their involvement in war and arms races (Cockburn 2007). The Namibian presidency was chosen because Namibia was a key actor in organizing the Windhoek international seminar (May 2000), which called for a review of gender issues in peace operations, and, more importantly, because the NGO Working Group saw the benefit of having a non-Western country taking the lead on women's issues in general and on Resolution 1325 in particular (Tryggestad 2009; Cockburn 2007). Sanam Anderlini points out that while some of the UNSC members, such as Canada, Namibia, Jamaica and Bangladesh, from the beginning strongly supported the idea of a Resolution on women, peace and security, others had to be convinced. She notes, 'Russia especially pushed back and argued that the role of women in conflict was not a security issue and therefore not within the remit of the Security Council.' Therefore, as Maha Muna points out, the first key task was to convince all of the individual UNSC members that a Resolution was required in the area of women, peace and security:

> The Security Council had already done some work on the protection of civilians in armed conflict and you know there was a reluctance – 'Do we need to have more thematic debates? Where is this taking us?' So there was a lot of discussion as to the merits of having a Resolution, especially among the more powerful members of the Security Council, the permanent five. So that was the more difficult lobbying that we had to do to convince them that there was this neglected area, that it could quickly be remedied and that it would have an impact on the peace and security field.

Several of our participants state that it wasn't just about meeting with UNSC members but how you communicated and presented your case when you met them that was of crucial importance. For example, Sheri Gibbings notes:

> there is already a particular format about how a Resolution can be drafted, what kind of language can be used, and I think that's really important ... UN language can be legal and technical ... you must be aware of the politics and cultural functions of language and importance of language.

This understanding was of vital importance to the success of the NGO Working Group and indeed played a part in the most startling aspect of the Resolution 1325 campaign – the fact that in the end the NGOs co-drafted the Resolution with the Chair of the UNSC, Namibia (Gibbings 2004). Once the NGO Working Group agreed upon the draft of the Resolution they wanted to see passed, Cora Weiss notes: 'Then we took our draft and started lobbying the fifteen governments ... We divided up and each of us went to see members of the Security Council and engaged in face-to-face lobbying.' Weiss suggests, however, that those they engaged with in lobbying activities had to be ready to listen:

To meet face to face you have to also have people who really want to know, who press for information, because you can take all of these publications and they get distributed and they just get on someone's shelf but Chowdhury [the Bangladeshi Ambassador] would ask us really tough questions and he really wanted to see what we had written and what we were thinking and how we would answer these points and so you do your advocacy where there are opportunities, where there are people listening, decisions-makers who are really engaged.

Arguably, the reason why the UN representatives were ready to listen was because they had met 'real' women, not just campaign coordinators for the different NGOs. Weiss notes:

It strengthens your argument ... you had women who came and said, 'This is my experience', and the Security Council wanted to know about that. They didn't just want a theoretical construct ... We had to justify why this was an important issue by making it real and grounded in people's lives.

Several participants highlighted that a key factor in the campaign was the fact that the NGOs had a permanent base at the UN in New York. Martens' (2009) study of Amnesty International's influence at the UN attributes much that organization's success to being permanently located at the UN, and Sheri Gibbings believes that this factor was highly significant in the success of the Resolution 1325 campaign, too. She argues a key 'reason it was effective was that all the organizations were located in the same building ... so there was a face-to-face dimension ... [I]t can't be underplayed how important that presence was.'

Conclusion

The passage of Security Council Resolution 1325 in October 2000 was an historic event that marked the beginning of a global agenda on women in conflicts, peacemaking, peacekeeping and post-conflict reconstruction. In the words of Radhika Coomaraswamy, the current UN Special Representative of the Secretary General for Children and Armed Conflict, it also marked a 'whole revolution' in the Security Council's behaviour towards civil society. Tryggestad (2009: 541) reminds us that 'with the adoption of Resolution 1325 a formal barrier was broken in terms of acknowledging a link between the promotion of women's rights and international peace and security – between traditionally soft socio-political issues and hard security'. Breaking this barrier was a necessary step for today's recognition of women and gender issues as part of the UN peace and security strategies.

Read through this lens, Resolution 1325 remains a groundbreaking achievement for women around the globe. Lobbying international organizations is crucially important in bringing about policy change at home but also abroad in conflict-ridden societies. The efforts of the activists in New York have the potential to improve the lives of people on the ground. In this study we have seen how the concentrated efforts of a group of women can lead the UNSC to absorb and reproduce new norms on human security. The communication management strategies of the NGO Working Group proved very effective and successful and can be extrapolated and used (indeed, they *are* being used) successfully by other groups to lobby the UN in areas of justice and human rights.

In the case of the Resolution 1325 campaign, of key significance was the traditional PR tactic of the provision of information subsidies to educate and influence UNSC delegations and face-to-face lobbying by high-profile NGO Working Group 'experts' from civil society, law, politics and academia. Our study also highlights the importance of framing organizational and societal discourse in PR and lobbying work. In such hegemonic struggles the role of norm entrepreneurs like the NGO Working Group is highly significant and especially when combined with access (through, in this case, a permanent presence at the UN in New York) can be very successful in bringing about policy change.

Acknowledgements

The authors would like to thank Christine Daymon and Kristin Demetrious and the anonymous reviewers for their helpful comments on an earlier draft of this chapter.

Notes

1 The NGO Working Group on Women, Peace and Security was a coalition of NGOs which consisted of the following core founder members: Women's International League for Peace and Freedom (WILPF); Amnesty International; Women's Commission for Refugee Women and Children; International Alert; Hague Appeal for Peace; and the International Peace Research Association. They were subsequently joined by eleven other human rights organizations. See http://www.womenpeacesecurity.org/about/.

References

Alison, M. (2004) 'Women as agents of political violence: Gendering security', *Security Dialogue*, 35(4): 447–63.

Anderlini, S. (2007) *Women Building Peace: What They Do, Why It Matters*, London: Lynne Rienner.

Arksey, H. and Knight, P. (1999) *Interviewing for Social Scientists: An Introductory Resource with Examples*, London: Sage Publications.

Aroussi, S. (2011) '"Women, peace and security": Addressing accountability for wartime sexual violence', *International Feminist Journal of Politics*, 14(4): 576–93.

Askin, K. D. (2003) 'Prosecuting war time rape and other gender related crimes under international law: Extraordinary advances, enduring obstacles', *Berkeley Journal of International Law*, 21: 288–349.

Brownmiller, S. (1994) 'Making female bodies the battlefield', in A. Stiglmayer (ed.), *Mass Rape: The War against Women in Bosnia-Herzegovina*, Lincoln: University of Nebraska Press: 180–3.

Bryman, A. (2012) *Social Research Methods* (4th edition), Oxford: Oxford University Press.

Cahn, N. (2006) 'Women in post-conflict reconstruction: Dilemmas and directions', *William and Mary Journal of Women and the Law*, 12: 335–76.

Campanaro, J. (2001) 'Women, war and international law: The historical treatment of gender-based war crimes', *Georgetown Law Journal*, 89: 2557–70.

Campbell, J. (1998) 'Institutional analysis and the role of ideas in political economy', *Theory and Society*, 27: 377–409.

Carpenter, R. C. (2007) 'Setting the advocacy agenda: Theorizing issue emergence and nonemergence in transnational advocacy networks', *International Studies Quarterly*, 51: 99–120.

Chinkin, C. (2003) *Peace Agreements as a Means for Promoting Gender Equality and Ensuring Participation of Women: A Framework of Model Provisions*, Ottawa: United Nations Division on the Advancement of Women. Online. Available HTTP: <http://www.un.org/womenwatch/daw/egm/peace2003/reports/BPChinkin.PDF> (accessed 19 May 2011).

Cockburn, C. (2007) *From Where We Stand: War, Women's Activism and Feminist Analysis*, London: Zed Books.

Cohn, C., Gibbings, S. and Kinsella, H. (2004) 'Women, peace and security', *International Feminist Journal of Politics*, 6(1): 130–40.

Entman, R. M. (1993) 'Framing: Toward clarification of a fractured paradigm', *Journal of Communication*, 43(4): 51–8.

Fairclough, N. (1992) *Discourse and Social Change*, Cambridge: Polity Press.

Fleisher, G. S. (2003) 'Managing the grassroots and assessing its performance', *Journal of Public Affairs*, 2(3): 167–72.

Fleisher, G. S. (2005) 'The measurement and evaluation of public affairs processes and performance', in P. Harris and C. S. Fleisher (eds), *The Handbook of Public Affairs*, London: Sage: 123–44.

Gibbings, S. (2004) 'Governing women, governing security: Governmentality, gender mainstreaming and women's activism at the UN', MSc thesis, York University, Toronto.

Gonzalez-Perez, M. (2006) 'Guerrillas in Latin America: Domestic and international roles', *Journal of Peace Research*, 43(3): 313–29.

Grant, W. (2000) *Pressure Groups, Politics and Democracy*, London: Macmillan.

Harris, P. and Moss, D. (2001) 'Editorial: In search of public affairs: A function in search of an identity', *Journal of Public Affairs*, 1(2): 102–10.

Joachim, J. (2003) 'Framing issues and seizing opportunities: The UN, NGOs, and women's rights', *International Studies Quarterly*, 47: 247–74.

Kakabadse, A., Kakabadse, N. and Kouzmin, A. (2003) 'Reinventing the democratic governance project through information technology? A growing agenda for debate', *Public Administration Review*, 63(1): 44–60.

Keck, M. E. and Sikkink, K. (1998) *Activists beyond Borders: Advocacy Networks in International Politics*, Ithaca, NY: Cornell University Press.

L'Etang, J. (2007) *Public Relations: Concepts, Practice and Critique*, London: Sage.
Lippman, M. (2000) 'Humanitarian law: war on women', *Michigan State University DCL Journal of International Law* 9(1): 33.
Machanda, R. (2001) 'Ambivalent gains in South Asian Conflicts', in S. Meintjes, A. Pillay and M. Turshen (eds), *The Aftermath: Women in Post-Conflict Transformation*, London: Zed Books: 3–18.
Martens, K. (2009) 'Explaining societal activism by intra-organizational factors: Professionalized representation of human rights NGO's at UN level' in C. McGrath (ed.), *Interest Groups and Lobbying in the United States and Comparative Perspectives*, Lampeter: The Edwin Mellen Press: 225–44.
McGrath, C. (2007) 'Framing lobbying messages: Defining and communicating political issues persuasively', *Journal of Public Affairs*, 7(3): 269–80.
Meintjes, S. (2001) 'War and post-war shifts in gender relations', in S. Meintjes, A. Pillay and M. Turshen (eds), *The Aftermath: Women in Post-Conflict Transformation*, London: Zed Books: 63–77.
Motion, J. and Weaver, K. (2005) 'A discourse perspective for critical public relations research: Life sciences network and the battle for truth', *Journal of Public Relations Research*, 17(1): 49–67.
Ní Aoláin, F. (2000) 'Sex-based violence and the Holocaust: Re-evaluation of harms and rights in international law', *Yale Journal Law and Feminism*, 12(1): 21.
Nowrojee, B. (2005) 'Making the invisible war crime visible: Post conflict justice for Sierra Leone rape victims', *Harvard Human Rights Law Journal*, 18: 86–105.
Olasky, M. (1987) *Corporate Public Relations: A New Historical Perspective*, Mahwah, NJ: Lawrence Erlbaum Associates.
Otto, D. (2006) 'A sign of "weakness"? Disrupting gender certainties in the implementation of Security Council Resolution 1325', *Michigan Journal of Gender and Law*, 13: 113–75.
Porter, E. (2007) *Peacebuilding: Women in International Perspective*, London: Routledge.
Rethemeyer, R. K. (2007) 'The empires strike back: Is the internet corporatizing rather than democratizing policy processes?', *Public Administration Review*, 67(2): 199–215.
Shepherd, L. (2008) *Gender, Violence and Security*, London: Zed Books.
Showlater, A. and Fleisher, G. S. (2005) 'The tools and techniques of public affairs', in P. Harris and C. S. Fleisher (eds), *The Handbook of Public Affairs*, London: Sage: 145–59.
Somerville, I. (2011) 'Managing public affairs and lobbying: Persuasive communication in the policy sphere' in D. Moss and B. DeSanto (eds), *Public Relations: A Managerial Perspective*, London: Sage: 167–92.
Spivak, G. (1988) 'Subaltern studies deconstructing historiography', in R. Guha and G. Spivak, *Selected Subaltern Studies*, New York: Oxford University Press: 3–34.
Stephens, N. (2007) 'Collecting data from elites and ultra-elites: Telephone and face-to-face interviews with macroeconomists', *Qualitative Research*, 7(2): 203–16.
True-Frost, C. (2007) 'The Security Council and norm consumption', *International Law and Politics*, 40(1): 115–217.
Tryggestad, T. (2009) 'Trick or treat? The UN and implementation of Security Council Resolution 1325 on women, peace, and security', *Global Governance*, 15: 539–57.

Weaver, C. K., Motion, J. and Roper, J. (2006) 'From propaganda to discourse (and back again): Truth, power, the public interest, and public relations', in J. L'Etang and M. Pieczka (eds), *Public Relations: Critical Debates and Contemporary Practice*, London: Lawrence Erlbaum Associates: 7–22.

Weiss, T., Carayannis, T. and Jolly, R. (2009) 'The "third"' United Nations', *Global Governance*, 15: 123–42.

8 Gender, culture and power
Competing discourses on the Philippine Reproductive Health Bill

Marianne D. Sison

Feminist perspectives in public relations have been explored in ethnocentric and organization-centric ways but very little research has examined the intersections of women's identities, power relations and social change, particularly within the context of postcolonial feminist theory. Except for the work of a few postcolonial public relations scholars (Bardhan 2003; Dutta-Bergman 2005; Munshi and Kurian 2005; Pal and Dutta 2008), public relations research has paid limited attention to postcolonial feminist perspectives.

This chapter considers postcolonial feminist theory in analysing the public discourse associated with the proposed Reproductive Health Bill in the Philippines. In addition, it suggests that public relations plays an important role in bringing about social change in these complex, sometimes opaque, contexts.

Postcolonial perspectives, it has been argued, reveal the colonialist and imperialist legacies that have influenced contemporary culture and discourse. Postcolonial theory aims to 'decolonize the mind at political, economic, and cultural levels' to achieve a fair and just world (Dutta and Pal 2011: 198). Applied to public relations, a postcolonial lens 'exposes attempts by PR theory and practice to communicate corporate goals that coincide with a dominant, largely Western, model of economic growth and development' (Munshi and Kurian 2005: 515). As such, postcolonial approaches aim to provide alternative and previously unheard viewpoints. However, Spivak worries that in postcolonial scholarship, 'ideological construction of gender keeps the male dominant' and 'if in the context of colonial production, the subaltern has no history and cannot speak, the subaltern as female is even more deeply in shadow' (1999: 274).

Postcolonial feminist scholarship focuses on finding the voices of marginalized women or the subaltern, 'the member of a subjugated group whose position has been hidden from history' (Lewis and Mills 2003: 10). Postcolonial feminists argue that Third World women are the ultimate 'Other', but caution against generalizations that they are homogeneous and powerless (Mohanty 2003; Spivak 1999).

Using a postcolonial feminist lens, this chapter examines how public relations interacts with gender, culture and power in the competing discourses surrounding the Reproductive Health Bill in the Philippines.

The Reproductive Health Bill, hereafter referred to as the RH Bill or the bill, was initially proposed by Philippines House Representative Edcel Lagman in 2008 to address the country's burgeoning population. Since then, recent versions of the bill have positioned reproductive health within the context of universal human rights and sustainable human development. Described as 'pro-poor, pro-women and pro-life', the bill aimed to provide parents, particularly women, the 'opportunity to exercise their right to freely and responsibly plan the number and spacing of their children'.[1] The current RH Bill referred to in this chapter comprises two consolidated bills: House Bill No. 4244 and Senate Bill No. 1865.[2]

While the topic of reproductive health might be regarded as *prima facie* a women's issue, the discourses surrounding the bill highlight complex issues of power, religion and politics. Woven into the Philippine complexity are 350 years of colonial history, to which public relations has contributed in the construction of historical and contemporary narratives. The debates in the Philippines provide a useful cultural platform to reflect on gender issues as they relate to the 'negotiation, construction and performance of masculine and feminine identities' (Daymon and Demetrious 2010: 1).

With Catholics accounting for 80 per cent of the Philippines' 94 million population, the bill generates much controversy. Numerous debates have ensued between supporters and opponents of the bill, with the latter backed by the powerful Catholic Church hierarchy. While this chapter focuses on discourses between two advocacy groups – the Catholic Bishops Conference of the Philippines (CBCP), who oppose the bill, and the Reproductive Health Advocacy Network (RHAN), who represent the bill's supporters – other emerging and underlying discourses are also discussed. (The CBCP is the official organization of the Catholic Church hierarchy and RHAN is a network of individuals and organizations advocating for rights-based reproductive health for women.)

Therefore, in this chapter I will: explicate the competing discourses surrounding the Philippine RH Bill; discuss how the discourses reflect notions of power and representation within Philippine society; and demonstrate how the country's colonialist history influences perspectives on family and gendered discourses. First, I will discuss why postcolonial feminist theories are appropriate for analysing this case, and then I will describe the approaches that were used in collecting the data. After providing a brief background on the Philippines and the RH Bill, I present the competing discourses before concluding with thoughts on how a culture-centred approach to public relations may encourage social change.

Postcolonial feminist lens

Feminist research 'probes questions of power, difference, silence, and oppression, with the goal of moving toward a more just society for women and other oppressed groups' (Hesse-Biber 2010: 129). This research aims to examine the 'differences between standpoints' to gain a 'more accurate explanation of the lives of the oppressed and their oppressors' (p. 31). Feminist approaches are particularly relevant in this case not necessarily because the topic relates to women's health issues, but because they reveal how women's reproductive processes and choices have become the subject of gendered discourses at national levels.

Liberal feminist perspectives are helpful in raising questions about reproduction but should not be the default perspective because women's health issues are fraught with cultural and value-laden suppositions. Postcolonial feminist scholars suggest that:

> The control of reproduction and the protection of sexual rights have been central to the agenda of European and North American feminism ... For white feminists, the right to control one's own body, for it not to be regarded as a man's property, was essential to the conceptualization of female sovereign subjectivity and citizenship.
> (Lewis and Mills 2003:11)

Davis (2003) posits that the notion of 'voluntary motherhood' emerged from white, middle-class, educated women in the US who viewed birth control as the route to higher education and careers. Mohanty (2003) argues that Western feminist theory tends to generalize about 'Third World' women and doing so is tantamount to colonialism. She suggests that two frames of analysis exist in feminist literature: the 'average third-world woman' – who is 'sexually constrained, poor, ignorant, uneducated, tradition-bound, religious, domesticated, family-oriented' – in contrast to Western women – who are 'educated, modern, having control over their own bodies and sexualities and the "freedom" to make their own decisions' (p. 53). These frames are important in analysing the discourses on reproductive health, especially with references to the 'poor women' of the Philippines as the beneficiaries when the bill is passed.

Postcolonial approaches interrogate the extent to which voices of 'poor women' are either represented or 'erased' in social, cultural and political discourse. As Spivak posits, 'Part of our "unlearning" project is to articulate that ideological formation – by *measuring* silences, if necessary – into the *object* of investigation' (1988: 296). Arguing that colonialist historiography can perpetuate male dominance and cause subalterns to lose their history and voice, Spivak questions the chance female subalterns have of participating in the political discourse. 'Subaltern' refers to people who are marginalized, do not have access to power, and do not belong to a country's elite group. Their voices are either silenced or 'erased' (Dutta-Bergman 2005; Spivak 1999). Subalternity refers to a 'condition of subordination brought about by colonization or other forms of economic, social, racial, linguistic, and/or cultural dominance' (Beverley 1999: 1). Spivak also warns against the possibility of the 'indigenous elite', such as the local intelligentsia or political leaders, participating in the 'the circuit of colonialist production' (1988: 284).

Postcolonial feminist theory argues that power relations, particularly in areas of representation, need to be addressed and gendered colonial systems should be overthrown. Postcolonial feminist scholarship usually asserts that: women's identities are referred to as 'others' and Third World women as 'ultimate others'; social injustice exists in the use of women in colonial patriarchies; and social change can emerge from subaltern speech (Rakow and Nastasia 2009: 260). While subaltern studies emerged from the work of South Asian scholars who explored history through the narratives and perspectives of the colonized, rather than the colonizers, this approach is particularly relevant in reconstructing women's identities from the viewpoint of Filipino rather than American historians.

Filipino scholar Diaz (2003) argues that postcolonial feminist literature must integrate the local–global trajectory. She reveals the paradoxes in postcolonial Philippines, where women still live with the effects of Spanish and American colonizers' use of education, religion and the law to subjugate women 'while seeming to promote greater equality and social justice' (p. 13). She asserts that colonial histories and postcolonial conditions shape women's identities in some countries, yet these experiences are not reflected in postcolonial feminist literature. She calls for postcolonial feminist scholars to examine how local and cultural conditions have an impact on global politics and economics and vice versa, and to recognize that the continued effects of colonialism exist to enable ways to subvert them. Diaz (2003) suggests that by acknowledging that 'feminist theorizing does not transpire within an economic and political vacuum' and by considering global contexts, postcolonial feminist scholarship can advocate for social change (p. 16). This study responds to that call.

Case-study analysis: contextualizing media texts

Because of the complexity of the issue of reproductive health and the need to 'pay close attention to the influence of its social, political, and other contexts' (Stake 2005, cited in Hesse-Biber and Leavy 2011: 256), the case-study approach is appropriate for this analysis. Case studies are useful in providing 'a holistic understanding of a problem, issue, or phenomenon within its social context' (Hesse-Biber and Leavy 2011: 256). For this reason, the case study employed an analysis of media texts and websites.

To explore how discourse constructs social identities and subject positions, social relationships between people, and systems of knowledge and beliefs (Fairclough 1992: 64), I also analysed media texts and the CBCP's and RHAN's websites.

For the media analysis, I collected media articles from the Factiva electronic database for the period 1 January 2008 to 30 November 2011. I selected this period because Rep. Lagman introduced the RH Bill in 2008 and news media have since covered the issue as parliamentary debates continue on the proposed legislation. Using the keywords 'reproductive health' and 'Philippines', I chose two English-language metropolitan newspapers with online versions available on Factiva, namely the *Philippine Daily Inquirer* and the *Manila Bulletin*, because of their general news slant and high circulations (Tuazon n.d.). After the search yielded 418 articles, I refined it to focus on 'Church' and 'RHAN', sorted the list for 'relevance' and chose the first 100 texts as the sample.

Following Fairclough's (1992) notion of discourse representation, I read and coded the texts based on *what* was reported, *who* were quoted as 'sources', the context of the article, and whether the media text, through its tone, reflected a stance for or against the bill. I used these texts to analyse the discourse surrounding the issue. Discourse is a 'form of social practice' that not only represents the world but also signifies it by 'constituting and constructing the world in meaning' (Fairclough 1992: 63–4).

Between September and November 2011, I analysed the message content, organizational profile, language and images used in the websites. Other documents, such as copies of the bills and blogs, were also accessed through various online sources. Because media articles are reports of events or interviews undertaken with key sources, and may also include references to previously reported events, they may be subject to intertextuality. Intertextuality refers to 'the property texts have of being full of snatches of other texts' and which the text may 'assimilate, contradict, ironically echo' (Fairclough 1992: 84). Thus, the analysis must consider that the media reports of the discourses have gone through several gatekeeping processes. Furthermore, media reports also tended to present voices of the elite and powerful, so this was taken into account in the analysis.

The Reproductive Health Bill

To understand why the bill generates so much debate, it is important to understand the political, economic, social and cultural context of the Philippines. I set this out below, then describe key elements of the bill and define some of the key terms.

Philippine context

Karnow's description of the Philippines' colonial past as '300 years in a Catholic convent and 50 years in Hollywood' (1989: 9) aptly reflects a culture characterized by religion and celebrity. While being the only predominantly Christian nation in Asia, the Philippines ranked only 134th (out of 178) on Transparency International's (2010) Corruption Perception Index. Almost a quarter of the population lives below the $1.25 per day poverty line.[3] Despite an American-style democratic government and robust free press, corruption has impeded the country's progress (Lim 2003).

The Philippine constitution recognizes the separation of Church and State, yet much of Filipino culture reflects the people's religious faith. The Philippine Trust Index of 2011[4] identified the Catholic Church as the most trusted institution in the Philippines, followed by media, business and NGOs. The report also found that the most trusted NGOs were those that advocated health, nutrition, and youth and children's issues. For the Church to maintain its trust levels, a third of the respondents said that it was important to have a separation of Church and State. Respondents interpreted this Church–State separation as 'not meddling in affairs of the state, leaving politics to politicians and leaving the RH bill alone' (EON Stakeholder Relations 2011).

Filipino culture is characterized by a strong focus on family that comprises one's parents, siblings, spouse and children (Jocano 1998; see also Dalisay 2000). As the core unit of Filipino society, the family often includes extended members. This context is important in understanding the politics between the government and the Church at a macro level and the family dynamics at a micro level.

The key players

This section provides background on the main protagonists who 'represent' the supporters and opponents of the bill. I acknowledge this is a limited representation of the various groups engaged in the discourse, as there are numerous 'breakaway' groups and individuals. Nevertheless, it is important to understand that the CBCP represents the Catholic Church hierarchy. Meanwhile, the RHAN is a coalition of many different organizations who share the same views on women's rights and women's health.

The CBCP began as a postwar Catholic welfare organization that aimed to unify, coordinate and organize Catholic education, social welfare, religious and spiritual aid under the Filipino bishops. It has since become the official organization of the Catholic Church hierarchy in the country. Directly reporting to the Vatican, the CBCP operates through eighty-six 'ecclesiastical territories', spreading its reach deep and wide across the archipelago. Each territory comprises several parishes and is led by bishops, archbishops and cardinals. The institutional structure includes a permanent assembly (similar to an executive board) and commissions that fall under five departments, including a Department of External Affairs. While the CBCP's webpage has links to most of the commissions, notably absent are links to the Commission on Family and Life, and the Office on Women.

The RHAN is a 'network of organizations and individuals advocating for RH policies and programmes at the national and local levels' which campaigns for reproductive health policies and programmes based on human rights and human-centred principles.[5] It works with several groups and operates its website and its secretariat through the Likhaan Center for Women's Health.[6] Likhaan is a collective of 'grassroots women and men, health advocates and professionals dedicated to promoting and pushing for the health and rights of disadvantaged women and their communities'.[7] The group's foci include community organization, women's clinics, and women's right to health advocacy.

Other participants in the discourse included legislators from the Lower and Upper Houses of the Philippine Congress, and the President, whose successful 2010 presidential campaign included his support of the RH Bill. Provincial and local government officials also featured in the discourse because once the bill is passed, they will be responsible for its implementation. The media discourse also included voices from medical practitioners, media commentators, business leaders, community leaders, leaders of other Christian Churches, academics, and international agencies. However, it featured few voices from the community members, such as young women, mothers and fathers with low socio-economic status, who were most likely to be affected by the bill.

Key elements of the Reproductive Health Bill

While earlier versions of the Reproductive Health Bill focused on population control, the 2008 proposed that legislation was framed in the context of sustainable human development.[8] Undoubtedly, the bill responded to United Nations (UN) agency reports about high incidences of pregnancy- and childbirth-related deaths and high maternity mortality ratios (MMR). The UN Population Fund (UNFPA) reported that a total of 4600 Filipino women died in one year, giving an MMR of 230 for every 100,000 live births.[9] Despite a lower MMR in 2008,[10] the Philippines reasserted its pledge to meet the UN's Millennium Development Goals (MDGs), set in 2000. Of the eight goals, which included poverty reduction, access to primary education, environmental stability and global partnership for development, four related to maternal and child health care, gender equality and sexual health issues. The Philippine government specified targets and provided funding for programmes to achieve each of the MDGs. Framed as an 'international obligation', the RH Bill aimed to address the goals of eliminating extreme hunger and poverty, reducing infant mortality and improving maternal health (*Philippine Daily Inquirer*, 31 January 2011).

After much consultation, debates and lobbying, the 2008 version of the bill underwent various iterations and amendments. The most recent version of the RH Bill (Senate Bill No. 2865, 6 June 2011) defined the key terms.

Reproductive health is defined as:

> the state of complete physical, mental and social well-being and not merely the absence of disease or infirmity, in all matters relating to the reproductive system and to its functions and processes. This implies that people are able to have a safe and satisfying sex life, that they have the capability to reproduce and the freedom to decide if, when, and how often to do so. This further implies that women and men attain equal relationships in matters related to sexual relations and reproduction.

Responsible parenthood refers to:

> the will and ability of a parent to respond to the needs and aspirations of the family and children. It is likewise a shared responsibility between parents to determine and achieve the desired number of children, spacing and timing of their children according to their own family life aspirations, taking into account psychological preparedness, health status, socio-cultural, and economic concerns.

The second sentence in each of these definitions was added in the final (Senate) version to clarify these contentious terms. (They had not appeared in the House bill.) In its preamble, the bill emphasized three key themes: universal human rights, gender equality and universal access to 'medically safe, effective, legal, affordable and quality' reproductive healthcare products and services.

The key principles guiding the bill's implementation focus on provision by the national and local governments of resources and information on family planning, reproductive healthcare, maternal and child health, affordable healthcare and freedom of choice on family size and spacing of children.

Competing discourses

In advocating for their respective positions on the RH Bill, proponents and opponents interpret it and define issues based on their varying motivations and respective agendas. Supporters feel that the bill addresses women's rights and women's health and will lead to women's financial security. In a culture that expects the man to be the head of the family and the main breadwinner, women often assume a submissive role even when it comes to their own health concerns. Filipino women and mothers in paid employment or in small businesses are also primarily responsible for home management, and this 'second shift' generates 'more stress and conflict' during which women 'suffer from physiological symptoms' (Ventura 2000: 53).

Opponents argue that the bill encourages immorality and misuses taxpayer money through the State subsidy of contraceptive products and services.

They believe that free government-subsidized contraceptive products encourage young people to engage in sexual activity, and that these products also induce abortion.

Quite clearly, differing interpretations of the various components of the bill remain at the heart of the debate. Because of the complexities of the issue, the supporting and opposing camps are not clearly delineated across political, economic, social and gender lines. However, several key discourses emerged from analysing the media texts and websites: namely, the politics of reproduction, the economics of women's health, the morality of women's rights, and the responsibility of parenthood. I will demonstrate how public relations activities contribute to the construction of these gendered discourses.

The politics of reproduction

The key debates focus on how reproduction is interpreted, particularly in relation to conception, contraception and abortion. Woven into the debates on contraception were questions about conception and definitions of when life starts. Regardless of religious affiliation, Filipinos take the sanctity of life very seriously and many women would rather go through an unwanted pregnancy than abort an unwanted child. Both earlier and current versions of the bill clearly articulate that abortion is to be prevented since it is illegal in the Philippines, yet the bill's opponents continue to confuse contraception with abortion. Whether this is a deliberate ploy to confuse and mislead or a simple misinterpretation of the differences is not quite clear. The opponents have argued that the contraceptive drugs may be 'abortifacient' and thus induce abortion.

> Contraception, by its very nature, and as a broad social phenomenon, tends to incline the heart of a nation towards abortion. As John Paul II put it in 'Evangelium Vitae', the contraceptive mentality strengthens the temptation to abort. Contraception and abortion are not the same thing, but as John Paul put it, they are as closely connected as 'fruits of the same tree'.
>
> (Guanzon-Apalisok 2010)

It is obvious that the Catholic Church has linked contraception to a propensity to abortion and therefore a disregard for life. However, other Christian Churches and faiths, such as the independent Iglesia ni Cristo and Protestant Churches, that are pro-life define contraception differently. They appear to support modern methods of contraception as a means of social justice and alleviation of poverty. These religious groups form part of the Interfaith Partnership for the Promotion of Responsible Parenthood (IPPRP), which proclaimed that the RH Bill is 'truly pro-life, pro-family, pro-poor and pro-national development' (*Philippine Star*, 26 April 2011).

Both the Philippine Medical Association's president and a well-regarded Jesuit priest agreed that life starts at fertilization, not at implantation, as the opponents suggested. Fr. Joaquin Bernas is one of a few Catholic priests who, through his newspaper column, has expressed support for the modified RH Bill (*Philippine Daily Inquirer*, 23 May 2011). The bill's advocates, however, framed their arguments not from the *start of life* but on *women's right to life*. Democratic Socialist Women of the Philippines (DSWP) chairperson Elizabeth Angsioco asserted that 'deprivation of life-saving reproductive health services is like a death sentence' (*Manila Bulletin*, 3 March 2011). She reported that poor women in her group without access to reproductive health services have died and left children motherless. While focused on maternal health in particular, advocates admitted to the 'utilitarian' dimension of their argument in connecting human resource and financial assistance issues with the orphaned family.

At the national level, reproduction has been framed as an instrument of the State in its pursuit of the MDGs despite the supporters' focus on human rights, women's health and sustainable development. The bill's author admitted that once the bill is enacted into law, it will 'enhance the country's achieving the Millennium Development Goals', particularly those relating to poverty reduction, maternal and child health, and universal access to family planning (*Philippine Daily Inquirer*, 31 January 2011). As previously suggested, the bill is part of the country's international obligations that attract funding grants for health-associated programmes.

At this point, it is also useful to examine the public relations activities used in the construction of discourse.

The Catholic Church's campaign against the bill has employed several strategies. The CBCP directed its parish priests to use the homily to state its position against the RH Bill, which is: 'to follow God's words is to oppose the RH Bill'. The use of the Sunday mass as a channel for delivering the anti-RH Bill message by the CBCP was a considerable advantage in the battle for public opinion (*Philippine Daily Inquirer*, 21 November 2010). In a country where 68 per cent of the population attends church,[11] the priest in the pulpit occupies a very powerful position. Church bishops and priests exercised this power when they urged churchgoers to attend protest rallies. In addition to a signature campaign, the CBCP encouraged acts of civil disobedience by instructing followers not to pay taxes. The media also reported that one priest had asked pro-bill churchgoers to leave during mass (*Manila Bulletin*, 22 April 2011).

Manila Archbishop Gaudencio Cardinal Rosales stressed that the anti-RH Bill campaign would not use celebrities even if world boxing champion and congressman Manny Pacquiao echoed the Church's position. Media articles have referred to Pacquiao as the 'Church's poster boy against the controversial reproductive health bill' (*Philippine Daily Inquirer*, 18 May 2011). In the social media arena, the CBCP website featured a banner promoting its position against the RH Bill. To reach the youth, the CBCP campaign also resorted to using 'jejemon' vocabulary. ('Jejemon' is a language commonly used by a group of youngsters 'where they manage to subvert the English language to the point of incomprehensibility' (*Manila Bulletin*, 1 September 2011).) Furthermore, the CBCP launched a campaign-specific website (www.cbcpforlife.com) in May 2011. The CBCP's Media Office director, Monsignor Pedro Quitorio, acknowledged the wider reach of the internet as an extension of the pulpit (*Manila Bulletin*, 26 May 2011).

RHAN's communication strategy combined mainstream and grassroots tactics. In 2008, through the DSWP, the organization initiated an online campaign to gain one million signatures to demonstrate the widespread support for the bill. The campaign messages focused on women's rights and the number of maternal deaths in the Philippines. They used the powerfully emotive key message 'Eleven women die every day from pregnancy or pregnancy-related conditions' in their discourse. RHAN created the purple ribbon as the symbol of the pro-RH Bill group and launched Purple Ribbon Day in May 2011. Spokespersons included celebrities and political leaders, such as former President Fidel V. Ramos and world-renowned *Miss Saigon* lead actress Lea Salonga. Their statements appeared on several websites, such as RHbill.org and http://rhanphilippines.multiply.com/.

RHAN's own website featured the campaign colour with feminine elements such as flowers, pearls, stars and butterflies, which seemed rather inappropriate for such a serious issue. Likhaan's website design was simpler and reflected a more serious and progressive tone, with images of rural women in protest. It has hosted RHAN on its website since 2009. The Likhaan website also provided an in-depth database which included copies of reproductive health bills proposed earlier in Congress. The Filipino-language version of the 'Community Voices' tab revealed more local stories than the English version. These women's stories, written in the vernacular with accompanying images, narrated the hardship of bringing up many children and the effects on their health, stories of young mothers who experienced unplanned pregnancies, and the concerns of the gay and lesbian community.

The disparity in the breadth of resources used to construct the discourse reflected the inequality between the rich and the poor and the cultural dimensions at play. While these discourses illustrated how reproduction has generated debates at the national level, they also revealed the politics that occur at the family level. While children's schooling, medical assistance to family members and family planning are areas of joint decision-making, the husband's decision usually prevails in the latter (Page 2000). For example, when pro-bill Lea Salonga suggested that the wife of anti-bill Manny Pacquiao took birth control pills, contradicting his stand on the matter, his response was to tell his wife to stop (*Manila Bulletin*, 20 May 2011).

From a postcolonial feminist perspective, the discourse of reproduction reflected the politics between the educated middle-class and the 'poor' women.

Traditional birth control advocates viewed birth control as a 'fundamental requisite for the emancipation of women' and as a route to careers and higher education (Davis 2003: 353). If population control programmes target 'poor' women, resources become more available for the elite and middle class. However, the lack of sufficient resources for the population could also be construed as government abdicating its obligation to provide appropriate services to its people. As in many developing countries, children in the Philippines are expected to contribute to the family income, and more children means more hands to work on the family farm, a theme which is examined in more detail in the next section.

The economics of women's health

The RH Bill has economic implications on the global, national and individual levels. UN agencies have previously provided the Philippines with grants to fund family planning programmes. However, the cessation of UN funding from 2012 has generated pressure to pass the bill (*Philippine Daily Inquirer*, 1 September 2011). Committing to the achievement of the MDGs comes with funding grants to run the programmes that relate to maternal and child health and women's health issues. Stating the Philippines' international obligations in the RH Bill's preamble reveals the underlying objectives of the proposed legislation.

The explanatory note with the bill's earlier version explicitly equated 'uncontained population escalation' with the 'debt menace' and the State's inability to provide enough resources for education. (These references have been removed in the latest version of the bill.) While supporters argued that a larger population will stretch the current resources and infrastructure of the country, opponents countered that a larger population will generate more labour to provide more services. Opponents asserted that the government's solution should be better governance and less corruption, not 'population control'. As American authors Potts and Hayden (2010: 372) noted, 'the woman's inability to choose to have a child also deepens the divide between the "haves" and the "have nots"'. They posited that high birth rates 'undermine economic progress even when sound economic policies exist or there is little or no corruption' (p. 372).

Another economic dimension in women's health is the lost or reduced productivity of women who become unwell during pregnancy or have complications related to pregnancy. Supporters argued that the bill benefits women, particularly 'poor women', by providing free medicines and healthcare. However, for the individual woman, the bill is also about gaining access to information and affordable healthcare services. One female student who attended an RH Bill forum in a provincial university said: 'For me, the RH bill will protect the health of women and not promote premarital sex' (*Manila Bulletin*, 21 August 2011). While the voice of a young female student was welcomed in the male-dominated media discourse, very little was heard from the 'poor women' who are meant to benefit from the services offered by the bill. The sample of media texts featured few stories on the plight of the women and families for whom the legislation was created. Only Likhaan/RHAN's website provided a channel for their stories.

One of the arguments that emerged in the debates was that the RH Bill is part of a US imperialist strategy to limit population in countries that may be deemed security risks. Potts and Hayden (2010) suggest that a link exists between large families and unemployment, and that the latter leads to lack of financial resources for education or unhappiness. Dutta (2011: 151) cites former US Secretary of State Madeleine Albright, who stated:

> International family planning also serves important US foreign policy interests; elevating the status of women, reducing the flow of refugees, protecting the global environment, and promoting sustainable development which leads to economic growth and trade opportunities for business.

Dutta (2011) agrees that uncontrolled population growth can be a security risk to the US because an increasing population disrupts the status quo and creates new consumers with whom the 'neo-liberal patriarchs' will have to compete. However, while it is true that US multinational manufacturers of prophylactics and contraceptives will benefit from the passage of the RH Bill, it is unlikely that the Philippines – with its allegiance to, and colonial ties with, the US – will be deemed a security risk.

The morality of women's rights

The discourse has also pitted morality against human, and in particular women's, rights. The Catholic bishops have framed the bill as a question of morality. In his New Year's address, Cebu Archbishop Ricardo Cardinal Vidal stressed that the Church's edict to teach morality included exercising the right to religious freedom. While he acknowledged that the Philippine constitution guaranteed that right, he also warned against

> the illusion that moral relativism provides the key for peaceful co-existence when it is actually the origin of divisions and the denial of the dignity of human beings. As such, the Church will continue to preach against abortion, divorce and same-sex marriage.
> (*Manila Bulletin*, 6 January 2011)

Another bishop said Filipino women who undergo tubal ligation[12] are sinful (*Philippine Daily Inquirer*, 13 May 2011). To demonstrate their opposition to the 'immoral laws', bishops have called for civil disobedience. One, from Sorsogon, is reported to have said:

We will have a civil disobedience. Those laws that are immoral, we tell the people not to obey. We bishops are willing to be imprisoned, together with our priests, and protest the immoral things there. We are willing to show our part ... to be firm in our teachings. Let them imprison us.

(*Manila Bulletin*, 4 February 2011)

By framing reproductive health as an issue of morality, the CBCP indirectly accused pro-RH Bill Catholics as immoral. Not only does this diminish women's rights to make their own choices; it labels women who practise contraception sinful and immoral. This kind of discourse may be construed as a form of oppression by encouraging feelings of guilt among men and women who support the bill.

While the CBCP said it would not argue with other religious groups to avoid religious conflict, another bishop referred to RH Bill advocates as 'no better than terrorists'. Fr. Melvin Castro, Executive Secretary of the CBCP's Episcopal Commission on Family and Life, said, 'The reproductive health bill is a moral issue so everybody has the right to speak on the matter regardless of religion' (*Philippine Daily Inquirer*, 26 April 2011). In the same article, CBCP Vice-President and Cebu Archbishop Jose Palma further suggested, 'Advocates of the reproductive health bill are no better than terrorists because the measure could lead to the death of innocents.' Clearly the CBCP discourse was using aggressive language as it stepped up its campaign against the bill. One bishop was quoted as saying on the Church-run Radio Veritas, 'It's natural for us to declare an all-out war against the RH bill. We should persist to campaign against it and to educate the people against the legislative measure' (*Philippine Daily Inquirer*, 12 May 2011).

When the bishops asserted that women should follow their conscience based on religious and moral teaching, they implied that women do not already do so. One female leader demanded respect from the bishops, asking, 'Whatever gave you the idea that we decide about our bodies or anything else in life without anchoring in our deepest inspirations, whether faith or humanism or the sheer sense of being a woman?' (*Philippine Daily Inquirer*, 16 February 2011).

As the Church discourse focused on morality and conscience, Lagman reiterated that the issue is not about religion but about rights, health and progress (*Philippine Daily Inquirer*, 13 May 2011). Other opponents countered the rights argument by stating that the right to life is the 'first and most fundamental human right' (former Chief Justice Hilario Davide Jr in *Philippine Daily Inquirer*, 26 March 2011). Again, this argument largely depends on how contraception is defined. Clearly absent in the anti-RH Bill discourse, however, is any reference to *women's* rights. By contrast, while supporters of the bill did not contradict the 'right to life' argument, they argued that the bill was beyond 'pills and condoms'; it was about 'women's rights to decide for themselves' (*Philippine Daily Inquirer*, 11 March 2011). Female advocates emphasized that women always had to fight even for their basic rights and that the RH Bill is one way to protect the rights of women workers, including their rights to information and benefits. As a newspaper editorial entitled 'A basic women's right' strongly argued, reproductive health is not just a basic need but a basic women's right, especially for poor Filipino women (*Philippine Star*, 19 October 1991, cited on the Likhaan website).

The responsibility of parenthood

As previously mentioned, the interaction of Church and State resulted in changing the bill within the context of 'responsible parenthood'. Key to this shift was President Aquino's support of the bill as long as it was about responsible parenthood. The latest versions of the bill reflect this new focus.

In the course of the debates, the 'Reproductive Health' Bill morphed into a 'Responsible Parenthood' Bill. This change in focus reflected the power relationships inherent in Filipino culture.

First, the use of the term 'responsible parenthood' was President Aquino's compromise to appease the powerful Church sector, especially during his presidential campaign, as opponents attacked him over his support of the bill. When he took office in 2010, he included responsible parenthood as part of his social contract with the people. It is also the second core value (the first is dignity of life and the third is natural family planning) in the Church's outreach programmes, according to Archbishop Antonio Ledesma (*Philippine Daily Inquirer*, 17 May 2011).

Second, the shift also reflected Filipinos' focus on family and the widespread belief that reproduction and reproductive health are issues that should be decided by families, not individual women. For the unmarried Filipina, 'family' refers to her parents, siblings and the rest of her extended family. Traditional conceptions of family view the father as the head of the household and the mother as the family treasurer (Dolan 1991). However, while Filipino women live within a patriarchal society, they hold power indirectly in their households, businesses and government. Women in rural areas still worked in small businesses or farms throughout the colonial and postcolonial eras. When farms were not perceived to provide enough income, women sought work outside the home and even abroad. Working as nurses and domestic helpers, women now account for 55 per cent of the country's recently deployed overseas workers.[13]

While the shift of responsibility to the family may be seen as a feature of the extended support network that prevails in Filipino culture, it may also be construed as society's lack of confidence in women's ability to make decisions. This lack of respect for women's abilities was implied by the bishops' call for women to be guided by their consciences. Supporters worry that the semantic shift might result in a watered-down version of the bill that maintains the status quo on 'natural family planning'.

The bill highlights the joint responsibility of the national government and local government to provide reproductive healthcare and information. But the bill states that the responsibility of determining the ideal family size rests with each family, taking into account its own psychological, socio-cultural, economic and health factors. Giving the responsibility of parenthood to families enables a more supportive environment for young women. The caveat, however, is that the State must provide families with the appropriate information to help them make informed decisions.

While President Aquino has confirmed his support for responsible parenthood, one female newspaper columnist asked, 'Has he talked with women, particularly poor women, whose health, lives and destinies are on the line on the matter of government subsidies or support for family planning commodities, services and information?' (*Philippine Daily Inquirer*, 16 February 2011). She also asked how much he had engaged with grassroots organizations in determining the need for family planning products and services. Although it is admirable that female journalists are raising such questions, the absence of poor women's voices in the media discourse raises much concern, especially in public relations efforts to advocate for social change.

Public relations for social change?

In considering how public relations might enable social justice and social change, a postcolonial feminist lens has been helpful in unpacking complex issues of gender, power and culture. This chapter reveals the political, economic and cultural dimensions of reproductive health in the Philippines. It also illustrates the crucial importance of public relations strategies in constructing public discourse.

If population control reflects a neo-liberalist frame (Dutta and Pal 2011), the semantic shift from 'reproductive health' to the more culturally acceptable 'responsible parenthood' reflects a clever discursive strategy. 'Responsible parenthood' suggests that premarital sex and artificial contraception are discouraged and that couples should decide whether they should have children based on their own personal capabilities and resources. However, 'responsible parenthood' marginalizes women who are single mothers, children born out of wedlock, and unmarried couples, all citizens who are currently stigmatized by society. The rationale underpinning reproductive healthcare concerns women's right to information and education that will help them and their children become healthier. It should not make judgements on how and why a woman got pregnant, her circumstances, or her marital status.

The key is in the rhetoric. Advocates of the bill use the term 'reproductive health' to appropriate the concern for maternal and women's health, while 'responsible parenthood' is used to frame the issue within a family context. 'Population control' is the old term associated with modernist approaches to development; it is used by the opposition. So the discourse becomes a debate of control versus choice, morality versus empowerment. As Rakow and Nastasia (2009) posit, the oppositional discourse reflects the gendered colonialist system, where 'control' becomes the operative word and notions of morality are used to subjugate the people. The CBCP's discourse does not make any reference to how it will address the plight of poor women who die during childbirth. Instead, the Church hierarchy has focused on maintaining the status quo and branding the supporters of the bill as 'terrorists', 'immoral' and 'sinners', reflecting the gendered, patriarchal colonial system that oppresses women and their families. Used in this way, public relations becomes a strategic, manipulative and oppressive tool (Dutta and Pal 2011).

Critical to the discussion is how power and control are overtly and covertly exercised by dominant social structures. By invoking fear and morality in its campaign, the CBCP has exercised power over its followers. It has done so by combining coercive, subtle and sophisticated means, including walking out of a meeting called by the country's president.

However, the opposition's argument that Western countries such as the US and organizations such as the UN are driving the bill forward must not be dismissed. If, as Dutta and Pal (2011) suggest, population control is a key topic in the development agenda set by neo-liberalist countries, then advocates of the bill may be perceived as puppets of the very global capitalists, and specifically the manufacturers of contraceptive products, against whom they would normally protest. Furthermore, suggesting that 'poor women' need access to health information to make the right decisions implies a colonialist proclivity. Supporters of the bill need to be mindful that their advocacy does not fall into the designs of Western neo-liberalist forces that focus on productivity and individual rights. Otherwise, they risk losing the authenticity of their advocacies. Herein lies the paradox. Communities and people's organizations in developing countries such as the Philippines rely heavily on funding from NGOs to undertake health, environment and education programmes. Yet when such funds come from Western countries and organizations, questions arise over whose interests are truly being served.

Supporters of the RH Bill run the risk of finding themselves in this awkward paradoxical position. To address this, RHAN's approach is to provide previously marginalized publics with a voice and a channel to participate in the development of public policy. By developing a website that shares their stories primarily in the vernacular, the RHAN campaign reflects a culture-centred public relations that 'explores participatory mechanisms, that creates avenues for listening to subaltern narratives and incorporates these voices to policy and campaigns' (Dutta and

Pal 2011: 220). How successful they are in shaping public policy also depends on their presence (or absence) in the media discourse.

Implicated in this process are media practitioners whose rhetoric in reporting these events perpetuates the hegemony of the elite. The sources appearing in news media outlets are considered to be 'experts', with sufficient authority that they are deemed worthy of quotation. They include legislators, bishops and 'celebrity' advocates from both sides of the debate. Unsurprisingly, leaders of NGOs and community organizations, as well as individual women with low media profiles, are not so widely reported by the news media. In 'measuring the silences' (Spivak 1988) in the media discourse, we find that the main protagonists featured in the media continue to be the elite members of society. This formulaic choice of news sources reflects how the media appropriate the expertise of the elites who wield authority and power, whether formal or informal (Fenton, cited in Macnamara 2012). Even the use of social media (by both camps) indicates that these techniques require a certain level of economic access. Lost in all the media discourses are the voices of the women and families who will probably be most affected by the bill. How can public relations practitioners facilitate the articulation of these voices so they may be heard, with a resulting development of relevant public policy, as Dutta-Bergman (2005) suggests?

The public relations techniques used by advocacy groups such as RHAN reflect more participative and progressive approaches. Much of the work that occurs in urban and rural communities incorporates communicative activities such as town meetings, focus groups, and ethnography within the framework of community development. These grassroots activities have empowered women in local communities to generate livelihoods, encouraged education, and provided access to information. Some of this work has involved awareness campaigns on what women's rights are within a human rights context. As Mohanty (2003) suggests, we cannot assume that 'Third World poor' people are necessarily uneducated and can be easily manipulated. They are aware and conscious of companies with deep pockets who wish to exploit the resources of their communities. However, when religion and family are integrated into the discourse, the arguments find the Filipinos' weak spots. Reflective of their collectivist and communitarian cultures, Filipinos' notions of kinship and faith take priority over individual rights and welfare.

In conclusion, a postcolonial feminist analysis of this case study revealed the complex intersections of gender, politics, economics and culture. It also confirmed postcolonial scholars' concerns about the 'erasure' of marginalized voices in social and cultural discourses. This finding emphasizes the need for further research on how public relations can ensure the authentic participation of marginalized publics in policy discourse.

A postcolonial feminist approach to public relations research requires reflexivity, so I am mindful of the limitations of this research, especially as

I was out of situ and observed mediated events. As a migrant researcher who examined issues in my home country from afar, I acknowledged the privileged position that I am in, albeit not a unique position with the increased diaspora of multicultural scholars. Undoubtedly my identity as a Filipino 'liberal' Catholic wife and mother who has lived and worked in the USA and Australia has influenced my worldview. This background has also shaped my pursuit of public relations practice and scholarship that engenders more inclusive, more culture-centric and more community-based approaches that will encourage social change.

On 21 December 2012, Philippine President Benigno Aquino III signed Republic Act 10354, also known as the Reproductive Health (RH) Bill, after the House of Representatives and the Senate passed it. The Catholic Bishops Conference of the Philippines' Commission on Family and Life vowed that it would challenge the law when it came into effect in January 2013. In April 2013, the Supreme Court voted to delay the implementation of the law after petitioners questioned its constitutionality. At that time, it appeared likely that a decision would not be reached until after June 2013, by which time the Supreme Court would have heard oral arguments from both camps.

Notes

1. http://www.likhaan.org/content/15th-congress-house-bill-96-hon-edcel-c-lagman.
2. The House bill entitled 'The Responsible Parenthood, Reproductive Health and Population and Development Act of 2011' put forward by Edcel Lagman is a revised version of House Bill No. 96, 'An Act Providing for a National Policy on Reproductive Health, Responsible Parenthood and Population and Development, and for Other Purposes', which he filed in 2008. The Senate bill is entitled 'An Act Providing for a National Policy on Reproductive Health and Population and Development' or the Reproductive Health Act of 2011. Given that the Senate is the higher office in the bicameral legislature, its version will be referred to as the definitive and most recent version.
3. http://www.ausaid.gov.au/countries/eastasia/philippines/Pages/statistics-philippines.aspx.
4. http://www.slideshare.net/EONStakeholderRelations/the-philippine-trust-index-by-eon-the-stakeholder-relations-firm.
5. http://rhanphilippines.multiply.com/.
6. The original RHAN website now seems to be inactive and its representation has moved to Likhaan's website: http://www.likhaan.org/rhan.
7. http://www.likhaan.org/content/about-likhaan.
8. http://www.likhaan.org/content/sec-2-declaration-policy-2.
9. http://www.unfpa.org/webdav/site/global/shared/documents/publications/2007/mm_update05.pdf.
10. http://www.unfpa.org/webdav/site/global/shared/documents/publications/2011/EN-SWOP2011-FINAL.pdf.
11. http://www.nationmaster.com/country/rp-philippines/rel-religion.
12. Tubal ligation is a medical procedure in which women's Fallopian tubes are cut to prevent pregnancy.

13 The Philippine Overseas Employment Administration (POEA) reports that over 1.4 million overseas Filipino workers are deployed in 208 countries (http://www.poea.gov.ph/stats/2010_Stats.pdf).

References

Bardhan, N. (2003) 'Rupturing public relations metanarratives: The example of India', *Journal of Public Relations Research*, 15(3): 225–48.

Bardhan, N. and Weaver, C. K. (eds) (2011) *Public Relations in Global Cultural Contexts: Multi-Paradigmatic Perspectives*, New York: Routledge.

Beverley, J. (1999) *Subalternity and Representation: Arguments in Cultural Theory*, Durham, NC: Duke University Press.

Dalisay, S. M. (2000) 'The Filipino family: An anthropological perspective', *State-of-the-art in Family Studies Lecture Series*: 1–8.

Davis, A. (2003) 'Racism, birth control and reproductive rights', in R. Lewis and S. Mills (eds), *Feminist Postcolonial Theory: A Reader*, Edinburgh: Edinburgh University Press: 353–67.

Daymon, C. and Demetrious, K. (2010) 'Gender and public relations: Perspectives, applications and questions', *PRism* 7(4). Online. Available HTTP: <http://www.prismjournal.org/fileadmin/Praxis/Files/Gender/Daymon_Demetrious.pdf> (accessed 11 January 2013).

Diaz, A. R. (2003) 'Postcolonial theory and the Third Wave AGENDA', *Women and Language*, 26(1): 10–17.

Dolan, R. E. (1991) *Philippines: A Country Study*, GPO for the Library of Congress. Online. Available HTTP: <http://countrystudies.us/philippines/> (accessed 13 November 2011).

Dutta, M. J. (2009) 'On Spivak: Theorizing resistance – applying Gayatri Chakravorty Spivak in public relations', in Ø. Ihlen, B. van Ruler and M. Fredriksson (eds), *Public Relations and Social Theory: Key Figures and Concepts*, New York: Routledge: 278–300.

Dutta, M. J. (2011) *Communicating Social Change*, New York: Routledge.

Dutta, M. J. and Pal, M. (2011) 'Public relations and marginalization in a global context', in N. Bardhan and C. K. Weaver (eds), *Public Relations in Global Cultural Contexts: Multi-Paradigmatic Perspectives*, New York: Routledge: 195–225.

Dutta-Bergman, M. J. (2005) 'Civil society and public relations: Not so civil after all', *Journal of Public Relations Research*, 17(3): 267–89.

Eon Stakeholder Relations (2011) 'The Philippine Trust Index'. Online. Available HTTP: <http://www.slideshare.net/EONStakeholderRelations/the-philippine-trust-index-by-eon-the-stakeholder-relations-firm> (accessed 20 November 2011).

Fairclough, N. (1992) *Discourse and Social Change*, Cambridge: Blackwell.

Guanzon-Apalisok, M. (2010) 'The culture of contraception', *Philippine Daily Inquirer*, 4 October.

Hesse-Biber, S. N. (ed.) (2010) *Mixed Methods Research: Merging Theory with Practice*, New York: Guilford Publications.

Hesse-Biber, S. N. and Leavy, P. (2011) *The Practice of Qualitative Research* (2nd edition), Thousand Oaks, CA: Sage Publications.

Jocano, F. L. (1998) *Filipino Social Organisation: Traditional Kinship and Family Organisation*, Metro Manila: Punlad Research House.

Karnow, S. (1989) *In Our Image: America's Empire in the Philippines*, New York: Random House.
Lewis, R. and Mills, S. (eds) (2003) *Feminist Postcolonial Theory: A Reader*, Edinburgh: Edinburgh University Press.
Lim, W. (2003) *Alternative (Post) Modernity: An Asian Perspective*, Singapore: Select Books.
Macnamara, J. (2012) *Public Relations: Theories, Practices, Critiques*, Frenchs Forest: Pearson Australia.
Mohanty, C. T. (2003) 'Under Western eyes: Feminist scholarship and colonial discourses', in R. Lewis and S. Mills (eds), *Feminist Postcolonial Theory: A Reader*, Edinburgh: Edinburgh University Press: 49–74.
Munshi, D. and Kurian (2005) 'Imperializing spin cycles: A postcolonial look at public relations, greenwashing, and the separation of publics', *Public Relations Review*, 31: 513–20.
Page, J. B. (2000) 'State-of-the-art in the sociology of the family', *State-of-the-art in Family Studies Lecture Series*: 33–47.
Pal, M. and Dutta, M. J. (2008) 'Public relations in a global context: The relevance of critical modernism as a theoretical lens', *Journal of Public Relations Research*, 20: 159–79.
Potts, M. and Hayden, T. (2010) *Sex and War: How Biology Explains Warfare and Terrorism and Offers a Path to a Safer World*, Dallas, TX: BenBella.
Rakow, L. F. and Nastasia, D. I. (2009) 'On feminist theory of public relations: An example from Dorothy E. Smith', in Ø. Ihlen, B. van Ruler and M. Fredriksson (eds), *Public Relations and Social Theory: Key Figures and Concepts*, New York: Routledge: 252–77.
Spivak, G. C. (1988) 'Can the subaltern speak?', in C. Nelson and L. Grossberg (eds), *Marxism and the Interpretation of Cultures*, Basingstoke: Macmillan Education: 271–313.
Spivak, G. C. (1999) *A Critique of Postcolonial Reason*, Cambridge, MA: Harvard University Press.
Transparency International (2010) 'Corruption Perception Index 2010 results'. Online. Available HTTP: <http://www.transparency.org/policy_research/surveys_indices/cpi/2010/results> (accessed 29 November 2010).
Tuazon, R. R. (n.d.) 'The print media: A tradition of freedom'. Online. Available HTTP: <http://www.ncca.gov.ph/about-culture-and-arts/articles-on-c-n-a/article.php?igm=3andi=221> (accessed 20 November 2011).
Ventura, E. R. (2000) 'Psychological perspectives on the Filipino family', *State-of-the-art in Family Studies Lecture Series*: 49–54.

9 'I want to voice out my opinion'
Bringing migrant women into union work

Maree Keating

Whilst there is a growing interest in critical public relations approaches which challenge dominant interests (Ihlen *et al.* 2009; McKie and Munshi 2005), there is remarkably little within public relations scholarship which examines trade union practice. However, critical public relations can contribute an important perspective on unions, as organizations that engage workers in the struggle for their rights. Further, union engagement activities can contribute to a 'new public relations agenda' (Weaver 2001) that challenges, rather than serves the interests of, global capital. Feminist activists within the Australian union movement have long drawn attention to the need for unions to challenge the discriminatory basis of labour relations (Acker 2000; Baird 2012), not only at the level of policies and laws, but also in relation to social norms, because these are instrumental in shaping broader power struggles in society (Pocock 1995; Franzway 2000; Probert 2002).

This chapter illustrates the negative consequences for a group of migrant women workers who became disengaged with workers' rights and trade unions. As a contrast, the chapter presents a case study of union activities that fostered collective identity, voice and visibility amongst a different group of migrant women. In analysing the two situations, the chapter draws attention to the interactions between gender, race and class, and the transformative power of trade union work that actively builds stakeholder engagement amongst migrant women workers.

Drawing on recent critical theory, which situates public relations as a potentially transformative practice (Weaver 2001; Dutta 2009; Holtzhausen 2011), this chapter positions low-paid migrant women workers in Australia as legitimate but marginal stakeholders in unions. It introduces the voices of three women who emerged from many years as passionate and vocal members of a unionized worker community in the textile industry to become casual workers as cleaners, carers and servers. They reflect on the sense of power they experienced through having a voice and being visible members of a largely migrant community of factory workers. These reflections provide a striking counter to their narratives on life since retrenchment, where silence, invisibility and marginality have led to a sense of personal disempowerment and disengagement from the struggle for their rights.

Whilst they often occupy the least protected and least rewarded jobs, low-paid migrant women have become less visible and vocal in trade unions with the restructuring of the Australian economy in recent decades (Webber and Weller 2001; Bertone 2007). Their lack of engagement with union activity can be said to contribute to a 'democratic deficit', which De Bussy and Kelly (2010) argue arises from low stakeholder engagement in matters of legitimate concern to them, and results in citizens feeling alienated from the political process. Whilst low-paid migrant women in Australia have much to gain through union advocacy on workers' rights, they remain largely inactive in unions and disengaged from union-led campaigns. From a critical public relations perspective, this lack of stakeholder engagement poses a challenge for trade unions seeking to promote worker resistance and transformations in labour relations.

Since the Industrial Revolution, trade unions have utilized public relations to counterbalance the power of employers in the formal employment contract. The Australian Fair Work Act (2009) affirms the role of trade unions as partners with the State in the enforcement of minimum standards for workers, although vigilance is required to protect and maintain this formal mandate (Hardy and Howe 2009). Traditional union activities have involved organizing workers, garnering public support and media coverage of issues and challenging government legislation and company practice on both legal and moral grounds (Hansen-Horn 2004). In recent decades shifting economic conditions have required trade unions in Australia to devise new approaches to workers' rights campaigns and worker mobilization. One of the drivers of this change is the growth of 'non-standard' employment, which includes work performed on a part-time, casual, seasonal or intermittent basis (Marten and Mitter 1999).

The Australian Council of Trade Unions (ACTU) has identified non-standard work and employment insecurity as major issues for the majority of Australian workers (ACTU 2012). As women's movement in and out of low-paid employment is a central feature of the global economy, trade unions and labour activists are compelled to address the gendered and racialized dimensions of this shift (Glucksmann and Nolan 2007). Growing numbers of women worldwide are working in non-standard jobs in low-paid, female-dominated occupations, and global production is dependent on a fluid supply of 'flexible' female labour (Chen *et al.* 2001; Glucksmann 2009; Moghadam *et al.* 2011).

In recent years the conditions of work for low-paid women have been highlighted in a number of Australian union activities and campaigns, resulting in improved access to better pay, workplace protections and skill recognition for many women (Muir 2008). However, whilst unions play a central role in securing these gains, many have only peripheral relationships with workers in low-paid, non-standard employment arrangements, creating a 'gap' in representation (Hill 2005). This is a troubling issue for Australian unions, and has also led many scholars to consider the conditions under which organized resistance can be fostered amongst growing numbers of workers in insecure and non-standard employment (Lambert and Webster 2010).

Aside from non-standard employment in 'formal' contract arrangements, there are a variety of ways in which non-standard employment arrangements also operate in the growing 'informal' or cash-in-hand sector. Some of the informal workers most vulnerable to exploitation are women who work in 'sweatshops' or alone at home as 'homeworkers' in global production chains or domestic industries (Delaney 2008). The expansion of the informal sector in Australia and elsewhere has gone hand in hand with regulatory shifts, which have reduced the overall bargaining power of trade unions across OECD countries (Chant and Pedwell 2008). It has not been possible for unions to organize and recruit informal workers without collaboration with grassroots organizations, or to challenge corporate practices across national borders without the cooperation of local and international non-government organizations with a focus on human rights. Strategic public relations activities in building stakeholder relationships have therefore been vital to the success of contemporary trade union-led campaigns (Bullert 1999).

Union-led global sweatshop movements have been responsible for a plethora of public relations campaigns in Australia, Europe, USA and Asia (Knight and Greenberg 2002; Garwood 2011). Whilst such high-profile international campaign work has resulted in some significant successes, unions have also started to highlight the impact on workers arising from the normalization of non-standard work (Chun 2005; Rea 2011).[1] As the distinctions between low-paid worker conditions in the formal and informal sectors have become increasingly blurred, in both developed and developing countries (Lund and Srinivas 2005), union campaigns have started to address this issue. In Australia, low-paid migrant women are often concentrated in those non-standard jobs which are most vulnerable to poor remuneration, visibility, job insecurity, and which lack social and industrial protections (Meagher 2000; Masterton-Smith *et al.* 2006). The lack of organization and voice amongst this group is reflected in their low level of power as stakeholders in firms. Their status in unions also remains marginal, even though they hold a legitimate stake in union work.

Whilst migrant women have often performed low-paid jobs, the downsizing of the Australian manufacturing sector over the past thirty years has resulted in large numbers of migrant women being retrenched from formal factory jobs and entering a variety of non-standard jobs in low-paid, female-dominated occupations (Weller and Webber 2001; Keating 2010). As many move into casual and cash-in-hand employment in occupations such as personal care, domestic service and retail (Keating 2012), they join a growing low-paid workforce, which has been described as 'invisible, powerless and politically inconspicuous' (Hill 2005: 84). Many who were previously in unionized jobs, workplaces and industries experience a significant loss of collective voice, industrial protection and social networks with the transition into more fragmented employment (Pocock et al. 2005). If unions are to engage these workers, it is likely that they will need to find ways to strengthen migrant women's voice and visibility in the social spaces which they inhabit beyond the sphere of paid work.

This chapter presents the voices of several migrant women, recently retrenched from a textile factory, as they reflect on their loss of engagement with unions and their decreased sense of themselves as stakeholders in workers' rights. In doing so it highlights the profound impact that decreased engagement with unions has on their power to negotiate, resist and act as workers. The Australian FairWear Campaign is then discussed, as it provides a model by which unions have built stakeholder engagement with groups of Vietnamese homeworkers and thereby challenged the relations of labour outside formal employment. This unique union–community campaign has utilized nuanced strategies for building worker resistance amongst women whose struggle for workers' rights is intensified by the intersecting power dynamics of class, race and gender.

Framing migrant women workers as stakeholders

A decade ago, Weaver challenged public relations practitioners to 'dress for battle' and place power, identity and discourse at the centre of a new public relations agenda which challenges, rather than serves, hegemonic global capital (Weaver 2001). Recently others, including Munshi and Edwards (2011), Heath *et al.* (2009) and Holtzhausen (2011) have called for public relations scholars to question the discipline's uncritical allegiance to powerful interests. Weaver goes so far as to suggest that the discipline should be realigned to serve the interests of 'the people who perceive themselves as disempowered by globalization or who oppose the philosophies and/or economic effects of globalization' (2001: 280).

Rakow and Nastasia (2009) have drawn attention to the need for women's 'invisibility' to be addressed through critical public relations work, claiming that women's experiences and work are often 'beyond marginal' since they remain unaccounted for in institutional discourses and practices. Institutional public relations plays a significant role in constructing the gendered and 'racialized' identities which reinforce the power relations of capitalism (Munshi and Edwards 2011). In countering this process, organizations can employ public relations activities to support broader social goals. Trade union-led campaigns discussed throughout this chapter have the potential to challenge the gendered and racialized relations of labour underpinning global capitalism. However, the engagement of migrant women workers as stakeholders in unions is crucial in this process.

Public relations scholars such as Hallahan (2000, 2001) have expanded early theories distinguishing stakeholders from 'active publics' (Grunig and Repper 1992), to suggest that organizations should see all publics as important. Further, De Bussy and Kelly argue that the primary focus of public relations should be on building 'stakeholder relationships', rather than simply managing organizational 'publics' (2010: 289). They claim that 'Ethical public relations practitioners should make a conscious effort to consult even the unorganised groups who have a legitimate interest or claim in a situation' (p. 305).

Migrant women workers are legitimate but usually unorganized stakeholders in the mandated work of unions. Despite this, it is ethically imperative for unions to build their engagement, and this necessitates increasing their voice and visibility.

Migrant women, alongside other workers retrenched from full-time employment in formal, unionized manufacturing jobs in Australia, usually cease being union members immediately after leaving the factory environment (TCFUA 2006). As casual employees, intermittent labourers or subcontractors, most workers from this group also cease being members of close-knit workplace communities (Keating 2012). The social isolation experienced by many casual workers has considerable negative impacts upon their experiences as active, vocal members of their communities beyond work (Pocock *et al.* 2005; Hearn and Lansbury 2006). Amongst retrenched factory workers, migrant women's options for work and social participation are particularly constrained by their lack of confidence in negotiating the labour market as well as their limited social networks, English language skills and capacity for self-advocacy (Webber and Weller 2001). These factors also compound their low bargaining power in the industrial arena once they secure employment. Migrant women are often disadvantaged in new ways as non-standard workers. Their jobs are often the least secure, visible and protected within female-dominated low-paid occupations (Meagher 2000), and their marginal employment status intersects with their other experiences of social marginality.

In order to engage this group in processes which build voice, visibility and agency, some trade unions have supported a range of activities beyond the industrial arena, such as post-retrenchment English language and literacy training and support programmes (Webber and Weller 1999; Keating and Robb 2005). However, whilst such programmes have made a significant difference to participants (Webber and Weller 1999), union support strategies commonly fall away in the years following retrenchment, leaving the overwhelming majority of retrenched workers completely disengaged from unions (Keating 2010).

Engaging women in union campaigns

It is relevant here briefly to highlight the ways in which union-led campaigns have engaged women as active stakeholders by drawing attention to social inequalities which impact on labour relations. Workers' rights campaigns often rely upon narratives which establish the incompatibility of corporate interests with those of other social institutions and values (Andriof *et al.* 2002). In circumstances where cleaners have faced exploitation and powerlessness in the US and Korea, for example, recent union-led campaigns have invoked shared values such as fairness, equal opportunity and human rights in order to challenge corporate practices which seek to marginalize low-paid, migrant women workers further (Chun 2009).

Australian unions have also pursued justice for low-paid women workers through appeals to broader social values. In pursuing a legal case on behalf of social and community service workers, the Australian Services Union (ASU) recently won a sector-wide pay increase by arguing that systemic low pay rates in the female-dominated sector are historically linked to the undervaluation of women's work (Cortis and Meagher 2012). This success drew upon women's rights activism beyond the sphere of industrial relations, utilizing notions of gender equality and fairness to challenge the discriminatory 'norm', enshrined in a modern industrial award, that care work is not skilful labour. As care work has been performed routinely by the majority of women without pay in the domestic sphere, legal recognition that caring involves skilled and valuable labour also contributes to the larger struggle for gender equality.

Union-led public relations campaigns have also engaged women as stakeholders by highlighting the interactions between broader gender relations and struggles in the industrial sphere. In Australia, the interaction between paid and unpaid labour is increasingly at the centre of feminist-led policy debate in relation to employment, care services and gender equality (HREOC 2007; Skinner *et al.* 2012; Baird 2012). This context informed the approach taken by unions in the highly successful 'Your Rights at Work' campaign between 2004 and 2007 (Muir 2008). From 2005 the campaign focused public attention on the new WorkChoices legislation, and in particular on the negative consequences it had for low-paid women workers and gender equality in Australia (Elton *et al.* 2007; Ellem *et al.* 2008). Unions engaged working women as key campaign stakeholders by focusing media attention on the ways in which decreased rights at work impacted on women's caring responsibilities at home (Muir 2008: 63).

Union activities which take women's broader concerns into account are vital in engagement strategies. The high mobility of many women workers in and out of low-paid employment makes it difficult for unions to organize this group in workplaces (Visser 2006). Further, women in fragmented, non-standard, low-paid employment often have weak perceptions of themselves as workers, as the skills involved in paid care and service jobs are often considered to be merely 'extensions of their identity as women' (Poynton 1993: 85) and are invisible to women themselves. Decreases in industrial protections for non-standard workers have exacerbated this tendency. Low-paid Australian women reported that their sense of control over their lives had been 'significantly diminished', and their 'identities' as workers had decreased, as a result of increasing insecurity and powerlessness over the conditions of their work under WorkChoices legislation (Bailey *et al.* 2012: 451). Union engagement strategies have needed to take into account women's perceptions of themselves and their values in relation to families and communities in order to engage them with their rights as workers.

Trade union public relations work which counters the claims and interests of dominant groups in this way works against a process by which women are 'erased' from view (Dutta 2009: 293). Such public relations work can activate marginalized groups of women workers to resist dominant discourses and challenge the status quo (Holtzhausen 2011). However, to achieve transformative ends, trade union public relations work must do more than resonate passively with marginalized women workers. It must build their collective power as stakeholders in workers' rights.

Migrant women and the conditions for resistance

Actors wishing to engage marginalized groups in a collective struggle must first examine the conditions under which their 'dispositions to resist' may be socially constituted, triggered and rendered effective (Bourdieu and Wacquant 1992: 82). The resistances of low-paid migrant women workers often take place in private and subjective ways (Shi 2008), although the study of their narratives can indicate how marginality impacts upon their self-perceptions and motivations for engagement. Unions seeking to engage this group as organized stakeholders who are both legitimate and powerful must gain an understanding of the conditions which might bring about their power and agency.

Bourdieu proposes that the possession of material, symbolic and cultural capital defines the 'probabilities of belonging to really unified groups, families, clubs or concretely constituted classes' (Bourdieu 1990: 75). One of the important aspects of union work is its capacity to build a sense of shared 'social capital' between workers through actions which unify those workers in pursuit of a goal. Drawing on Bourdieu's work, Chun (2009) claims that low-paid migrant women workers can exercise 'symbolic power' which they collectively draw from their marginal positions in society to challenge the claims of institutions. Also drawing on Bourdieu, however, feminist theorists have noted that the persistent association of femininity with 'selfless caring' can make it particularly difficult for workers to effect transformative resistance in female-dominated occupations, where the highly prized cultural capital is associated with attributes of femininity (Adkins and Skeggs 2004: 24).

Subjective, private resistance, fostered through shared experience or sense of belonging as women, mothers, migrants, factory workers or residents in working-class suburbs, does take place amongst women in low-paid jobs. In this way, working-class women can and do refuse 'the perspectives of the powerful' (Adkins and Skeggs 2004: 25) by 're-valuing' identities which are portrayed by dominant interests as marginal and without value.

However, resistance rarely effects social transformation unless it is collectivized in a struggle around 'legitimate ways of seeing, knowing and believing in the world that is autonomous from structures of the state' (Chun 2005: 498). Processes which legitimate migrant women's shared ways of 'seeing, knowing and believing' are crucial to fostering their engagement with collective struggle, and this is evidenced by the consequences for those who lose their involvement in such processes.

In the next section, I identify a number of issues which emerged from interviews with a group of migrant women who were retrenched from long-term jobs in a textile factory in 2005. The interviews took place nearly three years after the retrenchment took place. In analysing their reflections on work I highlight the ways in which their disengagement from unions impacted upon their sense of themselves as workers and their notion of their rights as workers. As a non-factory worker coming from outside, I observed these workers during reunions and classes they attended over a twelve-month period. Likewise, they observed me and scrutinized my perspectives as a white, university-educated, Australian researcher. As a union employee in an advocacy role, I used my position to build connections between workers, potential employers and agencies. Also, as a teacher in union-based English language programmes, I worked with the women as they developed shared meanings and critiques in relation to the unfamiliar labour market.

Beyond Feltex Carpets: migrant women's (dis)engagement with workers' rights

In October 2005, 165 textile machine operators were retrenched from a single site in Braybrook, an inner western suburb of Melbourne, Australia. The majority of the retrenched machine operators had worked at the Feltex factory for an average of fifteen years. Most lived in the surrounding suburbs and had come to Australia from a range of European, Asian and African countries, arriving with various waves of migration throughout the 1980s and 1990s. Both men and women worked the machines in roughly equal numbers, with most engaging in the physically demanding and noisy labour in day, afternoon or night shifts.

Like many Australian textile factories, Feltex Carpets had been a highly unionized workplace, and the Textile Clothing and Footwear Union (TCFUA) had engaged in intense industrial disputes throughout the 1990s, focused on protection of pay and conditions for factory workers during periods of workplace change and downsizing (Keating 2010). A number of women had been strong and vocal union organizers in these struggles. Only one-third of the retrenched workers found ongoing work in the year after leaving Feltex. In almost every instance this work was casual or 'cash in hand'. Only two men – who found full-time work in the manufacturing and transport sectors – rejoined a union (Keating 2012).

Most women employed at Feltex Carpets left the company with a strong commitment to the TCFUA, as well as to fellow workers, who were often described in terms of 'family'. Over many years they had engaged in vigorous assertion of their collective rights at work throughout numerous industrial disputes in the 1990s and early 2000s. All the women interviewed had left Feltex hoping for exposure to a larger social world through new jobs that brought them into contact with the public, but most found that their new jobs had isolated them further and eroded their self-confidence beyond the workplace. Prospective employers were perceived as not wanting to hear or understand them; their qualifications and experience were not valued in the labour market; they had lost a sense of belonging to a sympathetic work community; and their daily experiences at work did not broaden their social networks. Unions were uniformly perceived as important and powerful organizations that were no longer able to take up their concerns as workers.

Losing voice and visibility

Many migrant women workers retrenched from Feltex experienced a loss of 'voice' as they entered new kinds of low-paid work. This happened in several ways. First, the collective strength of being part of a largely migrant workforce had previously countered the diminishing impact of not being heard or understood in the broader community. Nearly three years after retrenchment, Florica was working alone as a night-shift cleaner on a cash-in-hand basis and she had all but abandoned her dream of working as a security officer. The loss of discursive community which migrant workers shared at Feltex was summarized by Florica when talking about her fear of looking for another job: 'There was people like me [at Feltex] so I don't really care if – I *knew* they gonna understand me. Now I'm scared maybe they no understand me.'

Second, union membership had previously provided women with a forum through which they developed confidence and knowledge, and learned to express their views at work. Through the provision of advice and support, union organizers had provided the factory workers with important resources to support collective resistance. Levy talked about the union in her working life at Feltex as playing the dual role of building her personal confidence that she had rights and providing an avenue through which her voice could be heard: 'I was active in the union. Union membership made a difference. It give me confidence that I have the right. I want to voice out my opinion because when I have problems I don't have to keep it in myself.'

Vesna had also been a strong unionist at Feltex, and valued the practical negotiating power that workers gained through knowing their legal rights:

> Make you a bit stronger member of union. You have more understanding for what's happening, the law. You have more understanding

of that stuff. You feel more stronger. You know how to answer it. They can't just tell you, 'No, that's how it is!'

None of the retrenched Feltex women had rejoined a union in the previous three years, despite their ongoing belief in the power of unions and their commitment to the principle of trade unionism. None of the women interviewed believed that they had rights at work as casual and cash-in-hand employees. Without rights, Vesna felt the union could not play any role in her working life. She said, 'I am a union supporter but when I am a casual they can't help me. They [the employer] can tell me "Go" and the union can't help me. It's not worth it 'cos, you know, they can't help me.'

Third, having a tenuous connection to the workplace led workers to experience a reduced sense of connection to other workers, and a corresponding sense that their interests were not important to other workers. Vesna explained it in this way:

[As a casual] not really same because [pause] sooner or later you have to finish, because you are not part of that place. When you are full time you feel different. Even with friends, with the job and everything. When I were full-time Feltex, I feel free for the job to ask something, to talk with people or everything, but when you are casual you can't talk much. You can't say something because you feel different.

Finally, loss of voice at work occurred through a reduced sense of self-confidence. For Florica this began with her sense that the work she was performing as a cleaner lacked dignity: 'I feel like, you know, before, people work for other people – poor people for rich people. I feel like that. In my country I *never* do this job.'

Vesna described the process as one whereby her confidence slowly disappeared over a period of time as she took on different temporary jobs. She explained it as a fundamental change in her sense of self: 'Because I passed through all these places I feel like more nervous! More [pause] jumpy. I dunno, like, I think I'm not the same person anyway.'

For most of the women interviewed, their sense of themselves had dramatically shifted since leaving Feltex. Having at first believed that, with qualifications, they would easily be able to access alternative ongoing jobs, their experiences in the labour market between 2006 and 2008 had diminished their belief in themselves as members of the community, their sense of connection to work and fellow workers, and their aspirations to find fulfilling work.

The sense of powerlessness manifested in various ways. Vesna described the acute powerlessness she had felt in customer service, which led her to leave the job and seek a casual warehouse position in a more familiar workplace culture. She felt unable to negotiate new power relations, which involved heightened surveillance and monitoring of individual worker behaviour: 'I felt like I was in the jail. They watch you every single step. You don't feel free at all. I just hate every single moment I spend there. It was my worst experience in my life.'

Levy, who had been very confident of finding work as a receptionist, because she was university qualified, with recent Vocational Education and Training (VET) qualifications and good English, summed up her loss of that confidence when evaluating her future options in the labour market: 'I'm getting old! No one's going to hire me. When they ask, "How old are you?", I say, "Fifty-five", and they think, "Oh no! What service can she be?" [Laughs.] It's a lack of confidence really.'

Once active in industrial struggles over rights, the women's engagement with labour rights had all but disappeared in the years following retrenchment. Lack of voice was a common experience, but unions were no longer perceived as organizations which were able to provide relevant advice or support – two aspects of union membership that had been crucial to them as workers in the Feltex workplace environment. In talking about what she needed as a worker, Florica articulated the different ways in which she believed that migrant women like her needed 'help' to build self-confidence:

FLORICA: I need somebody to push me or otherwise I not gonna start.
INTERVIEWER: What do you mean by 'push'?
FLORICA: I think it's 'help'. You feel like nobody care of you any more and nobody help you – and that's it ... Like with the English. I always said, 'I am not good' and you always said, 'Yes you are.' And this one made me to *believe*. And er – you always talk with us what to do, where to go. And I think *people like us* need – *I* need – somebody like this. Now is different. Now I have to push myself and the only thing is English – I'm scared I think I don't understand. See if you ask I can answer but I can't *start* to talk. I don't know *how* to start. And I still don't know why so I prefer to shut up all day if I'm with somebody. I don't say nothing.

Migrant women workers entering casual and informal employment in the retail, service and care sectors described their positions in ways that could be considered 'beyond marginal' (Rakow and Nastasia 2009). Their engagement with ethnic communities and immediate families remained strong, but these networks and interests no longer intersected with their working lives as they had at Feltex. Indeed, whilst they remained committed to what they saw as the important work of unions, rights at work were not seen as relevant to them, as they did not believe they had many rights to protect, as casual and cash-in-hand workers. As non-standard workers with few rights, they all felt marginal to the work of unions, as unions were not seen as organizations that could 'do anything' to help them.

Individual narratives on low-paid work can inform union campaigns in Australia, because when taken together they provide a composite story of the altered relations of labour for low-paid migrant women leaving factory-based employment. The story of retrenched Feltex women highlights the new interactions between migrant women's identities as low-paid workers and their broader experience of diminishing voice and visibility.

How can migrant women like Florica, Vesna and Levy become engaged as stakeholders with unions under circumstances where their opportunities to work in secure jobs with social and industrial protections are extremely limited as a result of their gender, class and migrant identities? Further, how can trade unions employ public relations practices to support women like them to resist the 'systematic marginalization' (McKie and Munshi 2009: 69) they experience as they attempt to negotiate more secure, dignified and rewarding working conditions?

The following section considers some of the strategies utilized in the Australian FairWear Campaign (FWC), which has had some success in building migrant women workers' engagement with unions and workers' rights campaigns by addressing their broader social needs.

The Australian FairWear Campaign

Situation background

There are an estimated thirty million people working in the textile, clothing and footwear industries worldwide, most of whom are women, employed under a variety of low-paid, non-standard and informal arrangements (Garwood 2011). In Australia, it has been estimated that homeworkers currently account for 70 per cent of all employment in the national textile clothing and footwear industry (TCFUA 2008).

When the Australian federal government started to reduce tariffs on imported textile, clothing and footwear (TCF) products in the early 1980s, it became clear that much of the garment construction work remaining in Australia would move into the cheaper 'sweatshop' or homeworker model of production (Weller 1999). Homeworkers in the garment industry in Sydney and Melbourne have predominantly been Vietnamese women, often procuring work through extended family members who act as 'middle-men' (Weller 2007). Because they are usually unable to find alternative work, and because they are reliant on any work they can get, homeworkers often find it difficult to resist exploitative employment conditions. One Melbourne-based homeworker, Hai, described the work in this way:

> The working hours and the pay are terrible. The law is there but I think employers take advantage because we need the job, so whatever they

pay we have to do it or we can't get the job. That's the point. If you say no, and you go to find another job, you can't. Staying at home is so stressful but you have to do it because you need money for life, for the family.

(Quoted in Spyrou 2009)

Growth of the global movement

Campaigns about homework started in Australia in the 1980s, spearheaded by the TCFUA. In the earliest campaign, the union focused on raising public awareness about the legal status of homeworkers, drawing public attention to 'the fiction of their portrayal as small business contractors' (Weller 1999: 205). The union's campaign focus on homeworkers as 'employees' resulted in important amendments to the Clothing Trades Award in 1987, which first extended industrial protections to homeworkers in the clothing industry.[2]

Meanwhile, the international anti-sweatshop movement started in the early 1990s, comprising trade unions, major international non-government organizations, including Oxfam International and Christian Aid, and hundreds of smaller organizations (Connor 2004). Since then, public awareness in Australia, Europe, Asia and the USA has been raised about abuse of workers' rights across the production chain, with over a thousand newspaper articles generated between 1996 and 2004 in relation to abuses within Nike's supply chain alone (Connor 2004: 64). Several initiatives grew out of the global movement involving collaborations between unions and non-government organizations as well as other community groups, and these have generally involved the mobilization of consumer and advocacy groups to apply pressure on the corporate sector to undertake commitments to ethical practices (Connor 2004). These collaborations have led to the emergence of several successful umbrella organizations, such as the Clean Clothes Campaign organizations in Europe and India and the FairWear Campaign in Australia (Connor 2004).

The emergence of the Australian FairWear Campaign

The Australian FairWear Campaign (FWC) began in 1996, involving the TCFUA, Asian Women at Work (AWatW), a range of faith groups, consumer groups, students groups and women's organizations (Burchielli et al. 2009). A variety of FWC activities over the past fifteen years have resulted in significant regulatory change, increased legal recognition of workers' industrial rights, successful union prosecutions of companies in breach of the award, and heightened consumer awareness of Australian company practice. The focus on corporate social responsibility (CSR) has also resulted in a number of corporate signatories to a voluntary Homeworkers Code of Practice (Hill 2005).

Despite these successes it has been observed that company transparency remained weak further along the supply chain, local organizing efforts amongst homeworkers were not improving, and homeworkers continued to experience poor pay and conditions (Burchielli *et al.* 2009). The reasons for this link to the social isolation, lack of networks and poor bargaining power commonly experienced by migrant women who work as homeworkers. Burchielli *et al.* (2009: 576) claim that, under conditions where women are working in extreme isolation and lacking in social protection, 'CSR lacks any real potency and is not a useful mechanism.' Whilst the campaign succeeded in raising awareness and in forcing the corporate sector to address reputational concerns (Knight and Greenberg 2002), traditional campaign tactics had not necessarily led to greater voice or collective strength for homeworkers themselves.

Building worker voice and visibility

Given the failures outlined above, a number of campaign activities were designed to increase the voice and visibility of homeworkers, taking into account the ways in which gender, race and social class interacted to create particular needs and perspectives amongst this group. The TCFUA played an important role in this work.

Homeworkers belong to close-knit migrant communities which are intricately involved in the flow of their work, they have few arenas in which to register complaints, abuses or problems experienced in relation to homework, and many are mothers with caring responsibilities at home. This context, combined with low levels of English language, confidence and labour rights awareness, compounded the disadvantages that homeworkers experienced (Delaney 2008). It was vital for Vietnamese homeworkers to have a forum in which to build shared understandings and legitimate the 'ways of seeing, knowing, and believing' (Chun 2005: 498) which might mobilize their collective action.

Voice through English classes

From early in the Australian FairWear Campaign, the TCFUA supported English language classes in community locations, bringing homeworkers together to meet one another socially and address their desire to improve their English. These classes are part of a broader English language and literacy programme which has been funded through the federal government Workplace English Language and Literacy (WELL) scheme, through which a number of Australian trade unions have accessed funding to deliver classes for workers in workplace settings (Keating and Robb 2005). Through such union classes, migrant workers have been able to meet and discuss issues of importance to them, develop networks and increase their knowledge and confidence with industrial issues as well as broader social issues taking place in Australia (Yasukawa *et al.* 2011).

Since 1999, the TCFUA-run English classes have provided many homeworkers with a forum through which the union could communicate directly with them on matters relating to breaches of their rights. In Spyrou's research with homeworkers (2009), she found that the TCFUA English classes resulted in numerous benefits for homeworkers and provided them with important rights information, although this has not necessarily led to homeworkers becoming union members, as precarious employment arrangements often result in a lack of confidence that their rights can be accessed. One of her participants, Diep, explains the risks for homeworkers who gain a reputation for speaking out: 'Even if we are union members ... and even if we get support, it means we are out of work because the owner will not give us the work if we complain about it' (Spyrou 2009: 60). Nonetheless, despite the lack of formal engagement with most homeworkers as members, the union has continued to support English classes and has provided opportunities for them to engage with FairWear Campaign activities, including information seminars, social networking events and public actions, forums and protests. This has been an important step in increasing homeworkers' sense of stakeholder power and legitimacy in union work.

Visibility through a homeworker network

Several other activities have facilitated the increased voice and visibility of homeworkers over the past fifteen years. Since the 1990s, AWatW has supported the development of a network that operated first as an advocacy group for Vietnamese homeworkers and a forum through which they could trade information about their experiences and the flow of work across the supply chain. Over time, this has become a self-representative group, wherein homeworkers attend meetings with ministers and company representatives to advocate for their own rights (Burchielli *et al.* 2009: 583). TCFUA-supported English language training programmes in Melbourne have also led to self-advocacy. In some cases, homeworkers who participated in TCFUA classes have given evidence at formal hearings, and in one recent case class participation has led to a homeworker becoming a union organizer (Spyrou 2009).

Through their engagement with the network, a number of homeworkers began to work closely with the TCFUA, passing on information which facilitated prosecution of companies through the courts and informing consumer group pressure on companies to monitor their supply chains diligently (Delaney 2008). Further, according to Delaney, the network has provided collective protection to workers experiencing reductions in pay or other problems with companies. Delaney points out such a network is vital for informal workers who are not union members as they 'are not required to be singled out' (Delaney 2008: 8) when they report underpayments or other issues. In these ways outworkers have been able to become a potent group of stakeholders in the FairWear Campaign, and in the work of the union.

Taking control through radio

Since 2003, *Outworker Voice*, a weekly Vietnamese language radio programme run by homeworkers, has been directly supported through the FairWear Campaign office in Melbourne. According to Delaney, this programme has expanded the possibility for a homeworker to 'self-identify as a worker' (2008: 2) by experiencing a sense of collective voice which links them to other homeworkers. Through such campaign activities, homeworkers have been provided with an opportunity to build a sense of engagement with workers' rights campaigns and exercise their own collective voice, whilst continuing to work in the informal, low-paid economy. According to Burchielli *et al.* (2009: 584), 'the engagement of homeworkers ... increased their levels of power as stakeholders, and this is seen as one of the most important outcomes, in ethical terms, of the FWC'.

Hill (2005) claims that such activities have enabled the union to embrace issues beyond women's employment, and, by adopting a 'whole person' approach, it has succeeded in increasing homeworker confidence and visibility.

The activities outlined in this section have been important to homeworkers and to the union for several reasons. They have facilitated a working relationship between the union and migrant women as a stakeholder group. They have assisted in the establishment of a legitimate role for the union in the eyes of a group of workers whose perspectives and agendas as migrants, as low-paid informal workers and as women with multiple responsibilities usually place them in a marginal position in union-led workers' rights campaigns. They have strengthened homeworkers' collective capacity to articulate and represent their own interests, and to share important information and advice amongst themselves. In increasing homeworkers' sense of themselves as a group of workers, their capacity to resist and to articulate that resistance have been strengthened. The creation of forums in which migrant women workers can address their own social priorities has been a vital component of the union's stakeholder engagement strategy in relation to this workers' rights campaign, and this has had transformative results. One homeworker, Hai, reflected on the impact of her engagement with TCFUA English classes in 2009: 'It's like going to a new world. You know, you get stuck inside and you don't know anything outside ... I feel my future now. I can grow' (Spyrou 2009: 56).

Discussion

In considering the importance of stakeholder engagement in ethical public relations work, De Bussy and Kelly have asked: 'What can and should practitioners do to ensure the process of stakeholder consultation in politics is sufficiently inclusive?' (2010: 289).

This chapter has considered this question from the perspective of Australian trade union work with marginalized migrant women. As public relations practitioners, many trade union activists are constantly engaged in processes to develop discursive communities around workers' rights. In Australia, trade unions have a formal mandate to represent and advocate on behalf of workers in workplaces and within the formal industrial arena. As such, they have an important role to play in ensuring that governments and companies monitor workers' access to minimum employment standards. As organizations, they have a vital role to play in nurturing stakeholder relationships with groups capable of furthering their goals, including the workers whose interests they serve.

Increasingly unions engage in campaign work which reaches beyond formal spaces. Whilst they have long been challenged to engage with the broader social and moral realms in which struggles over power take place, contemporary union work now actively depends upon engaging women, consumers, migrant workers, students and other stakeholders in the community by drawing upon shared social values such as fairness, equality and justice. This public relations work takes place on the global stage, where unions work with other actors to build a groundswell of public support for vulnerable workers across corporate supply chains (Bronfenbrenner 2007), at the national level, where unions work with grassroots and advocacy organizations to build public concern about protections for workers' rights (Muir 2008), and at the local level, where forums are developed with the express purpose of assisting retrenched workers to build shared social capital (Keating 2012).

Knight and Greenberg (2002) have argued that unions can use public relations to build 'shared meaning' and 'shared interests', which focus on the wellbeing of others. Australian union campaigns have done this by utilizing a variety of tactics, targeting particular audiences and exploiting the social, cultural and institutional dynamics at different times. Campaign strategies have sought to build common ground between Australian women, care workers or consumer groups in order to build their engagement as 'stakeholders' in union efforts to influence workplace legislation, corporate practice and federal elections. In this way, union strategies have maximized the discursive dynamics in the Australian context, sometimes with great success. At the same time, unions currently face challenges in engaging the most vulnerable workers themselves in the struggle for workers' rights.

Critical public relations scholarship has much to offer trade unions, because it places public relations practitioners at the centre of transformative work which builds voice and visibility amongst those who 'perceive themselves as disempowered by globalization' (Weaver 2001: 280). The gendered–classed relations of labour are increasingly identified as central planks to successful, union-led public relations campaigns (Bailey *et al.* 2009). However, for a variety of reasons, low-paid migrant women have lost ground as stakeholders in Australian unions. Retrenched textile workers like Levy, Florica and Vesna often find cash-in-hand employment with few social or industrial protections. They often work in isolation, and have no recourse to advice, information or support about how to stand up for their rights at work, negotiate with employers or find alternative employment. Many women in this situation wish to stay connected with unions. As Florica said, this connection is important in helping migrant women 'to *believe*' in themselves; and as Vesna emphasized, it is also important so that employers cannot simply say, 'No, that's how it is!'

More than ever, unions must find ways to reconnect with the women who inhabit the margins of non-standard employment. For many retrenched Feltex workers, English language and literacy classes after retrenchment provided opportunities to share information and find advice from a trusted source, to plot a path to a better job, and to network with others like themselves (Keating 2012). Through post-retrenchment classes, many maintained discursive communities, made sense of their options and gained the confidence to re-enter the labour market. As this support fell away over time, women retrenched from Feltex became disengaged from their sense of themselves as workers. As they entered new, private struggles for self-belief and self-respect, many ceased to be engaged in a struggle for workers' rights. Importantly, whilst they still longed for support and advice, they no longer saw trade unions as relevant organizations with a role to play in their lives. As non-standard workers, they had come to consider themselves marginal in union activities.

As Australian unions start to devote campaign attention to the widespread issues arising for workers because of non-standard employment (ACTU 2012), it is urgent for them to develop strategies for engaging non-standard migrant women workers. As De Bussy and Kelly (2010) suggest, organizational inattention to stakeholder engagement can lead to deficits in the democratic process. The evidence from research with Feltex's ex-employees suggests that many low-paid migrant women in non-standard employment need a forum in which to exchange ideas, seek advice, discuss alternatives with others like themselves and regain a sense of dignity and self-respect. These are important steps towards their re-engagement with social and political processes around the conditions of their work. The consequences of unions not developing stakeholder strategies are that this group of workers will not engage with union campaigns around rights and their voice and visibility as citizens will continue to erode. Tentative work status, low self-confidence and isolation are identified by the migrant women workers in this research as compounding their experience of marginalization. Although they are clearly legitimate stakeholders in union work on job security, the isolation they experience decreases their sense of power as workers and inhibits their engagement with union activities.

As worker advocates and leaders in workers' rights campaigns, unions are ethically compelled to find ways to bridge this gap.

The Australian FairWear Campaign provides a model by which one union has been able to develop connection and legitimacy with informally employed migrant women workers. By responding to the relations of labour outside the realm of formal employment, the TCFUA, in collaboration with AWatW has built strong stakeholder engagement with a group of women whose powerlessness as workers is compounded by the intersecting dynamics of class, race and gender in the Australian context.

In order to draw 'symbolic power' from their marginal identities (Chun 2005), low-paid migrant women workers must engage with the struggle for their rights as workers. Unions are critical actors in this process. This chapter has demonstrated that by building voice and visibility, and engaging with their broader struggles, unions can increase the potential for low-paid migrant women workers to convert their marginality into 'a concrete form of leverage' (Chun 2009: 5). This leverage increases union capacity to challenge the status quo for non-standard workers effectively.

Whilst public relations campaigns often engage powerful stakeholders in firms in order to influence legislation, codes of practice and corporate responsibility, trade unions have an ethical responsibility to engage disempowered workers in the struggle for their rights, so that they can claim legitimacy and exercise power as stakeholders in union work. By creating spaces for low-paid migrant women to identify themselves as workers, learn about their rights, and develop skills and confidence, unions can engage in ethical public relations practice and contribute to a new, transformative public relations agenda.

Notes

1 The Australian Council of Trade Unions (ACTU) claims that half of all Australian workers are now employed on fixed-term, casual, labour-hire and non-permanent employment, and the country is outranked amongst OECD countries only by Spain in terms of work insecurity (Rea 2011).
2 The Fair Work Amendment (Textile, Clothing and Footwear Industry) Act 2011 was only recently passed into law, after fifteen years of union advocacy, commencing on the 1 July 2012. This act provides a way for homeworkers to recover unpaid amounts up the supply chain and extends union right of entry into premises operating under sweatshop conditions. It will make it easier for the Fair Work Ombudsman to identify businesses that engage outworkers and investigate breaches of the Fair Work Act and the Textile Clothing and Footwear Award (Shorten 2012).

References

Acker, J. (2000) 'Revisiting class: Thinking from gender, race, and organizations', *Social Politics*, 7(2): 192–214.

ACTU (2012) 'Secure jobs, better futures'. Online. Available HTTP: <http://www.actu.org.au/Campaigns/SecureJobsBetterFuture/default.aspx>.

Adkins, L. and Skeggs, B. (2004) *Feminism after Bourdieu*, Oxford: Blackwell.
Andriof, J., Waddock, S. Husted, B. and Sutherland Rahman, S. (eds) (2002) *Unfolding Stakeholder Thinking, Theory Responsibility and Engagement*, Sheffield: Green Leaf Publishing.
Bailey, J., Macdonald, F. and Whitehouse, G. (2012) 'No leg to stand on', *Economic and Industrial Democracy*, 33(3): 441–61.
Bailey, J., Townsend, K. and Luck, E. (2009) 'WorkChoices, image choices and the marketing of new industrial relations legislation', *Work, Education and Society*, 23: 285–304.
Baird, M. (2012) 'Women, work and policy settings in Australia in 2011', *Journal of Industrial Relations*, 54(3): 326–43.
Bertone, S. (2007) 'Unions, the workplace and social cohesion', in J. Jupp and J. Nieuwenhuysen (eds), *Social Cohesion in Australia*, Cambridge: Cambridge University Press: 124–35.
Bourdieu, P. (1990) *In Other Words: Essays towards a Reflexive Sociology*, Stanford, CA: Stanford University Press.
Bourdieu, P. and Wacquant, L. (1992) *An Invitation to Reflexive Sociology*, Cambridge: Polity.
Bronfenbrenner, K. (2007) *Global Unions: Challenging Transnational Capital through Cross Border Campaigns*, Ithaca, NY: Cornell University Press.
Bullert, B. (1999) 'Strategic public relations, sweatshops and the making of a global movement', working paper 2000–2014, Washington: The Joan Shorenstein Centre on the Press, Politics and Public Policy.
Burchielli, R., Delaney, A., Tate, J. and Coventry, K. (2009) 'The FairWear Campaign: An ethical network in the Australian garment industry', *Journal of Business Ethics*, 90: 575–88.
Chant, S. and Pedwell, C. (2008) *Women, Gender and the Informal Economy: An Assessment of ILO Research and Suggested Ways Forward*, Geneva: International Labour Organization.
Chen, M. (2001) 'Women in the informal sector: A global picture, the global movement', *SAIS Review*, 21(1): 71–82.
Chen, M., Jhabvala, R. and Lund, F. (2001) 'Supporting workers in the informal economy: A policy framework', paper prepared for ILO Task Force on the Informal Economy, Geneva: International Labour Organization.
Chun, J. (2005) 'Public dramas and the politics of justice: Comparison of janitors' union struggles in South Korea and the United States', *Work and Occupations*, 32(4): 486–503.
Chun, J. (2009) *Organizing at the Margins: The Symbolic Politics of Labor in South Korea and the United States*, Ithaca, NY: Cornell University.
Connor, T. (2004) 'Time to scale up cooperation? Trade unions, NGOs, and the international anti-sweatshop movement', *Development in Practice*, 14(1–2): 61–70.
Cortis, N. and Meagher, G. (2012) 'Recognition at last: Care work and the Equal Remuneration case', *Journal of Industrial Relations*, 54(3): 377–85.
De Bussy, N. and Kelly, L. (2010) 'Stakeholders, politics and power: Towards an understanding of stakeholder identification and salience in government', *Journal of Communication Management*, 14(4): 289–305.
Delaney, A. (2008) 'Accounting for corporate social responsibility: Does it benefit workers across the supply chains?', paper presented at the 21st AIRAANZ Conference, Melbourne, February.

Dutta, M. (2009) 'On Spivak: Theorising resistance: Applying Gayatri Chakravorty Spivak in public relations', in Ø. Ihlen, B. van Ruler and M. Fredriksson (eds), *Public Relations and Social Theory: Key Figures and Concepts*, New York: Routledge: 278–99.

Ellem, B., Baird, M., Cooper, R. and Lansbury, R. (2005) 'WorkChoices: Myth-making at work', *Journal of Australian Political Economy*, 56: 13–28.

Ellem, B., Oxenbridge, S. and Gahan, B. (2008) 'The fight of our lives: An evaluation of Unions NSW and the Your Rights at Work campaign 2004–7', report for Unions NSW, University of Sydney.

Elton, J., Bailey, J., Baird, M., Charlesworth, S., Cooper, R., Ellem, B., Jefferson, R., Macdonald, F., Oliver, D., Pocock, B., Preston, A. and Whitehouse, G. (2007) 'Women and WorkChoices: Impacts on the minimum wage sector', report for Centre for Work and Life, University of South Australia.

Franzway, S. (2000) 'Women working in a greedy institution: Commitment and emotional labour in the union movement', *Gender, Work and Organization*, 7(4): 258–72.

Garwood, S. (2011) *Advocacy across Borders: NGOs Anti-Sweatshop Activism and the Global Garment Industry*, West Hartford, CT: Kumarian Press.

Glucksmann, M. (2009) 'Formations, connections and divisions of labour', *Sociology*, 43: 878–95.

Glucksmann, M. and Nolan, J. (2007) 'New technologies and the transformations of women's labour at home and work', *Equal Opportunities International*, 26(2): 96–112.

Grunig, J. E. and Repper, F. C. (1992) 'Strategic management, publics, and issues', in J. E. Grunig (ed.), *Excellence in Public Relations and Communication Management*, Mahwah, NJ: Lawrence Erlbaum Associates: 117–57.

Hallahan, K. (2000) 'Inactive publics: The forgotten publics in public relations', *Public Relations Review*, 26(4): 499–515.

Hallahan, K. (2001) 'The dynamics of issues activation and response: An issues processes model', *Journal of Public Relations Research*, 13(1): 27–59.

Hansen-Horn, T. (2004) 'Labour public relations', in R. L. Heath (ed.), *Handbook of Public Relations*, Thousand Oaks, CA: Sage: 565–70.

Hardy, T. and Howe, J. (2009) 'Partners in enforcement? The new balance between government and trade union enforcement of employment standards in Australia', *Australian Journal of Labour Law*, 23(3): 306–36.

Hearn, M. and Lansbury, R. (2006) 'Reworking citizenship: Renewing workplace rights and social citizenship in Australia', *Labour and Industry*, 17(1): 85.

Heath, R., Toth, E. and Waymer, D. (2009) *Rhetorical and Critical Approaches to Public Relations 11*, New York: Routledge.

Hill, E. (2005) 'Organising "non-standard" women workers for economic and social security in India and Australia', conference proceedings, *Reworking Work: 19th AIRAANZ Conference, Sydney*: 83–90.

Holtzhausen, D. (2011) *Public Relations as Activism: Postmodern Approaches to Theory and Practice*, New York: Routledge.

HREOC (2007) 'It's about time: Men, women, work and family', Canberra: Australian Government Publishing. Online. Available HTTP: <http://www.hreoc.gov.au/sex_discrimination/its-about-time/index.html>.

Ihlen, Ø., van Ruler, B. and Fredriksson, M. (eds) (2009) *Public Relations and Social Theory: Key Figures and Concepts*, New York: Routledge.

Keating, M. (2010) 'Learning from retrenchment: Textile workers redefine themselves after global restructuring', Melbourne: RMIT University. Online. Available HTTP: <http://researchbank.rmit.edu.au/stat_details.php?action=show_detail&pid=rmit:978>.

Keating, M. (2012) 'Developing social capital in "learning borderlands": Has the federal government's budget delivered for low-paid Australian workers?', *Literacy and Numeracy* Studies, 20(1): 5–18.

Keating, M. and Robb, A. (2005) 'What do I do next? Developing an integrating literacy strategy for retrenched textile clothing and footwear workers', report, Melbourne: Australian National Training Authority.

Knight, G. and Greenberg, J. (2002) 'Promotionalism and subpolitics: Nike and its labour critics', *Management Communication Quarterly*, 15: 541–70.

Lambert, R. and Webster, E. (2010) 'Searching for security: Case studies of the impact of work restructuring on households in South Korea, South Africa and Australia', *Journal of Industrial Relations*, 52(5): 595–611.

Lund, F. and Srinivas, S. (2005) *Learning from Experience: A Gendered Approach to Social Protection for Workers in the Informal Economy*, Geneva: International Labour Organization.

Marten, M. and Mitter, S. (1999) *Women in Trade Unions: Organizing the Unorganized*, Geneva: International Labour Organizsation.

Masterton-Smith, H., May, R. and Pocock, B. (2006) 'Living low paid: Some experiences of Australian childcare workers and cleaners', Discussion Paper 1/06, Hawke Research Institute for Sustainable Societies, Centre of Work and Life, University of South Australia.

McKie, D. and Munshi, D. (2005) 'Tracking trends: Peripheral visions and public relations', *Public Relations Review*, 31: 453–57.

McKie, D. and Munshi, D. (2009) 'Theoretical black holes: A partial A–Z of missing theoretical thought in public relations', in R. Heath, E. Toth and D. Waymer (eds), *Rhetorical and Critical Approaches to Public Relations 11*, New York: Routledge.

Meagher, G. (2000) 'Struggle for recognition: Work life reform in the domestic services industry', *Economic and Industrial Democracy*, 21: 9–37.

Moghadam, V. M., Franzway, S. and Fronow, M. (2011) *Making Globalization Work for Women: The Role of Social Rights and Trade Union Leadership*, Albany: SUNY.

Muir, K. (2008) *Worth Fighting for: Inside the 'Your Rights at Work' Campaign*, Sydney: University of New South Wales Press.

Munshi, D. and Edwards, L. (2011) 'Understanding "race" in/and public relations: Where do we start and where should we go?', *Journal of Public Relations Research*, 23(4): 349–37.

Pocock, B. (1995) 'Women in unions: What progress in South Australia?', *Journal of Industrial Relations*, 37(1): 3–23.

Pocock, B., Prosser, K. and Bridge, K. (2005) 'The return of "Labour as Commodity"? The experience of casual work in Australia', paper delivered at 19th AIRAANZ Conference, University of Sydney, February.

Poynton, C. (1993) 'Naming women's workplace skills', in B. Probert and B. Wilson (eds), *Pink Collar Blues: Work, Gender and Technology*, Melbourne: Melbourne University Press: 85–100.

Probert, B. (2002) 'Grateful slaves or self-made women: A matter of choice or policy?', *Journal of Australian Feminist Studies*, 17(37): 7–17.

Rakow, L. F. and Nastasia, D. I. (2009) 'On feminist theory of public relations: An example from Dorothy E. Smith', in Ø. Ihlen, B. van Ruler and M. Fredriksson (eds), *Public Relations and Social Theory: Key Figures and Concepts*, New York: Routledge: 252–77.

Rea, J. (2011) 'Casuals: Insecure work, anxious lives: ACTU launches campaign and inquiry into secure work', *Advocate: Newsletter of the National Tertiary Education Union*, 18(3): 2.

Shi, Y. (2008) 'Chinese immigrant women workers: Everyday forms of resistance and "coagulate politics"', *Communication and Critical/Cultural Studies*, 5(4): 363–82.

Shorten, W. (2012) Media release, 30 June.

Skinner, N., Hutchinson, C. and Pocock, B. (2012) 'The big squeeze: Australian Work and Life Index 2012', report for the Centre for Work and Life, University of South Australia, Adelaide.

Spyrou, H. (2009) 'The experience of homeworkers in relation to their participation in accredited training', unpublished Master's thesis, Monash University.

Sriramesh, K. (2009) 'Globalisation and public relations: The past, present, and the future', *PRism* 6(2). Online. Available HTTP: <http://www.prismjournal.org/fileadmin/Praxis/Files/ ... /SRIRAMESH.pdf>.

Standing, G. (2011) *The Precariat – The New Dangerous Class*, London: Bloomsbury.

Textile Clothing and Footwear Union of Australia (TCFUA) (2006) 'Empty promises', report, Melbourne: TCFUA.

Textile Clothing and Footwear Union of Australia (TCFUA) (2008) 'Submission to the Review of the Australian Textile Clothing and Footwear Industries', report, Melbourne: TCFUA.

Visser, J. (2006) 'Union membership statistics in 24 countries', *Monthly Labor Review*, January. Online. Available HTTP: <http://digitalcommons@ilr.cornell.edu/key_workplace>.

Weaver, K. (2001) 'Dressing for battle in the new global economy: Putting power, identity, and discourse into public relations theory', *Management Communication Quarterly*, 15: 279–88.

Webber, M. and Weller, S. (1999) 'Re-employment after retrenchment: evidence from the TCF industry study', *Australian Economic Review*, 32(2): 105–29.

Webber, M. and Weller, S. (2001) *Refashioning the Rag Trade: Internationalising Australia's Textile, Clothing and Footwear Industries*, Sydney: UNSW Press.

Weller, S. (1999) 'Clothing outwork: Union strategy, labour regulation and labour market restructuring', *Journal of Industrial Relations*, 41(2): 203–27.

Weller, S. (2007). 'Regulating clothing outwork: A sceptic's view', *Journal of Industrial Relations*, 49(1): 67–86.

Weller, S. A. and Webber, M. J. (2001) 'Precarious employment and occupational change', in J. Borland, R. Gregory and P. Sheehan (eds), *Work Rich, Work Poor: Inequality and Economic Change in Australia*, Melbourne: Victoria University Press: 160–95.

Wick, I. (2005) *Workers' Tool or PR Ploy? A Guide to Codes of International Labour Practice*, Bonn: Friedrich-Ebert-Stiftung.

Yasukawa, K., Brown, T. and Black, S. (2011) 'Exploring the role of Australian trade unions in the education of workers', paper delivered at 14th AVETRA Conference, University of Technology, Sydney, April.

10 'Mammography at age 40 to 49 saves lives; just not enough of them'

Gendered political intersections in communicating breast cancer screening policy to publics

Jennifer Vardeman-Winter, Hua Jiang and Natalie Tindall

In this chapter, we investigate ways that gender – and other identities – are complicated as a result of policymaking processes. Public relations is integral to policymaking processes as communication practitioners often strategize and implement new policies as well as communicate policies to relevant groups (Heath and Palenchar 2009). Public relations is also characterized by gender (Aldoory and Toth 2002) and racial (Pompper 2007; Sha and Ford 2007) discrepancies among its practitioners and miscommunications based on cultural gaps between practitioners and publics (Sison 2009; Vardeman-Winter and Tindall 2010). Thus, we propose that gender and other identities are intimately tied to the inequitable consequences that result from politicized relationships.

The policies that result in inequitable consequences are due, in part, to cultural gaps between policymakers/communicators and publics. The particular mixes of identities influence and maintain these cultural gaps, which impede communication. For example, those enacting and communicating policy change have sophisticated levels of specialized education about social issues whereas publics represent a wide spectrum of literacy on public health, education, politics, and economics. These distinct levels of knowledge may also be intricately tied to other identities, such as race, class, age, and nationality.

Public relations activities can have significant implications for gendered relationships and social practice. This was evident when a long-standing, widespread health policy was changed in the United States in 2009. Breast cancer screening guidelines were changed by a small group of medical professionals with specialized medical knowledge, and this change in mammography screening guidelines affects all women who reside in the United States (and potentially globally). Although these guidelines are specific to US policies and publics, US federal agencies and NGOs work with international health groups to establish knowledge sharing of best practices in healthcare screening guidelines and to provide funds for reducing morbidity and mortality rates of health disparities globally.

The revised policy left the media and other publics with myriad questions. Chiefly, women and public health advocates fear that mammograms may not be recommended for women aged between forty and forty-nine and that this will likely adversely affect women from non-white, non-middle-class backgrounds. As the health policy carries significant potential consequences for many different groups, we sought to learn what the consequences were of the policy communication for the identities of the publics of this policy.

This case study offers insight into the role public relations plays in producing problematic gendered policies that exacerbate problems for women publics of different races, ages, and classes. We propose that gender identity matters in policymaking and communication about policy change. As such, this study orients gender as a salient identity from which to examine how both powerful and marginalized groups negotiate policy change. At a surface level, gender emerges as relevant to public relations because of the overwhelming majority of women as the corpus of US communication practitioners, which designates public relations as a gendered industry (Aldoory 2009; Daymon and Demetrious 2010; Wrigley 2010). Thus, the nexus between public relations and policymakers indicates that we should begin questioning what public relations practitioners can do to address this as a problem.

To critique these processes, we explain the background to the controversial policy change in the public health realm. Then, to ground the work theoretically, we provide a fundamental understanding of gender-only analysis, race-only analysis, and the convergence of those two analytical structures – the intersectional approach. Our main propositions about gendered political intersectionality are presented to explain the connection between gendered intersections, policymaking, and communication, followed by details of how we studied the phenomenon. Having talked to publics about the cancer screening changes and after examining documents by the policymaking group, we present a number of challenges that reveal how the assumptions about gender and identity that are made by policymakers influence their decision-making and can lead to inequitable consequences for gendered publics. The chapter closes with a discussion about how political intersectionality can provide a useful critique of evaluations of policies enacted by communicators.

Breast cancer screening guidelines controversy

In 2011, more than 39,500 women in the United States of America were expected to die from breast cancer, and more than 288,000 women from that country were expected to be affected by breast cancer (American Cancer Society 2011). Although more non-Hispanic white women are affected by breast cancer than any other racial group, African Americans have the highest mortality rate from breast cancer. This disease also disproportionately affects women from racial minorities and women with low incomes more than white women earning middle- or upper-class incomes, largely because of poverty and lack of health insurance (American Cancer Society 2011). In 2006, the national breast cancer care expenditure (at all stages) in the United States was greater than US$13.8 billion, making it the most costly of all cancers (National Cancer Institute 2010).

In 2009, the US Preventive Services Task Force (USPSTF) proposed new recommended guidelines for breast cancer screening for women. This new information was presented to lay publics and health-provider publics alike via a press release. The revised guidelines conflicted with traditional recommendations for breast cancer screening. Rather than starting mammograms at forty years old and having them performed annually, women were told they can wait until they are fifty years old to begin mammograms and should then have them performed only biennially (USPSTF 2009a). US breast cancer advocacy groups like the American Cancer Society (ACS) rejected the recommendations and urged women to continue screening annually, starting at forty (Kolata 2009).

The reliance of policymakers on absolute risk reduction is a major point of departure from the stance of cancer advocacy groups, such as the ACS and the Susan G. Komen for the Cure Foundation. Dr Otis Brawley, the chief medical officer of the ACS, spoke out vehemently against the USPSTF's new guidelines (as well as against the USPSTF's prostate cancer screening guidelines): 'With its new recommendations, the [task force] is essentially telling women that mammography at age 40 to 49 saves lives; just not enough of them' (quoted in Dellorto 2009).

Although the original guidelines were revised later in 2009, discussion continued for the next few years about this and similar healthcare screenings (Brownlee and Lenzer 2011). As this is a problem that has disproportionately affected socially disadvantaged women from a racial minority, we propose that identity is an essential element of this communication that must be investigated.

Gender, public relations, and political intersectionality

Gender of publics in public relations

The relationship of gender and public relations is largely unquestioned (Daymon and Demetrious 2010) as issues like the 'feminine fallacy' (Grunig, Toth and Hon 2001; Wrigley 2010) and the consequences of gendered publics (Aldoory 2009) remain problematic. As such, gender persists as the primary identity studied in public relations, above race, nationality, and sexual orientation (see Aldoory 2009 for a review of gender-based public relations research; Sison 2009).

Furthermore, most identity research has focused on practitioners' identities rather than publics' identities (Vardeman-Winter, Tindall and Jiang 2010). This trend of exploring practitioner identities exposes two problems in public relations: it perpetuates a dominance of practitioner voices rather than empowering public voices and it assumes that gender is the primary involvement factor in which publics connect with messages. These limited perspectives tell part of the story of the struggles practitioners face, one significant challenge being why campaigns targeting a primary consumer group (i.e. women as mothers, partners, care-takers, activists in communities) often fall short of their goals.

In this section, we address the competing theories that address the gender gap in public relations, which are gender-only and race-only approaches to understanding publics. Then we introduce the intersectional approach as an advanced way to understand the complexities of identity, as grounded in gender critiques. First, however, we must highlight a unique contradiction of identity conflict for practitioners-as-publics that complicates the basic problem of gender in public relations.

Identity conflict[1] for practitioners-as-publics

Gender research[2] has proposed competing liberal and radical feminist theories to elevate the status of women practitioners (e.g. Aldoory 2005; Aldoory and Toth 2002; Grunig *et al.* 2001; O'Neil 2003; Pompper 2007; Wrigley 2002). Briefly, liberal feminist strategies advocate the individual changing herself to fit better into the current social structure and cultural norms of the organization, whereas radical feminist strategies reject that individuals need to change and instead promote the transformation of the surrounding systems that enable marginalization of women practitioners (Grunig *et al.* 2001).

When campaigns and communication relationships are focused on women's issues, women practitioners span the boundary between organizations and publics to a questionable level. Simply, women practitioners may be designing campaigns that apply to their lives as well as to other women's lives. The quandary is that women practitioners must step outside their practitioner selves to create meaningful messaging to women publics to which they belong; meanwhile, women practitioners must also stay grounded in their organizational roles, committed to the mission of organizations as dedicated to efficiency, strategic planning, and the bottom line. Women practitioners may experience a journey with an impossible goal: to be a producer and consumer of messages, both of which encompass potentially conflicting purposes. As a consequence, some studies have found that campaigns targeting women often miss connecting with them in meaningful ways (Aldoory 2001; Vardeman and Aldoory 2008; Tindall and Vardeman-Winter 2011; Vardeman-Winter and Tindall 2010). Thus, the identity conflict for practitioners-as-publics emerges as an important site for questioning what happens in the dual identity of women practitioners that disconnects them from effectively communicating with other women about risks.

One feasible explanation for how gaps are created and perpetuated between practitioners and publics (despite obvious similarities like gender or race) has been theorized using the critical-cultural studies (Hall 1997) approach. To explain how public relations is produced, consumed, and represented by different groups according to shared cultural meanings of issues, Curtin and Gaither (2005, 2007) introduced the cultural studies model, the *circuit of culture* (du Gay et al. 1997) into public relations research. This model de-centres public relations as a purely managerial function and refocuses the act and products of public relations as a site of shared meaning for different groups (e.g. consumers, media, regulatory bodies). As in the tradition of cultural studies, the concept of power is central to learning how different cultures/groups perceive a common object/ idea differently. In cultural studies of public relations, gender has been conceptualized as a site of power struggle, particularly in how cultures of publics and cultures of practitioners diverge (Acosta-Alzuru 2003; Aldoory 2001; Curtin and Gaither 2007; Tindall and Vardeman-Winter 2011; Vardeman-Winter 2010; Vardeman-Winter and Tindall 2010). This model provides scholars and practitioners with a way to empower publics by equalizing their voices with practitioners' voices.

Single-identity analyses

However, cultural studies tell only part of the story about how identity and power influence public relations. Cultural studies in public relations have not explored the complexity that multiple, overlapping identities bring to practitioner–public gaps. We discuss next that the problem of single-identity approaches (gender-only and race-only analyses) to understanding problems within the practice has exposed the need to learn how multiple identities simultaneously complicate public relations.

Gender-only analyses of publics

For understanding publics' perspectives, few studies have explored how gender affects how decisions are made concerning the introduction of health topics into the media (Aldoory 2001; Vardeman and Aldoory 2008). As parts of a women's theory of health communication, cultural factors like the salience of everyday life, putting others' needs before their needs, and negotiating costs and benefits of health interventions characterize women publics (Aldoory 2001). These studies did not explicitly interrogate how race, class, age, nationality, religion, sexual orientation, and other identities relied on gender to complement and complicate women's experiences with mediated health topics. A gendered analysis of other identities would help practitioners better understand the general complications that segments of women (e.g. those from racial minorities, working-class women, ageing women, immigrant women) face in communication.

Race-only analyses of publics

Likewise, race has been touched on in public relations literature. From a publics perspective, only a handful of studies purposefully sampled participants from non-white/Caucasian races and ethnicities (Aldoory 2001; Sha 2006; Vardeman-Winter and Tindall 2010). Findings show that publics' recognition of race guides many of their communication behaviours because of heightened problem recognition and involvement recognition around racio-ethnic issues (Sha 2006; Vardeman-Winter and Tindall 2010).

Addressing this dearth of research in public relations, Pompper (2005) suggested that by adopting more critical race theory-driven studies, public relations scholarship makes fewer assumptions about the realities of public relations from the perspectives outside the white, hegemonic worldview. As with gender-only studies, race-only analyses cannot observe complex barriers to communication that stem from cultural stereotypes of shared meanings of certain multiple identities. For example, being an African-American woman from a low-income neighbourhood indicates entirely different social issues and communication outlets than being an African-American man from a middle-class background (in other words, being black is not a common experience across genders, classes, nationalities, etc.).

These competing types of analysis are relevant in enabling academic, organizational, and social activists to improve the status of women in the field and women as important publics. However, these analyses fall short of engaging in a nuanced discourse about the limitations of gender-only or race-only analyses. Furthermore, very little work in public relations has investigated and theorized about the nature and limitations of publics based on their identities (relative to the amount of work done to uncover the nature and limitations of identity among practitioners). Thus, this project explores the communication problems that occur at the nexus of public relations and the multiple identities of publics. It also seeks to suggest that gender-only frameworks are limited and that a multiple-identity (i.e. intersectional) framework is more useful in understanding publics.

Intersectionality: gender and beyond

The term 'intersectionality' refers to the presence of multiple identities, all at once (Weber 2001). It refers to an understanding that gender does not exist alone in an individual's life, and nor does race, class, age, sexual orientation, or other important identities (Dill, McLaughlin and Nieves 2007). Instead, identities rely upon one another to exist in sociocultural environments

(Mattis *et al.* 2008). In other words, a person cannot only be a woman or a low-income person. Based on their multiple identities, some groups are privileged by social systems, while other groups are marginalized (Zinn and Dill 1996). Multiple identities should be taken into account when communication is implemented with publics as well as when policies are made for publics (Weber and Parra-Medina 2003).

Media studies have shown that some groups are disproportionately and consistently negatively portrayed in media and in campaign work because of their overlapping, multiple identities (Crenshaw 1991; Ehlers 2004; Holland 2009; Meyers 2004). For example, in her intersectional analysis of the media portrayals of Janet Jackson after her Super Bowl XXXVIII halftime performance in which Justin Timberlake exposed Jackson's breast, Holland (2009: 147) argued that the 'marketing of Black female sexuality via mass media exacerbates the difficulties associated with image subversion'. Jackson's black, female identity served as the 'deceptive Jezebel' to Timberlake's 'innocent White man':

> [H]er racial and gendered Otherness was often juxtaposed with the 'normalcy' of Timberlake's White masculinity ... she emerged in public discourse as the primary (if not sole) instigator of the lewd act, a scheming seductress who manipulated Timberlake for her own economic gain.
>
> (Holland 2009: 130)

The principles of intersectionality are important in disciplines where our ideas of audiences and others impact how knowledge is produced and disseminated (Cheney and Ashcraft 2007). These consequences result in social inequities (Yuval-Davis 2009), such as public health disparities and epidemics (Weber 2007; Weber and Parra-Medina 2003).

Uncovering intersectionality in the context of health disparities and inequitable policies begins with identifying one pivoting identity and exploring issues related to that identity's creation by other identities and how it contributes to the effects of other identities. Intersectionality, then, provides an important theory to incorporate into the critical discourse of public relations and gender because of the salience of consequences resulting from cohesion or dissonance between organizational and public identities.

Gender as pivoting identity

Key to understanding intersectionality is that it relies on time and space as contexts that can change how identities are accomplished and transformed. Intersectionality theory proposes that salient, situational identities determine incremental privilege or oppression (King 1988). Alternatively, some have argued that race, gender, and class are continuous and ongoing accomplishments in the daily lives of individuals (West and Fenstermaker 1995). The relevance of these dynamic processes and how they influence publics' communication cannot be understood unless researchers acknowledge the context in which identities are achieved and accomplished.

Some intersectional work supports the extraction of a single identity and places it at the centre of analysis, initiating examination of its interactions with other identities (Dottolo and Stewart 2008; Luft 2009; West and Fenstermaker 1995; Yuval-Davis 2009). An anti-sexist singular approach avoids 'the risk of flattening difference' (Luft 2009: 104), which 'impedes intersectional social change' (p. 100). It also avoids discrediting independent social oppressions by using the trendy moniker of 'race, class, and gender' work, which confuses consciousness-raising activities because separate identities may not be attended to intellectually but rather as an unthoughtful whole (Luft 2009). This study, using intersectional analysis, examines the nuances of gender as it relates to other identities such as race, class, and age.

Intersectionality research in public relations

Gender alone cannot account for how publics make decisions and should not be studied as isolated from other identities. Instead, gender is an oppressed, marginalized, or privileged social interaction *because of its intersection* with race, class, sexual orientation, and age, among other identities (Vardeman-Winter and Tindall 2010; Vardeman-Winter et al. 2010). In a study with women from racial minorities, participants expressed structural barriers to engaging in heart-healthy behaviours because campaign messages failed to speak to the multiple identities influencing their health decision-making. Women illustrated their inability to adopt healthier behaviours due to a lack of money to buy expensive produce (class identity), which influenced their ability to feed their family properly (gender identity), particularly since the family may not eat the 'white' or American foods suggested in the messages (racial and ethnic identities) (Tindall and Vardeman-Winter 2011; Vardeman-Winter and Tindall 2010). This evidence of the relevance of intersectionality in public relations practice has been validated in similar identity research (Khakimova et al. 2011; Tindall 2009; Vardeman-Winter 2012; Vardeman-Winter et al. 2011).

Political intersectionality and practitioner–publics gaps

In an early, influential conceptualization of intersectionality, Crenshaw (1991) outlined three social realms where intersectionality has large-scale consequences:

1 *Political intersectionality* involves how organizational and legal policies and procedures are made, implemented, and maintained in ways that

consistently subdue the rights of some groups according to their mix of identities.
2 *Structural intersectionality* entails the physical, cultural, social, and legal systems that suppress the power of some groups because of the relationship a marginalized group has with dominant groups.
3 *Representational intersectionality* comprises how mediated texts represent some groups as disempowered because of their multiple identities, and how these texts, over time, contribute to stereotypes of marginalized groups.

Representational intersectionality as it relates to public relations publics has been evidenced in studies when publics perceived that campaign messages were not useful to them because the messages focused on singular identities and neglected important facets of their needs and motivations (Aldoory 2001; Sison 2009; Vardeman-Winter *et al.* 2011; Vardeman-Winter and Tindall 2010). However, political and structural intersectionality have not yet been linked to public relations; nor has a public relations study conducted a comprehensive analysis of the different levels of intersectionality within a public relations problem.

Political intersectionality in public relations is worth exploring because communication about policies among various groups (affected organizations, legislators, publics) indicates power flows. Furthermore, policies impact how groups experience health, education, politics, law, economics, workforce dynamics, and myriad other social relationships. Physical limits to opportunities reflect structural intersectionality, and how media and organizations demonstrate groups' experiences with these relationships displays representational intersectionality. Thus, political intersectionality of public relations – or how the communication practitioner holds power differently from publics based on social stereotypes of multiple identities – indicates to researchers areas we can study for intellectual, practical, and pedagogical interventions.

This chapter extends previous efforts to understand political intersectionality. Vardeman-Winter, Jiang and Tindall (2011) talked to women of various racial, socioeconomic, age, health status, and family structure backgrounds about how their identities influenced their decision-making about new breast cancer screening guidelines. The data suggested that structural intersectionality of communication shapes disparate health public relations because of gendered socioeconomic disparities and restricted gendered physicality, which made active health-seeking near impossible for some women. Also, women said their multiple identities were missing in the news and campaign messages. This suggests a lack of race–class contextualization in media portrayals and a negligence of gendered and community roles.

From these data, Vardeman-Winter *et al.* (2011) proposed specific tenets to connect public relations' practices of campaign design and messaging to intersectionality. Based on these publics' perceptions that gaps exist between those making the policies and publics, the authors suggested the following theoretical proposition through which to study political intersectionality in public relations:

> Political intersectionality of communication exists in how policies inequitably impact dominant and marginalized publics. A cultural gap exists between communicators and policymakers, and their publics, which results in policies with questionable intent and potential limited efficacy for those most in need of intervention.
> (Vardeman-Winter *et al.* 2011: 24)

'Cultural gap' refers to differences in perceptions of issues between producers and consumers of public relations campaigns (Curtin and Gaither 2005, 2007, as previously discussed). Shared meanings result from how a culture commonly gives meaning to objects, ideas, events, and relationships (du Gay *et al.* 1997). Some meanings dominate and become hegemonic discourses because of the powerful authorities that adopt that meaning, and other meanings become subaltern discourses because their advocates hold less social power (Hall 1997).

In public relations, hegemony is achieved in three major ways:

1 Campaign messages transmit discourses; the messages that carry dominant meanings often succeed more in being placed in prominent media and reaching larger publics than do subaltern meanings.
2 Messages are placed in prominent media depending on the quality of the relationships practitioners have with journalists, editors, and bloggers.
3 Campaigns are produced by people whose identities differ from those of many of their publics; therefore, race, gender, and class are largely problematic identities in public relations practice (Curtin and Gaither 2007).

We argue that the identities of practitioners and publics make a difference in which messages are deemed dominant, and the dominant discourse produces a view of risk that is partial and political.

The purpose of this study is to extend the proposition of political intersectionality to encompass the notion of public relations as a gendered industry that aids in creating policies with inequitable consequences. When policymakers do not understand this and communicate accordingly, then policies are ineffective for organizations and publics (Heath and Palenchar 2009). Inadequate policies and misrepresented meanings contribute to the perpetuation of systemic structural inequities (Heath and O'Hair 2009). Researchers must then explore what outcomes result from inequitable policies. The question 'What consequences occur in the public relations process and for the gendered identities of publics when a large-scale health policy is changed?' guided data collection and analysis.

A triangulated approach to exploring political intersectionality

To answer the question of how the revised breast cancer guidelines influenced publics' cultural understandings of gender and identity, we used multiple exploratory methods. First, we conducted individual interviews and focus groups with thirty-one women of various races, ages, income and educational levels, and health statuses to find out how they perceived the guidelines influenced their understandings of their genders and other identities. (See Table 10.1 for participant demographics.) The interviews and focus groups occurred in the interviewers' offices, the participants' offices or homes, and other public places, such as coffee houses. Interviews lasted 45–75 minutes, and focus groups lasted 75–120 minutes.

A health topic was introduced during interviews and focus groups to ground participants' understandings of how their identities affect their health decision-making. We chose a topic that was relevant to women, that received significant media coverage, and that introduced policy change. Women were asked to watch a brief television news segment about the revised guidelines. Afterwards, women were asked questions such as 'Which identity of yours do you think the screening guidelines decision-makers considered most [or least] important?[3] Why?' and 'To what extent do you feel the decision-makers know the situations in your life that are complex?' The researchers have used pseudonyms for the participants when reporting their responses.

To triangulate the publics' perspectives of the revised guidelines, we also conducted a qualitative content analysis of the task force's public documents about the revised guidelines. Codes were given to repetitive themes, and coders evaluated whether identities or cultural cues were embedded in the messaging. Coders also considered what important factors or messages were absent in the documents. The purpose of analysing the documents was to dissect the latent meanings about gendered intersections infused in the guidelines. We suggest that these meanings were created and communicated by the task force (the policymakers), either intentionally or unintentionally. The knowledge that was used to change policy largely depends on the groups involved in the policymaking, which is a significant power consideration (Heath and Palenchar 2009).

To accomplish this, we examined fourteen online documents produced by the task force (found at http://www.uspreventiveservicestaskforce.org) about the breast cancer screening guidelines, and how the task force is proceeding with changing and enacting the new guidelines. Documents covered biographies of the task force members, the history and current organization of the task force, a list of partners, explanations for how the task force employs research in its decision-making, public-facing documents about

Table 10.1 Participant demographics

	Number of women
Race	
African American	12
Asian/Pacific Islander	2
Latina/Hispanic	3
White	14
Household Composition	
Live alone	5
Live with a romantic partner/spouse	7
Live with family (parents, siblings, aunts, children, etc.)	12
Live with children and partners/spouses	7
Total Household Income Level	
Under $20,000	3
$20,001–30,000	8
$30,001–40,000	3
$40,001–50,000	2
$50,001–60,000	3
$60,001–70,000	2
$70,001–80,000	1
$80,001–90,000	1
$100,000 or above	7
Missing	1
Highest Level of Education Attained	
Some high school	2
Earned a high school diploma or GED	7
Some technical/junior college	3
Some college	3
Earned a bachelor's degree	8
Earned a master's degree	6
Earned a doctoral degree	1
Earned a JD degree	1
Sexual Orientation (self-identified by participants)	
Heterosexual/Straight	30
Missing	1
Problems with Breast Cancer	
Yes	5
No	26
Age	
Range of ages	23–63 years
Average	41.23 years

breast cancer screening, and procedures lay publics can take to suggest future topics for the task force to review.

To interpret the two types of data together (the publics' perceptions and the documents' statements about procedures, etc.), a thematic analysis (Miles and Huberman 1994) and narrative analysis (Lawler 2002) were used.

Themes told the consistent stories across the interviews and focus groups, whereas narratives described individual experiences as resonant with or remote from the themes. In reporting, multiple narratives from individuals are used to explain how different contexts precipitate the emergence of variable salient identity mixes (Valentine 2007). To illustrate the existence of intersectionality, narratives from women of different identities exhibit women's simultaneous opportunities and marginalizations within a common political health issue.

Differently, textual analysis was conducted to discover how power is employed in the documents and the policies. A textual analysis was chosen because, 'instead of focusing on people as constructors of culture, texts themselves can be viewed as cultural influencers ... where the focus is not on an independent piece of work ... but on the symbolic structures and the systems of relationships among these symbols that create meaning' (Potter 1996: 62–3). We looked for how the communication of the policies reflected different gender intersections, cultural gaps evident in the policies/communication, and contradictions between the policy communication and the impact on diagnosis and death by breast cancer.

Findings from the case study

Consequences for cultural understandings about gender and identity

The purpose of this study was to examine the consequences that occur in the public relations process and for the gendered identities of publics when a large-scale health policy is changed. We found that the policymakers and communicators neglected how women live at the convergence of multiple identities where marginalization occurs because of gender, race, and age. Also, limited efficacy of communication about the policy confused women; they were unclear about the relevance and significance of the change to their lives. The data suggested that policymakers generally assumed that communication was not an important part of the policymaking process.

The loss of the everyday woman

The data were analysed according to how gender was the basic 'cultural gap' felt by participants that intersected with other identities. One focus group captured this sense of gender difference between policymakers and themselves:

GLORIA: I bet they were all men ... men don't perceive women or breast cancer or ovarian cancer or cervical cancer as important because it hits us.
MEREDITH: ... We need to have early detection ... There's still a lot of men in the field, and they tend to discount some things.

Women saw men as the creators of the guidelines for the breast cancer policies, with limited or no input from women and with no perspective or understanding of women's experiences with cancer as either a scare or a true diagnosis. Thus, what was largely missing from most participants' understandings was a lack of contextualization about gender.

Related to the lack of communication to or with women, participants felt that policymakers did not account for their identities, such their genders, races, income levels, health insurance access, education levels, ages, lifestyles, and social roles. In other words, gender was only part of the story missing from how women believed policymakers considered them. Some women perceived their gender–class intersectional identities were neglected. Some of the interviewees expressed beliefs that medical and insurance companies' interests pushed the agenda and the decision, which contradicts their needs as working-class women. Specifically, a focus group of African-American women believed the doctors were the targets of the policy changes. As a result of such communication inequities, these women considered that they receive questionable treatment when they enter an emergency room or doctor's surgery, based on their level of health insurance:

RHONDA: Doctors, really and truly, are being taken by the corporate world right now. So whatever the corporate world says, this is what we're gonna do, because they pay them a certain percentage of what the fees are.

MONIKA: One nurse told [a friend], if you come in here with CHIPs or with Aid,[4] you just assumed step to the side of the building, you know what I'm saying? They don't care. People can't afford it.

RHONDA: The number of the people in the ER sitting out there with their kids just waiting and waiting ... [She then tells a story of waiting in a waiting room for hours without being helped.] I gave you my HMO card[5] – I didn't give Medicaid, I didn't give you CHIPs. I paid for my insurance! But no matter whether I paid for it or not, I got insurance to take care of it.

VERA: It's sad you have to have insurance to be taken care of. What if I can't get the care I need?

Participants had many reasons for feeling those in powerful policymaking positions were not in tune with their needs for better policies and better information. In general, the participants believed the task force lacked interest in the needs and wants of the women, particularly those who had limited access to healthcare. These women's words suggested that the task force's communication approach is largely goal-oriented and does not account for consumers' experiences with healthcare. Because lay publics were not part of policymaking and communication, the women were considered by policymakers to be 'passive' publics.

Furthermore, even in the clinical documents, the panel did not address or consider how publics would react to the new breast cancer screening recommendations. There is no evidence that qualitative or ethnographic research was conducted to determine the negative effects of false positives[6] and biopsies, or the negative effects that may occur when women learn that breast cancer screening results have been dramatically revised. Policymakers informed decisions with studies that employed sophisticated statistical analyses that pointed to the magnitude and certainty of net benefit (USPSTF 2009a), and the discussions of these studies were highly technical (i.e. the cultural, jargon-filled language of clinicians and policymakers) (USPSTF 2009b). The lack of lay language exacerbates a cultural gap between policymakers and non-clinical publics.

When considerations for intersections of gender–class are removed from the process, the revised policy may be moot to most women. This policy change largely neglected the needs of women who lacked access to healthcare. As a consequence, this lack of representation of working-class women in decision-making discounted the complexity of privilege and marginalization created by the confluence of women's identities.

Privileging white women with resources

The intersection of race and gender was also complicated in participants' understandings of breast cancer communication. Although the US mortality rates for black women indicate that more of them die from the disease (American Cancer Society 2011), one participant was troubled by the representations in the well-known, higher-profile media and advertising campaigns. One consequence of this is the perception that breast cancer is a white women's disease. Ronnie – a thirty-eight-year-old single mother with a master's degree who earns between $40,001 and $50,000 annually – talks about this problem in her community:

> Unless they have a commercial that specifically talks about it, or, you know, addresses African Americans or Latinos, then they're really not going to, you know, pay attention to it, as closely as they would say, 'There's X amount of Latino women that are dying each year. There's X amount of African-American women dying every year.' You know, I know [breast cancer] is a problem or becoming an issue in our community but I don't think, umm, people realize how big of an issue it's becoming in our community.

Some participants saw the gender–race intersection further problematized by class. Victoria – a single Filipina in her early twenties with a bachelor's degree who earns between $20,001 and $30,000 – agreed that the communication sent by policymakers was targeting white women *because of* their financial access:

Caucasian women. I don't really know statistics, but I would say probably minorities are more likely to not be able to afford to pay for the care themselves ... probably it is a discriminatory policy ... it's probably not considering women of minority and it's probably figuring that Caucasians can afford to carry the burden. They want to shift the burden onto the public to pay for something else to save money for the government. If the women can't afford it, I guess because they are in the minority, they don't care about it.

These women perceived that none of their identities beyond gender were represented in the communication, yet they felt their race mattered in how they understood this issue. To their point, task force documents revealed that there were no guidelines about how women experiencing racial and socioeconomic health disparities (and other relevant identities) should approach breast cancer screening. The documents displayed no considerations for women's races, nationalities, immigrant status, locations, years in the United States, reproductive status, income level and healthcare access, languages spoken, or religions (all factors that may influence women's perceptions of cancer risk).

Document analysis also revealed that the policymakers largely ignored the intersecting identities of women by excluding public communication experts from the task force and its list of target audiences. There is no evidence to indicate that diverse identities beyond professional backgrounds were considered when recruiting the USPSTF members.[7] Furthermore, there were no communicators or health educators on the task force.[8] When the task force designed the new screening guidelines, it mainly targeted 'busy physicians in many areas of medicine', 'researchers', and 'policymakers and others concerned with coverage issues' (USPSTF 2007), rather than women of different backgrounds.

Overall, gender and age were the only identities considered when the policymakers changed screening policies. The women interviewed felt that the policies privileged white women with resources to access healthcare. As strategic communicators and decision-makers, the policymakers of new screening guidelines are called upon to build relationships with the USPSTF's culturally diverse publics. But without understanding how multiple identities co-construct women's perceptions of breast cancer screenings, the policymakers failed to reach into the complex social situations of women (e.g. barriers that working-class women from minority groups face when attempting to access healthcare). Consequently, the interests and needs of target audiences were misrepresented in the devising of the policy and in its communication.

Limited efficacy of policies and communication

The lack of communication of the policy and the subsequent media questioning of it (Kolata 2009) resulted in ineffective messages about cancer screening that left participants confused. Most women interviewed said the new guidelines contradicted traditional information about breast cancer and their personal experiences. As one white woman in her fifties explained:

> I was told you have to have a mammogram starting at the age of forty and every year. So I had my baseline at thirty-five or whatever and I've had two since then. And now they're saying, 'Oh! You don't have to have it until you are fifty'? Well, I've actually had a couple of friends who have had mammograms and found cancer in their forties. So it's like, it's one of those that's very contradictory.

Several women also said they would continue to get screened at forty or even earlier. One African-American woman felt that people become routine in their behaviours and are not likely to adopt new behaviours later in life. Therefore, she felt the guidelines were ineffective in helping older women but should instead target younger women so they can start mammograms at twenty-five years of age:

> I just think if you start young, you can get women in the habit of doing. Because once you hit fifty, you're kind of stuck in your ways. You're probably not really thinking about it. I think if you start the pattern or start early, women will already – like pap smears. You already know you are supposed to get a pap smear every single year. If you start the breast cancer, you know, evaluations or whatever earlier, it will already be ingrained ... As a black women and just me, I don't know anyone that's been affected by it, so it's not really on my radar. But, you know, I don't – but I've known you need a pap smear. So that's always something that I plan to do.

To this participant's point, women who are confused by the new guidelines may seek additional information about the 'bottom line' of breast cancer screening. However, if they had looked to other major breast cancer organizations, such as the American Cancer Society or the Susan G. Komen for the Cure Foundation, for answers, they would have found statements by these groups that reiterated traditional screening guidelines and decried the new recommendations. For example, on the same day the USPSTF released its recommendations, Susan G. Komen for the Cure issued a press release, citing a vice-president who objected to the new guidelines:

> Susan G. Komen for the Cure wants to eliminate any impediments to regular mammography screening for women age 40 and older. While there is no question that mammograms save lives for women over 50 and women 40–49, there is enough uncertainty about the age at which mammography should begin and the frequency of screening that we would not want to see a change in policy for screening mammography

at this time ... Our real focus, however, should be on the fact that one-third of the women who qualify for screening under today's guidelines are not being screened due to lack of access, education or awareness ... For African-American women this is particularly urgent, because too few African-American women are getting annual mammograms and breast screenings under the rules that exist today. Additionally, with the African-American population facing diagnosis at younger ages, getting screened early is critical.

(Susan G. Komen for the Cure 2009)

Because of opposition from the breast cancer advocacy community to the policy change (Kolata 2009), women may have perceived profound conflicting information about the 'official' recommendation of breast cancer screening. Women may feel panic, anxiety, and dissonance about a risk, such that they may 'turn off' further messages about it (Covello and Peters 2002; Cozzens and Contractor 1987; Lupton 1992; Vardeman and Aldoory 2008). The convergence of the three major issues at the heart of this topic – the conflicting messages about the guidelines, the lack of communication about the guidelines, and the negligence of considering how women of different backgrounds should adhere to the guidelines – suggests potentially dangerous consequences for morbidity and mortality rates of breast cancer.

Conclusion

Identity is a complicated influence that should be further problematized by researchers and practitioners. Gender emerged as the salient identity from which to study how multiple identities form privileged and marginalized groups. Without explicit efforts to analyse the intersections of gender with other identities, we may not have learned the extent of the problem with the policymaking and policy communication, such as the belief that the policies privileged the experiences of those women who were white and middle or upper class. Understanding of these gendered intersections informed our analyses of the policy documents, which revealed that policymakers – as predicted by the participants – made little or no explicit effort to include women publics of any backgrounds in the policymaking and policy communication processes.

The data suggested that influential health policies were made based in financial concerns, political agendas, and statistical analysis, and that decision-makers discounted and even neglected the opportunity to take into account the realities of lived gendered intersections which deter women from being able to follow health guidelines. Since the convergence of identities influences, shapes, and frames women's experiences, their perceived realities and lived experiences were discounted and ignored, leaving groups of individuals even more vulnerable to breast cancer, as well as other health disparities. At the macro level, the political decisions made regarding breast cancer screenings affect the public health system, which may exacerbate public health disparities and public confusion in the long term.

Gender and publics in public relations: more research needed on practitioners-as-publics

Our findings also reiterated the need to explore how the dual identity of women practitioners (or the identity conflict for practitioners-as-publics) is accomplished and negotiated. Some participants suggested that no women sat on the USPS policymaking board, yet our analysis found that women clinicians *were* members of the board. However, the head of the board admitted that communication was not considered in the rolling out of the policy. These two findings – that women clinicians were involved in policymaking and that communication was neglected – suggest that the cultural gap between practitioners and publics discussed in previous studies (Curtin and Gaither 2007; Vardeman-Winter *et al.* 2011) still exists, is largely dependent on gendered intersections (with socioeconomic status), and potentially results in ineffective policy communication.

In summary, intersectional studies are important for understanding the relationship between gender and public relations because, without policies and communication that take into account all the intersecting identities of women, the status of women as publics and as producers of information is relegated to a passive position (or made absent).

Sociopolitical consequences of neglecting gendered intersections

Inequitable outcomes may occur based on the overarching assumption (by the producers, as implied in the documents) that gender is the only connection women have to this breast cancer issue. Differently, participants in our study suggested instead that the development of the guidelines should start with considering their gender and speak directly to the complex barriers that their other identities present to healthcare situations. Neglecting the ways in which class, race, age, and social role intertwine with gender may render the policy change detrimental to women's health. When policymakers and communicators do not collect and analyse data according to intersections – rather than gender alone – health disparities are perpetuated (Weber and Parra-Medina 2003). Intersectionality rests on temporal and spatial contexts through which to understand multiple identities (King 1988; Mattis *et al.* 2008); as such, the creation and careless dissemination of ineffective, meaningless information without intersectional contextualization is considered irresponsible in times of global economic trouble and social inequality.

The consequences of policymakers' decision-making and communication which this study has identified do not reflect well on the field of public relations as an ethical discipline purporting to work in publics' interests. By examining only gender or even taking additive approaches to multiple identities of relevant players in public relations, researchers tell a partial story of identity and marginalization in the field of public relations. Recognizing and remedying public relations only as a gendered industry rather than a *gendered-intersecting industry* aggravates the social problems public relations works to alleviate, as solutions rely on the power of strategic, public-informed communication (and this case study is an example of the consequence of neglecting intersectional communication).

Political intersectionality and gendered disruptions

Vardeman-Winter *et al.* proposed that 'a cultural gap exists between communicators and policymakers and their publics, which results in policies with questionable intent and potential limited efficacy for those most in need of interventions' (2011: 24), and this proposition and its merits are made evident by *the decontextualization of policymaking*. The standalone, unconnected manner by which the USPSTF presented the revised guidelines to publics and neglected to respond to critics served to medicalize women's lived experiences and everyday issues (e.g. lack of access) with breast screening.

The decontextualization of policymaking also represented women's bodies as only medical and financial objects that carry risk. Policymakers' disregard for public participation signifies women's health as a collection of medicalized gendered disruptions, as breast cancer screening seems to bother – or interfere – with policymakers' attempts to conduct business efficiently. Gender is not problematized in decision-making because of the norms associated with different political affiliations: the culture of clinicians holds local knowledge of medicine and procedure, whereas the culture of patients knows the experience of survivorship or scheduling, paying for, and emotionally managing mammograms; the culture of policymakers manifests in technical, legal languages and the focus is process-driven, whereas the 'everyday woman' speaks a language of lived negotiations of health risks and limited time to seek adequate information about health (Vardeman-Winter *et al.* 2011). Worsening this point, women living at the margins experience hardships that are ignored by the policy communication; the policy language is not only technical and therefore potentially hard to understand but leaves marginalized women to navigate difficult decision-making about when they can or cannot request mammograms. Furthermore, they have to research the implications of the policy for insurance, alternative screening tools, and preventative measures, since the guidelines do not offer any such guidance.

To policymakers and communicators, publics from whom these gendered disruptions emerge exist a world apart from their programme and campaign goals. Coupled with the state of women as the majority of public relations practitioners and the identity conflict for practitioners-as-publics, the policymaker–public cultural gap must be actively negotiated in two major ways: publics should be part of policy task forces throughout the duration of projects because of their local knowledge on the topic; and policymakers and communicators must consider women beyond their gender, noting salient intersections with race, age, and education, for the purposes of making guidelines meaningful and useful.

Finally, based on the findings from this study, we present a revision to our previous proposition about political intersectionality that necessarily includes gender as a problematic site of policymaking and its communication. Gendered political intersectionality of communication exists in how policies inequitably affect marginalized publics, namely women publics. A cultural gap exists between communicators and policymakers and their publics, largely because of gender identity conflicts for practitioners-as-publics. The results are policies with questionable intent and potential limited efficacy for those most in need of policy intervention.

Notes

1 This conflict is translatable to identities other than gender, namely race. For example, practitioners from racial minorities are pigeonholed into communicating with publics of racial minorities, and, thus, experience a double bind (Tindall 2009).
2 The vast majority of gender studies in public relations have focused on women (Aldoory 2009). That creates a fallacy that women are the only people who are gendered and thus reinforces the standard binaries.
3 We anticipated that some participants would struggle with naming an identity they felt represented them. Therefore, at the beginning of the interviews, during rapport-building, we asked them to write down what their identity was as a way to make certain attributes salient throughout the interview. The prompt asked, 'If you were to describe who you are to someone that cannot see or hear you, how would you describe yourself?' If participants did not write down the major identities we hoped to explore, such as gender and race, we asked about these explicitly later in the interviews. Also, because participants did not discuss multiple, overlapping identities organically, we asked such questions as: 'To what extent do the different parts of you overlap in this piece? In other words, when you read this piece, how much do you think of yourself only as a [gender] reading it, or only as a [race] person reading it?'
4 This participant is referring to two healthcare insurance assistance programmes in the United States of America. The first is the Children's Health Insurance Program (colloquially known as 'CHIPs'), which 'provides low-cost health insurance coverage for children in families who earn too much income to qualify for Medicaid, but can't afford private health insurance' (Medicaid and the Children's Health Insurance Program n.d.). 'Aid' refers to Medicaid, a federally funded programme that offers free or low-cost health insurance to those struggling to pay for private health insurance. Medicaid eligibility is based on income and other circumstances, and is mandated by state guidelines. Overall, 'children in families with incomes up to $44,100 per year (for a family of four) are likely to be eligible for Medicaid coverage' (Medicaid and the Children's Health Insurance Program n.d.).

5 An 'HMO' is a 'health maintenance organization', a type of managed care health insurance option in the United States. These plans typically cost less than other plans, but users have less choice about which doctors they can visit (ConsumerReports.org 2011). This participant is referring to the health insurance card she uses when visiting her doctor.
6 A false positive is considered a 'false alarm'. When a test screens for a health condition and this indicates the health condition exists when in actuality it does not, the result is known as a 'false positive'. In this case, a false positive occurs when mammogram results suggest cancer is present, but after follow-up tests clinicians conclude that cancer, in fact, is not present.
7 Members were involved in various aspects of the medical profession: paediatrics, public health, health management and policy, family and community health systems, medicine, epidemiology, and biostatistics (USPSTF 2011).
8 To this point, the task force admitted problems with communication in the release of the new guidelines. The first author attended a panel discussion in Houston, TX, sponsored by the Texas Medical Center Women's Health Network (www.tmcwhn.org/) in January 2010, titled 'New Recommendations for Mammography and Cervical Cancer Screening: What They Really Mean'. The chair of the USPSTF, Dr Virginia Moyer, discussed the revised recommendations for breast cancer screening. Amid criticism from breast cancer advocacy groups, patients, and healthcare providers during the panel discussion, Dr Moyer admitted that the task force did not consider communication in its release of the guidelines. She also noted that communication about the issue would be important for future changes to screening guidelines.

References

Acosta-Alzuru, C. (2003) '"I'm not a feminist ... I only defend women as human beings": The production, representation, and consumption of feminism in a telenovela', *Critical Studies in Media Communication*, 20: 269–94.

Aldoory, L. (2001) 'Making health messages meaningful for women: Factors that influence involvement', *Journal of Public Relations Research*, 13: 163–85.

—— (2005) '(Re)Conceived feminist paradigm for public relations: A case for substantial improvement', *Journal of Communication*, 55: 668–84.

—— (2009) 'Feminist criticism in public relations: How gender can impact public relations texts and contexts', in R. L. Heath, E. L. Toth and D. Waymer (eds), *Rhetorical and Critical Approaches to Public Relations II*, New York: Routledge: 110–23.

Aldoory, L. and Toth, E. (2002) 'Gender discrepancies in a gendered profession: A developing theory for public relations', *Journal of Public Relations Research*, 14: 103–26.

American Cancer Society (2011) *Breast Cancer Facts & Figures 2011–2012*, Atlanta: American Cancer Society. Online. Available HTTP: <http://www.cancer.org/acs/groups/content/@epidemiologysurveilance/documents/document/acspc-030975.pdf> (accessed 26 October 2011).

Brownlee, S. and Lenzer, J. (2011) 'Can cancer ever be ignored?' *New York Times Magazine*, 5 October. Online. Available HTTP: <http://www.nytimes.com/2011/10/09/magazine/can-cancer-ever-be-ignored.html> (accessed 29 October 2011).

Cheney, G. and Ashcraft, K. L. (2007) 'Considering "the professional" in communication studies: Implications for theory and research within and beyond the boundaries of organizational communication', *Communication Theory*, 17: 146–75.

Collins, P. H. (2000) *Black Feminist Thought: Knowledge, Consciousness, and the Politics of Empowerment*, London: HarperCollins Academic.
ConsumerReports.org (2011) 'Insurance: PPOs vs HMOs'. Online. Available HTTP: <http://www.consumerreports.org/health/insurance/health-insurance/how-to-pick-health-insurance/hmo-vs-ppo.htm> (accessed 15 February 2012).
Covello, V. T. and Peters, R. G. (2002) 'Women's perceptions of the risks of age-related diseases, including breast cancer: Reports from a 3-year research study', *Health Communication*, 14: 377–95.
Cozzens, M. D. and Contractor, N. S. (1987) 'The effect of conflicting information on media skepticism', *Communication Research*, 14: 437–51.
Crenshaw, K. (1991) 'Mapping the margins: Intersectionality, identity politics, and violence against women of color', *Stanford Law Review*, 43: 1241–99.
Curtin, P. A. and Gaither, T. K. (2005) 'Privileging identity, difference, and power: The circuit of culture as a basis for public relations theory', *Journal of Public Relations Research*, 17: 91–115.
—— (2007) *International Public Relations: Negotiating Culture, Identity, and Power*, Thousand Oaks, CA: Sage Publications.
Daymon, C. and Demetrious, K. (2010) 'Gender and public relations: Perspectives, applications and questions', *PRism* 7(4). Online. Available HTTP: <http://www.prismjournal.org/fileadmin/Praxis/Files/Gender/Daymon_Demetrious.pdf> (accessed 11 January 2013).
Dellorto, D. (2009) 'Task force opposes routine mammograms for women age 40–49', CNN.com, 16 November. Online. Available HTTP: <http://www.cnn.com/2009/HEALTH/11/16/mammography.recommendation.changes/index.html#cnnSTCText> (accessed 31 March 2011).
Dill, B., McLaughlin, A. E. and Nieves, A. D. (2007) 'Future directions of feminist research: Intersectionality', in S. N. Hesse-Biber (ed.), *Handbook of Feminist Research: Theory and Praxis*, Thousand Oaks, CA: SAGE Publications: 629–37.
Dottolo, A. L. and Stewart, A. J. (2008) '"Don't ever forget now, you're a black man in America": Intersections of race, class and gender in encounters with the police', *Sex Roles*, 59: 350–64.
du Gay, P., Hall, S., Janes, L., Mackay, H. and Negus, K. (1997) *Doing Cultural Studies: The Story of the Sony Walkman*, London: Sage Publications.
Ehlers, N. (2004) 'Hidden in plain sight: Defying juridical racialization in *Rhinelander* v. *Rhinelander*', *Communication and Critical/Cultural Studies*, 1: 313–34.
Grunig, L. A., Toth, E. L. and Hon, L. C. (2001) *Women in Public Relations: How Gender Influences Practice*, New York: The Guilford Press.
Hall, S. (ed.) (1997) *Representation: Cultural Representations and Signifying Practices*, London: Sage in association with the Open University.
Heath, R. L. and O'Hair, H. D. (2009) 'The significance of crisis and risk communication', in R. L. Heath and H. D. O'Hair (eds), *Handbook of Risk and Crisis and Crisis Communication*, New York: Routledge: 5–30.
Heath, R. L. and Palenchar, M. J. (2009) *Strategic Issues Management: Organizations and Public Policy Challenges* (2nd edition), Los Angeles, CA: Sage.
Holland, S. L. (2009) 'The "offending" breast of Janet Jackson: Public discourse surrounding the Jackson/Timberlake performance at Super Bowl XXXVIII', *Women's Studies in Communication*, 32: 129–50.

Khakimova, L., Briones, R. L., Madden, S. and Campbell, T. (2011) 'The Letting Girls Glow! communication campaign: Methodological and conceptual lessons for segmenting teen publics', *PRism*, 8(2). Online. Available: <http://www.prismjournal.org/fileadmin/8_2/Khakimova_Briones_Madden_Campbell.pdf> (accessed 15 January, 2013).

King, D. K. (1988) 'Multiple jeopardy, multiple consciousness: The context of black feminist ideology', *Signs: Journal of Women in Culture and Society*, 14: 42–72.

Kolata, G. (2009) 'Panel urges mammograms at 50, not 40', NYTimes.com, 16 November. Online. Available HTTP: <http://www.nytimes.com/2009/11/17/health/17cancer.html> (accessed 31 March 2011).

Lawler, S. (2002) 'Narrative in social research', in T. Mays (ed.), *Qualitative Research in Action*, Thousand Oaks, CA: Sage: 242–58.

Luft, R. E. (2009) 'Intersectionality and the risk of flattening difference: Gender and race logics, and the strategic use of antiracist singularity', in M. T. Berger and K. Guidroz (eds), *The Intersectional Approach: Transforming the Academy through Race, Class, & Gender*, Chapel Hill: University of North Carolina Press: 100–17.

Lupton, D. A. (1992) 'From complacency to panic: AIDS and heterosexuals in the Australian press, July 1986 to June 1988', *Health Education Research*, 7: 9–20.

Mattis, J. S., Grayman, N. A., Cowie, S.-A., Winston, C., Watson, C. and Jackson, D. (2008) 'Intersectional identities and the politics of altruistic care in a low-income, urban community', *Sex Roles*, 59: 418–28.

Medicaid and the Children's Health Insurance Program (n.d.) 'Need health insurance?' Online. Available HTTP: <http://www.medicaid.gov/Need-Health-Insurance/Need-Health-Insurance.html> (accessed 15 February 2012).

Meyers, M. (2004) 'African American women and violence: Gender, race, and class in the news', *Critical Studies in Media Communication*, 21: 95–118.

Miles, M. B. and Huberman, M. (1994) *Qualitative Data Analysis: An Expanded Sourcebook* (2nd edition), Thousand Oaks, CA: Sage.

National Cancer Institute (2010) *Cancer Trends Progress Report: 2009/2010 Update*. Online. Available HTTP: <http://progressreport.cancer.gov/doc_detail.asp?pid=1&did=2007&chid=75&coid=726&mid=> (accessed 26 October 2011).

O'Neil, J. (2003) 'An analysis of the relationships among structure, influence, and gender: Helping to build a feminist theory of public relations', *Journal of Public Relations Research*, 15: 151–79.

Pompper, D. (2005) 'Difference in public relations research: A case for introducing Critical Race Theory', *Journal of Public Relations Research*, 17: 139–69.

—— (2007) 'The gender–ethnicity construct in public relations organizations: Using feminist standpoint theory to discover Latinas' realities', *Howard Journal of Communications*, 18: 291–311.

Potter, W. J. (1996) *An Analysis of Thinking and Research about Qualitative Methods*, Mahwah, NJ: Lawrence Erlbaum Associates.

Sha, B.-L. (2006) 'Cultural identity in the segmentation of publics: An emerging theory of intercultural public relations', *Journal of Public Relations Research*, 18(1): 45–65.

Sha, B.-L. and Ford, R. L. (2007) 'Redefining "requisite variety": The challenge of multiple diversities for the future of public relations excellence', in E. L. Toth (ed.), *The Future of Excellence in Public Relations and Communication Management*, Mahwah, NJ: Lawrence Erlbaum Associates: 381–98.

Sison, M. D. (2009) 'Whose cultural values? Exploring public relations' approaches to understanding audiences', *PRism*, 6(2). Online. Available HTTP: <http://www.prismjournal.org/fileadmin/Praxis/Files/globalPR/SISON.pdf> (accessed 15 January 2013).
Susan G. Komen for the Cure (2009) 'Susan G. Komen for the Cure recommends no impediments to breast cancer screening', media release, 16 November. Online. Available HTTP: <http://ww5.komen.org/News/SusanGKomenForTheCureRecommendsNoImpedimentsToBreastCancerScreening.aspx> (accessed 15 February 2012).
Tindall, N. T. J. (2009) 'The double bind of race and gender: Understanding the roles and perceptions of black female public relations faculty', *Southwestern Mass Communication Journal*, 1: 1–16.
Tindall, N. T. J. and Vardeman-Winter, J. (2011) 'Complications in segmenting campaign publics: Women of color explain their problems, involvement, and constraints in reading heart disease communication', *Howard Journal of Communication*, 22: 280–301.
USPSTF (2007) *How to Read the New Recommendation Statement: Methods Update.* Online. Available HTTP: <http://www.uspreventiveservicestaskforce.org/uspstf07/methods/methupd.htm> (accessed 20 October 2011).
—— (2009a) *Screening for Breast Cancer.* Online. Available HTTP: <http://www.uspreventiveservicestaskforce.org/uspstf/uspsbrca.htm> (accessed 20 October 2011).
—— (2009b) *Screening for Breast Cancer: Clinical Summary of 2009 US Preventive Services Task Force Recommendation.* Online. Available HTTP: <http://www.uspreventiveservicestaskforce.org/uspstf09/breastcancer/brcansum.htm> (accessed 20 October 2011).
—— (2010) *Role of Partners.* Online. Available HTTP: <http://www.uspreventiveservicestaskforce.org/partners.htm> (accessed 20 October 2011).
—— (2011a) *About the USPSTF.* Online. Available HTTP: <http://www.uspreventiveservicestaskforce.org/about.htm> (accessed 31 October 2011)
—— (2011b) Biographical Sketches of Members. Online. Available HTTP: <http://www.uspreventiveservicestaskforce.org/uspstbio.htm#Moyer> (accessed 20 October 2011).
Valentine, G. (2007) 'Theorizing and researching intersectionality: A challenge for feminist geography', *Professional Geographer*, 59: 10–21.
Vardeman-Winter, J. E. (2010) 'Using the cultural studies approach to understand health decision-making among a teen public', *Public Relations Review*, 36: 383–5.
—— (2012) 'Medicalization and teen girls' bodies in the Gardasil cervical cancer vaccine campaign', *Feminist Media Studies*, 12: 281–304.
Vardeman, J. E. and Aldoory, L. (2008) 'A qualitative study of how women make meaning of contradictory media messages about the risks of eating fish', *Health Communication*, 23: 282–91.
Vardeman-Winter, J. E., Jiang, H. and Tindall, N. T. J. (2011) 'Representational, structural, and political intersectionality of public relations' publics', paper presented to the Public Relations Division of the Association for Education in Mass Communication and Journalism, St Louis, MO, August.
Vardeman-Winter, J. and Tindall, N. (2010) '"If it's a woman's issue, I pay attention to it": Gendered and intersectional complications in *The Heart Truth* media

campaign', *Prism*, 7(4). Online. Available HTTP: <http://www.prismjournal.org/fileadmin/Praxis/Files/Gender/VardemanWinter_Tindall.pdf> (accessed 28 February 2013).

Vardeman-Winter, J., Tindall, N. and Jiang, H. (2010) 'The possibilities and realities of studying intersectionality in public relations', paper presented to the Public Relations Division of the Association for Education in Journalism and Mass Communication, Denver, CO, August.

Weber, L. (2001) *Understanding Race, Class, Gender, and Sexuality: A Conceptual Framework*, Boston, MA: McGraw-Hill.

—— (2007) 'Future directions of feminist research: New directions in social policy – the case of women's health', in S. N. Hesse-Biber (ed.), *Handbook of Feminist Research: Theory and Praxis*, Thousand Oaks, CA: Sage Publications: 669–79.

Weber, L. and Parra-Medina, D. (2003) 'Intersectionality and women's health: Charting a path to eliminating health disparities', in M. T. Segal, V. Demos and J. J. Kronenfeld (eds), *Gender Perspectives on Health and Medicine: Key Themes*, Advances in Gender Research Series 7, Amsterdam: Elsevier: 181–230.

West, C. and Fenstermaker, S. (1995) 'Doing difference', *Gender and Society*, 9(1): 8–37.

Wrigley, B. J. (2002) 'Glass ceiling? *What* glass ceiling? A qualitative study of how women view the glass ceiling in public relations and communications management, *Journal of Public Relations Research*, 14: 27–55.

—— (2010) 'Feminist scholarship and its contributions to public relations', in R. L. Heath (ed.), *The SAGE Handbook of Public Relations* (2nd edition), Thousand Oaks, CA: Sage Publications: 247–60.

Yuval-Davis, N. (2009) 'Intersectionality and feminist politics', in M. T. Berger and K. Guidroz (eds), *The Intersectional Approach: Transforming the Academy through Race, Class, & Gender*, Chapel Hill: University of North Carolina Press: 44–60.

Zinn, M. B. and Dill, B. T. (1996) 'Theorizing difference from multiracial feminism', *Feminist Studies*, 22: 321–31.

11 Ex-journos and promo girls
Feminization and professionalization in the Australian public relations industry

Kate Fitch and Amanda Third

This chapter examines the experiences of female public relations practitioners in Australia in order to understand the impact of professionalization and feminization on both the identities of individual female practitioners and the industry's professional identity and status. We focus on these experiences during the 1980s because this decade represented a pivotal period for the Australian public relations industry, in which women entered public relations practice in greater numbers and first came to dominate the industry numerically (Rea 2002; Zawawi 2009). Reflective of large-scale transformations in the gendering of work in the Western world, this 'feminization' of public relations is partly attributable to the rise of second-wave feminism, and the consequent entry of increasing numbers of women into the paid workforce (Fitch and Third 2010). At the same time, the status and role of public relations as an occupational practice was rapidly transforming. It gained increasing recognition in the corporate sector, and its domain expanded beyond media relations to include such areas as government relations, investor relations, and corporate communication. This period also witnessed, as part of broader attempts to improve the professional standing of the industry, the increasing introduction of public relations to universities as a programme of study, and the implementation of practitioner examinations by the Public Relations Institute of Australia (PRIA). These twin processes of feminization and professionalization have framed professional discourses around public relations, and the gendering of the field continues to have a significant impact on its professional identity.

Considering the personal experiences of women practitioners during this decade allows us to understand how the gendered tensions shaping the public relations industry intersected with its increasing professionalization. We draw on interviews with women who were involved in the public relations industry in Australia during this time. We asked participants to reflect upon their everyday experiences as practitioners and their perceptions of the impact of gender on their careers. This approach enabled us to reflect upon the ways in which feminization and professionalization have impacted on individual female public relations practitioners' identities. Further, the analysis of this data provides a window on how those same processes have impacted upon the identity of the public relations profession.

Investigating Australian female practitioner perspectives in the 1980s: research design

Between August and October 2011 we interviewed six female practitioners who worked in public relations in Australia in the 1980s, using in-depth, semi-structured interviews to elicit the perceptions and insights of the participants. Interviewees were recruited by a snowball sampling technique, yielding a small sample of high-profile women in the field. Their insights must be understood through the lens of these women's success. That is, the way that these women understood both their own identities as professional women and the identity of the public relations profession may differ significantly from the understandings of women who either left the industry before they established a reputation or enjoyed less professional success.

The participants had diverse experiences and backgrounds. Collectively, they worked in New South Wales, Victoria and Western Australia, although some of their campaigns, clients and activity were national or interstate. Two participants had international experience (in the UK and the US) prior to, or during, the 1980s. Although it was not a requirement for this study, all participants were members of the professional association, the PRIA, in the 1980s. All but one served on state or national councils, and some as state or national presidents (although some held these positions after the 1980s). We conducted in-depth face-to-face interviews with two participants and telephone interviews with four participants. Interviews, lasting on average ninety minutes, were recorded and transcribed. Participants had the opportunity to review and, if necessary, amend their transcripts, allowing a member check (Lincoln and Guba 1985). We invited participants to talk about their attitudes, perceptions and experiences regarding events that occurred three or even four decades prior to the interviews. It is not surprising, then, that some participants struggled to remember precise dates and timelines. We sought to clarify dates in the interviews, and later through email, and to cross-check dates and other information to validate the information provided by participants.

Drawing upon our different disciplinary backgrounds in public relations and feminist cultural studies, we used the participants' perspectives to inform our understanding of how the professional identity of public relations was constructed in the 1980s, and to identify themes and patterns in how female practitioners negotiated their professional identity. We then compared and discussed our initial identification of themes emerging from analysis of the data, and re-analysed the data. We adopted a critical approach, avoiding the assumption that an interview provides an accurate insight into participants' innermost thoughts (Atkinson and Silverman 1997; Daymon and Holloway 2011). Rather, we approached oral history as useful for understanding 'the lived experience of ... women's ... history' (Thomson 2007: 52), which we believe is ill-documented in standard evolutionary histories of public relations in Australia (see, for example, Morath 2008; Zawawi 2009). While we acknowledge that asking participants about their experiences and perceptions in the 1980s relies on memory, which has almost certainly been influenced by their continuing and long-term participation in the public relations industry (all but one still work in, or recently retired from, public relations), we draw on Thomson to argue interviews encourage 'active remembering and meaning-making' (2011: 88). Therefore, the stated experiences of the participants, even interpreted through the lens of their later experiences in public relations, offer valuable insights into the construction of personal and professional identity.

The gendering of work in Australia in the 1980s

To understand the links between feminization and professionalization, and the shifts in the professional identity of Australian public relations immediately before and during the 1980s, it is important to situate them within broader societal shifts around women and work in the same era.

In the 1970s, second-wave liberal feminism's calls for equal opportunity led to widespread social change with a rapid rise in numbers of women pursuing higher education and entering the paid workforce. As Currie notes, 'the overall participation rate of women in work increased from 40 percent in 1970 to 45 percent in 1980 to 52 percent in 1990' (1990: 1). However, despite the overall increase in women entering the Australian labour market, women 'still worked in a strongly sex-segregated market and under job conditions men would have rejected' (p. 2). Currie's longitudinal study of 1984 graduates' incomes and careers in Australia between 1986 and 1990 found not only that the labour market was sex-segregated in that 'women were relegated to subordinate positions' but that women working in the same kinds of jobs in the same fields as men earned less and received fewer fringe benefits (p. 20). Similarly, Curthoys (1987) found that gender played a significant role in job segregation across occupations and industries. She notes in the public service, 'men tended to enter the administrative positions with good avenues for advancement, women continued to enter the clerical jobs which had few avenues for promotion' (p. 11). However, while women found new professions, such as public relations, offered fewer barriers to entry (for example, a US publication, *Careers for Women in the 70's*, identified public relations as offering significant opportunities for women with a college education [US Department of Labor 1973]), institutional barriers to career progression for women increased as these professions matured (Gower 2001).

Research investigating the impact of feminization on professional identity suggests complex responses in a range of fields. Feminized occupations such as teaching (Acker 1989) and nursing (Witz 1992; Rafferty 1996) struggled to gain professional recognition and experienced declining salaries in the 1980s and 1990s. In a more recent example, the ways in which female journalists are accommodated in Australian newsrooms is arguably gendered (North 2009), with male journalists linked with higher-status stories and hard news (Cann and Mohr 2001), acknowledged more through the use of by-lines, and better represented at senior levels (Strong and Hannis 2007).

Greater numbers of women assuming public relations roles in the 1980s did not produce substantive changes in the gender relations underpinning work cultures. Rather, the incorporation of women contained the feminist challenge to patriarchal order. Research into gender in public relations highlighted gender inequities, particularly in terms of salaries, status and roles (see, for example, Broom 1982; Broom and Dozier 1986; Cline *et al.* 1986; Serini *et al.* 1997; Toth and Cline 1989; Toth and Grunig 1993; Weaver-Lariscy *et al.* 1994). More recent research explores how this gendering continues to influence the professional identity of public relations. For example, Tsetsura (2011) investigated how female practitioner discourses around 'women's work' and a 'real job' shape perceptions of public relations in Russia. In Germany, Fröhlich and Peters (2007) found many practitioners reproduce stereotypical discourses, concluding that the feminization of agency work results in its lower status.

With the feminization of public relations in the 1980s in Australia, there was renewed interest in professionalization (Fitch and Third 2010), with attempts to define it as a strategic practice and management discipline (Hatherell and Bartlett 2006). The processes of professionalization resulted in an industry whose labour is stratified along gendered axes. An increase in the number of women employed, and indeed the over-representation of women in highly feminized fields, such as public relations, does not mean that gender is no longer an issue. Rather, feminization masks 'the continuing reality of gender inequality' (Rea 2002: 2).

One way of framing the feminization of public relations is to interpret it through the theoretical lens of gendered readings of professionalization. Drawing on sociological approaches allows us to recognize occupational attempts to gain professional status (Pieczka and L'Etang 2006), by 'defin[ing] and control[ling] their work' (Macdonald 1995: 5). As feminist scholars have noted, processes of industry professionalization frequently operate to marginalize women and their work (Witz 1992; Davies 1996). The concept of profession is embedded in 'a specific historical and cultural construction of masculinity and a masculinist vision of professional work ... repressing ... those qualities culturally assigned to femininity' (Davies 1996: 661, 669). It is therefore important to recognize professions as processes of occupational closure that marshal exclusionary and demarcatory strategies to control access to and regulate professional practice, reinforcing gender boundaries (Witz 1992).

As one example, the masculinity of the professions has played out in the demarcation of 'the professional' from 'the technical', resulting in 'an occupational division of labour' (Witz 1992: 47), and this is visible in feminized occupations. As Davies (1996: 663) writes:

> A central issue for an understanding of gender and profession in the contemporary era turns not so much on the *exclusion* of women, but on a particular form of their *inclusion*, and on the way in which this inclusion is masked in a discourse of gender that lies at the heart of professional practice itself.

In public relations, the demarcation is evident in the split between management and technical functions, and between professional and technical tasks, first outlined in Grunig and Hunt's (1984) models of public relations and later refined in the research by Broom (1982) and Broom and Dozier (1986) into public relations 'roles'.

From a gender perspective, it is significant that the professionalization of public relations gained momentum in the 1980s. At this time, the increase in women working in public relations threatened the industry's claim to be a legitimate profession and the role and influence of public relations in organizational and corporate settings (Fitch and Third 2010). Drawing on Davies (1996) and Witz (1992), we investigate the ways in which women practitioners negotiated their professional identities in the decade the industry was rapidly feminizing. We also consider the impact of feminization on the professional status of public relations, and the particular ways in which women were included.

The experience of gendered public relations work environments in the 1980s

Three participants – hereafter referred to by number – commenced their careers in public relations in the 1970s. Although the focus of this chapter is primarily the 1980s, it was difficult for participants to discuss their experiences in public relations in that decade without a discussion of their career prior to that time. These three women entered the field from diverse backgrounds: stenography/secretarial work (1); university education and marketing (2); and university education and diplomacy (3). In the 1970s, public relations was primarily perceived as publicity and promotion: 'And how you got experience was on the job. I didn't have any journalistic skills, and a lot of people ... came out of jobs like secretarial roles into publicity' (1).

The other participants, all university educated, began working in public relations in the 1980s, with backgrounds in journalism (4); academic research (5); and publishing (6). Despite the diverse backgrounds of the study participants, the most common route into public relations was journalism, and this was perceived to skew the gender composition of the industry:

> When I started in the early eighties, I came from a journalistic career, which was more commonly the way people came into the profession. Not surprisingly, most of the people who came into the profession were men; there weren't that many women coming into the profession from journalism.
>
> (Participant 4)

Women also entered public relations via marketing, as they could build on their understanding of 'customer relationships' and 'consumer behaviour' (5). Two participants described their move into public relations as 'accidental', expressing surprise at their ability to get public relations work without formal training or experience, and attributing their success to personality or common sense:

> Then I took a job which was a more serious job now, but keep in mind I've had no formal training during all of this, it's all pure instinct, intuition, common sense, and learning from the journalists in the early days.
>
> (Participant 1)

> I'm a natural, I'm quite outward going, I'm an extrovert, I've got lots of energy, I enthuse people, without even thinking about it … it's not something I've had to work at at all … I love communicating with people.
>
> (Participant 6)

These comments confirm research findings which show practitioners' understandings of professionalism focus on personality and their ability to serve clients (van Ruler 2005) and perceptions that women, as 'natural born communicators', are well suited to public relations (Fröhlich and Peters 2007). These interviewees framed their capacities in terms of 'feminine' abilities such as 'intuition' and 'instinct', constructing their employability in terms of gendered, personal characteristics.

Nearly all the participants found in their early careers that professional women were a minority:

> I was absolutely unique … to have a woman there at that time who wasn't a secretary. The librarian was a woman too, but other than that I really don't think there was anybody else.
>
> (Participant 2)

> I was the only woman [in the agency] and the office manager, she was of course a woman. She did the accounts, that was a woman's job. She did the books; she made sure that all the correspondence was done. She also made the cups of tea.
>
> (Participant 5)

The participants reported a range of experiences which we can identify as strategies of demarcation and exclusion in operation (Witz 1992), sometimes in highly subtle ways. For example, one participant hinted at the way her work was aligned with secretarial duties through physical proximity:

> It was a very male corporate workplace and there was one other woman who worked quite closely to me who was ... the PA to the Managing Director and she and I had offices quite close.
> (Participant 6)

Strategies of exclusion were often explicit, with several participants citing examples, especially from early in their careers. The following comment, which relates to the 1970s, is compelling:

> The brewing industry was very male dominated, the business was literally conducted over a glass of beer, the company had a bar where everybody would go ... but, of course, women weren't allowed there.
> (Participant 2)

This exclusion continued into the mid- to late 1980s, although more subtly: 'So I was the only woman, yet again, on a board of five blokes, who told ribald jokes at the board table' (4).

Not surprisingly, few participants had female role models. One notable exception was a participant who worked with a highly regarded female public relations practitioner from overseas:

> They brought out a woman from New York ... who was a public relations specialist, she was about forty years of age and had worked for many different companies and really was just amazing to have in Australia and I was employed to be her graduate assistant ... She was incredibly professional ... She was also very strategic and very creative and was highly regarded by the men in the centre and was called in for all sorts of problems, not just the promotional aspects but right through to the regulatory and corporate affairs side.
> (Participant 2)

In contrast to the corporate world, the public sector offered significant employment and management opportunities. One participant described her work in a 'predominantly female' government department after several corporate roles in the 1970s:

> Now that was a very different environment in that they had a marketing services department and it was run by a woman ... I went there as a marketing projects officer looking at special projects and really writing strategy for them and managing a variety of campaigns ... I think

> it probably took less than a year [before] I was ... in a managerial role, managing twenty people.
>
> (Participant 2)

However, the same participant described a stratified and gendered working environment in the public sector with a separate 'public affairs section which was run by a gentleman ... because our work was very public education/ promotional' (2). Thus, this participant suggests even government had two kinds of public relations work: public affairs – 'they were really the ones who were dealing with the company's CEO and the ones that were working on the big issues' (2) – and marketing communications, which was predominantly run by women. This observation evidences the strategies of demarcation shaping public relations roles that were emerging in the late 1970s and early 1980s, and supports the thesis that gender had a significant impact on the status of different kinds of public relations activity.

Understanding the ways our participants experienced their work as gendered, we now consider the ways that gendering shaped the identity of the public relations profession more broadly.

Identity of PR: tensions around the professional standing of PR and its changing role

On the one hand, the diversity of entry points allowed women to make careers in public relations and this was a significant factor in the feminization of the industry. On the other hand, given that professions are defined in part precisely through the regulation of education and membership, the lack of a credentialing process undermined the professional standing public relations sought. As we discuss later in this chapter, the industry responded by successfully lobbying for tertiary qualifications in public relations and regulating practitioner accreditation via a professional body, the PRIA. However, the perception that public relations was 'not quite a profession' endured, offering a sense of the complex ways in which feminization and professionalization resonated together in the 1980s.

Our participants noted that the dominance of (mostly male) former journalists had a profound effect on the ways in which public relations was understood and practised:

> In the seventies [public relations] was almost all done by ex- or failed journos who thought it was about media relations and about mates that they knew who'd write up the story for them if they could get them to have lunch and flog the line to them and so it was seen as a bit of graft.
>
> (Participant 5)

> The majority of public relations people in [Australian city] in the eighties were ex-journalists. That was one of the things that [male boss]

I think didn't like about me ... that I hadn't been a journalist, I didn't have that background of media, because a lot of the PR consultants had come from journalism and they thought PR was media.

(Participant 6)

These observations suggest media relations was coded as masculine and, along with corporate affairs, was a significant and high-status area of public relations activity. Given the dominance of male ex-journalists in the early and mid-1980s, the gender of one participant who applied for a role in corporate affairs was considered a problem by the prospective employer:

'One of the things that you're going to have to do is every night after work or a couple of times a week you'd have to go down to the Exbar opposite the *Herald and Weekly Times* newspaper and drink with the journos' – so he obviously saw that as a weakness in that I was a woman and that I wouldn't be able to do that part of the job as well as the other parts which, with my degrees, I was eminently suited [to do].

(Participant 2)

Further, participants unanimously described public relations in the corporate sector as 'a very male-dominated environment' (3), 'a very blokey, macho environment' (4) and 'totally blokey' (5). Participants, who worked in both the public and corporate sectors found the public sector '1000 per cent' (5) more positive in terms of opportunities for women.

In the 1980s, a broader range of work expanded the understanding of what constituted public relations activity. Participants described engaging in community relations and internal communication (6); research and report writing (2); project managing and writing annual reports and newsletters; and investor relations (3). However, participants identified a discrepancy in status related directly to the kind of public relations work they performed:

I guess I had more of a back-room role ... you're not really taken to the important meetings or allowed to input, or be a part of a lot of the more strategic discussions, you really are just a technician and I was just a technician there.

(Participant 2)

I was ... writing their newsletter ... We were also doing media for [corporation], but [male boss] wouldn't let me touch it because it was his bag. So I got the menial tasks to do, like go and take photographs of the staff and write the newsletter.

(Participant 6)

One participant worked independently in a corporation in the 1980s, before a male manager was appointed to oversee her work:

> They employed him ... as the Public Relations Manager, so he then became my boss. They needed someone – I think, to be quite honest, they needed someone with more journalistic skills and he was an ex-journo and I wasn't. Although I could write corporate material, I wasn't writing media or journalist material.
>
> (Participant 6)

Another participant, who in the 1980s worked in a consultancy, returned from leave to find a male consultant had been appointed:

> I thought to myself, 'What's he doing here?' and [boss] said, 'Well, I've decided to do all of this political stuff and government stuff more directly and so I'm going to get him to run that side of the business.'
>
> (Participant 5)

When the researcher queried whether participant (5) – who had been politically active throughout her career – might have been considered for that role, the participant replied in the negative: 'Well, I was a mum and blokes did ... the "blokes' work"' (5) of public affairs and government relations.

This division of labour draws upon and reproduces a long-standing gendered split between the public (politics and commerce) and the private or domestic (as 'mums', in the words of our interviewee) realms in Western culture (Pateman 1988; Lloyd 1993). An identical strategy of exclusion is at play in participant (5)'s description of the ways that 'the upfront presentation of material' to clients was deemed something appropriate only for male consultants: 'I don't think in all those years I ever went to a pitch.' Her exclusion constitutes a spatial demarcation that relies on a notion of the public space of business as inherently masculine. When asked what kind of work women did, she replied: 'Fast-moving consumer goods, FMCG ... Because it was about soap and make-up and clothing and festivals and race meetings and all the stuff you would see in the women's magazines' (5).

The utility of female practitioners was seen to lie in their capacity to offer insights into the 'peculiarly feminine' experience of domestic consumption and other 'feminine' consumption activities.

One participant described a similar gendered division of labour in an agricultural company:

> I did internal relations, they had some staffing issues, motivational problems ... I did a staff survey ... I had to organize a big staff party.

I wrote a regular newsletter, I organized their corporate functions, but then the sort of more serious stuff, i.e. the media management ... [male name] did. As the manager, he started writing a magazine ... he did more of the farmer liaison ... They didn't send me out to talk to the customers.

(Participant 6)

In this example, the participant performed emotional labour – the emotive work such as negotiation and smoothing of relations thought natural for women, and often found (but rarely acknowledged) in jobs segregated by gender (Guy and Newman 2004) and consequently devalued (Gilligan 1982). Again, we can see a gendered public/private dichotomy at play. In this way, women were not merely excluded from performing particular tasks coded as masculine but actively assigned tasks coded as feminine.

An analysis of the participants' perceptions and experiences reveals a clear demarcation in the roles and status of different kinds of public relations activity, as the industry expanded its domain from promotion and media relations to corporate and strategic work, such as government relations and public affairs. The public relations industry offered many opportunities for women in the 1980s. However, in the experiences of the participants in our study, these opportunities occurred along 'gendered fault lines' (Fitch and Third 2010: 2). Whereas men did the so-called 'serious' work of corporate affairs, strategy development, media management and dealing with external stakeholders, women tended to perform internal and community relations, marketing, promotion and public education roles, and, only later in the 1980s, media relations. Women did have more opportunities in the public sector to move into management positions, albeit – as in the experience of participant (2) – in public education and community relations rather than corporate affairs.

Given the gendering of public relations roles in both corporate and public sectors, it is not surprising that women from the mid- to late 1980s increasingly moved into or established consultancies where there was potentially a broader range of work. However, even then, women tended to work on particular kinds of campaigns, such as fast-moving consumer goods, suggesting women's public relations roles were closely associated with marketing and promotion, arguably lower-status public relations activity, peripheral to strategic and professional public relations practices. In contrast, corporate affairs and government relations – the 'blokey' stuff, as several participants described it – was recognized in public relations scholarship, and in the industry itself, through the professional association, as professional and strategic public relations, and therefore more deserving of full recognition as a management discipline.

The ways in which women were included in public relations work in the 1980s suggests a demarcation along gender lines, in that women and men tended to be assigned different roles and different kinds of public relations work. As we have already noted, such demarcatory strategies are typically found in professional projects in rapidly feminizing occupations (Witz 1992; Davies 1996).

Women negotiating professional identities: dynamics, contradictions and ambiguities

Participants experienced and responded to the gendered constraints of working in public relations in the 1980s in diverse ways. The success of their strategies shaped the ways they actively remembered the impact of gender on their experiences as professional women. Several participants maintained they never faced blatant discrimination. Others described how their professional life unfolded against a backdrop of persistent sexism. For example, one participant described how she operated within a context of 'totally 1950s behaviour, where people drank too much and behaved unacceptably, where some men ... believed that women were inferior' (4).

Whether or not the participants noted explicit gendered obstacles to their professional success, their comments revealed wide-ranging but subtle strategies of gendered demarcation and exclusion at play. For example, despite the increasing work opportunities for women, their prospects for promotion remained limited. One participant claimed that, whilst women today are advancing further in government and agency contexts, a 'glass ceiling' persisted – and still persists – within the corporate sector:

> [It is] very easy to advance in agency and easy to advance in government, but I think in the corporate sector it is still very hard when you look at the number of women who are the top corporate affairs directors. There are very few.
>
> (Participant 2)

Participants reported mixed experiences in terms of negotiating their professional identity. Drawing on our interview material, we identify six key strategies (outlined below) that female practitioners mobilized successfully – either in isolation or in combination – to navigate, and sometimes subvert, the gendered practices underpinning public relations work cultures in the 1970s and 1980s. Remembering our participants' success at negotiating gendered workplace cultures, it is in the context of these same strategies that these women constructed professional identities for themselves as women.

Embracing the 'promotional girl' identity

One way of surviving the gendered structures shaping women's engagement in public relations was to play upon stereotypical notions of femininity. That is, participants sometimes chose to mobilize what Judith Butler (1999) describes as the 'performative' dimensions of binarized gender constructions.

Although one participant constructed an identity that was 'quite conservative', she recognized others 'had to ... be something extra, whether it was wear a miniskirt or wear lipstick' (6). Another described the way she 'always dressed very femininely ... I used to wear a fresh flower every day ... I used to wear very tiny minis. I would use my femininity without realizing that's what I was doing' (1).

For these women, performing classical femininity in the workplace enabled them to present themselves as non-threatening, affording certain kinds of freedom to operate as professional women. Interestingly, these participants were among those who perceived little overt discrimination in their careers.

Tolerating bad behaviour

Another participant reported her determination to further her career necessitated bracketing the inappropriate behaviour of male colleagues and getting on with the job. She noted that, in the 1980s, she prioritized ambition above the desire to respond to sexist behaviour:

> I mean, you've got to remember I was twenty-six, I was in this corporation that was really starting to go places, I could see the job was really starting to open up for me. On most days it was a great day. [Then] you get cornered in a lift by somebody who has had too many glasses of beer, and you sort of think this is just disgusting. Yes, it's unacceptable, he's usually a pretty OK guy that you've worked with, you know it's unacceptable. Nobody said anything in those days. So you just got on with it. And I was so ambitious, I never would have said anything.
>
> (Participant 4)

In this logic, 'getting ahead' equated with tolerating sexist behaviour and working within the gendered structures of power.

Playing like a boy

Another strategy was to downplay one's femininity and adopt a more 'masculine' identity. The following description of the successful, female practitioner recruited from the US in the 1970s is revealing:

> She was a divorcee, she was very good looking, she would use the occasional swear word, really she did a lot. She turned off a lot of men, because she was quite different. Whereas what she was then today would be quite normal in terms of a high-achieving public relations female professional, she was quite different in that she wasn't your normal promotional girl.
>
> (Participant 2)

We can detect the sexual/gender economy underpinning workplace relations in the observation that this woman 'turned off a lot of men'. This strategy, perhaps more than those described earlier, directly confronted the gendered assumptions shaping women's participation in public relations.

Moving to greener pastures

In response to a perceived lack of recognition or financial reward, women often opted for a career move. For example, one participant explained why she left a consultancy in 1987, despite the flexibility it offered:

> I went to [my boss] and said, 'Well, if you can pay [male colleague] that sort of money, you can pay me a lot more,' and he basically said I should be so grateful. He'd been the most accommodating employer. If my children were sick, he would let me go, which was true. He never expected me to be at work in the mornings on the days that I was supposed to drop the kids off to school, it was true ... And so he said on the basis of all those great tolerances that he'd demonstrated that I should be grateful that I had a job.
>
> (Participant 5)

This comment suggests the employer perceived a female practitioner should expect a lower income in exchange for job flexibility. Configuring childcare primarily as a woman's responsibility, masculinity is implicitly reasserted as the precondition for workforce participation.

A change in workplace was often a productive way to circumvent the lack of opportunity: 'I just left and moved on ... but back in the eighties there were a lot of jobs' (1). In part, the opportunities were linked to shifts in the kinds of activity perceived to be public relations, beyond media relations, and in the growth in the corporate sector, creating 'employment opportunities, which were almost all taken up by women' (5).

Opting out: the lure of consultancy

In response to persistent obstacles to promotion within the corporate sector, particularly from the mid- to late 1980s, women increasingly joined or set up consultancies. Consultancy work, like the public sector, appeared to offer more opportunities for women. Participants articulated a sense of feeling more valued for their work:

> I was pretty much running my own show from a very early age, so it must have been much harder for the women in corporate roles. But then going into [corporate client] as somebody who was running your own PR agency, you were seen as quite different to somebody who was working in-house.
>
> (Participant 1)

When you're going in as a consultant, because you're going in from outside and they were paying you externally as a consultant, they then listened to you. So I didn't have the problems that people in-house had.

(Participant 3)

Positioned outside the formalized structures of power within corporate workplaces, a move into consultancy work was perceived by some participants to offer greater career opportunities, as well as more challenging and diverse work.

Mobilizing the professional body

All participants were members of the PRIA in the 1980s, regarding their membership as an important component of their success. For all the women we interviewed, membership offered a way of asserting and giving substance to their sense of professional identity, and for some it led to recognition via the PRIA's national awards, as winning an award brought significant professional acclaim: 'It was demonstration and recognition of your skill and clients loved it' (5).

The institute offered professional development opportunities, and gave women access to a professional community:

You got involved in that kind of professional circle which was good because you didn't have your own personal network of women because there weren't that many women ... It gave me a network in so much as I think people got to know who I was and that was very useful for me.

(Participant 2)

Thus, the PRIA offered an alternative to the 'old boys' network' of ex-journalists through opportunities to network with other practitioners and share professional knowledge: 'I did it more, I guess, to keep up with best practice and to expand and advance my knowledge' (2). One participant described the value of discussing public relations issues with practitioners in similar roles or industry sectors:

'Say we're putting together a corporate social responsibility programme, how have you done yours at [corporation], it looks fantastic.' And very open, very sharing, 'Oh you really want to look at this', 'Don't forget to do that', or he would ring and say, 'Loved how you handled this crisis.'

(Participant 4)

While the participants credited the PRIA with playing an important role in their individual careers, this did not always mean that women's relationship to the professional association was straightforward. One participant, who joined in 1985, noted the membership was divided between 'smart folks' who were progressive in their thinking about gender dynamics and had a strategic grasp of the field, and 'dinosaurs' who were much more conservative in their attitudes: 'he had a very old blokey school view of how PR was done, and it was that the men meet with the men who run the company. And there weren't many women in his office, it was all blokes' (4).

Industry responses to the feminization of public relations

By the mid-1980s, women comprised a significant percentage of the public relations workforce. There was widespread industry concern that a feminized workforce would devalue the work of public relations and dash attempts to establish it as a profession. While the *individual* women we interviewed appeared to receive mostly strong support from their (male) colleagues within the PRIA's informal mentoring structures, the issue of women *collectively* entering the industry appears to have been a source of anxiety. This anxiety became particularly marked when new tertiary public relations degrees began producing large cohorts of female graduates. One participant was told that women 'are pouring out of the universities' (5) and into public relations, while a second noted 'how many more women were coming into communication public relations courses than males, because it was not seen as a high-paying career track for young males' (3). Another described how these concerns dominated discussions at the PRIA state council:

> So most of the guys were ex-journalists, and not a lot of women went down that track. But once the graduate courses became available, they were predominantly, 96 per cent, women doing the courses, and no guys. And it did become an industry problem, it became a major industry problem, and one that was discussed at numerous meetings.
> (Participant 1)

The number of women graduating with public relations degrees was viewed as problematic for the status of the industry even though, paradoxically, those degree courses had been instituted to help professionalize the industry and enhance its status by insisting upon tertiary qualifications as entry criteria. Our interviewees were in no doubt that the industry's feminization was an ongoing concern within the PRIA in the 1980s, with a perceived need to guard against public relations being thought of as a 'pink profession' (2). This dilemma illustrates the ways the industry's feminization and professionalization sat uncomfortably with one another. Ultimately, the feminization could not be reconciled with the industry's desire for professionalization. Or, to put it differently, precisely because professionalization signifies as masculine, it could not be an antidote to the industry's feminization.

One participant, familiar with US scholarship promoting public relations as a strategic, management discipline, identified why the feminization of public relations in Australia was a concern:

> Our everyday experience was that women were really being more employed as tacticians. That women were the ones that were being employed as the publications officers ... event organizers or as promoters, and weren't really being promoted to the positions that had the most influence within an organization, or the positions where you could be very strategic and be on the same table as the other business functions, be it strategy or finance or legal ... We didn't want PR to be left in that kind of situation where we were very much seen as support people rather than as professionals who really could help an organization achieve its business objectives very strategically.
>
> (Participant 2)

One PRIA state council considered campaigns 'to attract more men into the profession so it would have more equal gender balance – what we could do to run campaigns like "real men *do* work in PR"' (2) while another discussed 'how can we make PR more attractive to young men, so they would ... want to study PR?' (1). Such strategies assumed raising the professional standing of public relations depended upon countering its feminization. The push for professionalization, in this sense, did little to address the structural problem at the heart of public relations' identity crisis: namely, that a feminized field of practice was not valued as a profession, largely because professions are, by definition, masculinized (Fitch and Third 2010).

Nonetheless, the solution to the industry's feminization was commonly thought to lie in its professionalization. One participant linked the expansion and redefinition of public relations through the introduction of rigorous practice standards as a direct response to the industry's feminization:

> Well, because was this going to become a totally feminized industry ... Well, then it would devalue. So the blokes had put a lot of effort into taking it beyond media management into something much more strategic and if it was taken over by women, well, then ... it would be downgraded again.
>
> (Participant 5)

Some participants advocated the need to move away from the personality-driven understandings of professionalism in public relations, seeking instead to establish it as a theoretically grounded profession. The use of research, the development of measurable objectives and a clear communication strategy were perceived as important in repositioning public relations away from promotion, media relations and 'common sense' to a more strategic professional, and indeed 'accountable', practice (5).

The industry's quest for greater professional recognition was underpinned by the fact that university degrees were increasingly viewed as prerequisites for entry into public relations. By the mid- to late 1980s, many employers were seeking university graduates, although not necessarily public relations majors. At the same time, several of the participants in this study were instrumental in the development of university courses in public relations, serving on university industry advisory committees and lobbying to have public relations taught at tertiary level. When asked about the significance of university education for the profession, one participant replied: 'Absolutely critical. We had no methodologies. I used to dream things up on the run' (5).

However, the introduction of more rigorous processes relating to membership and accreditation by the PRIA, as well as raising standards in industry practice, was not always popular, as one participant explained:

> It was blokes, particularly all of the ex-journos who had done an apprenticeship and didn't have any qualifications, feeling that they would be excluded in an accreditation process that demanded that you had qualifications and their argument to me was ... how we would protect those who were already in ... and that's why even when you got your degree you weren't allowed to automatically become a member. You had to do an apprenticeship before you could.
>
> (Participant 5)

Furthermore, another participant described how her PRIA state council threatened to withhold members' fees from the national body, demanding recognition for senior members in the industry who lacked professional qualifications:

> Where you are starting up an organization that hasn't had any formal accreditation, and you have a lot of people in the industry who have a lot of experience, you can't expect them to go and do accreditation exams and things; it's an insult. So I think they are called a grandfather clause, where ... you're recognized in the industry as a leader in the industry, and so on that basis you get your accreditation.
>
> (Participant 1)

These examples demonstrate the ways in which senior practitioners were not required to meet the same standards being demanded of new entrants to the field, who were predominantly women. Such strategies reproduced the gendered hierarchies of power that defined the public relations industry.

The twin processes of feminization and professionalization can be seen in concerns about the professional identity of public relations as women – partly in response to broader societal changes and expectations relating to women, work and education – increasingly found employment in the industry. As public relations, which was initially dominated by ex-journalists and focused on media relations, changed and expanded in response to the growth of the corporate sector, the different job roles were stratified along gendered fault lines, validating Davies' (1996) theory that women's marginalization within the masculine construct of the professions turns upon a particular form of their inclusion, rather than their exclusion.

The response of the professional association, the PRIA, to concerns about the feminization of public relations was to introduce strategies to regulate the field and improve the standards in, and correspondingly the status of, the industry. Our participants identified the need for particular strategies to professionalize the industry by raising standards and regulating membership through accreditation examinations, supporting the introduction of public relations as a university subject, and developing more rigorous practices based on research and evaluation. Ironically, then, through their involvement in the PRIA, the participants in this study were actively involved in establishing what Witz (1992) identifies as exclusionary strategies in the professionalization of public relations.

Conclusion

In this chapter, we have reported on the feminization and professionalization of public relations in Australia in the 1980s, drawing on the perceptions and experiences of six female practitioners. Participants described diverse experiences, particularly in terms of how they negotiated their professional identity, in a decade when ever more women were employed in public relations.

The industry's response to the rapid feminization of public relations was ambiguous. Given concerns that public relations was rapidly becoming a 'pink-collar' occupation and would therefore be devalued in terms of status and salaries, the professional association worked to raise the standard of industry practices through the introduction of public relations to universities and the development of more rigorous membership criteria. At the same time, public relations broadened its range of activities, moving away from an emphasis on promotion and media relations at the start of the 1980s towards corporate communication, investor relations, government relations and public affairs. The feminization of public relations resulted in a demarcation along gender lines between 'professional' and 'technical' roles, and different kinds of public relations activity, with women more likely to work in internal relations, community relations, public education and promotion or marketing. Not surprisingly, these roles were considered to be low status or technical. Meanwhile, men were more likely to do media relations and political and government communication, and advise senior management on corporate strategy. These roles became the high-status, professional activities of public relations.

These findings suggest the link between feminization in the 1980s and the lived realities of women with respect to economic and cultural divisions of labour needs to be understood beyond the limited remit of second-wave liberal feminism. In addition, the strategies of exclusion and demarcation position public relations as a highly gendered industry, where the effects of that gendering occurred in complex and nuanced ways and continue to have ramifications for the public relations industry. The impact of feminization was ambiguous: at the same time as women were offered significant employment opportunities and, in some sectors, pathways into management, the professionalization of the industry resulted in the separation of public relations activity into professional and technical roles where certain roles tended to be marginalized and public relations activity in the corporate sector was perceived as more professional. This process of demarcation relegated what was primarily constructed as 'women's work' to the function of technician or assistant, rather than strategist or manager. At the same time, the drive towards professional recognition led to the development of the PRIA's individual accreditation examinations. However, 'grandfather' clauses ensured existing members were exempt while new graduates still had to serve an apprenticeship before gaining full membership. Such exclusionary strategies have been common in feminizing occupations.

The gendering of public relations must therefore be understood as a complex process, and one response to the feminization of the field. The impact of large numbers of women entering the industry renewed attempts to ensure professional status for public relations and to position it as a strategic and corporate activity. The impact of this gendering continues to shape the professional identity of public relations today, and deserves further research.

Acknowledgements

Our thanks go to Candy Tymson (1), Marjorie Anderson (3), Wendy Yorke (6) and the three participants who chose not to be identified. All six women were enthusiastic contributors to this research and willingly shared their experiences.

References

Acker, S. (1989) *Teachers, Gender and Career*, London: Falmer Press.
Atkinson, P. and Silverman, D. (1997) 'Kundera's *Immortality*: The interview society and the invention of self', *Qualitative Inquiry*, 3(3): 304–25.
Broom, G. (1982) 'A comparison of sex roles in public relations', *Public Relations Review*, 8(3): 17–22.

Broom, G. and Dozier, D. (1986) 'Advancement of public relations role models', *Public Relations Review*, 12(1): 37–56.
Butler, J. (1999) *Gender Trouble: Feminism and the Subversion of Identity*, New York and London: Routledge.
Cann, D. and Mohr, P. (2001) 'Journalist and source gender in Australian television news', *Journal of Broadcasting and Electronic Media*, 45(1): 162–74.
Cline, C., Masel-Walters, L., Toth, E., Turk, J., Johnson, N. and Smith, H. (1986) *The Velvet Ghetto: The Impact of the Increasing Percentage of Women in Public Relations and Business Communication*, San Francisco, CA: IABC Foundation.
Currie, J. (1990) 'Women, wages and the need for pay equity legislation', paper presented at the National Women's Conference, University of Canberra, 30 September.
Curthoys, A. (1987) *Women and Work* (monograph), Hawthorn, Victoria: Curriculum Development Centre.
Davies, C. (1996) 'The sociology of professions and the profession of gender', *Sociology*, 30(4): 661–78.
Daymon, C. and Holloway, I. (2011) *Qualitative Research Methods in Public Relations and Marketing Communications* (2nd edition), London: Routledge.
Fitch, K. and Third, A. (2010) 'Working girls: Revisiting the gendering of public relations', *Prism*, 7(4). Online. Available HTTP: <http://www.prismjournal.org/fileadmin/Praxis/Files/Gender/Fitch_Third.pdf> (accessed 5 October 2011).
Fröhlich, R. and Peters, S. (2007) 'PR bunnies caught in the agency ghetto? Gender stereotypes, organizational factors, and women's careers in PR agencies', *Journal of Public Relations Research*, 19(3): 229–54.
Gilligan, C. (1982) *In A Different Voice: Psychological Theory and Women's Development*, Cambridge, MA: Harvard University Press.
Gower, K. (2001) 'Rediscovering women in public relations: Women in the *Public Relations Journal*, 1945–72', *Journalism History*, 27(1): 14–21.
Grunig, J. and Hunt, T. (1984) *Managing Public Relations*, New York: Holt, Rinehart and Winston.
Guy, M. and Newman, M. (2004) 'Women's jobs, men's jobs: Sex segregation and emotional labor', *Public Administration Review*, 64(3): 289–98.
Hatherell, W. and Bartlett, J. (2006) 'Positioning public relations as an academic discipline in Australia', *Asia Pacific Public Relations Journal*, 6(2): 1–13.
Lincoln, Y. and Guba, E. (1985) *Naturalistic Inquiry*, Newbury Park, CA: Sage.
Lloyd, G. (1993) *Man of Reason: 'Male' and 'Female' in Western Philosophy*, Minneapolis: University of Minnesota Press.
Macdonald, K. (1995) *The Sociology of the Professions*, London: Sage Publications.
Morath, K. (2008) *Pride and Prejudice: Conversations with Australia's Public Relations Legends*, Elanora, Queensland: Nuhouse Press.
North, L. (2009) 'Gendered experiences of industry change and the effects of neoliberalism', *Journalism Studies*, 10(4): 506–21.
Pateman, C. (1988) *The Sexual Contract*, Cambridge: Polity.
Pieczka, M. and L'Etang, J. (2006) 'Public relations and the question of professionalism', in J. L'Etang and M. Pieczka (eds), *Public Relations Critical Debates and Contemporary Practice*, Mahwah, NJ: Lawrence Erlbaum Associates: 265–78.
Rafferty, A. (1996) *The Politics of Nursing Knowledge*, London: Routledge.
Rea, J. (2002) 'The feminisation of public relations: What's in it for the girls?', paper presented at *Communication: Reconstructed for the 21st Century*, proceedings of

the Australia and New Zealand Communication Association International Conference, Gold Coast, Queensland, 10–12 July. Online. Available HTTP: <http://www.anzca.net/conferences/anzca02.html>.

Serini, S., Toth, E., Wright, D. and Emig, A. (1997) 'Watch for falling glass ... women, men and job satisfaction in public relations: A preliminary analysis', *Journal of Public Relations*, 9(2): 99–118.

Strong, C. and Hannis, G. (2007) 'The visibility of female journalists at Australian and New Zealand newspapers: The good news and the bad news', *Australian Journalism Review*, 29(1): 115–25.

Thomson, A. (2007) 'Four paradigm transformations in oral history', *Oral History Review*, 34(1): 49–70.

Thomson, A. (2011) 'Memory and remembering in oral history', in D. Ritchie (ed.), *The Oxford Handbook of Oral History*, New York: Oxford University Press: 77–95.

Toth, E. and Cline, C. (eds) (1989) *Beyond the Velvet Ghetto*, San Francisco, CA: IABC Foundation.

Toth, E. and Grunig, L. (1993) 'The missing story of women in public relations', *Journal of Public Relations Research*, 5(3): 153–75.

Tsetsura, K. (2011) 'Is public relations a real job? How female practitioners construct the profession', *Journal of Public Relations Research*, 23(1): 1–23.

US Department of Labor (1973) *Careers for women in the 70's*, Washington, DC: Women's Bureau, Employment Standards Administration, Department of Labor.

van Ruler, B. (2005) 'Professionals are from Venus, scholars are from Mars', *Public Relations Review*, 31: 159–73.

Weaver-Lariscy, R., Cameron, G. and Sweep, D. (1994) 'Women in higher education public relations: An inkling of change?', *Journal of Public Relations Research*, 6(2): 125–40.

Witz, A. (1992) *Professions and Patriarchy*, London: Routledge.

Zawawi, C. (2009) 'A history of public relations in Australia', in J. Johnston and C. Zawawi (eds), *Public Relations: Theory and Practice* (3rd edition), Crows Nest, New South Wales: Allen and Unwin: 26–46.

Index

abortion 185, 189
accessorizing 22, 29, 32, 38
account handlers 92–4, 96
activism: as fashionable 116; hostility towards 13; identity strategies for 111; privileged groups in 118; research on 108–9, 161–2; use of term 109–10
actresses 72
ACTU (Australian Council of Trade Unions) 199, 215
addictions, respectable 52–3, 62n4
advocacy, and public relations 12–13, 194
advocacy groups, and migrant workers 210, 212
affirmative action 70–1
African-American/black people, in public relations work 71–2, 74–5, 77–8
African-American/black women: and breast cancer 223, 234–5, 237–8; sexuality of 227; social issues of 226
age discrimination 72, 78, 144, 150
ageism 72, 144–6, 148
agency directors 93–4, 96–8, 101, 103–4
AgResearch 118–19, 125
American Cancer Society (ACS) 222–3, 235, 237
Amnesty International 159, 163, 165, 169, 172
Anderlini, Sanam 162, 168–9, 171
anger 96, 98
Aquino, Benigno 191–2
Ashby, James 36–7, 39–40, 41n2
Australia: economic transformation of 199–200; gendering of work in 249–50; non-standard employment in 216n1; paid and unpaid labour in 203; power relations in media 30;

public relations industry in 247, 249, 263; sexual harassment in 21–2, 30–1, 34–7; textile homeworkers in 209–12; trade union movement in 198–9, 203, 211, 214–15 *see also* Western Australia
authority: fictional re-distribution of 98; modality of 29, 40
AWatW (Asian Women at Work) 210, 212, 216

B2B (business-to-business) 95
Baillie, Georgina 144
BBC: conventions of presentation 137–9; corporate culture of 149–50; financing of 134–5; media opposition to 135–6, 148; reputational crises at 132–3, 135–6, 140–2; women presenters in 144–7, 149
Beijing Declaration and Platform for Action 159
Bernas, Joaquin 186
binary dualisms 69
birth control 188
blackmail 27
body, vulnerability of 121
Bourdieu, Pierre 50, 204, 61n1
Brand, Russell 133–4, 138–9, 142–4, 149, 150n4
branding: origins of 134; personal *see* personal brands
brand values, protecting 133
breast cancer screening guidelines: changes in 221–3, 238–9; communications on 236–8, 240, 242n8; and ethnic identity 235–6; and gender identity 229, 233–4; research on 231–3, 232
breasts, mother's 117–18

brinkmanship 102
broadcasting, charismatic norms in 137
business leadership 71
Butler, Judith: on gender 88; on language 61n1; on sexual harassment 21; and gender construction 22–3; and sexual hierarchy 20; and sexuality 24

capitalism: authority in 29, 33; identity construction in 201; public relations in 23; reification of 11
care, ethics of 11, 46, 55–61
career advancement: barriers to 67; and social sexuality 11, 39; suitability for 103
careers, strategies for navigating 79–81
care work 203
carnivalesque 112, 137, 143, 147
cash-in-hand work 200, 206–8, 215
casual workers 198, 202
Catholic Church: in the Philippines 178, 181–2, 189–90; and reproductive health 13, 185–7
cattle, transgenic 118
Caucasian/white people: in activism 118; and affirmative action 70; and employment barriers 80; in leadership 71–2, 81; norms created by 68; in public relations 67, 69, 71
Caucasian/white women: and breast cancer 222–3; Latino attitudes to 77; in PR 67; as privileged 6, 14, 235–6
CBCP (Catholic Bishops Conference of the Philippines) 178, 181–2, 186–7, 190, 193, 195n14
CEDAW (Convention on the Elimination of All Forms of Discrimination against Women) 158
celebrities, sexualization of 133
celebrity, gendered power relations of 136, 139
celebrity branding 132, 134, 137, 142–3, 149
celebrity careers 132
celebrity idealization 139, 149
celebrity status, achieving 134
childcare 51, 53, 65, 260
CHIPs 234, 241n4
Church–State separation 182
civil disobedience 186, 189–90
CJD (Creutzfeld–Jakob disease) 115
cleavage 22, 26, 33

clients: challenging 98–9; education of 96; emotions of 97–8
clothes-body complex: and acculturation 25–7; fixed identity in 40; and job interviews 30; and lifestyle 33; and public relations 22; as text 11
clothing: casual 93; as creative expression 40
Cohn, Carol 162, 166–7
colonialism 11, 177, 179–80, 193
color-blindness 71–2
comedy 137–8, 141, 143
Commission on the Status of Women (CSW) 164
communication: and cultural gaps 221; political intersectionality of 230; sexy 32, 38–9; strategic 108, 126, 168
communication management strategies 161, 163, 173
communication styles 70
community relations 59, 255, 257, 265
consciousness, bifurcated 8
consent: creating 3–4; orchestrating 7
constructionist studies 92
consumption: as activism 117–18; and gender 49
contestation 110, 125
contraception 21, 184–5, 189–90, 192–3
Coomaraswamy, Radhika 160, 162, 172
core brand values 135, 146, 149
corporate branding 134
corporate social responsibility (CSR) 62n3, 210–11, 261
cowgirl image 118–19, 121–6
Craven, John 145–6
creative innovation 132, 135, 138, 147, 150
creative risk 134–5, 141
credentialing, in public relations 254
Crenshaw, Kimberlé 68
critical-cultural studies 225
critical feminism 1, 6, 9–11, 14–16
Critical Race theory (CRT): and intersectionality 68–9, 226; and public relations 14, 71, 81
critical scholarship 6
CSW (Commission on the Status of Women) 164
cultural gaps: policymaker–public 221, 240–1; use of term 230
cultural intermediaries 11, 46–51, 55, 59–61, 61–2n2, 65
cultural meanings, shared 225
cultural studies model 225

Currie, Alannah 115–16, 124–5
cyborg image 119

Daily Mail 140, 147–8, 154
David Jones department store 22, 34–5
decision-making, gender in 240
DEDAW (Declaration on the Elimination of Discrimination against Women) 158
deep acting 98, 103
democracy, and public relations 3–4
democratic deficit 199
developing countries 27, 188, 193, 200
disability, and gender 15
disciplinary myopia 6
discourse: commoditization of 3; construction of 186–7; corporate 11; hegemonic struggles in 166, 173; organizational 11, 46; in public relations 11–12, 166; as social practice 181; subversive patterns of 12; transforming 13
discourse representation 181
discrimination: legislation against 71; and public relations 11, 72, 78–9
discursive communities 206, 214–15
disruptive space 112
diversity: and the BBC 133–4, 136, 138, 145; challenging use of term 81–2, 87; as marketing ploy 68
diversity training 76–7
Dixon, Alexha 145
Douglas, Lesley 142
dress codes 32–3
DSWP (Democratic Socialist Women of the Philippines) 186–7
Dyfan, Isha 162, 169

eating, cultural representations of 116–17
Edinburgh Television Festival 135–6
elites: and media hegemony 181, 194; in transnational advocacy 161
emotional labour: obscuring role of 57; of professionals 88–9; in public relations 12, 87–8, 91, 93, 102–4; as women's work 257
emotion management 98, 102, 104
emotions, validation of 58
empathizing 98–9, 102
employment, non-standard 199–200, 215
English language classes 211–12, 215

Entwhistle, George 132, 136, 142, 150n5
ERA (Equal Rights Amendment), defeat of 2
ERMA (Environmental Risk Management Authority) 118
essentialism, strategic 168, 170
essentialization 82, 112, 114
ethical behaviour 27–8
ethics, in public relations 40–1, 60
ethnic identity, self-described 74
ethnicity in, in public relations 71
ethnic minorities: in public relations 68–9, 241n1; women from 228
everyday life, salience of 225
Excellence Theory 68, 81
exclusion, in public relations 12

face-to-face lobbying 170–1, 173
FairWear Campaign 201, 209–13, 216
false positives 235, 242n6
family planning 188–9, 191–2
fashion: and gender 25–6; as social practice 20, 22, 41
feeling rules 88, 94, 101
Feltex Carpets 205–8, 215
female body: domination and control over 13, 127; in health policy 240; naked 109, 112–13, 119–23, 125–6; in women's activism 112–14
female genital mutilation 169
feminine fallacy 223
femininity: and caring 204; distancing from 102; performing classical 258–9; policitized use of 14
feminism: essentialism in 168; impact of 1–3; liberal 82, 92, 179; and MAdGE 115; postcolonial 177–80, 187–8, 192, 194–5; and public relations practice 224; as research standpoint 6–9; second wave of 3, 21, 111, 247, 249; and sexuality 24
feminization: and demarcation 258; and professionalization 12, 247, 249–51, 262–3, 265; use of term 79
Feminization Theory 69–70
focus group research 127n2
food, and ethnic identity 228
Ford, Anna 144–5
Fourth UN World Conference on Women 158–9
framing: of difference 67; and lobbying 170; process of 165
Fraser-Kirk, Kristy 34–40
functionalism 29, 40–1

Index

gay men, and sexual harassment 11, 22, 39
GE (genetically engineered) products 108–9, 114–20, 122–5
gender: carnivalesque disruptions of 137; construction of 20, 22, 38; and cultural intermediation 50–1; intersections of 7; as pivoting identity 227–8, 238; and power struggle 225; problematization of 6, 10–11, 16; in public relations thinking 4–5, 24–5, 27; and salaries 69; teaching of 104; use of term 47–8, 88; Western intellectual tradition of 15
gender biases 5–6, 78, 80
gender conformity 20, 24
gender displays 89, 95
gendered identities 20–1, 47, 60
gendered performance: in PR consulting 99, 103; in service occupations 87
gendered policies 222
gendered relationships 34, 41, 221
gender identity: binary opposition of 144; in global sphere 54; literature on 89–90; negative effects of 75–6, 79; as ongoing project 88; and organizational leadership 70; and policymaking 222; in PR consulting 89–90, 102–3
gender inequality: in corporate jobs 72; and feminization 250; perpetuation of 26, 38
gender performance: sexual aspects of 11; in the workplace 29, 258–9
gender performativity 25, 38, 41, 103
gender representations, in Australian media 30
gender research 1, 3, 6, 16, 224
gender roles, and emotional labour 89
Germany 6, 91, 250
Gibbings, Sheri 162, 164–5, 168, 171–2
glass ceiling, in public relations 69, 72, 74, 80–1, 258
globalization: affluent professionals under 52; gender in 54–5; structure of values under 60; victims of 201
globalization discourses 47, 55
'gold digger' 35, 39
Greenham Common 112
guilt 46, 58, 66, 190

habitus 22, 26, 31, 38
Harding, Sandra 8

health communication: effectiveness of 236–7; and policymaking 239
health communications, gendered 15, 225–6, 233–4
hegemonic power 166
hegemony: construction of 26, 230; forms of 25
heteronormativity 23–4, 39
Hill, Felicity 162, 164, 167, 169
HMOs 242n5
homeworkers 200–1, 209–13
homosexuality, and sexual harassment 37–8
human rights: in trade union campaigns 203; universal 178, 184
human rights lobbying 163–4
Human Security Network 166–7
Hunt, Jay 147–8

identities: intersecting 15, 225–7, 241; marginal 216; overlapping 241n3
identity work: in public relations 95, 101; use of term 87–8
ideological domination 25
image repair 136, 146
impression management 134
independent production companies 138–9, 143, 149
indigenous elites 180
individual experience, subversive accounts of 12, 15
individual standpoint 8–9
inequality, sexualized forms of 20, 23, 38
informal sector 200
information subsidies 162, 173
injustice, problematization of 6
innovation, in public relations 29–30
international organizations 166, 172–3
internet, Catholic Church use of 187
intersectionality: and health policy 235, 238–40; as research lens 67–9, 72; social realms of 228–9; use of term 226–7
intertextuality 31, 38, 181
IPPRP (Interfaith Partnership for the Promotion of Responsible Parenthood) 185
IR (international relations) 160, 163, 166

Jackson, Janet 227
James, P. D. 145
jejemon vocabulary 187
job interviews 30

journalism: gender norms in 138; and public relations 252, 254–5, 262
journalists: female 192, 250; relationships with 99–101

Kinsella, Helen 162, 167–8
knowledge, gender-biased systems of 7–8
Ku Klux Klan, women in 111

labour, sexualisation of 28
labour market, women's experiences in 202, 206–8
labour relations 198–9, 202
Lagman, Edcel 178, 181, 190
language, and public relations 61n1
Latinas/Latinos, and sexual harassment 77
leadership, and gender 74–5
leadership styles 71
Leveson Inquiry 142
licence fee 133–6, 138, 140–1
lifestyle public relations 33, 40
Likhaan Center for Women's Health 183, 187, 189, 191, 195n6
little black dress (LBD) 22, 32
lived experience: and knowledge 48; and public relations 9–11; as research category 73; and women's history 249
low-paid work, narratives on 209

MacKinnon, Catharine 2, 20–1, 38
MAdGE (Mothers Against Genetic Engineering) 108, 114–16, 118–21, 123–7
male sexuality 144
mammograms 222–3, 237–8, 240
management consulting, discourses in 89, 99
man's jobs 27
Maori culture 120–4, 126
marginalized groups 12, 110, 204, 222, 229, 238
marketing, and public relations 252
Martin, Florence 169
masculine performance 142, 149, 178
masculinity, and professionalization 263
masculinized thinking 7–8
maternity mortality ratios (MMR) 183
McInnes, Mark 34–5
meaning, construction of 8
media relations, as masculine 254–5
Medicaid 234, 241n4

men: as celebrities 140, 142; as entrepreneurs 79–80; gender identity of 89–90; identity work of 102; as public relations practitioners 16, 70, 74; younger 76–8
migrant communities 211
migrant women workers: and FairWear 209; invisibility of 14, 198–9; in non-standard jobs 200–2, 208–9, 215–16; resistance of 204–5; retrenched from Feltex 206–8; and trade unions 199, 202, 214–15
Millennium Development Goals (MDGs) 183, 186, 188
minorities, use of term 81
MMR (maternity mortality ratios) 183
modernity, late 13, 29
motherhood: and children's health 116–17; voluntary 179; and women's activism 111–12, 114, 126
mothers, identity of 13, 109
multiculturalism, use of term 81
Muna, Maha 162, 164, 167–9, 171

naked protests 113–14, 124, 127
Namibia 170–1
negotiating strategies, gendered 91
neo-liberalism: and the BBC 135; caring under 60–1; and celebrity 139; and gender 30, 51, 57; lifestyle consequences of 49; and political advocacy 163; and population control 192–3; in public relations 46; in Western Australia 48–9
networking 80
News International 135–6, 142
New South Wales 248
New Zealand: anti-GMO campaign in 13, 109, 114–16, 124–5; public surveys in 120–1
NGOs (non-governmental organizations): access of 170, 172; framing processes of 165–6; media reporting on 194; in the Philippines 182, 193; and public relations 12–13; and the UN 160; and union organising 200; women's 156, 161
NGO Working Group 158, 160–5, 167–71, 173n1
non-conformism, imperative to 29–30
norm entrepreneurs 161, 165–6, 169, 173
NZ Advertising Standards Authority (ASA) 109, 119–20, 123–4, 126–7

the objective professional 89, 102
Ofcom 135, 140–1
older women: advice from 80; in broadcasting 133, 144–6, 150; mammograms for 222; political resistance by 149; and workplace discrimination 72, 77
O'Reilly, Miriam 133, 139, 144–6, 148–9
organizational culture 12, 27
organizational inequalities 67, 82
organizational leadership, literature on 70–1
the Other 14, 180, 227

Pacquiao, Manny 186–7
Pakeha 120–4, 127n1
parenthood, responsible 184, 191–3
patriarchy 11, 69, 71
peacekeeping 159, 165, 172
peacemaking 156–60, 165, 167–70, 172
performance, and social movements 112
personal brands 132, 134, 137, 139, 143–4
personal identities 12, 25
personal subjectivities 66
Perth 48–9, 51, 65
petite bourgeoisie 50–1
phenomenology 92
Philippines: colonial legacy of 178, 180; communications strategies in 186–7; media texts from 180–1; politicians in 183; population control in 188–9; religious faith in 181–2; reproductive health in 13; role of family in 185–6, 188, 191, 194
Philippines Reproductive Health Bill *see* RH Bill
Phillips, Arlene 145, 147
policymaking processes 221, 233, 240–1
policy sphere 163, 165
political intersectionality 222–3, 228–31, 240–1
political opportunity structure 166–7
politicized relationships 221
politics, stakeholder consultation in 214
poor women: in Philippines 179, 186, 188–9, 192–3; and UN Security Council 169
population control 183, 188–9, 192–3
postcolonial theory 177
power: in cultural studies 225; problematization of 6; and public relations 13–14; subversion of 25

power hierarchies 7, 14, 71
practitioner–publics gaps 225, 228
practitioners-as-publics 224–5, 239, 241
PR bunnies 17, 27, 91
pressure group politics 164
PR girl image 32, 100, 102
PRIA (Public Relations Institute of Australia) 247–8, 254, 261–6
privilege, and gender 74–5, 79
professional identities: and fashion 23; and feminization 249–50; and gender 88; and professionalism 12; of PR practitioners 58, 258
professionalism: emphasizing 103; gendered 133–4, 137–8, 147–8, 150; hegemonic notions of 12; practitioner understandings of 252; and work clothes 31
professional practice 12, 94–5, 250–1
professional roles 46, 88
professionals: feeling rules for 88–9; salaries of 69
professional women: children of 58; identity of 248; juggling roles 56; as minority 252; sense of guilt 54
professions, gendered notions of 89, 250–1
PRSA (Public Relations Society of America) 69, 82, 110
public holidays 52
public relations: and activism 12–13, 108–10, 126; classic 31–2, 38; critical research in 15–16; and CRT 68; and cultural intermediation 49–50; cultural studies of 225; demarcation of roles in 251, 254, 257–8; effects on individuals 14; effects on relationships 61; as feminized field 67, 69–70, 87–8, 92, 247; frames of difference in 67; as gendered industry 230, 266; and gendered policies 222; history of 249; identity and marginalization in 103, 239–40; inclusion and exclusion in 9; of the NGO Working Group 162–3; political intersectionality in 229; power structures in 81; professional development in 261; professional identity of 248, 250–1, 262–6; progressive and traditional 95; purposive communications of 149–50; and ruling 8; sexualization of work in 23, 32–3; and social change 192–5, 198, 201, 204, 214–15; stakeholder engagement in 202, 213–14; use of

term 3; work–home relationship in 11, 46–7
public relations agencies 73, 76, 78, 93–6, 138
public relations consultancy work 16, 48, 89, 260–1
public relations education 1, 4–6, 104
public relations practitioners: in Australia 49, 247; availability for work 52–3; and celebrity news 139; diversity among 221; emotion management of 102–3; gender roles of 27, 70–2; genders of 224; and globalization discourses 47, 55; identity work of 89, 93–6, 101–2; Latina 71; negotiating relationships 87, 92, 96–101, 103; perceptions of field 27; as relational beings 55–7, 60–1; response to power relations 25; senior 264; on social identities 74–6; surveys of 65–6, 73–4, 92–3; work–family relations of 58
public relations theory 9, 15, 81, 109
public relations workplaces: gendered disadvantage in 14–15, 30–1, 35, 103–4; gender identity in 20, 25, 27–8, 255–6; gender roles in 20–1, 76–8, 89, 253, 265–6; internet tips on 30–3; relationships in 12; sexual harassment in 11, 21–3, 34; sexuality in 28, 38–40; social identity in 79; women's identities in 91
publics: active 201; commodification of 24; gendered 222–5, 231, 233; racialised 226
public sector, woman professionals in 253–5, 257, 260
public service broadcasting 133
public sphere: gender in 51, 62n3; motherhood in 112; statements circulating in 3
Purse Power 117, 120, 125

queen bee syndrome 71

racism 67, 71
Radical Public Relations roundtable 1, 16
rape 157
reformation, public relations used for 11–12
reification 11
Reith, John 136, 150n2
relational practices 89, 99

relational responsibilities 60
relationships, interdependence of 59
representational intersectionality 229
repression, politics of 20, 24
reproduction: control of 179; politics of 185–7
reproductive health: definitions of 184; as human right 178, 191; media texts on 181; and morality 190; role of state in 192; semantic shift from 192–3
reputational damage 135, 138
reputation management, at the BBC 133–4
requisite variety 68–9, 81–2
resistance, dispositions to 204
RHAN (Reproductive Health Advocacy Network) 178, 181–3, 187, 193–4, 195n6
RH Bill 13, 177–8, 181–6, 188–91, 193–4
Rippon, Angela 144
risk reduction, absolute 223
Rolleston, William 119
Ross, Jonathan 133–4, 136, 139, 142–3
Russia 6, 91, 171, 250

Sachs, Andrew 139–40, 144
salary gaps 75, 80, 82
Salonga, Lea 187
Savile, Jimmy 132, 136, 140, 149–50, 150n5
scandals, gender politics of 133
self: gendered 15, 23, 26, 40; promotion of 40
self-confidence 206–8, 215
self-image 14
self-presentation 25–6, 134, 137
self-profiling 94
self-promotion 134, 138
self-reliance 52, 55
selling-in 99–100
service culture 12
sexist behaviour, tolerating 259
sexual assaults 136, 157
sexual domination 20, 26
sexual harassment: and gender performance 11, 21, 23, 38; public reaction to 39; workshops on 77
sexual hierarchy 20, 22–3, 33, 38, 40
sexuality: in Australian media 30; and gender 24; social 11, 21, 24, 38; transgressive 144
sexualization 28, 33, 114, 133–4, 139, 149

sexual rights, protection of 2, 179
sexual violence 21, 156–7, 159–60
shared meanings 205, 214, 226
silences, measuring 179, 194
Slipper, Peter 36–7, 41n2
Smith, Dorothy 7–8, 48
social capital 94, 204, 214
social identity: intersectionalities of 68, 71, 80; and personal identity 25; in public relations 73–4
social identity dimensions 67, 72–3, 76–7, 80, 82
social isolation 202, 211
socialization, and social identity 69, 76, 81
social life: cultural economy of 50; economic capture of 53
social media 96, 194
social spaces 3, 16, 26, 29, 201
softly-softly approach 99
Spivak, Gayatri 168, 177, 179–80
stakeholders: and active publics 201–2; in activism 108; in BBC 132, 134–5; multiplicity of 68; women as 203–4; in workers' organisations 198–200, 214, 216
stationery items 32
Strictly Come Dancing 145, 147
structural intersectionality 229
Stuart, Moira 145
studying up 48
subaltern 177, 179–80, 193, 230
subjects, culturally scripted 25
subordination 2, 23–6, 180
surface acting 97, 103
Susan G. Komen for the Cure 223, 237–8
sweatshops 200, 209–10
symbolic power 50, 126, 204, 216

taste, hierarchy of 147
TCFUA (Textile Clothing and Footwear Union) 202, 205–6, 209–13, 216
technology, gendered attributes of 102
textual analysis 233
'that dress' 33
third UN 160
Thompson, Mark 136, 140–1, 145–6
tokens 82
trade unions: and discursive communities 214; engaging with women 203–4; and migrant workers 211–13; and non-standard employment 200–1, 209, 215–16; and public relations 14, 198–9, 214; and retrenched workers 202, 206–8
transgression: licensed 137; mythopoetic 112
transnational advocacy 12–13, 156, 158, 161, 163–4
trusted advisers 89, 99, 102

union-led campaigns 14, 199–203, 215–16
United Nations: funding of Filipino programmes 188; and women's rights 158–9
United States, breast cancer screening in 221–3
universities, public relations studies in 247, 251, 262, 264–5
UNSC (United Nations Security Council): appropriate discourse for 168–9; and human security 166–7; lobbying of 162–4, 170–1; other important resolutions of 160; Resolution 1325, 13, 156, 159–61, 171–3
USPSTF (US Preventive Services Task Force) 223, 236–7, 239–40

Vanity Productions 143
Victoria 248
Vietnamese homeworkers 201, 209, 211–12
vintage clothing 29, 33
violence, symbolic 60, 61n1
voice, loss of 206, 208
vulnerability, performing 114

war: gender roles in 157–8; sexual violence in 156–7, 159
Weiss, Cora 162, 164, 169, 172
Western Australia 11, 46–9, 51, 56, 59, 248
WFTV (Women in Film and Television) 148
whole person approach 213
WILPF (Women's International League for Peace and Freedom) 159, 162, 164–5
woman: everyday 233, 240; politicized use of word 13–14
woman/man dichotomy 11
woman's jobs 27, 252
women: as activists 109–11, 114; appearance norms for 23–4, 28; and armed conflict 156–9, 167–8;

battle for social rights 2–3; in the BBC 12, 133–4, 136–8, 144–7; in broadcasting 12, 133–4, 136–8, 144–9; as communicators 252; competition between 76; as decision-makers 190–2, 229; differences among 14; and gender studies 241n2; as homeworkers 211; identity work of 101; images of 119–20, 122; intersecting identities of 236, 239; as invisible 201; and leadership 75, 80; lived experience of 7–9; in low-paid employment 199; at management levels 70; and neo-liberalism 54–5; in paid workforce 249; in the Philippines 184–5; and policy communication 234, 236; political use of images of 168–70; and professionalization 251; public relations in lives of 9, 24–5; responses to barriers 79–80; as retrenched workers 207, 215; sexualization of 114; social embedded patterns of abuse 21; Third World 177, 179–80; as TV presenters 12; and the UN 159–60, 167; work–family relationship for 56, 58–9

women of color 67, 80, 243

women PR practitioners: beginning of careers 251–2; career paths of 39, 260; challenge to existing order 250; disadvantage for 69, 74, 258; identities of 224–5, 239, 251, 258–60; perceptions of utility 256–7; in professional associations 261–2; research on 247–9; role and status of 257–8

women's health: and contraception 182, 184; economics of 185, 188–9

women's rights: activists for 158, 168; awareness campaigns on 194; and contraception 182, 184, 190–1; and image of women 168; morality of 185, 189; and trade unions 203; and UNSC 156, 172

women's work 99, 102–3, 203, 250, 266

WorkChoices legislation 203–4

workers: exemplary 54; informal 200, 212–13; organising 201, 211; retrenched 202, 205, 214–15; retrenchment of 202, 205, 214–15

workers' rights campaigns 202–3, 210, 213

work–home relationship: caring practices in 59–60; and gender 51, 56–7; and salaries 69; under neoliberalism 11, 46, 52–5

workplace communities 202

workplaces: clothes and accessories in 26; discrimination in 72, 80; feminized images of 90; gender relations in 21; homogeneity in 68, 70; inequalities in 67, 81–2; in late modernity 29–30; sexualized 40; tenuous connection to 207

young adults 72
young women 11, 104, 139, 183, 192

New eBook Library Collection

Taylor & Francis Group
an **informa** business

eFocus on Gender

30 day free trials available!

Gender has been at the forefront of academic debate for the last four decades and this exciting new resource offers access to some of the most important contributions to the subject. With works by scholars from more than twenty academic disciplines, the work addresses issues such as:

- The rise of feminism
- Masculinity as a distinct area of study
- Women's social, cultural, religious, political and economic position
- Debates around sexuality and identity.

Gender is considered from an international perspective with coverage of both the Western and non-Western worlds.

Contributions from renowned authorities, the very best in academia...

The collection includes some of the most important single contributions to the field, such as Judith Butler's *Gender Trouble* and Patricia Hill-Collins' *Black Feminist Thought*, as well as titles by Hélène Cixous, bell hooks, Victor J. Seidler, Sheila Rowbotham, Haleh Ashfar and Mary Maynard. It also features several key works of reference including the four volume *Routledge International Encyclopedia of Women*.

eFocus on Gender is available as a subscription package with 10 new eBooks added per year.

Order now for guaranteed capped price increase.

Recommend this package to your librarian today!

www.ebooksubscriptions.com

For a complete list of titles, visit:
www.ebooksubscriptions.com/eFocusGender

For more information, pricing enquiries or to order a free trial, please contact your local online sales team:

UK and Rest of the World
Tel: +44 (0) 20 7017 6062
Email: online.sales@tandf.co.uk

United States, Canada and South America
Tel: 1-888-318-2367
Email: e-reference@taylorandfrancis.com

Taylor & Francis eBooks
Taylor & Francis Group